T0046215

THE BEST
AMERICAN
MAGAZINE
WRITING

2022

THE BEST
AMERICAN
MAGAZINE
WRITING

2022

**Edited by
Sid Holt for the
American Society
of Magazine
Editors**

Columbia University Press   New York

Columbia University Press
Publishers Since 1893
New York   Chichester, West Sussex
cup.columbia.edu
Copyright © 2022 the American Society of Magazine Editors
All rights reserved

Library of Congress Cataloging-in-Publication Data
ISSN 1541-0978
ISBN 978-0-231-20890-1 (hardcover)
ISBN 978-0-231-20891-8 (pbk.)
ISBN 978-0-231-55768-9 (e-book)

Columbia University Press books are printed on permanent and durable
acid-free paper.
This book is printed on paper with recycled content.
Printed in the United States of America

Cover design: Julia Kushnirsky
Cover image: Shutterstock

Contents

Jeffrey Goldberg

Introduction

I n the mid-1990s my wife served as the United Nations human rights officer in Liberia. At the time, I had just started writing for *New York* magazine, and my editor did not have the Liberian civil war high on his list of most urgent topics. But I was lucky—my editor was understanding enough to let me write about the war for the *New York Times Magazine*, my first legitimate foreign assignment.

Everything about the Liberian civil war was unusual and terrible and fascinating: the malicious warlords, the overwhelmed peacekeepers, the indifferent Western aid workers in their gleaming white Land Cruisers, the resilient but beat-up Liberian civilians. I was especially taken, though, by the Liberian press—a group of reporters, editors, and photographers who were pugnacious, resourceful, and indefatigable. There was not enough food in Monrovia, no clean water, barely any electricity, yet the press somehow found enough ink and paper to produce some stupendous journalism.

The strange thing is that, after all this time, it is an advertisement from these papers that I remember most clearly. It was an ad that helped me understand—in a real lightning strike of comprehension—the best way to approach magazine writing and editing, which I was just then learning.

The ad was for a local butcher shop and read "All Parts of the Cow." I don't remember if this was the name of the butcher shop or its marketing slogan or simply a statement of fact, but it doesn't matter. "All Parts of the Cow" has stayed with me for almost thirty years because it became the way I explain the difference between newspaper writing and magazine writing.

Like many magazine people, I started in newspapers, and I loved the work: the adrenaline, the urgency, the high-wire collaboration. When I was a cub reporter on the night police beat at the *Washington Post*, I once left the newsroom at four a.m., wandered to the basement pressroom, and grabbed an actually hot-off-the-presses copy of the morning's paper, one with my byline on the front page. Below the fold but whatever. It still felt great.

By then, though, I had really started caring about my sentences, and I was worried about the limitations of newspapering. What I'm about to say is not meant to be a knock on newspapers or newspaper people. Obviously, newspapers, especially the big national papers (which is to say, the only newspaper that will undoubtedly survive the Great Cull), are stuffed with creative, brave, and talented people who are also, by the way, helping to save our democracy, which is no small thing.

The problem I had was twofold: First was the ubiquity of clichés. On the police desk, we joked that the city had only two types of streets: "quiet, tree-lined streets" or "trash-strewn, drug-infested streets." I once asked a bedraggled editor if I could describe a particular street as "tree-lined yet trash-strewn," but he didn't have time to get the joke.

Cliché is everywhere, especially in writing. Clichés are one of the prices we pay in journalism for speed, but vigilance and a brisk pre-edit scrub will eliminate most of them. I'm no great sentence maker, but I wanted—and still want—to try to be one, and I hoped to work for people who wanted me to try.

The second problem: In newspaper editing it is common to shear away unruly feeling, weird detail, discordant observation, and the unavoidably jangly Heisenbergian moments that occur when writers interact with their subjects and the world. A smart *New Yorker* editor, the late John Bennet, once told me that the real bias in journalism is toward coherence, and though there are other biases—of course—this seemed unambiguously true. This unexamined bias causes us to think that stories have beginnings, middles and endings, that all questions must be answered, and that everything that happens in the universe happens for a reason.

Magazine people, generally speaking, have a different understanding, a sideways understanding: Not every story has an ending; not every story even has a beginning. Not everything has to make sense. Not everything is knowable. And the big one, something that always and forever adds confusion and complexity to story making: the presence of writers (and their experiences, beliefs, personalities, histories, and predispositions) inevitably changes the reality of whatever the writers are observing and describing.

I learned, over time, that the best magazine editors don't fear complication but run to it. "Put it in, put it all in," is an efficient way to describe this style of editing. Another way to describe it: "All parts of the cow."

Last year, when I asked Jennifer Senior, who had just joined the staff of *The Atlantic*, if she had anything original to say about the twentieth anniversary of the 9/11 terrorist attacks (originality traditionally being scarce on anniversaries of world-historical events), she thought for a minute and then said, "Maybe, but it's complicated." The story she sketched for me then was something more than complicated. It was mind-bending and exquisitely personal and something beyond fraught, and it featured—as a protagonist—a 9/11 truther. "A good man," Jen said, something never previously said by sane people about 9/11 truthers. We talked and talked and talked. And then I thought, "All parts of the cow," and I said, "Let's try it." Just put it all in. And then Jen and her editor, Scott Stossel, made something magical happen, and we published her story and it won the National Magazine Award for Feature Writing and the Pulitzer Prize for Feature Writing and now can be found in this book. It's impossible to describe, except to say that it contains all the mess of life and that it is written like poetry but in prose. Jen, Scott, and I realized, late in the process, that the story didn't even have anything resembling a nut graf—a term, borrowed from newspapering, for the paragraph that explains why you, the reader, should continue reading this story. Sometimes a magazine piece is so mesmerizing that the entire thing is its own nut graf, and this was true in Jen's case.

I understand that I shouldn't use the opportunity of this introduction to praise stories that appeared in the magazine I edit, though I would be remiss if I didn't mention that Ed Yong, one of the world's great science writers and also an *Atlantic* staff writer, has a story in this book, "We're Already Barreling Toward the Next Pandemic" and that it is stupendous.

But back to the cow.

Many of the brilliant stories collected in this book are written by people rushing to complexity, writers who are unafraid to introduce readers to their intricate, jumbled, knotty thoughts and contradictory experiences. Their whole selves saturate their work. Such is the case with the article "What Do We Do About John James Audubon," from, remarkably, *Audubon* magazine. The piece, by the Black birdwatcher and academic J. Drew Lanham, is an astonishment, and only in part because the editors had the nerve necessary to commission a piece dismantling their namesake and, until publication of this piece, patron saint. A patron saint, Lanham notes, who was a slaveholder and may have been mixed-race himself.

"Deconstructing holiness is hard work," Lanham writes. "As I made the speaking circuits . . . talking bird science but also trying to connect dots between conservation and culture, I began to float the idea of Audubon's questionable heritage. 'What about holding him up as a multiracial role model?' I asked. After all, there was a Black POTUS (half-white) and a 'Cablinasian' (Tiger Woods's contrived name for Caucasian, Black, Indian, and Asian heritage) golfer who found widespread acceptance and acclaim. There seemed to be a different standard for John James, though. The first time I posed the question at a meeting in Arizona, I could almost hear squirms. There were plenty of other issues to dredge up that dealt more immediately with making birding more colorful; why this?"

Self-distancing, of the sort we see to good effect in professional newspaper reporters, has its place—restraint and detachment often aid the cause of believability. But ferocious honesty builds credibility as well. The sort of frankness modeled by Lanham is one reason I read magazines.

Another reason I read magazines can be found in Matthieu Aikins's article for the *New York Times Magazine*, "The Collapse," about the Taliban's return to power in Afghanistan. Aikins's piece is a concise 20,000 words. I do not state that mockingly. When people complain about the length of certain magazine pieces, I ask them to do a bit of mental reframing: think of the article in question as an exceedingly short and wildly cheap book rather than a long-winded act of journalism.

Every word Aikins and his editors chose for this story belongs in this story. It is brilliant and, yes, (cliché alert) magisterial, but it is its intimacy and human scale that make it so noteworthy. Here is a short passage I appreciated because the magazine allows Aikins to become a character in his own story:

> I didn't understand how quickly things were falling apart; maybe I was in denial, too. I went to Hamid Karzai International Airport . . . on the morning of August 11. It was busier than I had ever seen it, a crush of passengers headed for the international terminal. The domestic side was quiet and tense. There were flights to the main cities of Herat and Mazar-i-Sharif, where, like Kandahar, battles were raging as the Taliban laid siege.
>
> I went through security and sat in the boarding lounge, but I couldn't get in touch with the fixer who was supposed to pick me up in Kandahar. I couldn't get in touch with anyone there, in fact. Finally, a journalist friend called using the internet at the military base at the airport there. The Taliban had shut down the mobile networks in preparation for an all-out assault.
>
> I got up and walked back out through security. The airline staff chased me down.
>
> "I'm leaving," I said. "My trip has been canceled." . . .
>
> "He's the third person to cancel like this," one woman whispered anxiously.
>
> When I got my documents back, I walked out against the flow of Afghans leaving their country. In the parking lot, there

were groups of families, some crying and some silent, people in their Western outfits for travel, suits and T-shirts, girls with big up-dos and painted faces, matrons taking photos, men in turbans and karakul hats and prayer caps, the families embracing and then dividing, one part walking away, the others left watching.

The next day, Kandahar City fell.

I read Aikins's piece in one sitting when it was first published. I did the same when Ann Patchett's "These Precious Days" appeared in *Harper's*. Patchett's piece, which also appears in this volume, is a work of genius, entrancing and uncategorizable, and you'll have to read it to understand why.

The two pieces have virtually nothing in common and everything in common. The writers are present in full; they are completely human—no Olympian detachment here. They wander; they pause over putatively unimportant things; they unassumingly saturate their narratives with profound observation. They do things, in short, that are only possible in magazines. And Patchett does something else, too: she lets us know that she has no ending. This is one of the most beautiful and truest ways to bring a story to a temporary conclusion:

Tell me how the story ends.
It doesn't.
It will.
It hasn't yet.

Nothing in this volume is finished. The stories—rich, messy, and complicated—all go on.

Sid Holt

Acknowledgments

The nineteen articles in this year's edition of *Best American Magazine Writing* include, as the title indicates, some of the finest examples of journalism published in print or online last year. Each of these pieces, either alone or as part of a series, was nominated for a National Magazine Award. Several were winners in their categories. Two also won Pulitzer Prizes: "The Webb Space Telescope Will Rewrite Cosmic History. If It Works," by Natalie Wolchover, originally published in *Quanta*, and "Twenty Years Gone," by Jennifer Senior, published in *The Atlantic*.

More, though, than examples of magazine writing at its best, each of these pieces explains, at least indirectly, what magazines and websites do, what makes them different from, say, newspapers. ASME, which sponsors the National Magazine Awards with the Columbia University Graduate School of Journalism, defines a magazine in part "as a print or digital publication issued or updated regularly in a consistent format, shaped by a distinctive editorial perspective and trusted by readers to provide timely information relevant to their interests."

The key words here are "perspective" and "interests." Magazine editors believe they have a unique relationship with their readers based on a shared understanding of American life. Each magazine and website expresses that understanding differently, of course. For some, it means a focus on politics or the arts; for others, an enthusiasm for fashion or entertainment, sports or travel. But whatever they do, whatever they cover, every magazine and website has one fundamental mission: to serve the interests of the reader in the sense of both what is good for the reader (like doctors, lawyers, and tax accountants, journalists are paid to tell people what they don't want to hear) and what the reader likes.

ASME—the American Society of Magazine Editors—was founded in 1963 with the goal of establishing the National Magazine Awards as a counterpart to the Pulitzer Prizes, which were then largely restricted to newspapers. The first National Magazine Award was presented in 1966 to *Look* magazine "for its skillful editing, imagination and editorial integrity, all of which were reflected particularly in its treatment of the racial issue during 1965." Originally limited to print magazines, the awards expanded in the following years to include recognition of magazine storytelling in any form and eventually in any medium, including newspapers and websites.

This year the National Magazine Awards were presented in sixteen categories, ranging from Reporting and Feature Writing to Video and Podcasting. Several of the publications nominated for the most prestigious award—the National Magazine Award for General Excellence—are represented in this edition of *Best American Magazine Writing*, including *The Atlantic*, *New York*, the *New York Times Magazine*, *Audubon*, the *Georgia Review*, and *Quanta*. A complete list of the 2022 finalists and winners is posted at https://www.asme.media/.

More than 200 media organizations entered the National Magazine Awards in 2022, submitting nearly 1,100 entries. Print and digital entries were split roughly evenly, attesting to the evolution not only of the National Magazine Awards but also of magazines. Some 200 editors, writers, art directors, and photo editors participated in the judging of the awards, which for the second consecutive year were judged virtually. But the presentation of the awards—that was live for the first time since 2019 as more than 300 editors and publishers gathered at a music venue called Brooklyn Steel, in

New York's Williamsburg neighborhood, to celebrate the best of print and digital journalism with their friends and colleagues.

Sixty-five media organizations were nominated for National Magazine Awards in 2022, led by *New York* with eight and the *New Yorker* with six. The *New Yorker* also won two awards, for Video and Profile Writing. Top finalists also included the *New York Times Magazine*, which received five nominations and won three awards, for Reporting, Essays and Criticism, and Public Interest, and *The Atlantic*, which received three nominations and won two awards, for General Excellence and Feature Writing.

But long before ASME received a single entry, hundreds of magazine journalists were already at work preparing for the National Magazine Awards. It is they—the editors who choose to enter the awards and the staff members who organize the submissions—who are largely responsible for the continued success of the National Magazine Awards. They and of course the judges, all of whom begin reading, watching, or listening to dozens of entries weeks before they meet with their fellow judges to pick the finalists and winners.

The lead judges are charged with guiding their fellows toward the selection of finalists and winners that exemplify contemporary standards of editorial excellence. The judging this year was led by a distinguished group of journalists, including Joe Brown, editor, *one5c*; Maile Carpenter, editor in chief, *Food Network Magazine* and *Pioneer Woman*; Ben Goldberger, executive editor, *Time*; Anna Holmes, executive vice president, Higher Ground Productions; Adi Ignatius, editor in chief, Harvard Business Review Group; Radhika Jones, editor in chief, *Vanity Fair*; Lauren Kern, editor in chief, *Apple News*; Amanda Kludt, editor in chief, *Eater*; Cindi Leive, cofounder, *The Meteor*; Alison Overholt, general manager, *Oprah Daily*; Puja Patel, editor in chief, *Pitchfork*; Debra Adams Simmons, executive editor, culture and history, *National Geographic*; Julia Turner, deputy managing editor, *Los Angeles Times*; Liz Vaccariello, editor in chief, *People*; Geoff Van Dyke, editorial director, *5280*; and Charles Whitaker, dean, Medill School of Journalism, Northwestern University.

The National Magazine Awards are judged in conjunction with three other ASME awards programs: the ASME Award for Fiction, the ASME Awards for Photography and Illustration, and the ASME Awards for Journalists Under 20. The journalists who led the judging of these awards included David Brindley, managing editor, *National Geographic*; Jonathan Dorn, vice president and general manager, Outside, Inc.; Jared Hohlt, editorial director, *T: The New York Times Style Magazine*; Clara Jeffery, editor in chief, *Mother Jones*; and Paul Reyes, editor, *Virginia Quarterly Review*. A complete list of the judges of the National Magazine Awards and the ASME Awards is posted at https://ellieawards.secure-platform.com /a/page/judges.

The ASME board of directors is responsible for overseeing the administration, judging, and presentation of the National Magazine Awards. The members of the 2021–2022 board—all of whom are journalism educators or the editors in chief of well-known publications—are listed at https://www.asme.media/board-of -directors1. The president of ASME, Clara Jeffery, deserves special recognition for the success of the 2021 awards. I also want to thank Jeffrey Goldberg, the editor in chief of *The Atlantic*, for writing the introduction to this year's edition of *BAMW*.

As director of operations at ASME, Nina Fortuna is responsible for the day-to-day management of the National Magazine Awards. Her efficiency and, yes, kindness now come as a surprise to no one associated with ASME or the National Magazine Awards. ASME members are also thankful for the work of David McCormick, who is our literary agent. The editors of *Best American Magazine Writing* at Columbia University Press, Philip Leventhal and Michael Haskell, are especially deserving of praise. Their enthusiasm for *BAMW* is a constant inspiration.

On behalf of ASME, I want to thank Steve Coll for his enthusiastic support of the National Magazine Awards during his tenure as dean and Henry R. Luce Professor of Journalism at the Columbia Journalism School. ASME looks forward to working with his successor, Jelani Cobb. I also want to thank Abi Wright, the executive director of professional prizes at Columbia, who not only coordinates the efforts of ASME and Columbia but, year in, year out, serves as a National Magazine Awards judge.

Finally, I want to thank the writers who gave their permission to use their work in this anthology. Without them, there would be no *Best American Magazine Writing*—in fact, there would be no magazines, period.

THE BEST
AMERICAN
MAGAZINE
WRITING

2022

New York Times Magazine

WINNER—ESSAYS AND CRITICISM

This edition of Best American Magazine Writing *begins with two stories about the impact of the* COVID-19 pandemic. In *"Bodies on the Line,"* Carina del Valle Schorske *explores the importance of public dance both as a means of overcoming fear (by way of comparison, Schorske depicts scenes of frenzied celebration among survivors of the Black Death in the fourteenth century) and claiming personal and political freedom. Described as "kaleidoscopic" and "joyful" by the ASME judges, "Bodies on the Line" was one of three* New York Times Magazine *entries that won National Magazine Awards in 2022. The others were "The Collapse," by Matthieu Aikins, in the Reporting category, and the series "Hidden Files Bare Military Failures in Deadly Strikes" and "The Human Toll of America's Air Wars," by Azmat Khan, in Public Interest.*

Carina del
Valle Schorske

Bodies on
the Line

For most of 2020, I passed the pandemic alone in my studio apartment. I turned thirty-three, then thirty-four, and my body seemed to grow old without bringing my spirit along with it. My right knee was clearly deteriorating—I couldn't sit cross-legged at my desk the way I used to—and because I wasn't wearing makeup, I could track each age spot as it bloomed to the surface. When I pulled my hair back in a tight ponytail, I could see a patch of scalp. But in that same period had my life evolved at all? Had I met anyone? Surprised myself? Stemmed the tide of collective crisis? My mother often urged me to dance, just a little, by myself in the kitchen—"It's good medicine," she said, "*despojo.*"

I've never known what "*despojo*" means, precisely, though it's a word I use with some frequency to express a physical craving for spiritual catharsis: "*Necesitamos despojo, quiero despojarme.*" Or, watching a friend gain momentum on the dance floor and begin to enter a self-forgetful trance: "*Esoooo! Des-po-jo!*" My Spanish-English dictionary has only the verb (to despoil, to shed leaves) and the plural noun (the spoils of war, mortal remains, rubble, waste). Google Translate: dispossession.

It's strange to discover that a word I associate with rejuvenation technically has more to do with death and disaster. I guess "*despojo*" comes to me, via Puerto Rican Spanish, in a register already worked through by ritual, by generations of people who've had to scavenge something good from the many losses of forced migration.

The "*despojo*" I've desired articulates a paradox. In order to repossess the body, it's necessary to dispossess it; in order to feel alive, it's necessary to get in touch with what's already dead. But when I say "*despojo*," I don't always mean to sound so serious. Sometimes I mean that I want very badly to pin somebody to the club wall with my butt.

Even though it's better, as my mother recommended, to dance alone than not at all, the "*despojo*" I'd been dreaming of was social. In isolation, I'd felt myself stiffen into a form so familiar it had come to seem inescapable. I wanted my body to influence and be influenced by other bodies—this time not as a vector of disease but as a vector of pure feeling.

This impulse has a history. According to the French historian Philippe de Félice, "Eras of greatest material and moral distress seem to be those during which people dance most." A medieval dancing mania swept through Europe following the height of the Black Death, when between 500 and 800 people died every day in Paris and Saint-Denis and when alternating waves of flood and drought caused widespread famine. In her book *Choreomania*," Kélina Gotman argues that the medieval frenzy was really a mix of phenomena transpiring over centuries—intensified midsummer celebrations, municipal feasts meant to placate the masses, traditional pilgrimages that surged with new enthusiasm. But historical accounts leave little doubt that the boom in public dancing had something to do with the proximity of death. In 1348, two monks traveling through Paris observed a band of people in the street frolicking to the music of drums and bagpipes. When the monks asked the revelers why they were making such a scene, they replied, "We have seen our neighbors die and are seeing them die day after day, but since the mortality has in no way entered our town, we are not without hope that our festive mood will not allow it to come here, and this is the reason for why we are dancing."

Occasionally, the dancing itself was fatal—there were those who dropped dead from exhaustion, and in Utrecht, 200 people danced on a Mosel bridge until the structure collapsed and many drowned. Folklore with roots in this period, like "The Pied Piper of Hamelin," warns of rhythm's seductive power. So do later tales like "The Red Shoes," in which the young girl who wears them must have her feet cut off to halt her cursed dancing. That story frightened me as a child, but it also shaped a lasting preference. When I go out, I find myself reaching for wine-colored suede ankle boots with a Cuban heel, as if to court the ecstasies of enchantment.

I thought of those shoes when New York City's second pandemic spring began to buzz with fantasies of freedom. Slowly, then quickly, people I knew lined up for the vaccines. By Memorial Day, the subways were crowded and the bars noisy again. We stumbled into the season's audacious promise exhausted, delirious and seething with desire. I listened to Stevie Wonder's "Love Light in Flight" on loop, as if the song—*we will fly forever and one hour*—could restore the time we'd lost together. I followed a dozen DJs on Instagram. I texted my most festive friends. I mapped out New York City—birthplace of bugalú, salsa, hustle, vogue, breaking, flexing— and traced possible paths through a series of summer parties. When I opened Uber on my phone, the corporation's new tagline amplified the siren song: "The world's opening up again. Where to first?"

Back then, the summer seemed luxuriously long. But our reckless rush to make the most of it told another story. Even before the sudden surge of the Delta variant, we knew whatever freedom we'd chosen to feel would be hyperlocal, most likely temporary, and possibly destructive. We were right to think it might be our only chance. At Papi Juice's Pride party, when Destiny's Child came on, the incandescent anxiety of our wish to be well made the bridge sound like a spell: *I'm doing so, so, so, so, so, so, so, so, so, so good / Good, good, good, good, goooood.* That very day at the Gotham Jazz Picnic in Central Park, where our feet disappeared in the dust kicked up by our Lindy-hopping, I danced with a widower in white linen who called me by his dead wife's name. At Coney Island in late July, the celebrated B-boy turned DJ Tony Touch overstayed his boardwalk set and called out to his remaining audience: "If you're still here, I want you to act like it. I want to see that."

We are still here. We are trying to find out what it means to act like it. Bourgeois propriety often seems to prefer a clear distinction between grief and jubilation. In Puerto Rico, nineteenth-century white criollos condemned the Afro-Indigenous practice of the *baquiné*, in which children who died very young were dressed in flowers, sometimes lace, and mourned with all-night vigils of drinking, drums, and dancing. But what always struck me as most mortifying was not the intensity of that display but the possibility that those of us left living do not love life enough to deserve our survival. I don't believe in deserving, but I do believe we owe the dead a little dancing.

· · ·

The first night I went out for real was the Friday before the Puerto Rican Day Parade. My friends and I rode up from Brooklyn to the Bronx Brewery for A Party Called Rosie Perez, to hear DJ Laylo, Sucio Smash, and Christian Mártir play together live for the first time since 2019. I don't like the parade—the corporate sponsorships, the political ring kissing—but I like how all the city's Puerto Ricans seem to turn up at once, rowdy and rebellious, for the annual roll call. And I'd been to A Party Called Rosie Perez twice before, so I played along when a woman I didn't quite recognize—long blond braids, little crystals at her tear ducts—threw her arms around my neck as soon I stepped inside the door. Later, when I passed her on the way to the bathroom, we locked eyes and both laughed: "I'm not your girl, right?" "No—I liked that you faked it though!"

None of us seemed to remember how long to look an unmasked stranger in the face, whether to speak up or simply drift into the orbit of someone else's rhythm until touch could take over. For me, the tension broke when DJ Laylo dropped the early crossover house hit "Show Me Love" and the off-key strain in the voice of Robin Stone—she had the flu at the studio session—cut through our second-guessing with the desperate power possessed by the sick. *Words are so easy to say. . . . / You've got to show me love.* It felt good to make our human needs known against the electronic grind, to remember machines could be our creative allies rather than our overseers. *It's been so long since / I touched a wanting hand.* The government had failed to protect us and lied about the gravity of our collective condition. *Don't you promise me the world / All that I've already heard / This time around for me, baby / Actions speak louder than words.* The only language that could reach us now would be the language of bodies assembling in tight quarters to show love, even if we fumbled when we reached for one another.

The really skilled salseros had gathered on one side of the stage, and some of us wandered over to watch, caught between envy and admiration. I could see one woman's training in her perfect spotting. A lanky dancer in a red bucket hat had incredible improvisational range, looked absolutely natural, even with the hint of show business I could see in the clean angle of his elbows. Andrew Avilá turned out to be a dancer for Lin-Manuel Miranda's movie *In the Heights,* which premiered the night before—a South Bronx Puerto Rican Colombian who grew up dancing salsa at home with his mother before he turned professional. In previous generations, his great-grandfather crafted and played the folk guitar called the *cuatro*; his uncles played congas; and almost everybody danced at the Palladium Ballroom during the midcentury mambo craze. Whatever genius he possessed did not begin and would not end with him.

I liked him best dancing with a radiant woman in a red crop top, loose black pants, and waist beads—she could have followed the turns I saw him spin other partners through, but instead she was eliciting his rhythmic playfulness, tremors traveling between their torsos. At one point—it wasn't salsa anymore, but merengue—he tapped out the beat on the small of her back, and I saw her toss her head back and laugh with delight. I laughed, too, when I asked her name and it turned out to be just two letters off from my own, as if I'd dreamed myself into her dancing. Later, I asked Corinna Vega to remember that merengue moment. She couldn't locate it precisely—of course not—but she remembered the feeling: "The beauty of not knowing what happens next, the beauty of messing up and just like, you're still going."

Especially now, we're tormented by the volatile future, the anxiety of adaptation. The uncertainty of the pandemic seems merciless. But dancing activates the pleasure in this roiling field of possibilities, makes it feel as if there will always be another chance to choose. To reset the connection. To find opportunity in error. Getting ready for her first night out in over a year, Corinna had wavered—"Like, do I still got it?" Once she was back in the moment, she remembered that dancing is not something you've got. It's something you have to let get you.

Christian Mártir took over the turntables for the last set. Palo crashed in, a ceremonial music, Congolese originally, developed in new directions in Cuba and the Dominican Republic. The drums in palo are made from hollowed-out logs. I'd seen—even learned a little—the corresponding dance, which is low to the ground, athletic, forceful, exhausting. Palo summons the dead, pounding the earth until they wake up and enter the living through the feet. At the party, it didn't seem strictly necessary to know the details of this tradition or its historical trajectory in order to appreciate the primordial power of percussion and the human voice, our original instruments. To hear the persistence of Africa in the Americas.

"When you play that, you have a spiritual intention," Mártir explained. "It's almost like people would say it's disrespectful to play at the club. . . ." He trailed off, shook his head, began again. "I can get the crowd hyped on whatever record's on the radio," he said. But to play something our grandmothers, great-grandmothers might recognize, "that, to me, is beautiful, because you're connecting all those generations, bringing them into the same space." He paused. "Nothing's guaranteed, right?" And I think he meant to say that the music might not have survived but did. We can't always afford to be precious about preserving the original context— better to get in where we fit in.

• • •

In 1975, Cuba's Orquesta Ritmo Oriental released a relentless charanga whose title makes a bold claim: "Yo Bailo de Todo." I dance to everything. I've always aspired to that universalism, even though I know the dances of the world are infinite, intricate and often impossible to replicate without a lifetime's immersion. But between June and August, I committed to the cause—every time the electric slide erupted at a cookout or club, I fell in line, and whenever a hand was extended to me, regardless of my feel for the form, I took up the proposition.

I followed the tangled lines of music around my neighborhood, finding stoops overflowing with hookah smoke and Latin trap, yards with high wooden fences where stringed instruments scored ceremonies I wasn't meant to see. When I passed teenagers blasting "Gasolina" on skateboards, I dropped to give them five or ten seconds of Y2K perreo from across the street—"OK! I see what you got!"—and sitting at my desk with the windows open, I let myself get up to dance to Doja Cat when the car idling at the curb sent her new single floating toward me like a bright balloon.

Biking through Prospect Park, I pulled over whenever I heard live drums, this time accompanied by a long wooden flute, and when a few women got up to dance—OK, cumbia—I tried to match their precision and restraint. For at least two minutes, the six of us strangers sustained the percussive line with our clapping and kept the chorus alive—*ay, turura*—while the flutist popped his knees "Single Ladies"–style to his own melody, and I could see that even the Hawaiian-shirt hipster who had paused at the periphery to watch was making the shapes of the words with his lips.

Nightclubs intimidated me (the scramble for tickets, the epileptic lasers), but still I found myself caught in the seam of nightlife between Bushwick and Ridgewood, where, making an early escape from the crush of Elsewhere just after midnight, I could hear the parties emanating from other rooftops—*do you believe in life after love?*—sign and symbol of all the lives I'd never live. Sometimes friends canceled last minute, spooked by the virus, and I'd have to brave the club alone. At Nowadays I squirmed into the dense knot of bodies holding down the indoor dance floor, and it felt as if the DJ, spinning hard techno, had us locked in the shuddering chamber of a bomb shelter.

I wanted love but settled, instead, for the brutal thrill of anonymity—a cold can against my back, the sting of a woman's straight
hair across my face. At the Brooklyn Mirage, where the crowd all
faced the DJ in supplication to a distant god, I turned against the
tide to watch the rows of ravaged faces revealed by the breaking
dawn, and their fingers all made the same sign, as if searching out a
thousand secret sweet spots in the sky. I was relieved, almost giddy,
to be released into the open panorama of the streets—bits of bright
trash floating here and there, an impersonal ballet.

Even when I didn't find the feeling I was cruising for, I never
tired of the sensuous display: a pearl-skinned punk with green
finger waves and a septum ring winding her waist with her eyes
closed, a pair of dirty blondes in gray tanks and chains jerking
along to music so metallic it made my molars hurt to hear it. On
an East Harlem sidewalk, I watched a father take his daughter out
to work the well-worn groove of "Calle Luna Calle Sol." The
slightest gesture from him was enough to imply the music's many
directions, and his feet never faltered, as if navigating by memory
alone the blue cobblestones of the old city the song describes.

Had New Yorkers always been this beautiful, or had isolation
turned my sight psychedelic? I was dazzled by all the details I
couldn't catalogue. Part of the joy of social dancing, especially out
in a broader public beyond the family home, is that we will never
be able to identify all the faces that spin by, the hands that nudge
our backs to pass. Nor can we name our exact relation to those
other bodies. I suppose the usual word is "strangers," but there's
always the possibility that they turn out not to be—that we visit
the same dentist, that our cousins are coworkers, or that we take
them home and they become beloved. There's a euphoria to all we
will not know but might, the way the whirling out-of-reachness of
the world makes it seem more real.

•   •   •

Nevertheless, I lamented all the names I didn't catch, the interviews I didn't schedule, and, most of all, the gestures that escaped

description. There were mornings I woke up empty-headed, trying to remember the twisting wrist I'd found so bewitching hours before. Social dance is improvisational and collective by definition, so unless it has been recorded—and even then, from what angle, for how long?—we must rely on memory to reconstruct the shifting mandala of figures on the floor, the flow of sensations that ripple through, exhaust, and energize the body. After all, social dance is not social if it is merely observed; it has not done its work if it does not incite the desire to participate. And participation demands a certain intensity of presence that runs counter to remembering.

The anthropologist, choreographer, and performer Katherine Dunham spent her life in service to the movement traditions of the African diaspora, studying anthropology at the University of Chicago, conducting fieldwork in the Caribbean, and establishing a celebrated dance school in Midtown Manhattan all before 1950. Even she struggled to write well about dance: "Verbalization is apt to end in sterility, and the aesthetic experience" of actual dancing "eludes explicitness with a tantalizing facility." But the difficulty of describing social dance, like most difficulty, is also due to lack of practice—and we would all have more practice if social dance enjoyed greater respect.

In Plato's "Protagoras," Socrates argues that dancing girls have no place in philosophical gatherings. So-called Western culture has carried on this derisive attitude: In the traditional hierarchy of art forms, social dance doesn't even rank. It's entertainment at best, vice and social scourge at worst. This judgment squares, conveniently, with the fact that modern social dance has been developed most richly by girls of all genders, teeny-boppers and the racial underclass. Dunham was well aware of the stigmatized status of social dance and lamented the "injury done to the American Black youth in the omission from school textbooks" of those artistic achievements, "which would have elevated his being and spirit rather than categorically depriving it." That's one reason it mattered, for Dunham, to attempt "verbalization," no matter how clumsy or insufficient.

Dunham was a scholar, and much of today's best writing about social dance remains confined to the academic disciplines of anthropology and performance studies. In the mainstream media, well, there's always party reporting—often an entry point for young femmes who aspire to more prestigious beats.

The great Jamaica Kincaid got her start by writing then-anonymous "The Talk of the Town" columns for the New Yorker, describing, for example, lunchtime dancing at La Marthinique, a Black discothèque in Midtown with a "dance floor that always seemed freshly sanded" and women who looked as if they styled their hair with "a great deal of Dixie Peach Bergamot." She reached beyond the constraints of the column to recall her schoolyard at Friday recess in Antigua, where the girls would "grab each other around the waist" and whirl around chanting "tee la la la, congo" until the teacher chastised them as savages. The delight she once took in transgressing respectability politics—"How I did want to be a little savage!"—showed up, reanimated, in resistance to the New Yorker's house style. She rejected the magazine's stilted, imperious "we" by putting her own body on the line.

On the New Yorker's expense account—she documented her charges, once, in the column itself—she toured the city's many subcultures generally governed by strict unspoken rules of comportment, from a luncheon at the Regency Hotel honoring the legs of the showbiz dancer Cyd Charisse to a party where the "older young white people" in attendance eschewed Talking Heads in favor of "any Motown record from 1965." All of these scenes—not just the white ones—were in some sense cross-cultural for Kincaid, and the pretext of journalism lubricated her passage through them. But she was also carried by her feel for a wide range of rhythms, rhythms she knew how to follow through new elaborations.

Journalism and social dance have always seemed linked to me—forms of structured improvisation for stepping out into a world full of potentially hostile strangers. My friend Sheila Maldonado took me to see Tony Touch for his birthday boat ride on the East River. She interviewed him twenty years ago for *Urban*

Latino. "We're not stalkers," she reasoned. "This is our job." On the top deck I spotted the celebrated choreographer Danielle Polanco, her hair tied up in a black bandanna, fooling around for her friend's camera in the light rain. I'd been in love with her loose waist, her multilingual hands, since I saw her in the video for Omarion's "Touch" a dozen years ago. In that moment, it was tempting to understand the world as a dazzling web of intergenerational synchronicities. As we passed beneath the Manhattan Bridge, I talked with a few dancers who had spent the year in Tony's weekly Zoom room, cameras on in kitchens with kids running through, mourning one another's many losses. Then suddenly one of them turned to me, her gaze cool and her communication clear: "Don't write some [expletive]." I promised I would not.

·   ·   ·

Throughout the summer, municipal and corporate advertisements have conflated the reopening of nightclubs with the reopening of hearts and minds, as if through sheer wishfulness we might manifest some kind of euphoric restitution for the losses we've endured. This "we" is itself wishful, implying we all suffered equally and will celebrate our survival together on some mythic dance floor "Uptown," where Prince promised "White, Black, Puerto Rican, everybody just a-freakin'." Many of the city's dance floors remain deeply segregated. This isn't necessarily a lament: there can be pride, pleasure, and protection in the self-containment of marginalized communities. But the segregation on display today is also evidence of our society's stark failure to integrate public space—schools, neighborhoods—or to ameliorate the inequality that often corrupts existing opportunities for joyful encounters across race, class, and sexuality, to say nothing of age and ability.

I don't mean to imply that such spaces have never existed or to underplay my own desire for them. One of the pandemic's unexpected pleasures has been the dancing in the streets (cue Martha and the Vandellas) that has claimed plazas and parks from Herbert

Von King in Brooklyn to Washington Square in Manhattan despite police-enforced curfews. This kind of dancing dramatizes the city's true diversity, forces simmering tensions over who belongs where into open conflict, and enables chance encounters. My mother's longtime friend José Mateo remembers the streets of his South Bronx childhood as a multicultural welter—"Jews, Irish, Black, Hispanic, you name it, Italian, everything in one block." All the kids would gather to practice the latest dances beneath a neighbor's open window where the radio rained down.

But scenes like that are exceptions to the rule. Movies like *Footloose* romanticize and whitewash the very real American history of racist laws limiting public dancing, which have roots in the eighteenth-century bans on African drums and nineteenth-century limitations on Indigenous gatherings imposed by the Court of Indian Offenses. Near the turn of the century, the messianic Ghost Dance spread rapidly among the tribes of the West, prophesying the return of the dead and the end of settler dominion. The U.S. military responded with the notorious massacre of Lakota men, women, and children at Wounded Knee. New York's Cabaret Law—which prohibited dancing in restaurants and bars without a special license—was on the books for nearly a century between 1926 and 2017. Throughout the eighties, police arrested breakers who held dance battles in the street. Agents of the state still tend to characterize public dancing as "a riot" waiting to happen, but I think the real threat has less to do with disorder and more to do with the potential power of coordinated movement.

For Andrew Avilá, the dancer I met at A Party Called Rosie Perez, one form of movement galvanized the other: initially paralyzed by pandemic despair, he recovered his desire to dance last summer, when he "marched the whole city" to protest police violence. It was a relief "to scream in the street and sweat" with strangers, to tune in to the pulse that precedes any choreography. Around the same time, DJs dropped beats below a viral video of a woman named Johnniqua Charles, popping her hip at a security guard who had her in handcuffs and wouldn't let her back inside the club to collect her purse. She freestyled, half talking and half rapping through the injustice of her predicament, until she locked into a persuasive rhythm, a hook worth repeating: "You about to lose yo job." In response to the nationwide protests, a few authorities were in fact placed on administrative leave. But the energy embodied by Charles aimed far beyond modest reforms. Her song-and-dance asserted a fundamental claim to freedom of movement: even if she was not permitted to move from here to there, she would keep moving, ingeniously, right where she was.

The marketplace is eager to appropriate and subdue this kind of anarchic energy. No one owns tango or twerking, but plenty of well-positioned people have found fame and fortune quoting the dances of the underclass out of context. Jayna Brown, an African American studies scholar at Pratt, has chronicled the history of this dynamic in America's clubs and cabarets. In her book *Babylon Girls*, she shows how the American vaudevillian Ruth St. Denis, often considered a mother of modern dance, built her reputation by adapting carnivalesque fantasies of Egyptian and Indian movement to the turn-of-the-century stage. Irene Castle, another white dancer who came up through vaudeville, established a lucrative business in the Roaring Twenties translating dances she learned from Harlem chorus girls like Ethel Williams for high-society parties. At midcentury, the Portuguese-born Carmen Miranda was the favored emissary of Afro-Brazilian samba. "With a few exceptions," Brown writes, Black dancers "had to work behind the scenes."

But the visibility afforded by contemporary technology hasn't really solved the problem of credit and remuneration. In late June, a group of TikTok's Black dancers—which grew to include Challan Trishann, Erick Louis, and Marcus Greggory—called for a creative strike organized around Megan Thee Stallion's latest single. They were tired of watching the dances they invented go viral via white influencers who usually failed to credit them as choreographers. But with key dancers sitting this round out, copycats struggled to come up with any choreography at all, despite the song's clear directions: *hands on my knees shakin' ass.* The strike made it very clear who was driving innovation on the app. Matthew D. Morrison, a musicologist at NYU, analyzed these digital developments in real time on Twitter: "Yes, of course, people have been watching Black folks dance since they forced us over here as captives on slave ships, to the invention of the TV, etc., but social media provides a wholly different level of access and possibilities than before." An almost frictionless experience.

The "social" in social media is not the same as the "social" in social dancing. Online, there's no face-to-face accountability. The real-world encounter once required outsiders and amateurs to risk embarrassment. Even Irene Castle had to let Ethel Williams see her sweat. The dance floor cannot be mastered like a phrase of choreography; improvisation demands something more than imitation.

It can be hard to admit that we sometimes need to be taught how to treat our own bodies and the bodies of others with curiosity, courage, and tenderness. The conceptual artist Adrian Piper, who was raised among upper-middle-class Black Americans in Washington Heights, had this in mind when she designed "Funk Lessons: A Collaborative Experiment in Cross-Cultural Transfusion." Between 1982 and 1984, she toured the country teaching large groups how to "GET DOWN AND PARTY. TOGETHER." Later, she chronicled the experience in her essay "Notes on Funk." Like Dunham and Kincaid, Piper found that her peers in the avant-garde elite had trouble squaring her formidable intellect— she earned a Ph.D. in philosophy at Harvard—with her unwavering commitment to Black popular culture. But her experience as a "go-go girl" and her lifelong study of rhythm and blues was an equally rigorous education.

She began by "demonstrating some basic moves" and then, with the audience along for the ride, "rehearsing, internalizing, rerehearsing and improvising on them." Now and then, she introduced bits of musical history and political context. When the collaboration was successful, what she purported to teach her audience "was revealed to be a kind of fundamental sensory 'knowledge' that everyone has and can use." But even when it was less successful, the experience provided a holding environment for the ugly feelings sometimes provoked by social dancing: "annoyance, self-consciousness, embarrassment, resentment, contempt, shame," all the interpersonal funk we usually try to avoid or scrub clean.

•   •   •

Following Adrian Piper, I began to crave a more structured environment that could mediate the social anxieties at play whenever people gather. Someplace I could go alone, sober, and still expect to dance in a sustained way—ideally, I fantasized, without self-consciousness. "Funk Lessons" were no longer on offer, but at my local coffee shop I saw fliers for 5Rhythms, a practice developed by Gabrielle Roth in the 1960s that seemed like a compromise between Piper's party and the repressed utopic longings of my New Age childhood.

Teachers trained in the technique, who serve as both DJs and guides, usher the group through cycles of self-directed movement structured by the eponymous five rhythms: "flowing," "staccato," "chaos," "lyrical" and "stillness." I scanned the New York website for an open class and chose Kierra Foster-Ba for the Judith Jamison quote underneath her photograph, remembering how I'd seen Jamison's white skirt fly in old footage of Alvin Ailey's *Cry*. In my own adolescent experience of modern dance, I'd never developed my technique enough to do justice to that choreography, but it still emerged sometimes in my dancing, rounding my spine or bending my elbows back like bird's wings.

The class I attended was held at the Joffrey Ballet School's studio downtown, and I was surprised by the devotional feeling that came over me when I left my shoes by the door and entered the high-ceilinged room where Foster-Ba was setting up behind the mixer. Many of the people sprawled on the floor in wide-legged folds looked like off-duty ballerinas, but I wasn't scared—sustained improvisation tends to level the playing field, exhausting the advantages of training. It felt good to sink to the ground and roll around like kittens in a litter. Slowly, as Foster-Ba let the beat build, people began to rise, to adapt their stretching to the shape of the music.

When I got tired of weaving between other dancers in the room, I made my way to the windows, stretched my back out on the ballet barres, circled my head in time with the blades of the box fan and traced the shapes of the buildings I could see outside—tall, sweeping arches I followed with my arms. Then I'd dive back in, trying to manage my irritation at the man clapping loudly and offbeat, past two heads of dark waves twirling too fast to tell apart, drawn, always, toward the woman in the gray dress engaged in a lithe duet with her own reflection, like Rihanna in the video for "Work." A voice emerged from the heavy bass as if to admonish me: *Are you really gonna stand there staring at me / all the way from across the room?*

At 5Rhythms there seemed to be a taboo against looking, as if locking eyes could break the spell of freedom. All the flickering, avoidant encounters made me feel a little lonely, as if I were the only one listening to the lyrics, the only one rattled by the confrontation they demanded. Later, when I asked Foster-Ba why the dancers seemed to guard their inner worlds so closely, she paused to think before answering: "I think there's a lot of suffering around not being able to look and actually enjoy having people look at you. I mean, you've seen children on the playground telling strangers: *Look at me, look at me, look at what I can do!* But then it gets socialized: Who do you think you are?"

In 5Rhythms, the goal is to explore movement from the inside, to surprise yourself, to risk strangeness and reach beyond beauty. For many people, reaching beyond beauty requires giving up the desire to be seen—because what else besides beauty, talent, or extraordinary grace could justify the intensity of that wish? It pleased me when Foster-Ba said, "You like to dance, and you look like you know how to lose yourself dancing, too." I'm sometimes praised for a freedom I don't feel. But it's true—I don't mind being seen as mediocre if being seen makes me available to the other bodies in the room. For a moment, I got caught up in a trio with two ballerinas, building an invisible bower of flowered branches.

Before the pandemic, I was just beginning to learn bomba in Puerto Rico, from Lío Villahermosa, who knows a thing or two about the stakes of the desire to be seen as the first man in living memory to enter the *batey* in a skirt. The *batey*, in the style of bomba local to Santurce, is the open space inside the circle where the dancer enters alone to greet the musicians and direct the drum in an improvised duet sustained by the call and response of the crowd. In Villahermosa's classes, amateurism is no excuse. Everyone must enter the *batey* from day one. Everyone must join the chorus: *Si no bailo esta bomba / me voy a morir.* If I don't dance this bomba, I just might die.

· · ·

Going out so much more than usual sabotaged my sleep schedule and therefore my writing routine. My nerves were live wires, and by the end of July, Delta was hard on our heels. But a desperate hunger had taken hold of my heart, and I couldn't call off the chase. The mundane disappointments I'd suffered on the summer's dance floors—misrecognition, failed seduction, finding myself at this party when I should have been at that one—only radicalized my demands. *Make me feel like paradise,* I sang along with Stevie. *Give me what I'm missing.* At the end of July, I blew off a deadline for Tony Touch's afternoon set at Coney Island. Both Sheila and I had lost beloved people and places in the pandemic, and we thought it might make us feel more human to touch the shoreline where she came up, to inhabit a familiar history together.

There was a commotion on the boardwalk by the Cyclone that resolved into patterned swirls of dancing as I approached. *Llegó el curanderooo*—Tony was playing his summer mix, "Sacude," and I had arrived just in time for my favorite part, when Tego Calderón announces himself as the healer, the witch doctor. I've always been good at finding friends in the crowd, especially someone like

Sheila, whose movement, carried low in the body but light in the feet, is so beloved to me. But she wasn't the only undercover Gen X priestess in a plain tank, loose shorts and off-brand sneakers holding down the center of the floor. I was finally able to recognize the dance, not just the music, as New York house.

I didn't grow up partying to house—millennial hip-hop, mostly—so I found myself faking the footwork by playing around inside a salsa structure. Something about the syncopation makes it feel like a natural fit. "Well," Sheila said, "house *is* salsa." Why hadn't anybody told me that before? There were a million Puerto Ricans there, and of course they wanted you to know it—the woman dancing next to me had the flag bedazzled on her fanny pack, and I liked the way the figure-eight of her hips made it wave. But Tony Touch shouted everybody out: Guatemala, London, DR, Orlando, Canarsie. "The whole world is here," he said, and it felt true—not because of some encyclopedic internationalism but because the cultures the people there had been involved in creating had traveled so far, to Sweden, Japan, South Korea.

Then there were younger women, mostly white, who had clearly taken studio classes, and one of them, a regal redhead in baggy jeans, helped block the wind so I could light my joint. Later, I saw her dance with an old head in a smooth, high style I slowly realized must be the hustle. When her arms accented the turns, her wrists swirled slightly—salsa—but there was less twist and shimmy in her torso. The dynamism was all in the languid, traveling turns, as if a gust of glitter had blown through the waltz. I could see why Christian Mártir had described the hustle as "what bridged everything—Latin rhythms with disco." Now and then someone at the edge of the cipher would cut in, and there would be a trio for a minute, weaving like birds finding the right formation to slice the sky.

Later, when I looked up the hustle at home, I learned it was yet another social dance born among New York Puerto Ricans; I was later told it might have developed as a respectable alternative to a slow grind popular with teenagers—maybe the bump. I'm thirsty for that dance even though I'm enchanted by what emerged in opposition to it. There's really no way to discipline social dancing because every prohibition becomes a form through which new freedoms are elaborated. There's still a hint of parody in the hustle's elegance, an adolescent send-up of grown-up glamour. And isn't that the way? The head held high, Spanish style, in bomba or the straight-backed prancing in cakewalk? Whatever's abstemious in aristocratic ways of moving gets critiqued through flawless mimicry until it emerges enhanced, almost unrecognizable, suddenly irresistible.

At Coney, dances kept emerging, dying, and coming back to life in fragments. For a while Sheila got involved in an extended exchange with a beautiful boy—sharp cheekbones, white Kangol—who clocked and matched her vintage footwork. Maybe he learned it at the studio like the white girls, or maybe his parents had been young at the Paradise Garage—either way, he knew how to address her in that mother tongue. There was a live drum playing off the DJ the way there was on the boat, and a girl in a yellow leotard danced alone in the semicircle sketched by the rhythm's range; I wouldn't quite call it a *batey*, but what else was it? Even though I was at the edge of the drummer's sight line, I couldn't resist throwing out a couple of elementary piquetes—embarrassed, a little, when he caught them and hit me back. He knew the language. Most people understand live drums as traditional, which they are, but the mistake would be to situate tradition in the past, on an evolutionary timeline that sees other musical technologies as more contemporary. It is precisely because the drums have survived so long that they imply futures we cannot imagine.

Across Africa, drums once sent messages from village to village, warning of wars and announcing celebrations, and in the vast diaspora—Cuba, Haiti, Honduras, Brazil—they speak beyond time to summon divinities or the dead. Particular percussive phrases invoke particular possibilities. In Indigenous communities from the Amazon to the Caribbean, the shaman's maraca opens the channel to the spirit realm. The stretched hide and callused hand, the scraped gourd and dried seeds, call out to the scratched record and the fingers dancing over the mixer's dials. "Tony Touch," he's called, "Tony Toca"—and even when the drum is an 808 and there's no live accompaniment, you can feel the human skin still in the game. Just as the live drums infused the party with a ceremonial energy, the party infused the inanimate world with dance. The wind caught the flowered sheet I held out for Sheila when she emerged, dripping, from the gray sea, and I began to swing my hips with it: "Janet," she said. Yes, Janet, but also—Yemaya—Isadora Duncan—Sail—Bride—Shroud.

.   .   .

By early August, I couldn't summon the same abandon. But even at summer's apocalyptic end, when I stayed at home to cook a quiet dinner with friends, the dance found a way to surface somehow. My friend Will Glovinsky and I were talking about rugs and chairs and paperweights, about the wish to claim objects from our grandparents—in this case, the photo album his grandfather compiled as a Jewish American GI in World War II's European theater. He hadn't been on the front lines when the camps were "liberated," but there were photographs of those places in the album, and the terror was close enough to touch. Will remembers his grandfather beginning to speak—he was old by then, in his nineties, his wife already gone—about a dance that was held for the GIs and the women who stumbled out, still thin and bald, from that dystopia. The survivors took to the floor with an enthusiasm he would never forget.

I wonder what kind of dance they were doing. The 1940s, American GIs—maybe it was swing, even Lindy. Those dances were international, at least in the cities. Or maybe many of the women came from rural villages and were more fluent in local variations of the polka (originally invented, as the story sometimes goes, by a Bohemian housemaid). I've never done the polka per se, but that raucous Old World cadence has carried me—almost always drunk and laughing—through the accordions of Mexican norteño. Most likely the GIs and the liberated women negotiated among styles, improvised with whatever shared vocabulary they could find. Or maybe they just slow-danced to the records the GIs had on hand. Bing Crosby, Nat King Cole. Now I'm singing along to a speculative music that belongs to someone else's story.

There's something a little scandalous about the notion of dancing after Auschwitz. We might wish, for those women, rest and recovery rather than an eroticized encounter with foreign men in uniform. But there has never been a program of rest and recovery that could completely restore the soul from genocidal trauma. Who are we to think we know when those women would have been ready to resume the rituals of social contact, to start seeking out joy? Their bodies had been used as automatons to perform unspeakable labors. Maybe it felt good and right to spend—to waste, in capitalist terms—what little energy they had left on pleasure without profit.

The stubborn intensity of that desire fortifies me now, archived alongside other distant scenes of dancing that have reached me secondhand. I never saw my own grandfather dance, but his rhythm is fundamental to the way I understand my own. And when I think of the afterlife, I think of José Mateo's days at the Saint, an early members-only megaclub for gay men—how the DJ "might play a beautiful ballad" between the disco sets "and everyone would pseudo waltz," gliding across the vast, slippery floor beneath the ceiling's starry dome. Even José can get lost in this collective dream: he can't always tell whether certain details he remembers come from the wild *comparsas* of his early years just north of Santiago de Cuba or the many stories his parents told him about them in the years that followed. Does it matter? Technically, our brains aren't capable of that distinction; either way, the same circuits play the scenes back.

These years of social distancing have been long, but our dances have survived longer years, greater distances, more punishing prohibitions. I can feel even the dances I've never danced pulsing gently, as pure potential, in my ordinary movements. One of Adrian Piper's earliest performances began this way: "I listened to Aretha's version of 'Respect' until I had it completely memorized and could hear the entire song in my mind at will. Sometimes it 'turned itself on' without my willing it." Going about her business "on line at the bank, at a bus stop and in the public library," she would tune in to that silent channel and begin to dance. And here we are, watching her from behind these words. But we don't have to just watch. We can do it too.

The Atlantic

In "We're Already Barreling Toward the Next Pandemic," Ed Yong investigates the effects of underinvestment in public health on both the course of the COVID-19 pandemic and the likelihood of future outbreaks. "COVID-19," writes Yong, "revealed that the United States, despite many superficial strengths, is alarmingly vulnerable to new diseases—and such diseases are inevitable." The ASME judges praised Yong for "the prescience of his reporting" and "his talent for synthesizing a complex and frightening set of problems." Yong's writing about the pandemic in The Atlantic was also nominated for the National Magazine Award for Public Interest last year and won the 2021 Pulitzer Prize for Explanatory Reporting. The Atlantic won two National Magazine Awards in 2022: the first for General Excellence, the second for Feature Writing for Jennifer Senior's "Twenty Years Gone."

Ed Yong

We're Already Barreling Toward the Next Pandemic

A year after the United States bombed its pandemic performance in front of the world, the Delta variant opened the stage for a face-saving encore. If the United States had learned from its mishandling of the original SARS-CoV-2 virus, it would have been better prepared for the variant that was already ravaging India.

Instead, after a quiet spring, President Joe Biden all but declared victory against SARS-CoV-2. The CDC ended indoor masking for vaccinated people, pitting two of the most effective interventions against each other. As cases fell, Abbott Laboratories, which makes a rapid COVID-19 test, discarded inventory, canceled contracts, and laid off workers, the *New York Times* reported. Florida and Georgia scaled back on reporting COVID-19 data, according to *Kaiser Health News*. Models failed to predict Delta's early arrival. The variant then ripped through the United States' half-vaccinated populace and once again pushed hospitals and healthcare workers to the brink. Delta's extreme transmissibility would have challenged any nation, but the United States nonetheless set itself up for failure. Delta was an audition for the next pandemic and one that America flubbed. How can a country hope to stay ten steps ahead of tomorrow's viruses when it can't stay one step ahead of today's?

America's frustrating inability to learn from the recent past shouldn't be surprising to anyone familiar with the history of public health. Almost twenty years ago, the historians of medicine Elizabeth Fee and Theodore Brown lamented that the United States had "failed to sustain progress in any coherent manner" in its capacity to handle infectious diseases. With every new pathogen—cholera in the 1830s, HIV in the 1980s—Americans rediscover the weaknesses in the country's health system, briefly attempt to address the problem, and then "let our interest lapse when the immediate crisis seems to be over," Fee and Brown wrote. The result is a Sisyphean cycle of panic and neglect that is now spinning in its third century. Progress is always undone; promise, always unfulfilled. Fee died in 2018, two years before SARS-CoV-2 arose. But in documenting America's past, she foresaw its pandemic present—and its likely future.

More Americans have been killed by the new coronavirus than the influenza pandemic of 1918, despite a century of intervening medical advancement. The United States was ranked first among nations in pandemic preparedness but has among the highest death rates in the industrialized world. It invests more in medical care than any comparable country, but its hospitals have been overwhelmed. It helped develop COVID-19 vaccines at near-miraculous and record-breaking speed, but its vaccination rates plateaued so quickly that it is now thirty-eighth in the world. COVID-19 revealed that the United States, despite many superficial strengths, is alarmingly vulnerable to new diseases—and such diseases are inevitable. As the global population grows, as the climate changes, and as humans push into spaces occupied by wild animals, future pandemics become more likely. We are not guaranteed the luxury of facing just one a century or even one at a time.

It might seem ridiculous to think about future pandemics now, as the United States is consumed by debates over booster shots, reopened schools, and vaccine mandates. *Prepare for the next one? Let's get through this one first!* But America must do both together, precisely because of the cycle that Fee and Brown bemoaned. Today's actions are already writing the opening chapters of the next pandemic's history.

Internationally, Joe Biden has made several important commitments. At the United Nations General Assembly last week, he called for a new council of national leaders and a new international fund, both focused on infectious threats—forward-looking measures that experts had recommended well before COVID-19.

But domestically, many public-health experts, historians, and legal scholars worry that the United States is lapsing into neglect, that the temporary wave of investments isn't being channeled into the right areas, and that COVID-19 might actually leave the United States *weaker* against whatever emerges next. Donald Trump's egregious mismanagement made it easy to believe that events would have played out differently with a halfway-competent commander who executed preexisting pandemic plans. But that ignores the many vulnerabilities that would have made the United States brittle under any administration. Even without Trump, "we'd still have been in a whole lot of trouble," Gregg Gonsalves, a global-health activist and an epidemiologist at Yale, told me. "The weaknesses were in the rootstock, not high up in the trees."

The panic-neglect cycle is not inevitable but demands recognition and resistance. "A pandemic is a course correction to the trajectory of civilization," Alex de Waal, of Tufts University and the author of *New Pandemics, Old Politics*, told me. "Historical pandemics challenged us to make some fairly fundamental changes to the way in which society is organized." Just as cholera forced our cities to be rebuilt for sanitation, COVID-19 should make us rethink the way we ventilate our buildings, as my colleague Sarah Zhang argued. But beyond overhauling its physical infrastructure, the United States must also address its deep social weaknesses—a health-care system that millions can't access, a public-health system that's been rotting for decades, and extreme inequities that leave large swaths of society susceptible to a new virus.

Early last year, some experts suggested to me that America's COVID-19 failure stemmed from its modern inexperience with infectious disease; having now been tested, it might do better next time. But preparedness doesn't come automatically, and neither does its absence. "Katrina didn't happen because Louisiana never had a hurricane before; it happened because of policy choices that led to catastrophe," Gonsalves said. The arc of history does not automatically bend toward preparedness. It must be bent.

· · ·

On September 3, the White House announced a new strategy to prepare for future pandemics. Drafted by the Office of Science and Technology Policy and the National Security Council, the plan would cost the United States $65 billion over the next seven to ten years. In return, the country would get new vaccines, medicines, and diagnostic tests; new ways of spotting and tracking threatening pathogens; better protective equipment and replenished stockpiles; sturdier supply chains; and a centralized mission control that would coordinate all the above across agencies. The plan, in rhetoric and tactics, resembles those that were written before COVID-19 and never fully enacted. It seems to suggest all the right things.

But the response from the health experts I've talked with has been surprisingly mixed. "It's underwhelming," Mike Osterholm, an epidemiologist at the University of Minnesota, told me. "That $65 billion should have been a down payment, not the entire program. It's a rounding error for our federal budget, and yet our entire existence going forward depends on this." The pandemic plan compares itself to the Apollo program, but the government spent four times as much, adjusted for inflation, to put astronauts on the Moon. Meanwhile, the COVID-19 pandemic may end up costing the United States an estimated $16 *trillion*.

"I completely agree that it will take more investment," Eric Lander, OSTP director and Biden's science adviser, told me; he noted that the published plan is just one element of a broader pandemic-preparedness effort that is being developed. But even the $65 billion that the plan has called for might not fully materialize. Biden originally wanted to ask Congress to immediately invest $30 billion but eventually called for just half that amount, in a compromise with moderate Democrats who sought to slash it even further. The idea of shortchanging pandemic preparedness after the events of 2020 "should be unthinkable," wrote the former CDC Director Tom Frieden and the former Senator Tom Daschle in *The Hill*. But it is already happening.

Others worry about the way the budget is being distributed. About $24 billion has been earmarked for technologies that can create vaccines against a new virus within one hundred days. Another $12 billion will go toward new antiviral drugs, and $5 billion toward diagnostic tests. These goals are, individually, sensible enough. But devoting two-thirds of the full budget toward them suggests that COVID-19's lessons haven't been learned.

America failed to test sufficiently throughout the pandemic even though rigorous tests have long been available. Antiviral drugs played a bit part because they typically provide incremental benefits over basic medical care and can be overly expensive even when they work. And vaccines were already produced far faster than experts had estimated and were more effective than they had hoped; accelerating that process won't help if people can't or won't get vaccinated and especially if they equate faster development with nefarious corner-cutting, as many Americans did this year. Every adult in the United States has been eligible for vaccines since mid-April; in that time, more Americans have died of COVID-19 per capita than people in Germany, Canada, Rwanda, Vietnam, or more than 130 other countries did *in the prevaccine era.*

"We're so focused on these high-tech solutions because they appear to be what a high-income country would do," Alexandra Phelan, an expert on international law and global health policy at Georgetown University, told me. And indeed, the Biden administration has gone all in on vaccines, trading them off against other countermeasures, such as masks and testing, and blaming "the unvaccinated" for America's ongoing pandemic predicament. The promise of biomedical panaceas is deeply ingrained in the United States psyche, but COVID should have shown that medical magic bullets lose their power when deployed in a profoundly unequal society. There are other ways of thinking about preparedness. And there are reasons those ways were lost.

．　　　　．　　　　．

In 1849, after investigating a devastating outbreak of typhus in what is now Poland, the physician Rudolf Virchow wrote, "The answer to the question as to how to prevent outbreaks . . . is quite simple: education, together with its daughters, freedom and welfare." Virchow was one of many nineteenth-century thinkers who correctly understood that epidemics were tied to poverty, overcrowding, squalor, and hazardous working conditions—conditions that inattentive civil servants and aristocrats had done nothing to address. These social problems influenced which communities got sick and which stayed healthy. Diseases exploit society's cracks, and so "medicine is a social science," Virchow famously said. Similar insights dawned across the Atlantic, where American physicians and politicians tackled the problem of urban cholera by fixing poor sanitation and dilapidated housing. But as the nineteenth century gave way to the twentieth, this social understanding of disease was ousted by a new paradigm.

When scientists realized that infectious diseases are caused by microscopic organisms, they gained convenient villains. Germ theory's pioneers, such as Robert Koch, put forward "an extraordinarily powerful vision of the pathogen as an entity that could be vanquished," Alex de Waal, of Tufts, told me. And that vision, created at a time when European powers were carving up other parts of the world, was cloaked in metaphors of imperialism, technocracy, and war. Microbes were enemies that could be conquered through the technological subjugation of nature. "The implication was that if we have just the right weapons, then just as an individual can recover from an illness and be the same again, so too can a society," de Waal said. "We didn't have to pay attention to the pesky details of the social world or see ourselves as part of a continuum that includes the other life-forms or the natural environment."

Germ theory allowed people to collapse everything about disease into battles between pathogens and patients. Social matters such as inequality, housing, education, race, culture, psychology, and politics became irrelevancies. Ignoring them was noble; it made medicine and science more apolitical and objective. Ignoring them was also easier; instead of staring into the abyss of society's intractable ills, physicians could simply stare at a bug under a microscope and devise ways of killing it. Somehow, they even convinced themselves that improved health would "ultimately reduce poverty and other social inequities," wrote Allan Brandt and Martha Gardner in 2000.

This worldview accelerated a growing rift between the fields of medicine (which cares for sick individuals) and public health (which prevents sickness in communities). In the nineteenth century, these disciplines were overlapping and complementary. In the twentieth, they split into distinct professions, served by different academic schools. Medicine, in particular, became concentrated in hospitals, separating physicians from their surrounding communities and further disconnecting them from the social causes of disease. It also tied them to a profit-driven system that saw the preventive work of public health as a financial threat. "Some suggested that if prevention could eliminate all disease, there would be no need for medicine in the future," Brandt and Gardner wrote.

This was a political conflict as much as an ideological one. In the 1920s, the medical establishment flexed its growing power by lobbying the Republican-controlled Congress and White House to erode public-health services including school-based nursing, outpatient dispensaries, and centers that provided pre- and post-natal care to mothers and infants. Such services were examples of "socialized medicine," unnecessary to those who were convinced that diseases could best be addressed by individual doctors treating individual patients. Health care receded from communities and became entrenched in hospitals. Decades later, these changes influenced America's response to COVID-19. Both the Trump and Biden administrations have described the pandemic in military metaphors. Politicians, physicians, and the public still prioritize biomedical solutions over social ones. Medicine still overpowers public health, which never recovered from being "relegated to a secondary status: less prestigious than clinical medicine [and] less amply financed," wrote the sociologist Paul Starr. It stayed that way for a century.

• • •

During the pandemic, many of the public-health experts who appeared in news reports hailed from wealthy coastal universities, creating a perception of the field as well funded and elite. That perception is false. In the early 1930s, the United States was spending just 3.3 cents of every medical dollar on public health, and much of the rest on hospitals, medicines, and private health care. And despite a ninety-year span that saw the creation of the CDC, the rise and fall of polio, the emergence of HIV, and relentless calls for more funding, that figure recently stood at . . . 2.5 cents. Every attempt to boost it eventually receded, and every investment saw an equal and opposite disinvestment. A preparedness fund that was created in 2002 has lost half its budget, accounting for inflation. Zika money was cannibalized from Ebola money. America's historical modus operandi has been to "give responsibility to the local public-health department but no power, money, or infrastructure to make change," Ruqaiijah Yearby, a health-law expert at Saint Louis University, told me.

Lisa Macon Harrison, who directs the department that serves Granville and Vance Counties, in North Carolina, told me that to protect her community of 100,000 people from infectious diseases—HIV, sexually transmitted infections, rabies, and more—the state gives her $4,147 a year. That's ninety times less than what she actually needs. She raises the shortfall herself through grants and local dollars.

Trifling budgets mean smaller staff, which turns mandatory services into optional ones. Public-health workers have to cope with not just infectious diseases but air and water pollution, food safety, maternal and child health, the opioid crisis, and tobacco control. But with local departments having lost 55,000 jobs since the 2008 recession, many had to pause their usual duties to deal with COVID-19. Even then, they didn't have staff to do the most basic version of contact tracing—calling people up—let alone the ideal form, wherein community health workers help exposed people find food, services, and places to isolate. When vaccines were authorized, departments had to scale back on testing so that overworked staff could focus on getting shots into arms; even that wasn't enough, and half of states hired armies of consultants to manage the campaign, the *Washington Post* reported.

In May, the Biden administration said that it would invest $7.4 billion in recruiting and training public-health workers, creating tens of thousands of jobs. But those new workers would be airdropped into an infrastructure that is quite literally crumbling. Many public-health departments are housed in buildings that were erected in the 1940s and '50s, when polio money was abundant; they are now falling apart. "There's a trash can in the hallway in front of my environmental-health supervisor's office to catch rain that might come through the ceiling," Harrison told me. And between their reliance on fax machines and decades-old data systems, "it feels like we're using a Rubik's Cube and an abacus to do pandemic response," Harrison added.

Last year, America's data systems proved to be utterly inadequate for tracking a rapidly spreading virus. Volunteer efforts such as the COVID Tracking Project (launched by *The Atlantic*) had to fill in for the CDC. Academics created a wide range of models, some of which were misleadingly inaccurate. "For hurricanes, we don't ask well-intentioned academics to stop their day jobs and tell us where landfall will happen," the CDC's Dylan George told me. "We turn to the National Hurricane Center." Similarly, George hopes that policy makers can eventually turn to the CDC's newly launched Center for Forecasting and Outbreak Analytics, where he is director of operations. With initial funding of about $200 million, the center aims to accurately track and predict the paths of pathogens, communicate those predictions with nuance, and help leaders make informed decisions quickly.

But public health's long-standing neglect means that simply making the system fit for purpose is a mammoth undertaking that can't be accomplished with emergency funds—especially not when those funds go primarily toward biomedical countermeasures. That's "a welfare scheme for university scientists and big organizations, and it's not going to trickle down to the West Virginia Department of Health," Gregg Gonsalves, the health activist and epidemiologist, told me. What the United States needs, as several reports have recommended and as some senators have proposed, is a stable and *protected* stream of money that can't be diverted to the emergency of the day. That would allow health departments to properly rebuild without constantly fearing the wrecking ball of complacency. Biden's $7.4 billion bolus is a welcome start—but just a start. And though his new pandemic-preparedness plan commits $6.5 billion toward strengthening the United States public-health system over the next decade, it might take $4.5 billion *a year* to actually do the job.

"Nobody should read that plan as the limit of what needs to be done," Eric Lander, the president's science adviser, told me. "I have no disagreement that a major effort and very substantial funding are needed," and, he noted, the administration's science and technology advisers will be developing a more comprehensive strategy. "But is pandemic preparedness the lens through which to fix public health?" Lander asked. "I think those issues are bigger—they're everyday problems, and we need to shine a spotlight on them every day."

But here is public health's bind: Though it is so fundamental that it can't (and arguably shouldn't) be tied to any one type of emergency, emergencies are also the one force that can provide enough urgency to strengthen a system that, under normal circumstances, is allowed to rot. When a doctor saves a patient, that person is grateful. When an epidemiologist prevents someone from catching a virus, that person never knows. Public health "is invisible if successful, which can make it a target for policy makers," Ruqaiijah Yearby, the health-law expert, told me. And during this pandemic, the target has widened, as overworked and under-resourced officials face aggressive protests. "Our workforce is doing fifteen-hour days and rather than being glorified, they're being vilified and threatened with bodily harm and death," Harrison told me. According to an ongoing investigation by the Associated Press and *Kaiser Health News*, the United States has lost at least 303 state or local public-health leaders since April 2020, many because of burnout and harassment.

Even though 62 percent of Americans believe that pandemic-related restrictions were worth the cost, Republican legislators in twenty-six states have passed laws that curtail the possibility of quarantines and mask mandates, as Lauren Weber and Anna Maria Barry-Jester of *KHN* have reported. Supporters characterize these laws as checks on executive power, but several do the opposite, allowing states to block local officials or schools from making decisions to protect their communities. Come the next pandemic (or the next variant), "there's a real risk that we are going into the worst of all worlds," Alex Phelan, of Georgetown University, told me. "We're removing emergency actions without the preventive care that would allow people to protect their own health." This would be dangerous for any community, let alone those in the United States that are structurally vulnerable to infectious disease in ways that are still being ignored.

•   •   •

Biden's new pandemic plan contains another telling detail about how the United States thinks about preparedness. The parts about vaccines and therapeutics contain several detailed and explicit strategies. The part about vulnerable communities is a single bullet point that calls for strategies to be developed.

This isn't a new bias. In 2008, Philip Blumenshine and his colleagues argued that America's flu-pandemic plans overlooked the disproportionate toll that such a disaster would take on socially disadvantaged people. Low-income and minority groups would be more exposed to airborne viruses because they're more likely to live in crowded housing, use public transportation, and hold low-wage jobs that don't allow them to work from home or take time off when sick. When exposed, they'd be more susceptible to disease because their baseline health is poorer, and they're less likely to be vaccinated. With less access to health insurance or primary care, they'd die in greater numbers. These predictions all came to pass during the H1N1 swine-flu pandemic of 2009.

When SARS-CoV-2 arrived a decade later, history repeated itself. The new coronavirus disproportionately infected essential workers, who were forced to risk exposure for the sake of their livelihood; disproportionately killed Pacific Islander, Latino, Indigenous, and Black Americans; and struck people who'd been packed into settings at society's margins—prisons, nursing homes, meatpacking facilities. "We've built a system in which many people are living on the edge, and pandemics prey on those vulnerabilities," Julia Raifman, a health-policy researcher at Boston University, told me.

Such patterns are not inevitable. "It is very clear, from evidence and history, that robust public-health systems rely on provision of social services," Eric Reinhart, a political anthropologist and physician at Northwestern University, told me. "That should just be a political given, and it is not. You have Democrats who don't even say this, let alone Republicans." America's ethos of rugged individualism pushes people across the political spectrum to see social vulnerability as a personal failure rather than the consequence of centuries of racist and classist policy, and as a problem for each person to solve on their own rather than a societal responsibility. And America's biomedical bias fosters the seductive belief that these sorts of social inequities won't matter if a vaccine can be made quickly enough.

But inequity reduction is not a side quest of pandemic preparedness. It is arguably the central pillar—if not for moral reasons, then for basic epidemiological ones. *Infectious diseases can spread*, from the vulnerable to the privileged. "*Our* inequality makes *me* vulnerable," Mary Bassett, who studies health equity at Harvard, told me. "And that's not a necessary feature of our lives. It can be changed."

"To be ready for the next pandemic, we need to make sure that there's an even footing in our societal structures," Seema Mohapatra, a health-law expert at Southern Methodist University, in Dallas, told me. That vision of preparedness is closer to what nineteenth-century thinkers lobbied for and what the twentieth century swept aside. It means shifting the spotlight away from pathogens themselves and onto the living and working conditions that allow pathogens to flourish. It means measuring preparedness not just in terms of syringes, sequencers, and supply chains but also in terms of paid sick leave, safe public housing, eviction moratoriums, decarceration, food assistance, and universal health care. It means accompanying mandates for social distancing and the like with financial assistance for those who might lose work or free accommodation where exposed people can quarantine from their family. It means rebuilding the health policies that Ronald Reagan began shredding in the 1980s and that later administrations further frayed. It means restoring trust in government and community through public services. "It's very hard to achieve effective containment when the people you're working with don't think you care about them," Arrianna Marie Planey, a medical geographer at the University of North Carolina at Chapel Hill, told me.

In this light, the American Rescue Plan—the $1.9 trillion economic-stimulus bill that Biden signed in March—is secretly a pandemic-preparedness bill. Beyond specifically funding public health, it also includes unemployment insurance, food-stamp benefits, child tax credits, and other policies that are projected to cut the poverty rate for 2021 by a third, and by even more for Black and Hispanic people. These measures aren't billed as ways of steeling America against future pandemics—but they are. Also on the horizon is a set of recommendations from the COVID-19 Health Equity Task Force, which Biden established on his first full day of office. "The president has told many of us privately, and said publicly, that equity has to be at the heart of what we do in this pandemic," Vivek Murthy, the surgeon general, told me.

• • •

Some of the American Rescue Plan's measures are temporary, and their future depends on the $3.5 trillion social-policy bill that Democrats are now struggling to pass, drawing opposition from within their own party. "Health equity requires multiple generations of work, and politicians want outcomes that can be achieved in time to be recognized by an electorate," Planey told me. That electorate is tiring of the pandemic, and of the lessons it revealed.

Last year, "for a moment, we were able to see the invisible infrastructure of society," Sarah Willen, an anthropologist at the University of Connecticut who studies Americans' conceptions of health equity, told me. "But that seismic effect has passed." Socially privileged people now also enjoy the privilege of immunity, while those with low incomes, food insecurity, eviction risk, and jobs in grocery stores and agricultural settings are disproportionately likely to be unvaccinated. Once, they were deemed "essential"; now they're treated as obstinate annoyances who stand between vaccinated America and a normal life.

The pull of the normal is strong, and our metaphors accentuate it. We describe the pandemic's course in terms of "waves," which crest and then collapse to baseline. We bill COVID-19 as a "crisis"—a word that evokes decisive moments and turning points, "and that, whether you want to or not, indexes itself against normality," Reinhart told me. "The idea that something new can be born out of it is lost," because people long to claw their way back to a precrisis state, forgetting that the crisis was itself born of those conditions.

Better ideas might come from communities for whom "normal" was something to survive, not revert to. Many Puerto Ricans, for example, face multiple daily crises including violence, poverty, power outages, and storms, Mónica Feliú-Mójer, of the nonprofit Ciencia Puerto Rico, told me. "They're always preparing," she said, "and they've built support networks and mutual-aid systems to take care of each other." Over the past year, Ciencia PR has given small grants to local leaders to fortify their communities against COVID-19. While some set up testing and vaccination clinics, others organized food deliveries or educational events. One cleaned up a dilapidated children's park to create a low-risk outdoor space where people could safely reconnect. Such efforts recognize that resisting pandemics is about solidarity as well as science, Feliú-Mójer told me.

The panic-neglect cycle is not irresistible. Some of the people I spoke with expressed hope that the United States can defy it, just not through the obvious means of temporarily increased biomedical funding. Instead, they placed their faith in grassroots activists who are pushing for fair labor policies, better housing, health-care access, and other issues of social equity. Such people would probably never think of their work as a way of buffering against a pandemic, but it very much is—and against other health problems, natural disasters, and climate change besides. These threats are varied, but they all wreak their effects on the same society. And that society can be as susceptible as it allows itself to be.

Harper's

The ASME judges described Ann Patchett's "These Precious Days" as "an enchanting first-person account of the life-affirming friendship that begins when Tom Hanks's assistant, Sooki Raphael, moves into the writer's home while undergoing chemotherapy at a nearby hospital." That is the heart of the story (and yes, it is that Tom Hanks), but what the judges left out—had to leave out, since "These Precious Days" is 20,000 words long—is acknowledgment of the unexpected gift that their friendship brought both writer and guest: "to find someone who could see us as our best and most complete selves." Patchett is the author of eight novels, including most recently The Dutch House, *a 2020 finalist for the Pulitzer Prize for Fiction. "These Precious Days" is the title piece in a collection of Patchett's essays published in late 2021.*

Ann Patchett

These Precious Days

I can tell you where it all started because I remember the moment exactly. It was late, and I'd just finished the novel I'd been reading. A few more pages would send me off to sleep, so I went in search of a short story. They aren't hard to come by around here; my office is made up of piles of books, mostly advance-reader copies that have been sent to me in hopes I'll write a quote for the jacket. They arrive daily in padded mailers—novels, memoirs, essays, histories—things I never requested and in most cases will never get to. On this summer night in 2017, I picked up a collection called *Uncommon Type*, by Tom Hanks. It had been languishing in a pile by the dresser for a while, and I'd left it there because of an unarticulated belief that actors should stick to acting. Now for no particular reason I changed my mind. Why shouldn't Tom Hanks write short stories? Why shouldn't I read one? Off we went to bed, the book and I, and in doing so put the chain of events into motion. The story has started without my realizing it. The first door opened, and I walked through.

But any story that starts will also end. This is the way novelists think: beginning, middle, and end.

In case you haven't read it, *Uncommon Type* is a very good book. It would have to be for this story to continue. Had it been a bad book or just a good-enough book, I would have put it down, but page after page it surprised me. Two days later, I sent an endorsement to the editor. I've written plenty of jacket quotes in my day, mostly for first-time writers of fiction whom I believed could benefit from the assistance. The thought of Tom Hanks benefiting from my assistance struck me as funny, and then I forgot about it.

Or I would have forgotten about it, except that I got a call from Tom Hanks's publicist a few weeks later, asking whether I would fly to Washington in October to interview the actor onstage as part of his book tour. As the co-owner of a bookstore, I do this sort of thing, and while I mostly do it in Nashville, where I live, there have certainly been requests interesting enough to get me on a plane. I could have said I was busy writing a novel, and that would have been both ridiculous and true. Tom Hanks needs a favor? Happy to help.

"Do you even realize your life isn't normal?" Niki said when I announced my trip. Niki works at the bookstore. She has opinions about my life. "You understand that other people don't live this way?"

• • •

How other people live is pretty much all I think about. Curiosity is the rock upon which fiction is built. But for all the times people have wanted to tell me their story because they think it would make a wonderful novel, it pretty much never works out. People are not characters, no matter how often we tell them they are; conversations are not dialogue; and the actions of our days don't add up to a plot. In life, time runs together in its sameness, but in fiction time is condensed—one action springboards into another, greater action. Cause and effect are so much clearer in novels than they are in life. You might not see how everything threads together as you read along, but when you look back from the end of the story, the map becomes clear. Maybe Niki was right about my life being different, but maybe that's because I tend to think of things in terms of story: I pick up a book and read it late into the night, and because I like the book, I wind up on a flight to DC.

• • •

I went by myself. I was going only for the night. I walked from my hotel to the theater and showed my ID to a guard who then led me to the crowded greenroom. I met the hosts of the event and a few people who worked for them. I was introduced to Tom Hanks's editor, Tom Hanks's agent, his publicist, his assistant, Tom Hanks himself. He was tall and slim, happily at ease, answering questions, signing books. Everyone was laughing at his jokes because his jokes were funny. The people around him arranged themselves into different configurations so that the assistant could take their pictures, each one handing over his or her cell phone. Audience questions arrived on index cards, were read aloud and sorted through. The ones Tom Hanks approved of were handed to me. I would ask them at the end of the event, depending on how much time we had. The greenroom crowd was then escorted to their seats, and we were ushered to the dark place behind the curtain—Tom Hanks, his assistant, and I. The assistant was a tiny woman wearing a fitted black-velvet evening coat embroidered with saucer-size peonies. "Such a beautiful coat," I said to her. We'd been introduced when I arrived but I didn't remember her name.

The experience of waiting backstage before an event is always the same. I can never quite hear what the person making the introduction is saying, and for a moment I wouldn't be able to tell you the name of the theater or even the city I was in. There's usually a guy working the light board and the mics who talks to me for a minute, though tonight the guy talking was Tom Hanks. He wanted to know whether I liked owning a bookstore. He was thinking about opening one himself. Could we talk about it sometime? Of course we could. We were about to go on.

"I don't have any questions," I whispered in the darkness. "I find these things go better if you just wing it." Then the two of us stepped out into the blinding light.

As soon as the roaring thunder of approval eased, he pointed at me and said, "She doesn't have any *questions*."

·   ·   ·

When the event was over and more pictures had been taken and everyone had said how much they'd enjoyed absolutely everything, Tom Hanks and his assistant and I found ourselves alone again, standing at the end of a long cement hallway by a stage door, saying good night and goodbye. A car was coming to pick them up.

"Come on, Sooki," he said, his voice gone grand. "Let's go back to the hotel. I need to find a Belvedere martini."

I hoped he would ask me to join them. I'd spent two hours on a stage talking to Tom Hanks, and now I wanted to talk to Sooki. Sooki of the magnificent coat. She had said almost nothing and yet my eye kept going to her, the way one's eye goes to the flash of iridescence on a hummingbird's throat. I thought about how extraordinarily famous you would have to be to have someone like that working as your assistant.

Neither of them asked me out for drinks.

.   .   .

Again it would appear this story had reached its conclusion. But a few months later, I got an email from Tom Hanks early in the morning. He was in Nashville. Could I meet him at the bookstore, Parnassus, in half an hour? I couldn't. My friend Sister Nena had just called. She'd fallen down some stairs outside of church the night before and twisted her foot and now that foot was swollen and sore. She needed me to take her to the hospital for an X-ray.

"I've got to take care of my nun," I told him.

"*Your* nun?" he wrote, as opposed to what most people would say, "Your *nun*?"

I told Sister Nena the whole story while we sat in the waiting room, her foot propped up on a wheelchair. She was disappointed. "I want to meet Tom Hanks," she said. I called the bookstore and let the staff know that Tom Hanks was on his way over. He thrilled them, buying stacks of books, signing books, posing for pictures, going next door to the Donut Den for an apple fritter. I had missed my chance. But months later there he was again. His wife, Rita

Wilson, is a singer who writes with people in Nashville, where songwriting is a group activity. It turned out that Tom and Rita came to town something less than regularly but more than I would have thought. On this visit, we sat in the cramped office at my bookstore and talked about the one he was considering opening in Santa Monica while my dog slept in his lap. I was already years ahead of myself, thinking of all the good Tom Hanks could do for independent bookstores. Could any business wish for a better spokesperson?

Here's a universal truth: people are interested in helping Tom Hanks. Our hearts have been filled with the comfort his films have given us, and that, coupled with the fact that he's a nice man, made it easy to line up a group of booksellers who were eager to pitch in. But over time the idea drifted to the back burner. Our correspondence was less about bookstores and more about books. One more reason to like Tom Hanks: he's a reader. He recommends books and asks for recommendations. I had just finished my latest novel, and on a lark of the highest order, I sent him an email asking if he might record the audiobook. He responded:

> March 17, 2019: Hey! I'm in Albuquerque shooting a movie. I'd love to do your audio book! But when? I have limited time as I work til mid May, then leave the US in June until I come back to start another movie in September. So what are the deadlines, days needed, etc? Books are fun!

I sat at my desk for a long time, trying to make sense of this: time when there was no time, and talent all out of proportion to the task. It hadn't occurred to me that he might say yes. Had I thought it through, I never would have had the nerve to ask in the first place. A year and a half had passed since I had picked up his book in my office, and this was where it had taken me: Tom Hanks was willing to read *The Dutch House*.

I'd been in touch with Sooki once or twice when there was talk of a bookstore in Santa Monica, and now I pinned my hopes on her as she dug into Tom's schedule at Playtone, his production company. Wonderful Sooki! She made the time, stitching days together. As we worked our way through trying to get contracts signed and making arrangements with the audio producer, our emails became an affectionate exchange.

April 30, 2019: I imagine your kindness comes from you being kind. Just a guess.

April 30, 2019: My kindness comes from sincerely wanting this recording to happen. I am a huge fan of your work (and Tom's, of course) and it just thrills me that you are collaborating on this! So happy to be the connector of good things.

This wasn't out of the ordinary for me, as I'm sure it wasn't for her. Email tilts toward the overly familiar. I tilt toward the overly familiar.

I'd written a children's book and was about to go on tour. Sooki had two young grandchildren in San Diego and made plans to bring them to an event I was doing there, but they didn't show. I lost her for a while, and then she was back again. She apologized for her late response, saying that she'd had a medical procedure and hadn't been in the office.

I asked whether she was okay. I had met Sooki, after all. We'd stood together in the dark of a Washington theater for a matter of minutes a year and a half earlier. I had liked her coat very much, those pink peonies as big as my hand.

May 21, 2019: Thank you for your concern about my medical procedure. I am doing my best to keep it pushed off to the side, but I was diagnosed with pancreatic cancer in November (caught it early) so I've been dealing with surgeries and chemo. I'm still here—at Playtone and in general.

She had been diagnosed with pancreatic cancer a year after we met. There was no reason for her to tell me this. We didn't know each other, and for the most part our correspondence had come after this defining fact. Ours was an ephemeral connection common to the modern world. Except it was Sooki, and I liked her very much.

A week later, Tom Hanks started recording *The Dutch House* at a studio in Los Angeles. Sooki went with him every day. She sent updates—chapter 8 now, chapter 12. The producer of the audiobook sent me an article about Sooki from a 1978 issue of *New York* magazine. Sooki had gone to work for the New York City Department of Health's Bureau of Animal Affairs right out of college. She was the bat squad. She was Batgirl. There were pictures of her at twenty-two, beautiful and dark-eyed, standing on somebody's desk in little canvas tennis shoes, her gloved hands holding a bat and a net. I was struck by an overwhelming sense of wanting to know her, of not wanting to miss Sooki while she was here.

•   •   •

This is what it's like to write a novel: I come up with a shred of an idea. It can be a character, a place, a moral quandary. In the case of *The Dutch House*, I'd started to think about a poor woman who suddenly became rich, and because she was unable to deal with the change in circumstances, she left her family and went to India to follow a guru.

Sister Nena shook her head. "Not a guru. She's Catholic. She doesn't have to go to India. She helps the poor like Dorothy Day."

We were sitting at the bar at California Pizza Kitchen at four o'clock in the afternoon. It was our place, what Sister Nena called "vacation." She ordered the house merlot and I had a seltzer with cranberry juice. She wanted to know about the book I was going to write next, the book I had just barely started thinking of.

"This woman goes to India," I said.

"She could be a nun." Sister Nena picked up a piece of bread and swiped it through the olive oil in the saucer between us.

I shook my head. "She's married," I said. "She has children. She has to have children."

"It could happen. Plenty of nuns were married before."

"They were widows, not divorced."

"You never know." Then she looked at me, her face suddenly brightened by a plot twist. "She could work for Mother Teresa. If she really wanted to go to India and she wanted to serve the poor, that's what she would do."

I wasn't sure why I was negotiating my character's future with my friend, but there I was, listening. Did my character want to be a nun?

When I'm putting together a novel, I leave all the doors and windows open so the characters can come in and just as easily leave. I don't take notes. Once I start writing things down, I feel like I'm nailing the story in place. When I rely on my faulty memory, the pieces are free to move. The main character I was certain of starts to drift, and someone I'd barely noticed moves in to fill the space. The road forks and forks again. It becomes a path into the woods. It becomes the woods. I find a stream and follow it, the stream dries up, and I'm left to look for moss on the sides of trees. For a time, the mother in this novel went to India to work for Mother Teresa. I tried it but it didn't work. What about the children who were left behind in that house she hated? What became of them? And what about the women who cleaned that house, who fixed those children their dinner? The ones who stayed turned out to be the ones I was interested in.

Putting together a novel is essentially putting together the lives of strangers I'm coming to know. In some ways it's not unlike putting together my own life. I think I know what I'm doing when in truth I have no idea. I just keep moving forward. By the time the book is written, there is little evidence of the initial spark or a long-ago conversation in California Pizza Kitchen. Still, I'm able, for a while at least, to pick up the thread and walk it back. Everything looks so logical going backward—*Yes, of course, that's what we did*—but going forward it's something else entirely. Going forward, the lights may as well be off.

·   ·   ·

Sooki and I kept up a sporadic email exchange once the audio-book was done. I thought of her time as precious now. We wrote about painting because she painted. I sent her books on color theory. We wrote about artists we liked, about Pantone and the color wheel. *Dear* gave way to *Dearest. Love* became *Much love.* Then this:

June 21, 2019: As of last week, my six-month chemo run is done, and I had a follow up CT scan. My doctor paired up some words I never thought I would hear together: "pancreatic cancer" and "you're in remission!" It seems like an early declaration, but I'll take it! Here's to more time to explore color and enjoy all the people—like you—who make life colorful.

Later in the summer there was radiation, just to be safe.

August 5, 2019: Radiation has become a fascinating routine over the last five weeks.

Twenty-two sessions down and six to go. Only on weekdays and not on the Fourth of July, because apparently cancer knows to take weekends off and observe federal holidays.

I leave the house at 6:30 am every weekday morning to make it down to the bottom basement—floor 2B—at UCLA's Westwood Medical Center by 7:30 am. There is a bright therapist named Hassan at my assigned machine, always the same, with a sweet attitude. He has me repeat my name, birth date and area of radiation each time before I enter the room. I want to envision it as a healing room, but it reminds me of a meat locker: freezing cold—I'm guessing the temperature favors the delicate machinery—with a rack of blue torsos lined up on hooks. My blue torso, the mold made on the day I came in for my fitting and tattoos, is already on the radiation bed and I need to bare my abdomen and slide onto the table so they can line up the laser beams with all my tattoos and red-sharpie x's before they cover me with a warmed flannel sheet.

I was impressed that first day when the therapists swarmed the table forming the mold around me and explaining about tattoos. I was told that although not everyone wanted to commit to having the tattoos, it was the most accurate way to align the radiation field that had been so meticulously laid out by a team of physicists working alongside my radiation oncologist. The only other option was to go with "stickers" which could shift or come off in the shower. Of course I opted for tattoos. Precision seemed like a good decision here. Three blue tattoos on the same plane as my prominent abdominal scar, it would hardly matter. So, I was surprised on my first scheduled day of radiation to have another technician pop in with a red sharpie to make three large x's near the tattoos as additional points of reference and stick clear round stickers over them.

Now I look like an improvised elementary school art project, and in addition to owning my permanent tattoos, I have to nurture my three little stickers and hand-drawn sharpie marks so they last six weeks. I feel like I could pop into Trader Joe's and have them replaced with those happy little stickers they hand out to well-behaved children—it undermines my confidence in the sophisticated nature of the whole process just a bit.

I sent more books: books I'd written, books I thought she'd like, Kate DiCamillo books to be read with her grandchildren. In return, she sent me pictures she'd taken of Los Angeles, a woman in an orange sari sailing past a city bus on a bicycle. The world that Sooki inhabited was electrified by greens and blues, purple bougainvillea draping over hot-pink walls, colors too vivid to be explained. She would pour color into my inbox for a while and then be gone again. Winter came without a word. I worried, and thought it was not my place to ask. Did Tom even know that Sooki and I were friends? Would he think to tell me if something had happened? I wanted to say hello very quietly so as not to bother her. I didn't want to be one more person tugging at her coat, but I was.

December 27, 2019: Sweetest Ann, I am traveling today—just for the day—up to Stanford for a second opinion, with the magician's elephant in my carry-on bag.

I didn't need to hear about the first opinion to know what that meant. I said good luck because there was nothing else to say. Could I say that I would like to come see her? That I would like to meet her in the way I had wanted to meet my pen pals as a child? This was what I knew about Sooki: She lived in Los Angeles. She had a son and a daughter-in-law with two children who lived south of her and a daughter and son-in-law who had recently moved north. She painted. She once caught bats for the City of New York. She worked for Tom Hanks.

I saw Tom and Rita in Nashville two more times. The second time they came because Rita was singing at the Grand Ole Opry. My husband, Karl, and I sat in a dressing room with them for an hour and a half between sets. Dionne Warwick came in with her son. We talked about singing and touring and about the Opry. I told them that when I was a child, my sister and I would come to the Ryman on Friday and Saturday nights with the man who was then the house doctor at the Opry. He would bring us with his own two small girls, and the four of us would sit in the coils of snaking power cords backstage and fall asleep in dressing rooms, in this very dressing room. Every childhood is strange in its own way.

February 7, 2020: When last we typed you were on your way to Stanford for a second opinion. I think about you often and hope for the best. Much love. Ann

February 8, 2020: I have wanted to write—every day—for forever. As I got ready to send the details of my second opinion, I was already looking to the third opinion and rethinking the story.

My cancer marker—CA 19-9—is nonspecific to pancreatic cancer (it can indicate other inflammation in the body), but it's an indicator and is supposed to be at 35 U/L or less. It was normal in October, three months post–chemo and radiation—great news—but then started rising.

It has been an exercise in creative storytelling to try to think up more and more reasons why the number might rise while the scans (CTs! MRIs! PET scans) were showing no sign of disease. I looked up every anomaly online, settling on too much black tea, or maybe the wrong color shoes. As the number spiked this week at 1700 U/L, I ran out of excuses, and my PET scan on Wednesday showed a return of the cancer to my liver.

I am now sitting at the airport waiting to catch a plane to my next opinion, at Sloan Kettering in NY. (It was not reassuring to know that one of the nurses at UCLA thought that "Sloan Kettering" was the name of the doctor I'd be seeing.) It looks like I'll have chemo and maybe a clinical trial ahead. I will keep you more closely posted as I move ahead (in the right color shoes).

The last few months, the oncologists were watching the numbers and Western medicine offered nothing to do but to wait and see where the cancer showed up. I was convinced it wouldn't show up and embarked on a full-scale exploratory mission into holistic healing, prayer, juicing, yoga, meditation, sound waves, and magnetic magic (this last one, highly recommended by a friend, but in a clinic run by a reality-tv star). I gained back twenty pounds, and have been back hiking the trails and at work full time. I feel great.

But the doctors say, as they expected, the cancer is back, and they are ready to start up chemo again.

My reading on this flight is a book called Radical Remission. I am hopeful and feeling radical.

I promise to be a more reliable friend and pen pal. I miss our emails.

Much love,

Sooki

That night as my husband and I walked our dog around the block in the cold dark, I told him about Sooki. This was what we did at the end of the day. "Tell me the news of the great world," Karl would say when he got home from work, and since many were the days I didn't leave the house, I relied on books and phone calls and emails in order to have something to contribute. As Sparky stopped and sniffed, I offered up Sooki's recurrence as a story to tell, not a problem to solve. Karl is a doctor, but Sooki had been treated at UCLA, Stanford, Duke, and Memorial Sloan Kettering. This wasn't about an inability to get good medical care; it was about not being able to find a clinical trial that both matched her cancer and could accept her immediately. The months she'd lost not being in chemo while they struggled to locate the new tumor had put her perilously behind.

"Tell me how you know her again?" he asked.

I told him she worked for Tom Hanks, that we'd struck up a little friendship over email.

Karl said she should send him her records if she wanted to, and that he would talk to Johanna Bendell, an oncologist at the hospital where he works. He said they were running more trials for pancreatic cancer than Sloan Kettering.

I had thought this was a story about Tom Hanks, the friendly actor-writer who had recorded my book, but I was mistaken. I kept up with a great number of people, and I didn't know to what extent I'd told Sooki's story to Karl before, and if I had told him, I didn't know whether he'd been listening, but now I had his full attention. To introduce Karl into this narrative as a general internist (he calls himself a pediatrician for adults) would be reductive. Simply put, Karl makes rain. He figures out problems that other people have tried and failed to solve for years. Other doctors are quick to do him favors because he's done so many for them. He holds a kind of medical currency, saved then spent, and when needed, he can marshal all necessary parties into immediate action, bringing them together so fast that whatever needs to happen can happen yesterday.

I told him about Sooki that night, but it was equally possible that I wouldn't have. He didn't know her, and I didn't exactly know her either. I made it a point not to tell Karl sad medical stories at the end of his long days of sad medical stories. I might have made the choice to let it go unmentioned had there been something else to talk about, maybe his mother or my mother or the spigot that had frozen in the garage. I could have forgotten Sooki altogether in that moment because even though I followed her story with interest, it was one of many stories. But I didn't forget. I told him.

When we got home from our walk, I emailed Sooki and said that if she wanted Karl to check on the possibility of a trial in Nashville she should send her medical records.

. . .

There is nothing more interesting than time: the days that are endless, the days that get away. There are days of the distant past that remain so vivid to me that I could walk back into them and pick up the conversation midsentence while there are other days (weeks, months, people, places) I couldn't recall to save my life. One of the last things I understand when I'm putting a novel together is the structure of time. When does the story start and when does it end? Will time be linear, or can it stutter and skip? At what point does our understanding of the action shift?

. . .

We have come to the point in this story when time changes. It had been more than two years since I met Sooki in a theater in Washington. We had never spoken on the phone. The emails we'd exchanged could be printed out and slid into a single manila envelope. But the clinical trial she needed was here in Nashville at the hospital where my husband worked. Karl's friend Dr. Bendell knew Sooki's oncologist at UCLA and her oncologist at Stanford and her surgeon at Duke. They reviewed her records together. I was copied on a barrage of emails I had no business reading, reports of molecular profiling, adenocarcinoma, tumor tissue for genetic analysis. I now knew that she'd had a Whipple at Duke and twelve rounds of FOLFIRINOX followed by twenty-eight days of radiation over five and a half weeks at UCLA. UCLA had plans to start the same clinical trial that was up and running in Nashville, but not for another month or two, a unit of time that could not be lost to waiting. Plans were made for Sooki to come to Nashville. I told her I would pick her up at the airport. I told her, of course, that she would stay with us.

Let's go back to Karl for a minute.

This wasn't the first time I'd invited someone we didn't know to live with us. I once invited the daughter of a woman who ran a lecture series in Pittsburgh to live with us when she found a job in Nashville and couldn't find an apartment. Nell stayed for six months, and we loved her. My friend Patrick, who lives in a tiny apartment in New York, spends a couple of weeks with us every year, writing in our basement, which, for the record, is nothing like a basement. He uses the library table to spread out his papers. Writers who do readings at the bookstore are often stashed in the guest room. Karl has never once complained. He claims our lives are better for all the people I bring into the house. He thanks me for it. Still, I wanted to double-check. Sooki was coming as a patient, and more than a little of the work was going to fall to him. I emailed him at work. I asked him how he would feel about my extending an invitation to stay.

February 14, 2020: PS—Just to be clear, I ran all this by Karl first, who said, "I favor having her here." (Very Karl.)

February. 14, 2020: Oh, Ann. I don't even know how to respond to such generosity.

I would love to stay with you for my first night or two in Nashville—it would be wonderful to spend some time with you.

Once I'm there for chemo, I will find a place where I won't be worried about being a good houseguest. I just can't stand the thought of being so disruptive to your and Karl's (and Sparky's!) lives. I know that after my last round of chemo I would sometimes get up and eat in the middle of the night, or get up early and make noisy smoothies. I'm self-conscious about being in the way, especially if I'm not at my best through chemo. I just would worry too much about being a bad friend.

My husband, Ken, will come down for at least part of the time, once I've started chemo, and I may have other visitors, so I think I will explore some other options in the area, but I can't tell you how touched I am that you've extended the offer.

Sooki was married? I had pictured her going through this alone, a conclusion I reached on account of a lack of information and a florid imagination. Had I known she had a husband, might I have assumed that she was taken care of and so not followed the story as closely? I tried to find a place for this new fact in the equation but all I could come up with was the obvious—I didn't know her. I didn't know how old she was, I couldn't remember her face, but there have been few moments in my life when I have felt so certain: I was supposed to help. I was overcome by a sense of order in the world: if I hadn't picked up that book, if I hadn't gone to DC, if we hadn't stayed in just enough contact for her to tell me a year after the fact that she had cancer, and if I hadn't mentioned it to Karl, she wouldn't have found her way to the only clinical trial in the country that both matched her cancer and could take her immediately. I wrote again.

February 15, 2020: I will try to keep this quick as I know you have many fish to fry.

I hear you, and I know that if I were in your shoes and you were asking me to stay with you it would seem impossible. But I think once you're here and see the setup you'll understand. The bottom floor of the house is an apartment, separate entrance, no kitchen. We call it the VanDevender Home for Wayward Girls. There is another guest suite on the main floor and we live on the top floor. There are people here all the time. You will not be called upon to be a good guest.

I live fourteen minutes from the airport and five minutes from the hospital. I will pick you up very late on Tuesday and take you to see Johanna on Wednesday. Kate DiCamillo is coming later on Wednesday. You will love her. We are Southern, and it is like this here, always. Some people stay for months. It's like a Noël Coward play but not as witty.

I didn't know you had a husband!! What a good idea. Ken will like it here, too. Wait and see. And you will be surprised by how comforting it is to be very sick with an actual doctor upstairs. Karl is the king of the hospital. He'll make sure you get everything you need.

They can't do the Stanford biopsy here?

Much love.

We went back and forth. She agreed to stay for a few nights, but after that she said she would rent a car and find a hotel. Ken would come later. I tried to imagine chemo while living in a hotel. Surely there were sadder things, but none of them came to mind. My childhood best friend was staying with us while this discussion was going on. Her father was in the hospital, and she had driven down from Kentucky to take care of him. "Don't worry about it," Tavia said. "Once she gets here and sees the way things are, she'll be fine."

Because if I didn't know that Sooki had a husband, how much did she know about me, about us? Nothing. We would meet on the level playing field of affectionate strangers.

• • •

Sooki arrived in Nashville on Sunday, February 23, just after Kate left. I had told her the make of my car, and she waved when I pulled up in front of the airport. She looked like a tiny rock star in her shaggy pale-pink coat and sunglasses and high boots. She looked like Los Angeles in winter. We hugged, and I hefted her enormous suitcase into the hatchback.

What had been a theory—*Sooki should come to Nashville for her chemo*—was now a fact. There she was in the passenger seat, a shy person with a quiet voice. I asked her about her trip to Stanford for the biopsy, her flight to Nashville. She repeated her gratitude, and I waved it away. We did our best to pretend that what we were doing was normal. I asked her whether she had ever been to Nashville before, and she said yes, once, with Tom a long time ago. There had been a meeting of some sort. She'd only been here for a couple of hours.

I was leaving the next day for an event in New York. I would be gone for the night, and once I got back my friend Emma Straub was coming to visit. Emma and I would be speaking at a librarians' convention downtown. I would leave again on Sunday for Virginia. I had warned Sooki about all of this before she arrived. Everything was planned so far in advance, and my spring was packed with speaking engagements. I would be in and out; other people would spend the night, which would be fine, plenty of room for everyone. We would all proceed with our lives except that now we would be together.

I had invited someone I didn't know to live with us for an undetermined length of time, and I was leaving the day after she arrived, leaving it all to Karl. Even if it wasn't a perfect plan, it was better than doing nothing.

Karl was home from work when we got to the house, and he and I showed Sooki around. There was a sitting room downstairs, the library, her bedroom and bathroom. I had cut a small bouquet of Lenten roses and put them on the night table. There was a bottle of water, a blue glass by the sink. I told her to take her time settling in. We would have dinner whenever she was ready. She gave us a giant furry blanket that I loved. She had brought a squeaky toy for Sparky.

"She seems very nice," Karl said once we were in the kitchen. As I was agreeing, there she was again.

"I'm sorry to bother you," Sooki said, looking around. "But have you seen my phone? It looks like a little purse on a long strap?"

I asked her if she could have left it on the plane, but no, of course not. She'd called me from outside the airport. "Let's try the car."

The cell-phone case also served as her wallet, containing her credit cards, cash, IDs, insurance cards—everything important. We looked in the car. We looked downstairs and in the kitchen and the den. She had been in the house for only a few minutes; there hadn't been enough time to lose anything. She gave me the number and I called it from the house phone, hoping we'd hear it ring. A man answered. The phone had been turned in to airport security.

"I must have dropped it. It must have fallen off my shoulder when I got in the car." Sooki was a tiny thing, with thick brown hair and olive skin. She told me she had gained back the twenty pounds she'd lost after the last chemo but she couldn't have weighed a hundred pounds now. "If I can borrow your car, I'll drive back to the airport."

I shook my head. "Then you'd have to park. It would be a nightmare."

Karl said he would go.

"They aren't going to give you her wallet," I said. "Go together. Karl can pull up and you'll run in. You two go, and I'll have dinner ready by the time you get back." It was the practical solution, and so they left. While they were gone I tried to imagine it: the cancer back, the wallet gone, strangers.

Or maybe it wasn't as bad as that. The phone hadn't been run over, nothing in the wallet was missing. Karl and Sooki came in the back door together in the middle of a conversation. They were talking like old friends. "Sooki's a pilot!" Karl said. He wanted to know why I hadn't told him this. How could I not have known? Karl had started flying in Mississippi when he was ten. He had a single-engine Cirrus that he kept at the small hobby airport not far from where we lived.

"My mother was a pilot," Sooki said, and there she was, suddenly at ease.

"Sooki got her pilot's license before she learned to drive," Karl told me.

"Whenever I came to an intersection I would look to the right, the left, then up and down."

I lit the candles on the table and served the cauliflower cake and tomato soup I'd made that afternoon. The phone sat beside her on the table quietly—the prodigal returned—while we asked the kind of questions people ask on first dates: Do you have siblings? What do your children do? Where were you born? All three of us had lost our fathers; all three of us were close with our mothers. Now that things were going right I felt the jolt of just exactly how wrong they could have been. But this was right, and we would all be fine.

.   .   .

I flew to New York early the next morning, took a car to New Jersey, signed several hundred books, attended a cocktail-party fund-raiser for the Book Industry Charitable Foundation, gave a talk in a crowded town hall, got to my hotel room in Manhattan at midnight, got up in the morning to tape a segment for the *Today* show, then was back on a plane. It was such a short trip it hardly counted as being gone.

The house smelled of chickpea stew and rice when I came in the door that night. Sooki was making dinner. She'd gone to an Indian restaurant and bought bread stuffed with apricots and dates. Everything was lit up bright, the table set. In the twenty-six years that Karl and I had been together, I'd never had the experience of coming home to dinner being made. It was a minor footnote considering everything I got from Karl, but still, the warmth of it, the love: to walk in the door after a long two days and see that someone had imagined that I might be hungry knocked me sideways. This was what marriage must look like from the other side.

Karl found a giant bright-blue tarp in the garage and Sooki spread it over the floor and table downstairs, setting herself up to paint. Our lives ran the way they always did, only with the addition of a quiet person who did her best to take up as little space and be as helpful as possible. We took turns cooking or cooked together. Back before she came, when she was still insisting on finding a hotel, I asked her if we could talk for just a minute on the phone. I wanted to know what her worst fear about staying here was, and after a pause she told me she was a vegetarian. I laughed. I should have thought of that one myself. It's why I don't like to go to other people's houses for dinner: I never want to tell people I'm a vegetarian.

We kept a common grocery list on the kitchen counter. Writers still came and spent the night; bookstore events were still packed. Most mornings, Sooki set out in the darkness to walk the two miles to a power-yoga class that started at six-thirty, despite the presence of my car keys on the kitchen counter and explicit instructions to drive. She walked to the hospital for chemo and then walked home. Treatments were on Wednesdays—three Wednesdays on, one Wednesday off—with immunotherapy (the trial) every other week. They took ten vials of blood on one visit, twenty-eight vials the next. How did she have twenty-eight vials of blood in her? When her white count was too low to get treatment, she would run up and down the stairs at the hospital, down from the seventh floor to the first and back up again, over and over, and then get retested. Sooki had been a marathoner, though her best event was a 10K trail run. Those she won. Miraculously, after a spate of vigorous exercise there would be enough white cells to slip her in just under the wire. She asked whether that was cheating and was told not to worry about it. It meant she didn't have to sit out chemo for a week. She liked the team in Nashville. She loved Dr. Bendell. The treatments left her tired, but she was managing. This chemo wasn't the nightmare FOLFIRINOX had been. She was painting. She was doing every part of her job that could be done over email or by phone. The plan was that she would go home to Los Angeles during her weeks off, and once UCLA started the trial, she could go home permanently. We were loaded with plans in those days.

I was leaving for Virginia. In bed the night before, I asked Karl, "How do you think this is going?"

He put down his crossword puzzle. "It's an honor, really. I think about all the people who would want her to live with them. It's almost unbelievable that she's here with us."

It made me think of something our neighbor Jennie had said. Jennie and I walked our dogs together after dinner, and Sooki came with us most nights, unless she had a phone call to return, unless she wasn't feeling up to it. "Do you ever miss being alone in your house?" she asked me once. "Just you and Karl?"

I thought about it for a minute, shook my head. "No, it's wonderful having her here."

"Know why?" Jennie said.

"Why?" I asked.

"It's because she's a saint."

Sooki exuded such an air of self-sufficiency that I scarcely thought to worry about her. Maybe it had something to do with her job. She had worked for Tom for almost twenty years, and part of her responsibility was to go out on location before he arrived, find a place to stay in Morocco, get a driver, figure out the food, figure out what there was to see if there was any time, which usually there wasn't. Figuring out Nashville was small potatoes for someone who had put together a Thanksgiving dinner for a film crew in Berlin.

• • •

I went to Virginia to see my friend Renée Fleming in concert. Afterward we sat up at the hotel and talked about this new coronavirus and whether the rest of her tour would be canceled. A couple of authors who were scheduled to have events at the bookstore had pulled out. At first we'd rolled our eyes, but now I was wondering if it would be melodramatic to cancel my April book tour of Australia and New Zealand. I surely would go ahead with the dates I had scheduled in the States. "Don't go anywhere you wouldn't want to get stuck," a doctor friend had told me. I didn't want to get stuck in Auckland, but if flights were canceled and I was stranded in Tulsa, Karl could always come and get me.

While I was in Virginia, a series of tornadoes hit Nashville. Karl's cousin was visiting from New Mexico, sleeping in the other guest room. As the warning sirens kicked in at four in the morning, only Sooki was awake. "I didn't know what I was supposed to do," she told me later. "Should I have woken them up and made them come down to the basement? Were they awake and choosing not to come to the basement?" She wanted to know what constituted being a good houseguest during a tornado.

What if you come to Nashville to take part in a clinical trial for recurrent pancreatic cancer only to be killed by a tornado? Sooki told me about evacuating for wildfires in the canyon where they lived in Los Angeles, a year and a half earlier, the night before she was scheduled to fly to North Carolina to have surgery. She and Ken put what mattered most in the car and started driving, waiting to see which way the wind would shift the wall of flame. They were lucky and the fire skated past. They were lucky to get up in the morning to fly across the country so Sooki could have a pancreaticoduodenectomy, also known as a Whipple procedure. Her best friends lost everything in that fire. All that was left was the wall around what had been their garden. But they had survived. She had her surgery at Duke and survived. Twenty-five people died in Nashville the night of those tornadoes.

• • •

I came back from Virginia and took Sooki to see the daffodils at the botanical garden, but we were too early. The grass was still brown and only a handful of the thousands of bulbs had opened. I took her to the J. M. W. Turner exhibition at the art museum. We saw two movies with my sister. One morning Sooki had coffee with Sister Nena and me before she went to a yoga class across the street from the restaurant we went to for breakfast.

"Oh, she's darling," Sister Nena said. Sooki left for yoga just as the waitress was bringing our eggs.

"She has pancreatic cancer," I said.

Sister Nena stopped for a minute to lock Sooki in her heart. I could see her doing it.

"I'd be grateful if you'd pray for her," I said, because while I was uncertain about prayer in general, I believed unequivocally in the power of Sister Nena's prayers. I'd seen her work in action.

Sister Nena nodded. "We all will."

Good, I thought. Get as many nuns on this as possible.

•   •   •

Every day Sooki came upstairs looking spectacular—embroidered jeans, velvet tops, a different coat, a perfect scarf. No outfit ever showed up twice. "How is it possible?" I said as I complimented her again and again. "You must have Mary Poppins's suitcase."

"The clothes are small," she said. "And I roll them all up. I'm a good packer." She told me she had packed for good cheer, having had the reasonable expectation that times would be hard and cheer a necessity.

I said, "I have access to every article of clothing I own and I couldn't pull myself together to look as good as you do going to chemo."

She told me she thought she'd put too much of her creative energy into her outfits over the years since she had stopped painting, though she might have said it to make me feel better.

I flew back to New York for two more events, the first one in Connecticut. I met an old friend from school who lived up in Harlem, and she drove me out. We left early, taking into account the traffic that turned out to be eerily absent. We found a diner down the street from where I would be speaking. Our conversation was continually derailed by the television hanging over the counter. It seemed we had just driven through the U.S. epicenter of the coronavirus.

"Looks like we're sitting on the edge of the apocalypse," Marti said, leaving her french fries on her plate. Marti and I had hitch-hiked through Europe together the summer we were nineteen. We had been in some scrapes before. We both agreed that if this was the brink of extinction, it was nice to be together.

•   •   •

Walking backward is an excellent means of remembering how little you know. On the morning of September 11, 2001, I was sit-ting in a café in the West Village with my friends Lucy and Adrian when a woman ran in and said a plane had just hit the World Trade Center. A plane? we asked. Like a Cessna? She didn't know. She hadn't seen it happen. We went out to the street on that bright morning to see a fire high up in the distance. The waiter came out and told us to get back inside. We hadn't paid the check. I paid the check. Lucy said she didn't have time for this. She was teaching at Bennington, in Vermont, and this was the first day of classes. She had to make her train. We said our goodbyes and Adrian and I walked downtown to see what had happened. We both wrote for the *New York Times*. Surely there would be a story there for one of us. We had just passed Stuyves-ant Park when the first tower fell. I would tell you we were idiots, but that's true only in retrospect. In fact we were so exactly in the middle of history that we had no way of understanding what we were seeing.

•   •   •

I had thought I was writing a novel about a woman who had left her family to go serve the poor in India. That didn't work. The mistakes I had made were so clear once I had finished. I was inter-ested in her children.

•   •   •

At the country club in Connecticut, the event organizers began to apologize as soon as we were through the door. What with all the news of this new virus they thought there was a good chance people weren't going to show up. But everyone showed up, all four hundred of them packed in side by side, every last chair in the ballroom occupied.

"Welcome to the last book event on earth," I said when I walked onstage. It turned out to be more or less the truth. By the time I was done signing books that night, the event I had scheduled in New York the next day had been canceled. I had breakfast with my editor and agent and publicist, and when we were finished they each decided not to go back to the office after all. I caught an early flight home. It was over.

After dinner that night, Sooki and I sat on the couch and tried to watch a movie, but her phone on its leash began to ding and ding and ding, insisting on her attention. Tom and Rita were in Australia, where he was about to start shooting a movie about Elvis Presley. He was to play Elvis's manager, Colonel Tom Parker. All the messages were about Tom and Rita. They both had the coronavirus.

I leaned over to look at her phone. "They've been exposed to it?"

She shook her head, scrolling. "They have it," she said. "The press release is about to go out." I sat there and watched her read, waiting for something more, something that explained it. Finally she went downstairs. She was Tom Hanks's assistant, and there was work to do. I floated upstairs in a world that would not stop changing. I was going to tell Karl what was happening but he was looking at his own phone. He already knew.

•   •   •

Wednesday's chemo hit Sooki on Friday afternoon. It took me a few weeks to figure this out, but soon I could track it, the way her voice got quieter, the way she was less likely to look me in the eye. "How's the painting coming?" I would ask.

"I fell asleep."

"Then you needed to sleep."

"I need to go home," she would say, like home was another place she could walk to.

"You can't go home, and we don't want you to go home."

"You've been so nice, but you didn't sign on for this." She stood in the kitchen, holding her cup of ginger tea.

"I signed on for this."

She shook her head. "I can't tell you how appreciative I am. But I can't just live with you and Karl for the rest of my life."

Direct flights to Los Angeles had been suspended, and even if she'd wanted to fly to Dallas to wait and see whether the connecting flight would be canceled (because that's what happened now), her weekly blood draws underscored the fact that she scarcely had enough white cells to qualify for chemo, much less protect her from a pandemic while on a commercial flight. And anyway, UCLA had suspended its plans to start the clinical trial for recurrent pancreatic cancer. All across the country clinical trials were being postponed or abandoned in an attempt to deal with the overflow of patients being treated for COVID-19. All resources were now directed at a disease that was not the disease Sooki had.

"You can't kill yourself because you're afraid of being an inconvenience."

"I need to go home," she said.

"Let's wait and talk about it on Sunday. You can't go home before Sunday."

She was serious, but she was also tired, and so I could get her to agree. By the time Sunday came the urgency would have passed. In time, all I would have to say was, "It's Friday. You always feel this way on Friday."

"I do?"

"That's what I'm here for," I said. "I chart your emotional life."

There was an important piece of information that hadn't been made clear to Sooki when she came to Nashville; it was that, unlike the FOLFIRINOX, which had carved twenty pounds off her over twenty-four weeks, this course of chemotherapy had no end. She was to stay in the trial, three Wednesdays on, one Wednesday off, until the regime was no longer effective or, to put it another way, until she died. Sooki, I found out, was sixty-four.

Karl was seventy-two. The other partners in his clinic asked him to stay home and practice telemedicine until there was a better sense of how the pandemic would be resolved. The risk was too high. He agreed and then kept finding reasons to go to work anyway. Old habits. I reminded him that in choosing to work, he ran the risk of killing our houseguest. That was how I saw the coronavirus—as something that could kill Sooki. Finally he stopped going in. I went to the grocery store and piled up the cart. I had come late to pandemic shopping, but fortunately the staples I relied on—chickpeas, coconut milk—were still plentiful.

•   •   •

If I knew nothing about Sooki before she arrived, I knew very little more three weeks later when we were spending all of our days together. Or maybe I should say I was coming to know her without knowing very much about her. People are not composed entirely of their facts, after all. Our interactions stayed in the present: Do you want to go for a walk? How's the painting going? While we pored over every detail of dinner (Sooki revealed herself to be a great cook), we didn't talk about her family. I knew that she worried about her ninety-four-year-old mother in Rye Brook, New York, and read to her grandchildren in San Diego over Zoom. When I asked her how she was feeling, she might admit to being a little tired or having a bit of a stomachache, nothing more than that. Tom Hanks was so completely absent from our conversations that I once asked her if he knew where she was. She looked startled.

"I mentioned it to him," she said.

Somehow I imagined that she had mentioned she was in a clinical trial in Nashville but not that she was living with us, which didn't feel like too much of an evasion, seeing as how she managed to live with us in the quietest way imaginable. She was indefatigably pleasant and warm while maintaining her distance. Whether she was trying to hold on to her own sense of privacy or what she perceived to be our privacy, I didn't know. The truth was that we had no idea how long we were going to be together. Daughter, husband, sister, friend—none of the people scheduled to visit her could come now that the world was on lockdown. She had set up her life in the basement of our house, a place we never went. She painted and slept and did her work; she had her Zoom meetings and her Zoom gatherings with friends. Many nights after dinner, I would ask Karl where Sooki was and then we would start looking around for her. "She was right here," Karl said. It was more like a magic trick than someone turning in for the evening. She was there and then she was gone and we wouldn't see her again until the next morning.

"I don't want you to feel like you have to stay downstairs," I said.

"Oh," Sooki said. "I don't."

"We're just reading. You could sit with us and read if you wanted, answer emails. We could all be boring together."

But she rarely stayed upstairs. On the few mornings she didn't come up at her usual time, I imagined her sick, needing something, not telling me because she didn't want to bother me. That had been one of her greatest fears about coming to stay with us in the first place, that she would be unable to take care of herself, that she would be a burden, that she would embarrass herself.

I didn't worry about her embarrassing herself. I worried about her dying. I finally asked her to write down the phone numbers of her husband and son and daughter, telling her that if she got sick, if she were in the hospital unexpectedly, I'd need to know how to get a hold of them. The truth was that I had no idea how Sooki was doing, and I had no confidence that she would tell me.

"I wonder," I said to her one night while we walked Sparky around the block, "do you think you're a good assistant because you're a private person, or did you become a private person because you've been an assistant for a long time?"

"I think this is just the way I am," she said.

"You know that you don't talk about yourself, right?" We were living together. We were in the middle of a pandemic. I didn't see how it could hurt to ask. "I'm just wondering if you got in the habit of not talking about yourself because of the work you do." I told her about a friend of mine who worked as an assistant for a hedge-fund manager in New York and how she parked every piece of herself at the door when she went to work in the morning.

Sooki thought about it, or she thought about having to tell me. "I hadn't meant this to be my career. I worked at the Bronx Zoo during school and then I did the whole bat thing. I made a documentary about my father. He had a program where he taught kids with Down syndrome and autism how to ride bikes."

As it turned out, Sooki had done a lot of things. She'd worked on a documentary about George Romero called *Document of the Dead* (she was a zombie in *Dawn of the Dead*). She'd been a location scout, made wedding cakes, started a children's clothing company, taught ceramics. For a while she filled in for a friend and was the assistant to a film director, and then another friend introduced her to Tom, who was looking for someone. Her kids were in school by then. She thought it would be fun for a while. But it turned out to be a good job, and Tom was a nice guy, and the travel was interesting. "Still," she said, "I can't help feeling like I should have done more with my life."

"Call me crazy, but that seems like a lot." We were well into March by then. The spring was cold and wet and endlessly beautiful because of it. The cherry blossoms hung on forever. Sooki hadn't answered the question, but that was the day I felt as though we started talking.

What Sooki thought she should have done with her life was paint. She had wanted to study painting in college, but it all came too easily—the color, the form, the technique—she didn't have to work for any of it. College was meant to be rigorous, and so she signed up for animal behavior instead. "I studied what did not come naturally," she told me. She became interested in urban animals. She wrote her thesis on bats and rabies. "My official badge-carrying title at the New York City Department of Health's

Bureau of Animal Affairs was 'public-health sanitarian.' The badge would have allowed me to inspect and close down pet stores if I wasn't too busy catching bats." Painting fell into the category of what she meant to get back to as soon as there was time, but there wasn't time—there was work, marriage, and children. And then pancreatic cancer.

Renée Fleming spent two years in Germany studying voice while she was in her twenties. She told me that over the course of her life, each time she went back to Germany she found her fluency had mysteriously improved, as if the language had continued to work its way into her brain regardless of whether she was speaking it. This was the closest I could come to understanding what happened to Sooki. After her first round of cancer, while she recovered from the Whipple and endured the FOLFIRINOX, she started to paint like someone who had never stopped. Her true work, which had lingered for so many years in her imagination, emerged fully formed because even if she hadn't been painting, she saw the world as a painter, not in terms of language and story but of color and shape. She painted as fast as she could get her canvases prepped, berating herself for falling asleep in the afternoons. "My whole life I've wanted this time. I can't sleep through it."

The paintings came from a landscape of dreams, pattern on pattern, impossible colors leaning into one another. She painted her granddaughter striding through a field of her own imagination, she painted herself wearing a mask, she painted me walking down our street with such vividness that I realized I had never seen the street before. I would bring her stacks of art books from the closed bookstore, and she all but ate them. Sooki didn't talk about her husband or her children or her friends or her employer; she talked about color. We talked about art. She brought her paintings upstairs to show us: a person who was too shy to say good night most nights was happy for us to see her work. There was no hesitation on the canvases, no timidity. She had transferred her life into brushwork, impossible colors overlapping, the composition precariously and perfectly balanced. The paintings were bold, confident, at ease. When she gave us the painting she had done of Sparky on the back of the couch, I felt as if Matisse had painted our dog.

. . .

Most of the writers and artists I know were made for sheltering in place. The world asks us to engage, and for the most part we can, but given the choice we'd rather stay home. I know how to structure my time. I can write an entire novel without showing a page of it to anyone. I can motivate myself without a deadline or a contract. I was happy, even thrilled, to stop traveling. I had spent my professional life looking at my calendar, counting down the days I had left at home. Now every engagement I had scheduled in 2020 was canceled. With each day, I felt some piece of scaffolding fall away. I no longer needed the protection. I was an introvert again. Sooki had come to our house thinking she'd be staying with someone who was gone half the time and busy the other half of the time. And there I was, going nowhere. It was just the three of us now, Sooki and Karl and me.

Sooki and I stood together in the kitchen, one of us washing the vegetables, the other one chopping, making it up as we went along. I wrote and she painted and then we made dinner. But our truest means of communication arrived in the form of old yoga DVDs. There was no more walking to a class in the dark of morning—everything was closed—and so I asked her if she wanted to exercise with me. I did kundalini yoga in the morning, a practice that was built around a great deal of rapid breathing, and then I went on to other things.

But once we had finished that first short practice, she turned to me, blooming. "This is what I need," she said, excited. "This is what's been missing."

. . .

This story—which begins and begins—starts again here. Of course we would exercise together; it was good for both of us.

Kundalini is nothing if not an exercise in breath, and as it turned out, breath was what Sooki was craving. More breath. Almost from the moment we finished that first practice, she identified it as part of her recovery, the thing she needed to stay alive.

I had never found a way of asking what having cancer had been like for her or what it meant to so vigorously refuse the hand you were dealt. With every passing day I seemed less able to say, Do you want to talk about this? Am I the person you're talking to, or are you talking to someone else downstairs late at night? I was starting to understand that what she needed might have been color rather than conversation, breath rather than words.

My continuous and varied relationship with exercise was an inheritance from my father. He was not one to miss a workout, and neither was I. I'd practiced kundalini devotedly for years and then drifted, picking up other things, and while I'd stuck with the short class, I had amassed no end of DVDs. Now Sooki and I sorted through them like old baseball cards. We did a different hour-long class every morning, identifying our favorites, order-ing more DVDs. All that breathing and twisting and flexing fed her, and the calm voice of the instructor seemed to be speaking directly to her. "This one is good for your liver." "This will help all your internal organs." "You are beautiful. You are powerful. You decide." We laughed at the simple optimism, but we also caught ourselves listening.

Every morning before breakfast, we waved our hands in the air. We danced. We did up dog and down dog in endless repeti-tion. And then one night, for reasons I cannot imagine, we decided to do it all again before we went to sleep. And that was that. Yoga and meditation for an hour in the morning was augmented with yoga and meditation for an hour at night. Surely we would take off the Wednesday mornings when she had to be at the hospital at seven o'clock. Never. She was going to be stuck in a chair all day, which was why it was necessary to do it again at night when she got home. We laughed at ourselves, at the practice, at the voice that told us we were flowers, we were leopards, but we didn't stop. I thought some nights my back would snap. I wanted to go to bed and read. But my sixty-four-year-old houseguest with recurrent pancreatic cancer asked for absolutely nothing but this. How was I going to say I was tired when she was never tired? She lit up with all that breath.

Or maybe it was the company. We had finally found a completely comfortable way of being together. I saw my mother and sister. I went to sleep with my husband. Most days I went to work at Parnassus for several hours, filling boxes. The bookstore was closed to the public, but we were still shipping orders. Yoga was Sooki's necessary social hour, and what I got in return was time with Sooki. There were so many other people who would have done anything to be with her—her mother and husband, her daughter and son and grandchildren, her sisters and all of her friends. How thrilled they would have been to have even a few of the hours she wasted with us. *These precious days I'll spend with you,* I sang in my head.

Pay attention, I told myself. Pay attention every minute.

Even as Sooki's white count continued to hover in the neighborhood of nonexistent, her CA 19-9 cancer marker number (that unreliable indicator we relied on) was dropping. "Maybe it's the trial," she said, "but I think it could just as easily be the food and the yoga."

I told her it was all an elaborate hoax. "You think you're getting chemo three Wednesdays a month but really it's a test to measure the effectiveness of kundalini yoga and kohlrabi." I had signed up for a farm-share box, and every week we were overwhelmed with pounds of mysterious vegetables.

I knew there was a part of her that believed that maybe what Nashville had to offer in terms of fighting cancer was happening in our house, that she was improving because she was with us.

•   •   •

The day I picked up Sooki from the airport in February she told me she would need to buy dry ice for Wednesdays. She was supposed to wear a complicated Velcro gel pack (unfortunately called a penguin cap) on her head on the days she had chemo. The four frozen caps were to be stored in a cooler filled with fifty pounds of dry ice. She was supposed to lug this cooler with her to the hospital every week. They clearly didn't understand she intended to walk, though knowing Sooki, she probably could have carried it. The caps had to be switched out every twenty-five minutes during treatment to ensure that her head stayed more or less frozen. "It's supposed to keep your hair from falling out," she said. "Or it's supposed to slow it down." She hadn't lost her hair on FOLFIRINOX, though she'd lost her sense of taste and smell, the feeling in her feet and hands, and twenty pounds. FOLFIRI-NOX had also given her a profound aversion to cold.

"And you're going to freeze your head for eight hours every week?" We'd been together for a matter of minutes. There was no reason to offer unsolicited opinions on a subject I knew nothing about to a person who had just gotten into my car, but the thought of a frozen gel pack on my own head struck me as boundless misery. Would it even work? I asked her. If she missed a session, would her hair fall out anyway?

Sitting there in her shaggy pink rock-star coat, Sooki told me how much she'd come to hate the cold. I said I thought it would be easier to be bald. The caps were in the Mary Poppins suitcase, along with her paints and easel, the large blanket she had brought us as a gift, and her extensive wardrobe.

A month later, I still hadn't seen all the clothes she had brought with her, and I never saw the cold caps.

"Just think," I would say to her on Wednesdays. "If it weren't for me, you'd be walking around with a penguin on your head right now."

Then one day she told me she was starting to shed. The next day she brought up the vacuum cleaner to vacuum off her yoga mat. The day after that she came upstairs wearing a sock hat.

"I'm going to have to have my hair cut," she said. "Something happened to it while I was in the shower."

"I can cut it."

She shook her head. "It's too weird."

"There is no weirdness left between us," I said. "And anyway, it's my fault. I was the one who talked you out of the fifty pounds of dry ice."

She took off her cap to show me the damage. It was as if 98 percent of her hair had fallen out, but somehow in the process, it had felted. The chemical tide that rose in Sooki's blood had not only caused her hair to fall out; it caused that hair to mat into a solid surface. Small, flat islands of boiled wool were resolutely attached to her scalp by the 2 percent of hair that had not fallen out. It was a science experiment that could never be replicated.

"See?" she said.

I picked up one of the bigger islands and moved it gently back and forth. It was anchored by a quarter inch of hair at most but it was indeed anchored. Sooki got a stool and a towel and went to sit on the back deck. I went upstairs to get the scissors out of my sewing basket.

"You have a pretty head," I told Sooki when the job was done. "I guess you never know if you're the person who's going to look good bald until you're bald."

She went inside to see for herself. She wasn't about to tell me she looked good, but it was clear what I was talking about. There was a delicacy about her that was well-suited to baldness.

"I need to go home," she said, looking at the pictures of herself she had asked me to take with her cell phone. Then she went downstairs and went back to sleep.

Later that day we sat side by side on our yoga mats, Sooki's head wrapped artfully in a scarf. With our hands on our shoulders we turned left and right, left and right, endlessly.

"It's so important to twist this way," the gentle voice of the yoga teacher reminded us. "You're detoxifying all your inner organs."

That was what we had to hold on to, and so we held on.

•　　•　　•

When I look back on those first few months of the pandemic, all I will remember is recurrent pancreatic cancer. Recurrent pancreatic cancer kept me focused on the present moment. I wasn't suffering the crashing waves of anxiety that battered down so many people I knew—though two hours of daily yoga and meditation also contributed to keeping panic at bay. While other people were left to worry about a virus that may or may not have been coming for them, I worried about Sooki. I had a concrete reason to be careful about the germs I was bringing into the house. It wasn't that I could kill someone; it was that I could kill her.

I was also greatly occupied by the bookstore. Unlike so many other small businesses, we had the means to pivot. We still had customers even if they couldn't come into the store, and they were fantastically loyal. I was packing boxes, writing cards, and making cheerful videos in which I extolled the virtues of the books I loved. I would save what I could save, and, along with my business partner, Karen Hayes, and a small, ferocious staff (including my sister Heather) who never backed down, I was determined to save the bookstore. Sooki was desperate to be helpful. There were mornings we would go to the store at first light, when no one was around, and tape up boxes and stick on labels together. She was thrilled to get the chance to work. She kept saying she wanted to be the one to help me for a change. But all Sooki did was help me. She was the magnet in the compass. The very fact of her existence in our house kept me on track.

"What Sooki is," Tom wrote to me in an email later, "is all that is good in the world."

We lived in that good world made up of yoga and chemo, the bookstore, cooking, painting, talking over dinner. We filled up the bird feeders twice a day, scrubbed out the birdbath every morning, tracked the relationship of a couple of lizards who lived in the planter on the deck. Sooki told me they were skinks. Stranded at home, Karl studied to get his instrument rating as a pilot. He watched classes on his computer and worked through calculus problems at the dining-room table. He talked to his patients on the phone. He would tell me how lucky we were, the three of us together. And we were. We knew it.

On the first Sunday in May, in the late afternoon, a storm kicked up, not expected but not a surprise either. Karl was sitting on the front porch and he called for me to come out. "Look at this."

I came and watched from the open door. The sky had turned a tenacious gray, the rain sheeting sideways. The wind was coming down the street like a train.

Karl spent a huge amount of time studying weather as part of his instrument-rating prep. "I've never seen a storm come up so fast." He leaned forward over the porch stairs.

"Come inside," I said.

He wasn't listening. He was watching the weather.

A tremendous explosion rocked the house, something far beyond thunder. A transformer must have blown up somewhere close by. Up and down the street the lights clicked off; our house went dark. All the neighborhood dogs began to howl and bark. On the porch, Sparky joined in.

"We need to go downstairs," I said.

"In a minute."

"Hey guys?" Sooki called.

"God damn it, get inside," I said to my husband. Twenty-five people had been killed in the last round of tornadoes in Nashville, two months before.

Sooki came outside and was caught in the spectacle. It would take nothing for her to blow away. I could already see her tumbling down the street. "Do you want to come downstairs?" she asked.

I tugged at Karl and the three of us went downstairs with the dog. By the time we sat down it was over. It had been no more than seven minutes start to finish. The rain went on for another half an hour, and when it gave up I put Sparky on his leash and the three of us went outside to wander and gape with our neighbors. About a quarter of the trees were down. Giant hackberries had fallen into maples and split them in half. A forest sprung up in the middle of the street. Telephone poles were down, and electrical wires snaked across the asphalt. They were dead, the wires, weren't they? Gingerly we picked our way forward. Catalpa flowers littered the sidewalk, though I hadn't realized the catalpa trees were in bloom. I scooped up a handful for no reason and carried them with me. It was a straight-line wind, a freak occurrence that came out of nowhere. The trees were down but not the houses, and the trees, from what I could see, hadn't fallen on the houses. They'd fallen on the mailboxes. They knocked one another down like dominoes. Karl looked up the name for it on his phone. *Derecho.* Spanish for straight, direct.

"First the tornadoes," Sooki said, taking picture after picture, the giant root systems pulling up slabs of earth taller than Karl, the bright spring grass meeting the sidewalk at right angles.

"Then the pandemic," I said.

"The freak wind," Karl said.

"And pancreatic cancer," Sooki said.

"Let's not forget the cancer," I said, and we laughed.

That night there was still no power, and so we lit candles. We lit the gas stove with matches and made dinner. We played Scrabble and did our yoga from memory after Karl went to bed. We breathed deeply and flexed our spines.

"Well," Sooki said when we were finished. We just kept sitting there in the stillness, the kind of dark that electricity wants us to forget ever existed. It was the last hour of a long day.

"Let's go outside," I whispered.

Sooki got her flashlight and blew out the candles. Sooki had been working for the bat squad in New York when a bicentennial parade passed in front of the Bureau of Animal Affairs. People were dancing, laughing, and so she went outside. She met a group of sailors who had sailed around the world. One of them was shirtless and had a colorful parrot on his shoulder. Sooki had had a toucan in college. Surely there was a piece of this story she was leaving out because the next thing I knew she'd sailed off with them. She was twenty-one. She joined the ship's crew. They sailed to St. Barts in a beautiful old wooden boat named *Christmas*. She had once shown me a picture of herself standing in the surf wearing a bikini, a sarong tied around her narrow hips.

I woke up the dog and the three of us left in the darkness. We weren't the only ones who felt restless. People were sitting in their cars, in their driveways, charging their phones. People were out with their dogs. They were on their porches, laughing. I didn't understand what it was, but something was in the air. Everyone was wide awake, waiting up to see if the world was going to end.

Sooki and I shined our flashlights on the smooth bark of the trees that lay across the streets. We shined them into the beds of purple iris that stood tall and straight, untouched. We climbed over branches, met an impasse, turned to walk another way. The water in the creek a block away skimmed the bottom of the foot-bridge. We talked and then we didn't. It was enough just to be together in all that darkness.

The power was out for four days, those rarest of days in Nash-ville when it was neither too hot nor too cold. I cleaned out the freezer and the refrigerator and at every moment thought, We are so lucky.

· · ·

Before I can start writing a novel, I have to know how it ends. I have to know where I'm going, otherwise I spend my days walk-ing in circles. Not everyone is like this. I've heard writers say that they write in order to discover how the story ends, and if they knew the ending in advance there wouldn't be any point in writ-ing. For them the mystery is solved by the act, and I understand that; it's just not the way I work. I knew I would write about Sooki eventually, I had told her so, but I had no idea what I'd say. I didn't know how the story would end.

"She'll die," Karl said. "People die of this."

But wasn't there also a scenario in which she didn't die? The chemo, the clinical trial, the yoga and the vegetables, the prayers of nuns and all the time to paint—what if it added up to some-thing? What if there was some strange alchemy in the proportions that could never be exactly measured and, as a result, she lived, only to die at some later point from the thing no one saw coming: a pandemic, tornadoes, a straight-line wind.

· · ·

There is a magnificent quiet that comes from giving up the regular order of your life. Sooki came to Nashville and stayed in one place, no more movie stars, no more trips to Morocco and Tan-Tan. In Tan-Tan there was no electricity at night, either. She and Tom would walk in the desert in the early mornings and she would feed him lines from a script while he memorized his part, cobras skating through the dust just in front of them. Death was there during those long, sunny days. Death was the river that ran underground, always. It was just that we had piled up so much junk to keep from hearing it.

•　　　•　　　•

Sometimes Sooki would leave money on the kitchen counter, "For groceries," she would say, "for gas, for the books."

I would shake my head. "Don't do this."

That was when her eyes would well up. Sooki, bareheaded, her silver earrings dangling down her neck. "I have to feel like I'm contributing. I can't always be the one who's taking everything."

But of course I was the one who took everything. Why couldn't she see that? The price of living with a writer was that eventually she would write about you. I was taking in every precious day. What Sooki gave me was a sense of order, a sense of God, the God of Sister Nena, the God of my childhood, a belief that I had gone into my study one night and picked up the right book from the hundred books that were there because I was meant to. I had a purpose to serve. The CA 19-9 had gone from 2,100 to 470. The tumor in her liver was shrinking. A hundred thousand people in this country had already died of the coronavirus. We were still at the beginning then. But thanks to Sooki, there was enough quiet in my house, in my own mind, that I could hear the river running underground, and I wasn't afraid.

Sooki worried about her mother, who had been admitted to a hospital near Rye Brook for a urinary tract infection. Sooki left messages for the doctors and put her phone at the end of her yoga mat, waiting for the call back while we practiced. When they called, she asked them all the right questions. She was an expert in dealing with the medical system, after all. It made her crazy not to be there to help.

"I can fly you up," Karl offered, once her mother was safely home. "We can go up and back the same day."

Sooki had twice flown down to Mississippi with us to visit Karl's ninety-eight-year-old mother. She liked to fly. The idea of the considerably longer trip to New York was good news. Sooki's mother lived two miles from the Westchester airport. From her patio, she could watch the planes take off and land. Once a pilot, always a pilot. Sooki's two sisters, one in Connecticut and one in Massachusetts, could meet them there, a family reunion at the airport. Everyone could bring his or her own sandwich and stay safely apart.

"It's too much," Sooki said.

Karl disagreed. "It's not too much. I'm supposed to be flying."

The trip came together quickly. They would leave in four days. Karl worked out the plans. He would bring a copilot to split up the hours. They would stop each way to refuel in West Virginia. Her sisters were in, her mother was thrilled.

The problem wasn't how the trip would be organized, but what it meant—pandemic, cancer, ninety-four. Implicit in the idea of everyone getting together was the reality that this could be the last time it would happen. How do you fly from Nashville to New York in a single-engine plane for a two-hour visit? How do you get back on the plane to come home?

Sooki hadn't lost weight but she was losing her ability to project her voice. It had been happening for a while. Sometimes I had to get right in front of her to hear what she was saying. "It's so amazingly generous of Karl," she whispered uncertainly. She kept to herself, sleeping and painting, trying to wrestle it out. "Of course I want to go. It's just . . ."

I waited but nothing came next. Nothing had to.

The next morning, we went to the bookstore early and picked out presents for everyone in her family. We went to the bakery across from the bookstore and bought spinach-feta bread and cinnamon-raisin bread. We went home and baked a spectacular cake that was especially well suited to travel. "It's like you're going home to the Ukraine for the first time in ten years," I said as we loaded up coolers and bags. I had gotten up in the dark to make stacks of sandwiches. Whether all of this together was what helped or whether she had made up her mind to see only the good, I couldn't say. Probably it was some combination of the two. But by the time Karl and Sooki left for the airport she was happy.

They told me the story later: How after they landed, when they were all standing together on the lawn outside the small airport, a police officer came and told them they had to disperse. Westchester was still a pandemic hot spot and there could be no congregating, even outside. Karl, being Karl, took the officer around the corner to explain the situation.

"We have some picnic tables outside the police station," the officer said. "No one will bother you there." The station happened to be next door to the airport, so everyone picked up their coolers and walked over. All day long Sooki emailed me pictures of her family with the subject line *Where is our other sister?* She meant me.

When Sooki and Karl got home that night, they were elated. Karl loved Sooki's family, and they all loved Karl. He and the other pilot talked flying with Sooki's mother. "She told me that she had to put Sooki on a leash when she was little because she ran so much. No one could keep up with her. Every time her mother turned around, Sooki was gone."

Sooki, the middle daughter. "What about your sisters?" I asked.

"No leashes on them," she said.

In bed that night, Karl told me about how happy they all were, how kind. He said that Sooki was good when they left. She had made up her mind that it was going to be okay.

I turned out the light and kept thinking about the leash, the marathons, the trail running, the yoga, the walking in the desert, the painting and painting and painting. The energy it took to stay alive, the impossibility of quitting. I didn't know what I would have done in her place, but I imagined that upon getting the news of recurrent pancreatic cancer I would go see my lawyer and settle up my tab with the house. Maybe I would find the fight in me, but I was never much of a fighter. Sooki wore a leash as a child, the energy in her tiny frame too much for her mother to control. Many were the mornings the yoga felt endless to me, and so I would give her a wave as I left the mat and headed off to my desk. To the best of my knowledge, she never quit.

•   •   •

More news about planes: friends of mine in Nashville who knew what was going on with Sooki, and who have a house in California and a jet that takes them there, the nicest possible friends, offered her a ride home. They were flying out at the end of May. It was her only chance of getting back safely anytime soon. The same trial she was part of in Nashville had finally commenced at UCLA, twenty minutes from her house. Her California and Tennessee oncologists had conferred so that she could transfer from one hospital to the other without missing a treatment. Everything was lined up—except Sooki didn't want to go.

My goal was to maintain neutrality. I told her as much. She shouldn't stay for us or leave for us. She was welcome. No one had ever been so welcome. "You can live here for the rest of your life," I said, and I meant it. These days were concentrated like no time I had ever known. She had moved in before the pandemic. We had been together for the duration of this new world. But of course the thing to do would be to go, wouldn't it? She must miss all those people she so rarely spoke of.

"I'm afraid if I leave I'll never see you again," she said in a voice I could barely hear.

It was possible, and I had no intention of thinking about it. "I wonder whether it isn't easier here because you don't have to comfort us, you don't have to make us feel better about the fact that you're sick. You can just concentrate on yourself."

She shook her head. "It isn't that."

It's funny, but all this time I was sure it was exactly that. I'd come up with the answer months ago. Our house was a holding pattern, a neutral space without expectation where all that mattered was her recovery.

We were standing in the kitchen in the late afternoon, the time before dinner and between two yoga sessions. "I like myself here," she said softly.

I had to listen to what she was telling me. I had to turn myself away from the movie of what I thought was happening, the movie I had made for myself, so that I could see her.

It was so hard for her to talk. I stood there, close, willing myself not to fill in her sentences. She told me that at home she had become impatient and angry. She had wanted her life to be different, and now it was. She had wanted to be a better person, and here she believed she was better. She liked herself again. She wasn't just her illness. She was an artist. I saw her as an artist. "The fact that the two of you want me here, that you love me, that you believe in me—it makes me believe in myself. I don't want to give that up."

"You'll never have to give up the friendship or the love," I said. "And if you decide you want to stay, well, you don't have to give that up either."

Sooki the Tireless, Sooki the Indefatigable, looked as if she was about to split apart. She said she didn't know what she was going to do. "I can't just stay here forever."

But she could. I had no idea whether it was a good idea, but she could.

That night I tried to explain it to Karl. "This whole time I've gotten it wrong. I thought I was helping, and now I wonder if I've made it worse."

"How could you have made it worse?"

"By showing her what her life might have looked like and then sending her home." By seeing what I wanted to see instead of what was actually in front of me. Mine was the sin of misunderstanding, of thinking that a clinical trial was the point of the story.

•   •   •

The days went on and I could feel Sooki slipping, hounded by her own indecision. Here she was an artist who lived with a writer. Here she was the person she had meant to be. One night after we'd finished our yoga and meditation, we were lying on our mats, staring up at the ceiling. Sparky had crawled onto my chest and gone to sleep. I asked Sooki if she had any interest in trying psilocybin.

It's essential to the life of a novel—to come upon the turn you never saw coming.

I knew people in college and graduate school who took mushrooms, and then about thirty years passed before I heard anything about them again. Now I knew several people who were using them as part of therapy. Plant medicine, they called it now. When you're young you're getting high, and when you're old you're using plant medicine, like herbal insect repellent. Still, wasn't it worth mentioning?

Sooki said she'd heard about it, too, and knew other cancer patients who'd tried it, but she was hesitant, as any right-minded adult would be hesitant about adding the X factor of fungi into an already complicated chemical mix. We started looking up articles on the Johns Hopkins website. The reports were overwhelmingly positive:

Psilocybin produces substantial and sustained decreases in depression and anxiety in patients with life-threatening cancer . . . High-dose psilocybin produced large decreases in clinician- and self-rated measures of depressed mood and anxiety, along with increases in quality of life, life meaning, and optimism, and decreases in death anxiety.

"Maybe," she said.

I don't drink. I'm a vegetarian. My only prescription is for vitamin D. If I'd had a coat of arms, it would have read quality of life, life meaning, optimism. "Would you feel better about it if I did it with you?"

She looked at me. "Aren't we talking about doing this together?"

"Oh," I said. "We are. Of course we are."

This is how we arrive at the next chapter of the story.

•   •   •

The trick wasn't getting the mushrooms. I knew how to do that. The trick was coming up with the nerve to confess our plans to Karl. I presented him with the studies from Johns Hopkins. Seventy percent of participants rated it among "the most personally meaningful and spiritually significant experiences of their lives." He rolled his eyes, but he kept reading. Marriage meant that he would hear out what on the surface may have appeared to be a spectacularly stupid idea. Marriage also meant that I would listen if he tried to talk me out of it. I wasn't looking for permission, but it was a matter of mutual respect.

He read several articles while I waited. "Okay," he said.

"Really? You don't think this is crazy?"

"I didn't say that, but I know you're trying to help Sooki."

When we turned out the light that night I felt myself buzzing with happiness: After nearly three months of lockdown, we were going to have an adventure. Travel while staying at home! I don't know why I didn't have the sense to worry, but I didn't. My friends who had tried it all had positive experiences, new books extolled the virtues of seeing the beauty and connectivity of all life, and there was a chance that this experience, coming so far out of left field, might be just the thing Sooki needed.

•   •   •

It took a while to get the mushrooms. A friend who was well versed in the experience brought them over early in the morning on Memorial Day. I had interviews scheduled all day on Tuesday, Sooki had chemo on Wednesday, and my friends were leaving for California on Thursday. It was now or never.

My friend told us we should wear eye masks and cover ourselves with blankets. There was a six-hour playlist that the Johns

Hopkins team had put together that was meant to somehow guide you safely through the experience. Sooki had downloaded it. We were ready.

"It's important to think about your intentions before you start," my friend told us. We were sitting in the den at seven-thirty a.m. My intention was to help Sooki. There was no other reason for me to be going on the cancer patient's journey.

"It's okay for us to be in the same room," Sooki said, a statement rather than a question.

My friend tilted her head. "I wouldn't. Things can get very confused. There aren't a lot of boundaries. Or I should say the boundaries you think are there tend to fall away. I wouldn't be on the same floor of the house."

She said we could expect to be in the thick of things for an hour and a half, maybe two hours, with some residual effects for another three or four hours after that. "And even when you're in the middle of it you can still get up and go to the bathroom. It's not like you're stuck in one place." I would have given her a hug but for the pandemic. I promised to call when it was over.

Then Sooki and I went to the kitchen, mixed our pre-measured packets of mushroom powder in with yogurt, and poisoned ourselves. We headed upstairs to lie side by side on our yoga mats, deciding to disregard my friend's advice about staying on separate floors. We were in this together. That was the point of everything. Karl and the dog went out on the front porch to read the newspaper.

We put on the music, the eye masks, covered up. We waited. Then came the moment one feels on a roller coaster just as the bar locks into place and the car starts to pull up, the body pressing back into the seat, knees out ahead, and you think, Wait a minute, was this the best . . .

"Ann?"

I pulled up my eye mask. Karl was standing in the doorway. He told me he was going to take his grandsons to the river to go boating. It was Memorial Day, after all.

"You're not staying?"

He shook his head. I felt the car pulling up and up, just about to tip over the cresting track. Had we not talked about the part where he stuck around to oversee our health and safety? Maybe not. Remember in the future not to make assumptions. Click, click, click. I rose as I pressed against the floor.

"Is it working?" he asked.

"It's working," Sooki said.

And then, it seemed, he left.

The car was taking me into yellow, not a field of yellow but into the color itself. There are no words here, I thought. I had put a notebook and a pen beside me on the floor before we started. Forget that. There was only color and the color was keeping time with the music, color breaking apart into tiles the size of Chiclets, the color of Chiclets, from which cathedrals rose in the sacred spirit of the Johns Hopkins playlist.

· · ·

It occurs to me that I should put that playlist on again and listen as I'm writing this, but I will not. Vivaldi, Vivaldi, Vivaldi—that's how it starts.

· · ·

There was never so much color, spinning, building, reconfiguring, splitting apart. I tried to enjoy it but it was difficult to breathe. The car I was locked into was now hurtling down through a million winking flagella, every one a different color. Who knew there was so much color? It was my intention to vomit, but the idea of getting past Sooki was overwhelming. Sooki, in her eye mask, was lying so serenely beneath the furry blanket she had brought us from California that I wondered if she was dead. Still, it seemed possible I could get off the ride early by expelling the mushrooms. I desperately wanted to vomit, to turn back time. I crawled around her as carefully as I could and collapsed in the hallway.

Reading about other people's hallucinogenic experiences is like listening to other people's dreams at a dinner party. What's fascinating fails to translate. Suffice to say the car I was strapped into followed a tunnel down into dark and darker colors, narrower spaces. Where I was going was death. My death. Two words I kept trying to bring up as I convulsed on the bathroom floor.

"You okay?" Sooki asked. There she was in the doorway, outlined in neon tubing.

"Sick," I said.

"Are you breathing? You have to remember."

Facedown on a bath mat, I forced myself to take a breath.

"You should come back to the music," she said sympathetically.

I couldn't muster whatever it would have taken to follow her, but I could hear the music fine from where I was, Górecki's Symphony No. 3, Arvo Pärt, pieces I had loved and would love no more. "We did this to ourselves," I said, or maybe I didn't say it. She was already gone. By the time the playlist had reached *Tristan and Isolde*, my skull was a horse's skull, dry and white and empty.

•   •   •

"I'm dying," my friend had said to me.

"I'll go with you," I said.

•   •   •

This was not a two-hour journey. This was eight hours of hard labor. I wanted Karl's comfort and was glad he wasn't there. I was sorry for what I'd done to him, by which I meant poisoning myself. We'd had a very good life. I felt like someone was slamming me against a wall, not in anger but as a job. My breath was roaring now, in and out, my lungs enormous bellows that would not tolerate my death. These months of exercise would save me. Save me. When I was very nearly at the end, I came to a beautiful lake, the kind you'd see on a Japanese postcard, or my imagined picture of a Japanese postcard. My little dog Rose, now ten years gone, came out to meet me, running giant circles of exuberance in the soft grass. There was my grandmother, my father. They were waving. That was my reward.

I had set my intention to help my friend, to hold her hand and go with her while she went to peer over the cliff, the cliff that, coincidentally, I fell off.

When it was over, I managed to make my way into the shower, perhaps the biggest single accomplishment of my life. Sooki went downstairs to her room. Karl came home and we sat on the couch and watched a storm tearing up the backyard. I thought he was angry, and at the same time I knew my judgment to be flawed. I was angry at myself. I thought he *should* be angry at me. I pushed my face into his shoulder, apologizing. "For what?" he asked. He knew. Didn't he know?

"For being careless with our lives."

He got me a can of ginger ale and I tried to eat half a banana. Was this what COVID-19 felt like? I couldn't stay upright, a hangover from the last eight hours in which I had been quite memorably deboned. I was no longer sick or well. Where was Sooki? She couldn't be alone.

After a while she drifted up to the kitchen, taking a stab at the half of banana I had abandoned. "Are you okay?" I asked. I was having trouble with my own volume now. "I was so afraid I'd killed you."

Outside the rain was dark and lashing. Sooki had brought her computer with her. She was checking email or trying to make notes. "It was so important," she said, her voice pretty much vanishing in her mouth. I was trying to read her lips. I knew I should sit with her at the table but I couldn't imagine it.

"Are you not sick?"

She looked at me. "No, I'm fine. Are you sick?"

I nodded.

"Maybe it's all the chemicals I have in me already. I'm good. It's just." She stopped. There were no words because it wasn't about words.

"Was it like they said it would be, life-changing? Are you not sorry you did it?" I felt like it took me two minutes to put that much together.

"There are so many things I understand now," she said. "All the people who love me and how hard this has been for them, the cancer. I could see them—my family and my friends. I felt their love for me. I could see what they needed and what they'd given me. I could see Ken and how he's always been there for me, how he steps back to let me shine. I could see what the cancer's given me. If it hadn't been for the cancer, I never would have come here. I wouldn't have had this time with you and Karl. That's worth everything."

"So it really was what they said, a definitive spiritual experience?" She'd seen people. She had felt their love and heard their voices while I was hacking up snakes in some pitch-black cauldron of lava at the center of the earth.

"Absolutely. I can't tell you how grateful I am. Did you have a hard time?"

"I had a hard time."

"What was it like?"

"Death," I said. I didn't say, Your death. I didn't say, This thing you live with every minute, this heaving horse's skull, I held it for you today so that you could talk it out with the people who love you. I had set my intention going in: I wanted to help my friend. In making the journey to Oz, she had found the strength and clarity she needed to go home again.

• • •

Someone wound the clock and suddenly the second hand, so long suspended, began to tick again, pushing us forward. Sooki let my friends with the plane know that she would be there on Thursday. She had to pack her boxes the next day, Tuesday. Wednesday was chemo. She'd scarcely left the house for more than three months, and yet it was impossible to push the world back into the Mary Poppins suitcase. On her last night we sat in my office after yoga and I asked her every last question I could think of—when did she work on the documentary about George Romero, and when did she marry Ken? What was the line of children's clothing called? When was she first diagnosed with pancreatic cancer? How had she known something was wrong? All this time I'd been afraid of prying, only to discover that Sooki was happy to talk, to tell me about the bats, the sailboat to St. Barts, the desert in Tan-Tan, the surgery. She told me that part of the reason she'd been hesitant to stay with us was that she didn't want to trade on Tom's friendship with me. That she'd always been so careful not to cross any lines, not to advance herself through connections she'd made through him.

"Not to advance your cancer treatment? Are you serious? Can you imagine Tom sitting at home saying, 'I can't believe Sooki used my connections to get into a clinical trial in Nashville'?"

"No, of course not, I'm just telling you. I remember when you asked me months ago if he knew I was here and I panicked. I try to keep all the parts of my life separate."

We will never know all the things other people worry about.

She told me how lovely it had been to lay down the burden of her own vigilance. That at home she felt responsible for overseeing every aspect of her treatment, researching cures, double-checking medical orders—she had caught a few harrowing errors along the way, near misses—but here she knew that Dr. Bendell and Karl always had their eyes on her. She had their protection, and that knowledge had opened up so much time in the day. We talked about the nightmare of health insurance—and how the percentage of treatment costs she and Ken had to pay out of pocket had wiped out their retirement, had wiped out everything. "I should have planned better," she said.

"You should have planned for the financial fallout of having pancreatic cancer twice?"

She said yes.

How had I not asked her all these things before? She was perfectly willing to talk, she wanted to, and now she was leaving in the morning. Why had I been so careful?

Because I was trying to protect myself. I had been afraid of how the story would end.

On Thursday morning I started to cry while walking Sparky. It came out of nowhere, like one of those weird storms that had plagued us in the spring. I never cry, and yet I had plans to do nothing else for the rest of the day and maybe the rest of the week. Sooki's impending departure touched a memory I made a point of not revisiting: My sister and I flew from Tennessee to Los Angeles for one week every summer to see our father, and on the morning of the day we were going back to Tennessee I would start to cry. There was no stopping it. It would be another year before I saw my father again, an unimaginable unit of time in the life of a child. There was no money or freedom or wherewithal to buy another ticket and see him sooner. And now there was a pandemic, recurrent pancreatic cancer, and so this goodbye reminded me of my father coming onto the plane with us, sitting with me and my sister, the three of us sobbing inconsolably until finally the flight attendant would tell him he had to go.

·   ·   ·

Sooki washed her sheets and towels, cleaned the bathroom, vacuumed. She lugged her suitcase out to the car without my knowing it. When she came upstairs ready to go she was wearing the black-velvet coat with the peonies on it.

"You had it here all this time?" The coat wasn't the way I had remembered it. It was so much more beautiful, the overlaying color of every petal, the very light pink against the blackness.

"I was saving it," she said.

How was that possible? How could anything have been saved? How could there still be so many things I didn't understand when our time was nearly over?

Karl had gone back to work by this point, but he canceled his afternoon appointments to drive us to the hangar where my friends kept their plane. We were early, they were late. I was grateful for both of those things. I was grateful. Karl went to talk to the pilots about the plane and Sooki and I sat in the little waiting area. We tried to be jolly and failed and cried again. Look at what a success this time had been! Her CA 19-9 was 170, down from 2,100 when she arrived in February. Now she would go home to her husband, her children, her grandchildren, her friends. Tom and Rita were back from Australia. They had recovered. There was work to do. UCLA would fold her into their trial, everything seamless. We had found each other, and we would not be lost. We repeated these facts, we made them a mantra.

My friends arrived and we waved at one another from a distance as they gathered Sooki up. Out on the tarmac, I could see her again exactly as she was, resplendent in her velvet coat, her black beret. Sooki, who was light and life and color itself. A minute later everyone was on the plane and gone.

May 31, 2020: I've already worked out this morning. I did a Pilates DVD we never got around to. It had zero spiritual component. Your hike looks gorgeous and loaded with spiritual component. If there were too many people there, you managed to crop them out. There are suddenly people everywhere. The park was packed this morning. What will happen?

Forget about the heartfelt letters. You yourself are heartfelt, and all the love in the world has been expressed. There is no sense in putting that burden on yourself. Karl is not waiting on a thank-you note, I promise. I understand the impulse but I also think we've transcended it. (I say this as someone who is spending my days trying to write about our friendship and what happened here. It's HARD. I keep throwing things out. I'll get there but it's no small task to try and sum this up.)

I sent you another book that will show up eventually, a tiny French novel I love called The Lost Estate (Le grand meaulnes) by Alain-Fournier. It may resonate.

I'm around if you want to talk. Just remember, Wednesday chemo left you very sad on Friday and Saturday, so it stands to reason that Thursday chemo will break your heart on Saturday and Sunday.

All my love.

May 31, 2020: I had the most unusual dream last night. I'm not sure I can describe it without it sounding like an extension of the mushrooms, but it had that kind of depth and clarity of message for me.

There was an abstract image, and it was clearly you—not in a physical way, but as a soul. The most important human qualities were being applied to this form. They would flow on in papery layers, in a creation act. It seemed to be key to the way humans were shaped, and I was aware that this was going on for others around you. But for you, there was also a vapor that would come in and fill in any gap that was left in the process, and I realized, "Oh, this is what is special here and so essentially Ann." There was a completeness. No empty spiritual space. Everything filled in.

I'm sure these words can't adequately convey what was such a radiant message, but it stayed with me so strongly as I woke up during the night, and that's the best I can describe it. I've never experienced anything like it, or you.

Have a wonderful day today. I'll send photos from San Diego. I think we'll be back tomorrow.

LOVE

•   •   •

As it turned out, Sooki and I needed the same thing: to find someone who could see us as our best and most complete selves.

Astonishing to come across such a friendship at this point in life.
At any point in life.

CA 19-9 is 66.7 as of this moment.

Tell me how the story ends.

It doesn't.

It will.

It hasn't yet.

Popular Science

WINNER—SINGLE-TOPIC ISSUE

"Venus Rising" is drawn from "The Heat Issue," which won Popular Science *the 2022 National Magazine Award for Single-Topic Issue. The ASME judges described "The Heat Issue" as "a thoughtful and engaging examination of climate change" and went on to say that it was "hopeful but realistic about the perpetual summer that will soon beset our planet." "Venus Rising" explains what fascinates researchers about the rock next door and why they believe it is important to understand how a planet similar to our own became, in the words of the* Popular Science *editors, "a hellscape." Megan I. Gannon writes frequently about not only space but also archaeology.* Popular Science *also won the National Magazine Award for Single-Topic Issue in 2019 for "The Tiny Issue," which looked at the small things that make modern life possible.*

Megan I. Gannon

Venus Rising

Jörn Helbert was standing outside a stranger's apartment in the north end of Berlin with a bouquet of yellow roses. It was June 2020, and the woman behind the door was in mandatory quarantine. She had just moved to Germany from the United States, and as a favor to Helbert, a fellow planetary scientist, she was acting as a courier, bringing rocks far too precious to be put in the care of international postal systems hopelessly backlogged because of the pandemic. Already one shipping snafu had sent the package to a nail salon in Tucson and nearly lost it. Helbert was familiar with the kind of questioning you might run into when carrying geologic samples through German customs, so the flowers were a gift for her trouble.

The handoff had involved so much effort and intrigue that he felt as if the parcel should be in a suitcase that got handcuffed to his wrist. Instead, Helbert was amused to see a rumpled plastic Walgreens bag left outside for contactless pickup. It held thirty disks made of various rocks analogous to those that might be found on Venus. They had been painstakingly collected and analyzed by Darby Dyar, an astronomy professor at Mount Holyoke College in Massachusetts.

Helbert, Dyar, and a team of colleagues were in the last stages of pitching NASA on a mission called VERITAS, which would send a satellite to map Venus at higher resolution than ever before. Despite the pandemic, their deadlines hadn't budged. NASA selects low-cost (around $500 million) projects through a program called

Discovery only every few years. The team was desperate to get the rock disks into Helbert's lab at the German Aerospace Center, where he was calibrating an instrument for the VERITAS spacecraft that could determine what sorts of rocks make up Venus's geological formations; getting a better sense of these would help write the planet's history. Granite could show us where there were oceans. Basalt could lead us to active volcanoes. Stitching the features together could show us the steps that turned the planet into an uninhabitable inferno.

If you imagine that our solar system is a cul-de-sac where Earth is our cozy home and Mars is the empty lot down the street where developers pitch a shiny future, then Venus is the haunted house a few doors down, camouflaged by an overgrown yard and drawn curtains. It's similar to Earth in size, density, mass, composition, and gravitational pull, but at its surface, it has lead-melting temperatures of more than 850°F and air pressure equivalent to standing under half a mile of ocean water. Its magnetic field is too weak to protect it from the solar wind, it spins backward, and it has a permanent layer of heat-trapping clouds that veil its face from view.

The best topographic radar maps we have were produced in the 1990s, and they're quite coarse compared to our charts of Earth and Mars. We know Venus's surface has mountains, valleys, volcanoes, lava fields, and bizarre geological goodies, but among its many mysteries, scientists still don't even really know what kind of rocks might reside there.

Venusophiles say it's embarrassing that we haven't gotten to know our neighbor better. *Magellan*, NASA's last expedition there, left Earth in 1989. Since then, the space agency has launched fourteen missions to Mars while researchers submitted about thirty Venus proposals to no avail. VERITAS was already in that ignominious club of the unchosen; earlier iterations had been put forward for more than a decade. During the last round, in 2017, VERITAS and DAVINCI, a very different Venus project aimed at sampling the planet's noxious atmosphere, had been part of a five-team Discovery shortlist but hadn't made the final cut.

After that disappointment, David Grinspoon, one of the DAVINCI scientists, wrote an essay titled "Not Venus Again," lamenting that he and his colleagues were like long-suffering Cubs fans but if the Cubs had made it to the World Series and lost.

In the spring of 2021, both teams were back at the plate, anxiously awaiting NASA headquarters to call with their Discovery decisions. "I've really put my heart and soul into this particular mission, so for me, it is now or never," says VERITAS principal investigator Sue Smrekar, a geophysicist at NASA's Jet Propulsion Laboratory in California. "I can't imagine investing this intense effort again into getting a mission selected."

Other countries are planning Venus missions because there are good reasons to go. As scientists have studied solar systems beyond our own with instruments like the recently retired Kepler Space Telescope, they've found dozens of exoplanets with Earth-like properties. That prospect has reawakened the question that has confounded astronomers and philosophers alike for millennia. Are we alone? Except here's the thing: We have a rocky twin world next door that looks nothing like ours. "I want to understand why Earth is the place where life can exist, and that's what Venus can tell us," says Martha Gilmore, a planetary geologist who is on both teams. "I think it's of the highest priority for understanding how we got to be here."

· · ·

Venus sometimes appears as a twilight star that chases down the sun; other times, as a morning star that rises at dawn. Early revelations about the planet gave just enough license for wild speculation about what—and who—might be living there. In 1761, the Russian physicist Mikhail Lomonosov observed Venus transiting in front of the sun like a roving freckle, a rare phenomenon that allowed astronomers to estimate its diameter. Lomonosov noticed a strange fuzziness around its edges. That haze, he concluded, was a thick atmosphere. Because clouds on Earth were made of water, it stood to reason that Venus should be a very steamy and swampy place.

In the late eighteenth century, astronomers also developed a theory that the orbs in our solar system got progressively older the farther from the sun they were. By the late nineteenth, some imagined Mars, the fourth planet, to be covered in ruins of abandoned canals dug by long-dead thirsty beings. Meanwhile, Venus, the second, enjoyed a reputation as our more primordial twin, full of landscapes that resembled our world in the Carboniferous Period 350 million years ago, when fern forests grew, freakish sharks dominated the seas, and four-limbed creatures were just beginning to stretch out across the land. Perhaps old myths that associated Venus with fertility goddesses contributed to this Edenic image. The Victorian poet Alfred, Lord Tennyson, gave it "never fading flowers." Ray Bradbury, in one short story, pictured the planet more grimly as covered in a sickly white jungle with "cheesecolored leaves," soil like "wet Camembert" and ceaseless rainfall that feels like a thousand hands touching you when you don't want to be touched.

Lush visions of Venus dried up as new evidence trickled in. One especially damning sign came in 1956, when a team at the Naval Research Laboratory in Washington, DC, pointed the fifty-foot dish of its radio telescope at the planet. They found it emitted the amount of radiation they would expect from an object hotter than 600°F. NASA's *Mariner 2* spacecraft—the first-ever successful planetary probe to leave Earth—confirmed the hot atmosphere during a flyby in 1962.

It was during this decade that the astronomer Carl Sagan made a name for himself proposing that a greenhouse effect was at work on Venus, with poison gases in the clouds locking heat in. In October 1967, the Soviets sent their *Venera 4* probe there, this being the first time a spacecraft entered another planet's atmosphere. It beamed back disconcerting data: the air was much denser than expected and was made up of 95 percent carbon dioxide with negligible amounts of oxygen and water vapor. So crushing was this result that in 1968, the science fiction authors Brian Aldiss and

Harry Harrison put together a mournful anthology called *Farewell, Fantastic Venus*, gathering suddenly unscientific essays and stories from researchers and sci-fi writers that had been set on the "no-longer magical" world.

Although astronauts lost any hope of planting their boots on Venus, exploration continued. In 1975, *Venera 9*'s descent vehicle delivered the first photograph of the surface, a 180-degree panorama showing a desolate field strewn with shattered rocks and boulders. NASA's 1978 Pioneer Venus mission produced the first crude radar maps. But in the decade that followed, NASA launched no planetary science missions. President Ronald Reagan, who took office in 1981, helmed this dark age, focusing the agency's efforts on near-Earth orbits reachable by the space shuttle.

One casualty was the planned Venus-mapping VOIR (Venus Orbiting Imaging Radar) spacecraft. When the news came in 1982, Dyar, now deputy principal investigator of VERITAS, was a graduate student in planetary science at MIT. She arrived that day to find classmates openly crying. Eventually the research community was able to patch together a simpler, cheaper version, which launched in 1989 as *Magellan*, an orbiting spacecraft that mapped what was beneath Venus's impenetrable cloud layer by bouncing radar waves off the planet's surface.

In the early 1990s, then–NASA administrator Dan Goldin established the Discovery program to fulfill his "faster, cheaper, and better" mandate, emphasizing the use of ready-made commercial hardware and software to get small missions off the ground. The second project to launch, in 1996, was Pathfinder, which included a Mars lander and the first-ever rover, a wagon-size vehicle named *Sojourner*. It was a huge success and drummed up public support for exploration of the red planet. NASA approved projects with increasingly big budgets: the Mars Odyssey orbiter (2001), the rovers *Spirit* and *Opportunity* (2003), the still-operating Mars Reconnaissance Orbiter (2005). Those undertakings paved the way for *Curiosity*, *InSight*, and now *Perseverance*. Since the 1990s, the guiding principle for these efforts has been to "follow the water," looking for conditions that could once have supported life—but undoubtedly driven by the tantalizing prospect of future human exploration.

With so much money going into Mars, that's where planetary scientists go. *Curiosity* alone has had nearly 500 working on its ten instruments, and untold numbers of grad students have cut their teeth on its data. Success begets success in the eyes of the public too. New Mars rovers aren't presented like $2.5 billion pieces of hardware but lovable extraterrestrial road-trippers who narrate their journeys on social media and share photos along the way. NASA knows how to sell Mars to taxpayers. It's less clear how to market Venus, hostile to human eyes and rovers alike.

. . .

Throughout the past couple of decades, interest in places beyond Mars hasn't entirely disappeared. NASA's next flagship mission, the $4.25 billion *Europa Clipper*, will launch in 2024 to spend about six years traveling to Jupiter to study the ice shell and ocean of the planet's sixth-farthest moon. But Venus has been a glaring blind spot, especially considering it's so close to Earth. (A spacecraft takes only about four months to get there.) Although NASA hasn't dedicated a line of funding to studying Venus since the 1990s, a passionate research effort has persisted. Scientists are still reanalyzing data from *Magellan* and even the Pioneer and Venera missions. They're also looking at info from the European Space Agency's Venus Express and the Japanese *Akatsuki* climate orbiter—the only two such undertakings since *Magellan*.

Sue Smrekar, the VERITAS leader, was a postdoc at MIT when *Magellan* sent the first results of its radar mapping to JPL. The whole team was assembled, along with many guest investigators from around the world, to look at what she recalls as the "familiar yet alien images." She thought it was the closest she would come to "setting foot on another world." Here were topographic surveys of geologic features found nowhere else, such as tesserae, strange upland regions with such chaotic-looking ripples that researchers named them with the Greek word for mosaic tiles. Some scientists think the formations could be the equivalent of Earth's continents; others believe they might be more like the scum on top of a pond of hardened magma.

Magellan also documented a small number of meteorite craters, most of which were quite pristine, suggesting that Venus's current surface is relatively fresh, around 500 million years old. Many think this overhaul happened in a planetwide volcanic event, perhaps on par with the end-Permian extinction that wiped out most species on our Pale Blue Dot. Volcanism on Earth is linked to plate tectonics; however, scientists have yet to find evidence of Venus's crust shifting, so what drives its eruptive properties remains opaque.

The data left gaps Venusophiles were determined to fill in. *Magellan*'s image resolution was around 100–250 meters across each pixel. VERITAS (short for Venus Emissivity, Radio Science, InSAR, Topography, and Spectroscopy) would improve that by an order of magnitude. Perhaps more impressively, it would boost the topographic resolution by two orders of magnitude. In its pitch to NASA, the VERITAS team showed how Hawaii's Big Island would look in *Magellan*'s view: like an unintelligible collection of pixels. The VERITAS view brought the volcanic island's ridges and valleys and the peak of Mauna Kea into sharp relief.

"I often compare where we are with Venus to where we were with Mars in the eighties," says Paul Byrne, a planetary geologist at North Carolina State University in Raleigh who's due to take up a new post soon at Washington University. He's not part of either mission but has advocated for more research on the planet in general. He leads the Venus panel of the Planetary Science Decadal Survey, which helps set the field's priorities for the next ten years. "We had global image coverage of Mars, but it was relatively coarse. And it was when we started to fly more capable instruments there we started seeing stuff that we could never have dreamed we'd see in terms of the detail. We don't have that for Venus yet."

VERITAS, which would launch around 2028, would also glean new data about the composition of Venus's geologic formations using spectroscopy, an imaging technique to identify matter based on how it absorbs and reflects light. Because Venus's thick clouds block most light, Dyar, Helbert, and their colleagues had to invent a whole new way to interpret the data that can squeeze through the narrow wavelength range that can penetrate the cover.

Helbert created a Venus-simulating chamber in his lab that would heat Dyar's rocks to ungodly temperatures to test a prototype of the Venus Emissivity Mapper, or VEM, one of the instruments proposed for VERITAS. COVID-19, of course, was the wrench in their international collaboration, especially considering the teams found out only in February 2020 that they were moving to the next level of Discovery program selections. They needed more data from various igneous rocks to expand their calibration of the instrument. During those early confusing months of the pandemic, Dyar sent frantic emails to colleagues across the country asking for samples and soon had a large collection from locations like Pikes Peak in Colorado, Mount St. Helens in Washington, and the Leucite Hills in Wyoming. Some of the samples were the size of softballs and needed to be cut into small disks to fit in the Venus chamber. With her college closed, Dyar appealed to a retired mineral collector who had special saws and grinders in his basement to do the job. In a rendezvous in a Friendly's parking lot, she received the thirty rock disks that would eventually make their way to Berlin.

•   •   •

While VERITAS would have its eyes on the ground, DAVINCI+— for Deep Atmosphere of Venus Investigations of Noble Gases, Chemistry, and Imaging (the plus sign added for this round of proposals)—is primarily designed to search for clues about the planet's history in its opaque atmosphere. The concept was born out of a Venus summit in late 2007 and early 2008, but the current principal investigator, Jim Garvin, chief scientist at NASA's Goddard Space Flight Center in Maryland, has been dreaming of a new expedition since he finished his Ph.D. in the 1980s. The space-craft would launch around 2029 and drop a parachute-equipped, aeroshell-protected spherical probe that would sail through the cloud cover. Using spectrometers similar to the ones developed for the chemistry lab aboard *Curiosity*, it would measure inert gases like krypton and xenon (think of them like fossils of the early processes that formed Venus's atmosphere) as well as hydrogen isotopes, which could determine when and at what rates the planet lost the oceans it is suspected to have had in its early history.

That water-loss data would be hugely important. Michael Way, a physical scientist at NASA's Goddard Institute for Space Studies in New York, and his colleagues produced models in 2016 suggesting Venus not only had water before Earth did but also was covered in a shallow ocean for some 3 billion years. Those findings have energized researchers and revived the image of a wet world, at least in its past. "You put that 3 billion years of water on Venus next to the 300 million years that Mars had water and you realize that if we've been looking for signs of life somewhere else in our own solar system, maybe we've been barking up the wrong tree," says Dyar.

The DAVINCI+ team also proposes to put a camera on its descent vehicle to capture views of the surface far better than the *Venera 9* images that hooked Garvin when he was a student. He's convinced his spherical probe can see mountains at scales not possible from orbit. To prove it, he hired a UH-1 (Huey) helicopter test crew in August 2016 to take him for a series of daredevil rides over a quarry in Maryland. As the aircraft plunged toward the ground, trying to mimic the path of the descent vehicle, he hung out the window taking pictures of the rocks below. This past winter the team heated a full-scale prototype in the lab to make sure it could operate in the atmosphere long enough to send readings home.

Coloring in our image of Venus's long-gone seas could help answer the Big Question. In the 260 years since Lomonosov watched the planet's transit, scientists have developed telescopes so sophisticated they can observe the transit of faint planets in systems thousands of light-years away. Based on their size, their motion, and the wavelengths of light they emit, astronomers can estimate the conditions of the orbs. Some sixty are considered potentially habitable, meaning they appear to have the right parameters to sustain liquid oceans. But by those same parameters, if we were observing our own solar system from afar, we might think Venus should be Earthlike too. "If you can't understand Venus, which is our closest Earthlike neighbor, what chance do you have of believing anything some astrophysicist tells us about exoplanets?" says the planetary scientist Sanjay Limaye of the University of Wisconsin–Madison.

Limaye is part of a contingent of Venus researchers interested in finding out whether its cloud layer could still host microbial life. In 2020, investigators reported in the journal *Nature Astronomy* seeing signatures of phosphine—a chemical known thus far only to come from biological sources—in the atmosphere. Though claims about the possible discovery didn't pan out, the news helped to spotlight the planet as an overlooked astrobiology target.

The Indian Space Research Organization plans to fly its own radar-mapping orbiter at the end of 2024—and it's not the only foreign space agency actively pursuing a Venus trip. The ESA intends to launch a satellite called EnVision in the early 2030s to look at recent geological activity. And Russia is considering a mission called Venera D that would sniff for signals of life. In 2016 NASA launched its HOTTech program to fund research into hardware that could survive at hellish temperatures for at least a couple of months; with such tech, a Venus lander or rover could be a possibility.

What the Venus research community needs most is more data. Lauren Jozwiak, a VERITAS volcanologist at Johns Hopkins University who got her Ph.D. in 2016, says she was told to look elsewhere in her studies since there were few prospects for Venus. An influx of new data, though, will feed the next generation. "There is so much that we don't know about Venus," she says.

In the early hours of June 2, 2021, Smrekar and Dyar were sitting in their respective kitchens on opposite sides of the country, texting back and forth. Neither had slept much. This was the morning they knew they'd find out which Discovery missions NASA had greenlit. Around five-thirty a.m. Pacific Daylight Time, Smrekar got the call: VERITAS had been approved.

"It is an indescribable feeling to work toward something for ten long years with heart and soul and finally have it come to fruition," Dyar says. She spent the day wandering around in shock until she could pop corks with her colleagues in a virtual fete. Smrekar was ecstatic. "I don't plan to stop celebrating for a while," she says.

When the agency phoned Garvin that same morning, he nearly fell off his chair. DAVINCI+ would be going to space too. The next few days were a blur—his team buzzing. Both missions had beaten out their competitors, spacecraft proposed to explore Jupiter's moon Io and Neptune's moon Triton. After a thirty-year drought of new NASA missions to Venus, two will rocket there within the decade, the product of countless hours of research and testing, rock fetching, helicopter riding—and relentless optimism.

"We've got this brilliant planet sitting next door with a giant atmosphere and a fascinating crust and a history that somehow didn't end up like our own planet's," says Garvin. "To look back in time at what that world was like—probably Earth-like and maybe even better—is an opportunity for the people of planet Earth at this point. Maybe thirty years ago we weren't ready. But now we are."

Quanta

FINALIST—REPORTING

" 'The Webb Space Telescope Will Rewrite Cosmic History. If It Works,' is an extraordinary feat of explanatory reporting," reads the ASME judges' citation. "Reconstructing the difficult history of the JWST while illuminating the mysteries of astronomical time that the telescope may reveal in the future, this absorbing piece combines meticulous research with elegant storytelling—and displays the writer's knack for memorable metaphor." The ASME judges weren't the only ones who were impressed: "The Webb Space Telescope Will Rewrite Cosmic History. If It Works" was one part of a two-part series that won the 2022 Pulitzer Prize for Explanatory Reporting. Natalie Wolchover is a senior editor at Quanta, an online magazine launched in 2012. Quanta was also nominated for the National Magazine Award for General Excellence this year—an award the magazine won in 2020.

Natalie Wolchover

The Webb Space Telescope Will Rewrite Cosmic History. If It Works

To look back in time at the cosmos's infancy and witness the first stars flicker on, you must first grind a mirror as big as a house. Its surface must be so smooth that, if the mirror were the scale of a continent, it would feature no hill or valley greater than ankle height. Only a mirror so huge and smooth can collect and focus the faint light coming from the farthest galaxies in the sky—light that left its source long ago and therefore shows the galaxies as they appeared in the ancient past, when the universe was young. The very faintest, farthest galaxies we would see still in the process of being born, when mysterious forces conspired in the dark and the first crops of stars started to shine.

But to read that early chapter in the universe's history—to learn the nature of those first, probably gargantuan stars, to learn about the invisible matter whose gravity coaxed them into being and about the roles of magnetism and turbulence and how enormous black holes grew and worked their way into galaxies' centers—an exceptional mirror is not nearly enough.

The reason no one has seen the epoch of galaxy formation is that the ancient starlight, after traveling to us through the expanding fabric of space for so many billions of years, has become stretched. Ultraviolet and visible light spewed by the farthest stars in the sky stretched to around twenty-times-longer wavelengths during the journey here, becoming infrared radiation. But infrared light is the kind of atom-jiggling light we refer to as heat, the same heat that radiates from our bodies and the atmosphere and the ground beneath our feet. Alas, these local heat sources swamp the pitiful flames of primeval stars. To perceive those stars, the telescope with its big perfect mirror has to be very cold. It must be launched into space.

The catch is that a house-size mirror is too large to fit in any rocket fairing. The mirror, then, must be able to fold up. A mirror can only fold if it's segmented—if, instead of a single, uninterrupted surface, it's a honeycomb array of mirror segments. But in order to collectively create sharp images, the mirror segments, after autonomously unfolding in space, must be in virtually perfect alignment. Spectacularly precise motors are needed to achieve a good focus—motors that can nudge each mirror segment by increments of half the width of a virus until they're all in place.

The ability to see faint infrared sources doesn't just grant you access to the universe's formative chapter—roughly the period from 50 million to 500 million years after the Big Bang—it would reveal other, arguably just as significant aspects of the cosmos as well, from properties of Earth-size planets orbiting other stars to the much-contested rate at which space is expanding. But for the telescope to work, one more element is required, beyond a flawless mirror that autonomously unfolds and focuses after being shot into the sky.

Even in outer space, the Earth, moon, and sun all still heat the telescope too much for it to perceive the dim twinkle of the most distant structures in the cosmos. Unless, that is, the telescope heads for a particular spot four times farther away from Earth than the moon called Lagrange point 2. There, the moon, Earth and sun all lie in the same direction, letting the telescope block out all three bodies at once by erecting a tennis court-size sunshield. Shaded in this way, the telescope can finally enter a deep chill and at long last detect the feeble heat of the cosmic dawn.

The sunshield is both an infrared telescope's only hope and its Achilles heel.

In order to unfurl to large enough proportions without weighing down a rocket, the sunshield must consist of thin fabric. (The

115

The Webb Space Telescope Will Rewrite Cosmic History. If It Works

whole observatory, for that matter, including its mirrors, cameras and other instruments, its transmitters, and its power sources, must have only about 2 percent of the typical mass of a large ground-based telescope.) Nothing about building a giant yet light-weight infrared-sensing spacecraft is easy, but the unavoidable use of fabric makes it an inherently risky affair. Fabric is, engineers say, "nondeterministic," its movements impossible to perfectly control or predict. If the sunshield snags as it unfurls, the whole telescope will turn into space junk.

Currently, the telescope—which has, incredibly, been built—is folded up and ready to be placed atop an Ariane 5 rocket. The rocket is scheduled for liftoff from Kourou, French Guiana, on December 22, more than thirty years after its payload, the James Webb Space Telescope (JWST), was first envisioned and sketched. The telescope is fourteen years behind schedule and twenty times over budget. "We've worked as hard as we could to catch all of our mistakes and test and rehearse," said John Mather, the Nobel Prize–winning astrophysicist who has been chief scientist of the NASA-led project for twenty-five years. Now, he said, "we're going to put our zillion-dollar telescope on top of a stack of explosive material" and turn things over to fate.

The story of JWST's development over the past three decades has paralleled the tremendous progress we've made in our under-standing of the cosmos, not least because of Webb's predecessors. With the Hubble Space Telescope, we've learned that stars, galax-ies, and supermassive black holes existed far earlier in cosmic history than anyone expected and that they have since under-gone radical change. We've learned that dark matter and dark energy sculpt the cosmos. With the Kepler telescope and others, we've seen that all manner of planets decorate galaxies like bau-bles on Christmas trees, including billions of potentially habit-able worlds in our Milky Way alone. These discoveries have raised questions that the James Webb Space Telescope can address. Astronomers also hope that, as with other telescopes, its sightings will raise new questions. "Every time we build new equipment," Mather said, "we get a surprise."

The launch will begin what the astronomer Natalie Batalha called "six months of pins and needles," as the staggeringly complex telescope will attempt to unfold and focus itself in hundreds of steps. The observatory will spend a month floating 1 million miles to Lagrange point 2. On the way, it will transform into a celestial water lily, positioning its giant blossom of gold-plated mirror segments atop an even bigger silver leaf.

"It will be our own 'dare mighty things' moment," said Grant Tremblay, an astrophysicist at Harvard University who served on the telescope's time-allocation committee. "It's going to do amazing things. We'll be in the *New York Times* talking about how this is witnessing the birth of stars at the edge of time, this is one of the earliest galaxies, this is the story of other Earths."

"Please work," Tremblay added, his eyes fluttering upward.

From Smooth to Lumpy

The last time NASA launched an observatory of such significance—the Hubble Space Telescope, in 1990—it was a disaster. "Absolutely catastrophic," the veteran astronomer Sandra Faber told me. Faber was on the team that camped out at NASA's Goddard Space Flight Center in Greenbelt, Maryland, to diagnose the disorder. From the way a star in one of Hubble's photos looked like a ring, she and a colleague inferred that the primary mirror—the big, concave one that bounced light to a secondary mirror that then reflected it onto a camera lens—had not been ground down to quite the right concavity to focus the light; it was half a wavelength too thick around the edge. If the primary and secondary mirrors had been tested together before launch, this aberration would have been noticed, but in the rush to get the long-delayed and over-budget telescope aloft, that testing never happened.

Some NASA leaders called for abandoning the telescope, which was already a controversial project. Instead, Senator Barbara Mikulski of Maryland secured the funds for a rescue mission. Fixing it was possible because, as an optical telescope that's sensitive to the colors of the rainbow rather than to infrared light,

117

The Webb Space Telescope Will Rewrite Cosmic History. If It Works

Hubble can get a clear view from low-Earth orbit, only 340 miles up, instead of having to travel a million miles away. In 1993, the space shuttle docked with Hubble, and astronauts installed a sort of contact lens. The telescope would go on to revolutionize astronomy and cosmology.

Perhaps the most important question about the universe for much of the twentieth century was whether it had a beginning or if it has always been this way. For the British cosmologist Fred Hoyle and other believers in the latter "steady state" theory, "the compelling logic was simplicity," said Jay Gallagher, an astronomer and professor emeritus at the University of Wisconsin, Madison. "That at one point something changed and the universe created matter, why did that have to be?" Hoyle, the steady-state proponent, attributed his rivals' belief in the "Big Bang" (as he dubbed it) to the influence of the book of Genesis.

Then came a hiss in a radio antenna at Bell Labs in New Jersey in 1964. The hiss was generated by microwaves arriving from everywhere in the sky, exactly as predicted by the Big Bang theory. (The light was released in an early phase transition as the hot, dense universe cooled.) The discovery of the cosmic microwave background, as it was called, did not immediately end the debate—steady-state folks like Hoyle distrusted its interpretation and clung to their theory for many more decades. But for others, who recognized the afterglow of the Big Bang when they saw it, the CMB created a puzzle. The near-perfect uniformity of microwaves coming from all parts of the sky indicated that the newborn universe was astonishingly smooth—a purée of matter. "The puzzle is we see a very lumpy universe today," said Faber, who was a graduate student studying galaxies in the late sixties. "So the first challenge in understanding galaxies is to understand how the universe goes from smooth to lumpy."

Cosmologists knew atoms must have gradually clumped together because of gravity, eventually fracturing into structures like stars and galaxies. But on paper, it seemed that the growth of structure would have been extraordinarily slow. Not only was matter initially smoothly distributed, and thus pulled in no particular direction by gravity, but the expansion of space and the pressure created by light itself would both have worked to separate matter, counteracting its weak gravitational attraction.

Enter dark matter. In the 1970s, Vera Rubin of the Carnegie Institute of Washington observed that the outskirts of galaxies rotate much faster than expected, as if whipped around by some extra, invisible source of gravity. This evidence for substantial missing matter in and around galaxies, dubbed dark matter, matched Fritz Zwicky's 1930s observations that galaxies seem to attract each other more than they should based on their luminous matter alone. Also in the seventys, Jim Peebles and Jerry Ostriker of Princeton University calculated that rotating galactic disks consisting only of stars, gas, and dust should become unstable and swell into spheres; they posited that invisible matter must be creating a stronger gravitational well within which the visible disk rotates. In 1979, Faber and Gallagher wrote an influential paper compiling all the evidence for dark matter, which they pegged at about 90 percent of the matter in the universe. (The current estimate is about 85 percent.)

These researchers realized that dark matter, with its substantial gravity and imperviousness to light's pressure, could have bunched up relatively quickly in the early universe. Peebles, who won half of the 2019 Nobel Prize in Physics for his contributions to cosmology, developed a qualitative picture in which dark matter particles would have glommed together into clumps (known as halos) that then combined into bigger and bigger clumps. The British astrophysicist Simon White demonstrated this "hierarchical clustering" process in primitive 1980s computer simulations. Though visible matter was at that time too complicated to simulate, researchers surmised that the conglomerating dark matter would have brought luminous matter along for the ride: corralled within dark matter halos, atoms would have bumped together, heated up, sunk toward the center, and eventually gravitationally collapsed into stars and disk-shaped galaxies.

Although most cosmologists became convinced of this picture, a big question was how variations in the density of matter initially

119

The Webb Space Telescope Will Rewrite Cosmic History. If It Works

set in, jump-starting the gravitational clustering process. "People had no clear idea about what were reasonable initial conditions about the formation of cosmic structure," White, who is now retired and living in Germany, told me over Zoom. "You could run these simulations, but you didn't have any idea what you should put in at the beginning."

"SPECTACULAR REALIZATION," the cosmologist Alan Guth scrawled in his notebook in 1979. He had calculated that if space suddenly blew up like the surface of a balloon at the start of the Big Bang, this would explain how it got so huge, smooth and flat. Cosmic inflation, as Guth dubbed the primordial growth spurt, quickly became popular as a Big Bang add-on. Cosmologists soon noted that, during inflation, quantum fluctuations in the fabric of space would have gotten frozen in as space blew up, producing subtle density variations throughout the universe. The putative dense spots created by inflation could have served as the seeds of future structures.

These tiny density variations were indeed measured in the CMB in the early 1990s—the feat that earned John Mather, the Webb telescope's top scientist, his Nobel. But even before they were measured, people like Faber were working the dense spots into the plot. In 1984, she and three coauthors published a paper in *Nature* that strung everything together. "It's the first soup-to-nuts description of how inflation can make fluctuations and what the fluctuations would do later to make galaxies," she said.

But the story was speculative from start to finish. And even if it was broadly true, key dates and details were unknown.

One of the Hubble telescope's most impactful discoveries, and a major impetus for building its successor, the Webb, occurred in 1995, two years after its corrective lens was installed. Bob Williams, then the director of the Space Telescope Science Institute in Baltimore, the operations center for Hubble as it will be for Webb, decided at the suggestion of some postdocs to devote all one hundred hours of his "director's discretionary time," with which he could point Hubble wherever he wanted, to pointing it at nothing—a dark, featureless little patch of sky narrower than a thumbnail moon. The idea was to look for any incredibly faint, distant objects that might have been hiding beyond the reach of less sensitive telescopes.

Colleagues thought this was a waste. The late John Bahcall tried to talk Williams out of it. Bahcall and his wife, Neta Bahcall, well-known astrophysicists, were typical in thinking that structures like stars and galaxies arose relatively late in cosmic history. If so, then trying to resolve faint, faraway, long-ago objects wouldn't work because none would exist. The Bahcalls and many other theorists thought Williams' photo would come out dark.

But during the one-hundred-hour exposure, the lid of a treasure chest opened: the small rectangle of space glittered with thousands of galaxies of all shapes, sizes, and hues. Astronomers were stunned.

Farther-away galaxies in the Hubble Deep Field photo appear redder since their light has traveled longer through expanding space to get here and therefore has been stretched, or "redshifted," to longer wavelengths. Through this color-coding, the Deep Field image provides a 3D view of the cosmos and a timeline of galaxy evolution. Galaxies appear at all ages and stages of development—proof that the universe has changed radically over time. "Gone out of the window, never to be heard from again, was the steady-state theory," said Faber. "That was a great intellectual breakthrough, that you could take one picture with a telescope, you could look back in time, and you could see that the universe was a different beast back then."

The photo showed that bright objects formed in the universe far more quickly than most experts expected. This bolstered the theory that they didn't form on the strength of their gravity alone but were carried on the backs of merging dark matter halos.

Galaxies in early times were strange-looking—small and disheveled, like ugly ducklings that would take billions of years to grow into swans. "The beautiful universe with the beautiful [spiral and elliptical galaxies] of today is really kind of a late development," Faber said, "and that too was visible in the picture." Some of the duckling galaxies were colliding and merging, supporting

121

The Webb Space Telescope Will Rewrite Cosmic History. If It Works

the hierarchical clustering theory of cosmic structure growth. And clumps of stars in the long-ago galaxies were surprisingly bright, indicating that the stars were far more massive and luminous than modern, sun-type stars.

Astronomers observed that most galaxies reached peak luminosity, forming stars most quickly, around "redshift 2"—the distance from which light has stretched to twice its emitted wavelength by the time it gets here, corresponding to about 2 billion years after the Big Bang. After that, for reasons now thought to relate to the mysterious supermassive black holes growing at galaxies' centers, many galaxies dimmed.

The most striking thing about the timeline of galaxy evolution visible in the Deep Field photo, though, was that there's no beginning in sight. As far as Hubble's glass eye could see, there were galaxies. In even deeper-field photos taken with upgraded cameras that astronauts installed on the telescope later, smudges of light have been tentatively spotted as far off as redshift 10, which corresponds to around 500 million years after the Big Bang. It's now thought likely that structures started forming hundreds of millions of years before that.

But galaxies in the process of forming, their matter somehow fragmenting into stars for the first time, are both too far and too faint for Hubble to detect, and too redshifted: the light from these galaxies has stretched straight out of the visible part of the electromagnetic spectrum and into the infrared. To see them, we need a bigger, infrared-sensing telescope.

"What Hubble succeeded in doing with the Hubble Deep Field is finding that there were galaxies at redshifts much higher than we thought," Neta Bahcall told me. "A question for James Webb is when did it start, and how did it start so early."

Planets Out the Wazoo

In October 1995, two months before Hubble stared at nothing and glimpsed the history of time, the Swiss astronomer Michel Mayor announced another major discovery at a conference in Florence,

Italy: he and his graduate student, Didier Queloz, had spotted a planet orbiting another star.

In the back of the auditorium at Mayor's talk, Natalie Batalha, then a graduate student from California, failed to register the importance of what she had just heard. "It's funny how these things happen because in retrospect it was a pivotal moment," Batalha said recently, framed by three planets orbiting a star in her virtual background. "It was the dawn of this new era of exoplanet exploration but was also a transformational moment in my life, and I didn't know it yet."

At the time, exoplanet searching was a scientific backwater, and Mayor and Queloz's method had seemed like a long shot. Using a spectrograph, which splits starlight into its color components, they monitored more than one hundred sunlike stars hoping to detect a Doppler shift, where an object looks bluer or redder when it's approaching or receding, respectively. This could indicate that the star is wobbling because it is disturbed by the gravity of an orbiting planet. The technique seemed far-fetched because a planet would have to be ludicrously heavy and close to its host star to set the star wobbling enough to be seen with the best available spectrographs. Yet when Mayor and Queloz looked at 51 Pegasi, a sunlike star fifty light-years away, the wobble was huge: eliminating other possibilities, they determined that a Jupiter-size planet whips around the star once every 4.2 days, eight times closer in than Mercury's distance from our sun.

Not only had Mayor and Queloz bagged an exoplanet (and, eventually, the other half of the 2019 Nobel Prize in Physics, shared with Peebles), the planet itself, 51 Pegasi b, single-handedly upended the textbook understanding of what solar systems are like. As the planetary scientist Heidi Hammel put it, "We had been taught a lovely fairy tale about how our solar system formed," one designed to explain why rocky planets lie close to a star while giant gas and ice planets form far away. So what was 51 Pegasi b, a "hot Jupiter," doing practically grazing its sun?

Batalha remembers the audience's reaction in Florence to Mayor's presentation—silence. Soon enough, though, skepticism

123

The Webb Space Telescope Will Rewrite Cosmic History. If It Works

gave way to more hot-Jupiter discoveries. And as telescopes and techniques improved, other exoplanets showed up as well. Sixteen years after that day in Florence, Batalha would lead the NASA team that discovered the first confirmed rocky exoplanet, Kepler 10b.

Growing up in California's East Bay, Batalha (then Natalie Stout) hardly thought about science, though she was thrilled, at age seventeen, by Sally Ride's trip to space in 1983. Though neither of her parents went to college, she was accepted at the University of California, Berkeley, entering as a business major. But then, while she was doing laundry one weekend sophomore year, she remembers suddenly saying to herself: "'Forget talent, resources. If I could do anything in the world, what would it be?' And surprisingly the answer came to me immediately, and it was to work for the space program."

She enrolled in a physics class. She struggled but loved it. That everyday happenings could be explained with mathematical equations "gave meaning to my life," Batalha said. "It made me see my place in the universe differently. I thought that if you could write an equation to explain the interference off of thin films"— the reason oily puddles create rainbow shimmers—"what limit is there to what we can know about the natural world?"

Batalha thought she'd combine science with business somehow. She continued taking classes then landed a summer internship at the Wyoming Infrared Observatory, one of the few ground-based infrared telescopes. When she got there, she told her adviser and cohort that she wasn't like them, that she wasn't planning on being a scientist. But when her adviser gave her a problem to work on and she solved it, which later led to a publication, he told her "not to sell myself short," she said, and to knock on Gibor Basri's door when she got back to Berkeley.

Basri, a stellar astronomer, put her to work analyzing star spectra. Experiencing the scientific method firsthand hooked her. She also fell in love with her office mate, Basri's postdoc, Celso Batalha. She married him, went to graduate school in astronomy at the University of California, Santa Cruz, and had a son, Nolan, and daughter, Natasha, in quick succession. Two more kids would follow. Over those years, she and Celso Batalha, who is Brazilian, moved the family back and forth between California and Rio de Janeiro. Life in Rio was beautiful but complicated; she remembers driving past some slums and seeing a charred corpse on the side of the road. They eventually settled in the Bay Area.

Considering herself primarily a mother who did astronomy on the side, Batalha never attended conferences. But when she was invited to present new data on star spots at a stellar spectroscopy meeting in Vienna in the fall of 1995, she made an exception, taking her parents along to Europe to babysit her youngest child. She decided to stay for another conference on planets that was taking place in Florence the following week. It was on the last day of the second conference that Batalha noticed a TV camera setting up for a talk that had been added to the schedule at the last minute. "Then Michel Mayor gets up and just so nonchalantly talks about this planet discovery," she said.

At first, Batalha thought little about the newfound hot Jupiter and kept studying star spots in Santa Cruz. Then a year or so later, she heard about a scientist at NASA's Ames Research Center in Silicon Valley named Bill Borucki who was determined to build a space telescope capable of detecting rocky, Earth-size exoplanets, not just gas giants. Borucki planned to use the transit method: instead of tracking changes in the color of starlight as Mayor and Queloz had done, he would look for periodic dips in the starlight's intensity caused by an orbiting planet crossing in front of the star, blocking a small bit of its light.

Batalha didn't think this would work. Star spots, as she happened to know, are about the same size as Earth. So she thought a small transiting planet would be indistinguishable from a star spot sweeping around on a rotating star. She wrote to Borucki about the problem. He wrote back and said NASA had rejected his proposal in part for that very reason, and would she come work with him at Ames to figure out how to tell star spots apart from rocky worlds?

125

The Webb Space Telescope Will Rewrite Cosmic History. If It Works

She would, and they did. Next time, NASA greenlit Borucki's proposal, and Batalha became a project scientist. The Kepler Space Telescope—designed by Borucki and his team to continually monitor the brightness of approximately 150,000 stars in search of the dips of transiting planets—lifted off in March 2009. The Batalhas took all four kids to Cape Canaveral, Florida, for the launch.

Kepler delivered on Earth-size planets. "Kepler 10b was identified in the first ten days of data we got back from the spacecraft," Batalha said. When they graphed the brightness of the host star over time, the dip was visible to the eye. Follow-up observations from the ground confirmed it was a genuine planet and one that, based on its mass and radius, had to be rocky. Batalha presented the unequivocal detection in January 2011, following a more tentative claim of a rocky exoplanet labeled CoRoT-7b by astronomers in Europe. Neither Kepler 10b nor CoRoT-7b earned the coveted designation "Earth-like" because they orbited near their parent star rather than in the "habitable zone," where water is liquid. (The first rocky, watery, and potentially Earth-like planet, Kepler 186f, made headlines in 2014. Batalha wasn't formally involved with the analysis.)

The Kepler telescope, before being prematurely hobbled by the failure of two of its motors, discovered more than 2,600 exoplanets. More than 4,500 have been counted in all, a sufficient number for astronomers to study their statistical properties. Just as 51 Pegasi b had suggested, our solar system is atypical. For instance, the most common type of planet in the galaxy is a size we don't have, in between rocky planets and giants. Planetary astronomers don't yet understand the surplus of these so-called super-Earths or sub-Neptunes or what these midsize planets are like or how they form. New principles of planet formation and evolution are needed.

Extrapolating the data so far, researchers think that our galaxy holds billions of rocky, watery planets, suggesting that life, too, might be common. Until we find evidence of life actually inhabiting another planet, though, it remains possible that its emergence on Earth was a fluke and that we are alone.

Happily, the Webb telescope will be powerful enough to probe the atmospheres and climates of other Earths—or even, if we're very lucky, find evidence of an actual alien biosphere.

"Infrared is fantastic for exoplanets," Batalha said.

One Strike and You're Out

One morning in 1987, the astrophysicist Riccardo Giacconi, who was then the director of the Space Telescope Science Institute (STScI) and of the yet-to-launch Hubble, asked deputy director Garth Illingworth to start thinking about Hubble's successor. "My immediate reaction is, 'Argh, we haven't even got Hubble launched yet, and we've got a million things to do on there—it has major problems—so how can we do this as well?'" Illingworth recalled recently. "He said, 'Trust me, you've got to start early because I know it takes ages to do this.'" Hubble had been under development since around 1970, spearheaded in its early years by the NASA astronomer Nancy Roman following decades of campaigning by Princeton's Lyman Spitzer; they are known as the mother and father of Hubble.

Illingworth, who is from Australia, got together with his STScI colleagues Pierre Bely of France and Peter Stockman of the United States to brainstorm about the next-generation space telescope. They had basically nothing to go on. "We started thinking about what would be good to go beyond Hubble and to complement whatever it did and explore new areas," Illingworth said, "and the IR was one clear area." Infrared light is prohibitively difficult to observe from the ground. The trio figured that in space, where the infrared background is more than 1 million times lower, there would be plenty to see. "When you put a powerful new capability out there, you open an immense number of scientific horizons."

For an IR telescope to be as sensitive as Hubble, which has a 2.4-meter-wide primary mirror, Illingworth, Bely, and Stockman realized that it would need to be significantly bigger, since it

127

The Webb Space Telescope Will Rewrite Cosmic History. If It Works

detects bigger wavelengths. They considered that the mirror might have to fold to fit in a rocket. They also knew it had to be cold, otherwise its heat would saturate its own sensors. Rather than actively cool the telescope, they thought to exploit the extreme frigidity of outer space by blocking the heat of the Earth, moon, and sun. Their vague conception of a large, passively cooled infrared telescope, greatly elaborated upon, would become the cargo now awaiting launch in Kourou.

Leading astronomers convened at STScI in 1989 to discuss the science that an infrared space telescope might be good for. Discussions slowed during Hubble's disastrous start and salvation, then picked up again in the midnineties. In 1995, John Mather, a reedy, gentlemanly astrophysicist at the Goddard Space Flight Center, got a call from NASA headquarters asking if he'd like to join the project. Realizing that an infrared telescope "would do so much for so many people," he dropped everything and signed on. He's been JWST's top scientist ever since.

Mather calls himself a "theoretical instrument builder." He started building telescopes as a kid in pastoral New Jersey, assembling parts from catalogues in the hope of getting a closer look at the surface of Mars. As a young man in the 1970s, Mather worked on a balloon-borne instrument that failed; he and his colleagues concluded that they hadn't tested it enough before launch. "Murphy's law had been proven one more time," he wrote in an autobiographical account. But lessons learned led to the triumph of COBE, the NASA satellite experiment for which he and George Smoot would share the Nobel. In the early nineties, COBE measured the subtle variations in the cosmic microwave background that are thought to have seeded all later cosmological structures. In Mather's mind, theorizing about the cosmos is fine, but you need ingenious instruments to know anything for sure. "So let's build the equipment," he told me this fall. "To me that's a heroic thing to do."

Mather had contemplated wild designs, including telescopes that fold. In the difficult budgetary climate of 1996, however, a committee of top astronomers studying the infrared telescope concept proposed a four-meter mirror, which would fit in a rocket fairing, dramatically cutting costs and complexity. Illingworth thought this was "stupid. It was not going to be as good as Hubble." NASA's leader at the time, Dan Goldin, evidently felt similarly. At the American Astronomical Society meeting that year, Goldin said in an address: "Why do you ask for such a modest thing? Why not go after six or seven meters?" As committee member Wendy Freedman remembers it, "Goldin essentially said, 'You guys are really a bunch of scaredy-cats.'" He got a standing ovation. "In my mind he saved the telescope," said Illingworth. It would be bigger. It would also have to fold after all.

After some heady talk about 8 meters, in 2001 NASA finally settled on 6.5 meters for the segmented mirror's diameter, giving the next-generation telescope more than six times Hubble's light-collecting area. The question was: How can you fit a 6.5-meter-wide mirror in a 5.4-meter-wide rocket fairing?

"A big part of the design is how do you fold it up," Mather said. Outside contractors developed competing mirror designs. Lockheed Martin's mirror folded like six petals of a flower, Ball Aerospace's like a drop-leaf tabletop. TRW proposed putting mirror segments in place the way an old jukebox puts records down. After mulling over the proposals for a year, Mather and his team adopted bits and pieces from each. The main contract went to TRW because of the company's extensive experience building complex satellites for the U.S. military and its successful construction of the Chandra X-ray observatory. (TRW was soon purchased by Northrop Grumman.) The mirror design would be closer to Ball Aerospace's: an array of eighteen hexagonal segments forming a larger hexagon that would fold on two sides. Mike Menzel, who spearheaded Lockheed Martin's proposal, was brought on by NASA as Webb's chief engineer.

The mirrors would be made of beryllium—light, strong, stiff stuff that's toxic in powder form ("Beryllium is a pain in the neck, but it's the only thing that would work," according to Mather). Powdered beryllium was pressed into blocks in Ohio, then cut to

129

The Webb Space Telescope Will Rewrite Cosmic History. If It Works

shape in Alabama. The eighteen mirror segments were then topped with a layer of gold, which is supremely reflective of infrared light, and polished in a California factory built specifically for the purpose. "Shaping and polishing telescope mirrors is a dark art that goes back hundreds of years," said Sarah Kendrew, a Belgian British astronomer who works on MIRI, one of Webb's instruments.

Motors with unprecedented finesse would be needed to bring the hexagonal mirror segments into collective focus in space. "That's something we had to invent right away," Mather said. "If you can't do that, you can't make the whole observatory work." Ball Aerospace delivered actuators capable of nudging each of the gold hexagons in ten-nanometer increments, one ten-thousandth the width of a hair. Mather said the motors work by "flexing," or "converting a big motion into a tiny motion," though Ball's design, despite being taxpayer-funded, is proprietary. "When we take a picture of the telescope we have to make sure no one could see the motors," he said.

In 2002, the telescope got a name. NASA administrator Sean O'Keefe broke a tradition of naming telescopes for scientists—the Hubble telescope, for instance, refers to the American astronomer Edwin Hubble—and instead honored an earlier administrator, James Webb, who was head of the space agency during the Apollo era. The choice was immediately unpopular with astronomers and has grown increasingly so. Last year, 1,200 astronomers signed a petition to rename the telescope after claims that Webb either aided or chose to ignore the firing of gay government employees during the Lavender Scare. After an investigation, NASA announced in October that historians found no evidence warranting a name change.

Various institutions, from the University of Arizona to the European Space Agency, signed up to build the cameras, spectrographs, and coronagraphs that will swivel into place at the focal point of the optics, slicing and dicing different chunks of the pooled infrared light. In exchange, these institutional partners will command extensive telescope time.

As for the sunshield, the flimsy material on which the infrared telescope's fate rests, the team quickly settled on Kapton, a slithery silver plastic that looks like the inside of a potato chip bag but has the thickness of a human hair. Since it might tear, the sunshield would need many layers for redundancy—the team decided on five—and the layers would have to be unfurled, separated and held taut by a system of booms, cables and strings. Propulsion systems and solar panels would go on the sunward side, and the optics and instruments, which must operate below minus 223 degrees Celsius, would huddle on the dark side. "JWST has a lot of firsts, an awful lot of significant firsts," Menzel, the chief engineer, told me, "but that sunshield is one of them."

Menzel, who is thickset with a neatly clipped gray beard, oversees thousands of people's work on one of the most complicated engineering projects in history; he's also the type of person who tells you right away where they're from. That would be Elizabeth, New Jersey—Exit 13 off the turnpike—where his father drove a cab. On a recent Zoom call, Menzel bent his arm back and forth at the elbow to explain the challenge presented by the sunshield. "If you take something rigid, like a door, and you build a nice hinge, you can predict the way that moves," he said. "That's a piece of cake." He stopped bending his arm. "Now you got blankets. They're floppy. Try to push on a blanket on your bed and predict the shape that it's going to go in. It's horrible. Same thing with a string—the strings that tension [the sunshield]. There's a million different ways that a string can move." It gets worse: "Now put all this experience in zero-G, where that stuff can go in places you just don't want it to go." Smoothly unfolding the sunshield "becomes a very tough problem."

Around 2004, the NASA engineers Chuck Perrygo and Keith Parrish came into Menzel's office at Goddard and said they had a way to do it. Perrygo picked up a piece of paper on Menzel's desk and folded it into the shape of a Z. The sunshield could be folded into many more such zigzags, in what's sometimes called an accordion fold. "I'm pretty good at recognizing a bad answer, and

131

The Webb Space Telescope Will Rewrite Cosmic History. If It Works

I'm pretty good at recognizing a right answer," Menzel told me, holding up a piece of paper he had folded into a Z shape. "So we all saw that and thought, that's a way to pursue it." Northrop Grumman was separately coming to the same conclusion.

The next question was how to hold the accordion fold in place until the sunshield was ready to unfurl. A Northrop Grumman engineer, Andy Tao, found the solution: 107 pins that retract like a cat's claws.

The pin approach sprouted another tricky problem: pins make pinholes. If, after unfurling, pinholes on all five Kapton layers were to line up, this would let a sunbeam through, heating the optics. "It was one of those arcane little details that you'd never guess until you start getting into it and you start finding out, ah, Christ, five of the pinholes are lining right up and that's going to let sunlight right in," Menzel said. "It doesn't sound like much, but it was driving Andy to drink. And God bless him, he figured it out." Tao diligently sought out a suitable configuration of pins so that the holes in the five slightly-different-size Kapton layers would never align from any angle.

The moles were being whacked so slowly that astronomers began referring to the situation as "the JWST problem." Back in 1996, Mather and his team estimated that the telescope would cost $564 million—a somewhat disingenuous guess aimed at getting Congress on board—and that it would launch in 2007. As the price tag soared and the launch date hopped ever farther into the future, Congress grew impatient. In 2011, JWST was nearly canceled, but elementary school students wrote letters to Washington and Senator Mikulski again came to NASA's rescue.

Glass, metal, and plastic gradually got bolted together in clean rooms at Goddard, Northrop Grumman, Ball Aerospace, and elsewhere. But the assembled hardware couldn't simply be sent skyward, because the telescope is going a million miles away, where astronauts with wrenches can't visit. As Northrop Grumman engineer Jon Arenberg once put it, "This is a one-strike-and-you're-out business." Webb must deploy flawlessly on the first and only try. That means it had to be extensively, painstakingly tested on the ground. And in 2017 and 2018, these tests turned up one problem after another.

After a "shake test," a bunch of screws and washers that had held the sunshield cover in place were found on the floor; they hadn't been properly torqued. Another time, the sunshield caught on a snag and tore. Once, it unfolded, but not without a string wrapping around something it shouldn't have.

The telescope got in another scrape when it was shipped to the Johnson Space Center in Houston, placed in the chamber where Apollo astronauts once practiced their moonwalks, and cryogenically cooled to simulate the conditions of outer space. While instrument builders like Sarah Kendrew were testing the cold hardware, Hurricane Harvey hit. The whole city catastrophically flooded, but the biggest worry for the Webb team was the liquid nitrogen supply. If it ran out, the telescope's temperature would rise too quickly, damaging the instruments. The liquid nitrogen suppliers had to be urged to send trucks through the floodwaters as a matter of national importance.

Problems continued. Earlier this year, the transponders that will blip data back to Earth were found to be faulty and had to be repaired. "A delay causes its own cascade of issues," Tremblay said—and more expense: "It costs $10 million a month just to keep James Webb on the clean room floor." As the investment rose, so did the need for the mission to succeed. "If NASA was willing to accept more risk, JWST would have been half the cost," Tremblay explained.

Finally, problems abated. Northrop Grumman engineers successfully unfolded the sunshield several times at its facility in Redondo Beach, California. But according to Menzel, even after the shimmery layers have spread smoothly open, "we aren't as elated as you might think. Because we all know that sunshield will only be as good as the last time it's folded."

Webb's final cost approaches $10 billion. That's nearly twenty times its sticker price but still a few billion less than an aircraft carrier. Following some final pandemic-related delays, late 2021

133

The Webb Space Telescope Will Rewrite Cosmic History. If It Works

became its target launch date. In September, the telescope passed a final test in Redondo Beach: gold ears pinned back and blanket stashed away, the whole observatory was turned on its side, then righted, then checked to see whether anything had changed. Then it was put back on its side into a shipping container and taken away. Garth Illingworth, who has been involved with the telescope in a range of capacities since the beginning, went to Redondo Beach to see it off. There it had stood, "tall and majestic," he wrote in an email. "By the next day the clean room was even empty of any JWST-related support hardware." The exact date of the shipping container's departure from California was kept quiet—a precaution against piracy on the high seas—but in early October it voyaged through the Panama Canal to French Guiana, a region near the equator where the European Space Agency launches its plus-size Ariane 5 rocket to exploit the extra kick of Earth's rotation.

The Webb team is busy rehearsing the routines they'll execute 24/7 out of Baltimore during Webb's monthlong journey to Lagrange point 2, followed by its five-month commissioning period. "Do I feel confident?" said Menzel. "Yes. I feel confident that we've done everything we possibly could. The risk is acceptably low. It's as good as it's going to be. And I'm pretty confident that we're going to do fine.

"Could something go wrong? Hell, yeah."

Reasonable Guesses

Once the Hubble got working, humanity soaked up the sight of the cosmos like near-sighted kids wearing glasses for the first time. We also learned there was stuff out there that we couldn't see.

In 1998, two rival teams of astronomers used the Hubble along with other telescopes to observe supernovas in distant galaxies and ascertain that the expansion of the universe is accelerating. This exposed the existence of an accelerating agent infusing all of space, known as dark energy. There's so much space that dark energy makes up 70 percent of everything. (Another 26 percent is dark matter, and 4 percent is luminous atoms and radiation.)

Other puzzles soon turned up. The astronomer Wendy Freedman used Hubble to observe pulsating stars called cepheids. From these, in 2001 she and her team measured how fast the universe is currently expanding, achieving 10 percent accuracy, a huge improvement over previous measurements. In the years since Freedman's measurement, the cosmic expansion rate has landed at the center of the biggest controversy in cosmology. The issue is that, based on the universe's known ingredients and governing equations, theorists infer that space should currently be expanding more slowly than the measurements suggest. Its fast expansion may point to additional unknown ingredients in the cosmos beyond dark matter and dark energy. But Freedman, who is calm and authoritative, isn't convinced yet that the measurements are right. She'll lead a team that will use the Webb telescope to scrutinize cepheids and other stars more closely; they hope to measure the expansion rate precisely enough to tell for sure whether there's an exotic fundamental ingredient afoot.

Meanwhile, the Hubble Deep Field photo told a rollicking story of galaxy evolution that dramatically expanded human knowledge of cosmic history. But it remains to Webb to read the crucial first couple of chapters of the story.

Marcia Rieke, a longtime professor at the University of Arizona regarded as one of the pioneers of infrared astronomy, has spent the last twenty years overseeing the design and construction of NIRCam (as in "near-infrared camera"), one of Webb's four main instruments. She and her team at Arizona are planning to use more than half of their whopping 900 hours of guaranteed telescope time to do a new deep-field survey, one that will peer deeper into the past than ever before. Whereas Hubble could see the faint smudges of galaxies at redshift 10, corresponding to 500 million years after the Big Bang, Webb should be able to see those smudges very clearly and spot brand-new galaxies germinating farther away, perhaps as far back as 50 or 100 million years after the Big Bang.

Rieke and her team will do one better than the Hubble deep field. After using NIRCam to get an image of their dark patch of

135

The Webb Space Telescope Will Rewrite Cosmic History. If It Works

the sky, they'll identify the galaxies in the patch that are farthest away and use NIRSpec, Webb's near-infrared spectrograph, to take the galaxies' spectra, from which Rieke and her colleagues can deduce their chemical compositions. Hubble didn't have a spectrograph.

The spectrum will show which elements of the periodic table existed in each proto-galaxy and how their elements evolved over time. The standard story is that early gas clouds, stars, and galaxies mostly consisted of hydrogen and supernovas and other explosive events gradually forged heavier elements. "But there are curious things," Rieke said. "Close to the limit that Hubble can go to, there are quasars"—super-bright centers of galaxies powered by supermassive black holes—"and it looks like they have almost the same elements as the sun. Which is hard to believe. So there's something that goes on early that we don't have a good handle on."

There are as many reasons for wanting to see the first stars and galaxies as there are astronomers, astrophysicists, and cosmologists. For Risa Wechsler, a cosmologist at Stanford University, it's a way to watch dark matter's handiwork. She and her colleagues will use the proto-galaxies to deduce the distribution of sizes of dark matter halos that must have existed in the early universe, and when they formed. This can reveal whether dark matter is "cold," that is, made of slow-moving particles, or "warm," since particles that whizz around would have taken longer to huddle into halos. This temperature check would be a significant clue to dark matter's nature.

Other researchers want to understand the first stars. Some think Webb will see so-called Population III stars, primordial beasts that are hypothesized to have been roughly 10,000 times heavier than our sun. Such stars would help solve another major mystery of galaxy formation: how galaxies' centers ended up with supermassive black holes—physically small yet incredibly powerful gravitational sinkholes that can weigh billions of times the mass of our sun. Nobody knows how supermassive black holes grew so heavy or when or why their properties are correlated with properties of their host galaxies. One theory is that Population III stars seeded the holes, but there are a million other theories. Webb will look for signatures of the different scenarios.

Theorists have simulated many possibilities for how structures might have emerged in the young universe. But they can't simply start with the cosmic microwave background and evolve that picture forward on the computer to see what happened. "A lot of the initial conditions are not well understood—things like the magnetic field and how much turbulence there is in the gas," said Peter Behroozi, a theorist colleague of Rieke's at Arizona who simulates star and galaxy formation. It's "a lot of work," he said, to get from a large, ever-so-slightly dense spot in the cosmic microwave background to a tiny cloud of gas that will gravitationally contract and make a star.

"Oftentimes what people will do is they'll just skip that," Behroozi said, and "start with a spherical cloud of gas. They don't know what the distribution of [dark matter] clump sizes will be, so they guess. They don't know about the magnetic field; they don't know anything about the spin or turbulence of the gas; so they'll fill all that in with guesses."

The guesswork has accelerated recently as researchers race to get their predictions on record before Webb shows how star and galaxy formation really went down. Even conservative guesses can produce simulations with wildly different outcomes. "The main conclusion from my research," Behroozi said, "is even if you try to make a reasonable guess, we still have no clue what James Webb will see."

Bridge Planets

Natasha Batalha, Natalie Batalha's second child, was eighteen when she went to Florida for the Kepler launch. She remembers tagging along with her younger sister in the viewing room where the NASA science team had gathered. "During the launch, the anxiety that was in that space was chilling," she said on a recent video call. After liftoff, the scene turned jubilant. She found it

137

The Webb Space Telescope Will Rewrite Cosmic History. If It Works

inspiring to see a team accomplish something so grand, but it was the possibility of discoveries being so close at hand "that was really what flipped on my brain to start thinking about exoplanets as a concept," said Natasha Batalha, who is serious and precise, like her mother.

Space wasn't a constant topic of discussion in the Batalha household. "I didn't want to saturate their lives with science," Natalie Batalha said. "I always wanted them to feel like they were number one." But she and Celso did have "a secret hope" about Natasha. One evening in 1996 while Celso was teaching a night class, Natalie loaded up the half-asleep kids to drive them to a meadow so they look for the passing comet Hyakutake. Before they'd pulled out of the driveway, five-year-old Natasha said from the back seat: "What's that?" She was pointing at the comet.

When Natasha was eight and living in Brazil, her mother asked her and her siblings to draw an astronomer. Natasha drew a white man, and Natalie asked her why. "This was crazy for me, the daughter of a Latinx scientist and a female scientist; I still had these stereotypes ingrained in my mind," Natasha said. She suddenly felt empowered by the thought that she could belong in science.

A couple of years later she read Sally Ride's autobiography. Just as her mother had been inspired by Ride, Natasha decided to become either an astronomer or an astronaut. She dreamed of being the first person on Mars. After the Kepler launch, as more and more exoplanets were discovered, she grew interested in the possibility of extraterrestrial life and how we might infer its presence on those planets through telescope observations of their skies. She got a dual Ph.D. in astronomy and astrobiology. Then, soon after Kepler ended and her mom left NASA Ames to become a professor at Santa Cruz, Natasha took a job at Ames studying exoplanet atmospheres.

Natasha Batalha is part of a growing research community whose ultimate goal is to detect "biosignature gases"—gases in a planet's atmosphere that could only be there because of life. Every kind of molecule has characteristic wavelengths that it absorbs.

So by collecting light from a star when a planet is and isn't transiting in front of it, and checking which wavelengths of starlight grow dimmer when the planet is there, you can see which molecules are present in the planet's sky.

Oxygen is an obvious candidate for a biosignature gas: It's so reactive that it's unlikely to be found unless the planet's oxygen supply is continually replenished by, say, a biosphere doing photosynthesis. Photosynthesis is such a simple and efficient energy-capturing procedure that astrobiologists think it's likely to evolve on any living planet, so oxygen is smart to look for.

But seeing oxygen by itself wouldn't necessarily be convincing. Computer simulations show that under some conditions, oxygen can fill the skies of lifeless planets. "The challenge is there's not one gas that's going to be a biosignature gas," said Hammel, the planetary scientist. "Methane on Earth is mostly produced by cows . . . but you look at Neptune, and you can see tons of methane there, and that's not produced by cows."

A better biosignature is a peculiar mix of gases. "It's not going to be a single gas, it's going to have to be a combination of gases in a configuration that tells us they are in a disequilibrium state," said Hammel. "They can't have formed that way naturally."

Existing telescopes have already spotted molecular fingerprints in the skies of hot Jupiters, but these are lifeless planets. Detecting the weaker signals from rocky, possibly habitable planets' skies will require JWST. Not only will the telescope have close to one hundred times Hubble's resolution, but it will see exoplanets far more clearly against the background of their host stars since planets emit more infrared than optical light while stars emit less. Importantly, Webb's view of exoplanets won't be obscured by clouds, which often prevent optical telescopes from seeing the densest, low-altitude layers of atmosphere. "Imagine being in a plane and looking down at an insane cloud deck, and you can't see the surface at all," Natasha Batalha said. "When you look at infrared light, you can all of a sudden see through the cloud deck."

Exoplanets will be among the targets in JWST's "Cycle 1" round of observations, which it will start tackling as soon as

139

The Webb Space Telescope Will Rewrite Cosmic History. If It Works

deployment and commissioning are complete—about six months after launch. The exoplanet community elected Natalie Batalha to lead transit spectroscopy studies of three gas giants as part of these early observations. Her team will also develop data pipelines and processing techniques for the community to copy.

Cycle 1 also includes observations for specific groups of astronomers. Last year, more than 2,000 groups submitted proposals to use JWST in the first cycle; a time allocation committee selected 266. Dozens of these programs will look at planets. When I videochatted with Hammel, she screen-shared PowerPoint slides highlighting various exo-worlds of interest that Webb will turn its eye toward on behalf of different observers: Kepler 16b, which orbits two stars; the suspected "lava world" 55 Cancri e; and the seven rocky planets of the nearby Trappist-1 star system. (Hammel, who gets one hundred hours of guaranteed observer time as a longtime member of the Webb science team, will browse our own solar system, including Jupiter's red spot, the mysterious, far-flung objects of the Kuiper belt, and Hammel's oft-overlooked favorites, Uranus and Neptune, which appeared as a pair of plush toys behind her on her office couch.)

Out of all the exoplanets that JWST will look at in Cycle 1, Natasha Batalha reckons that the three Trappist planets that orbit in their star's habitable zone probably have the best shot at featuring detectable biosignature gases. "The Trappist system is unique in that the star is very small, and so the relative feature size of the atmospheres doesn't need to be big in order for you to be able to see it," she said. Whether Webb has a realistic chance of spotting biosignature gases is debatable, however. "Often the controversy comes up over the detection of oxygen," she said. Oxygen absorbs one infrared wavelength in Webb's range of sensitivity, and so theoretically an oxygen-rich transiting planet could put a noticeable dip in its star's spectrum at that wavelength. "However," she said, the wavelength "is just at the edge where the detector loses sensitivity." Other types and combinations of gases will be easier to detect but might be harder to definitively attribute to life.

Webb might just identify possibly living planets, which would then be examined more closely with future space telescopes. Astronomers are busy planning those now. NASA's Nancy Grace Roman Space Telescope, slated to launch later this decade, is mostly designed to study dark energy; Earth-like exoplanets are the purview of a future telescope concept provisionally known as LuvEx, an ultraviolet, optical, and IR telescope that (if funded by Congress) will launch in the mid-2040s.

What we will look at then depends on what we learn in the next few years.

One morning this spring, Natasha Batalha woke up to a text from fellow exoplanet astronomer Johanna Teske: "We got it!" The 266 selected Cycle 1 programs had just been announced, and a proposal led by Batalha, with Teske as her deputy, made the list.

Theirs will be the most extensive of all the exoplanet observing campaigns in the first cycle: a 142-hour survey of super-Earths and sub-Neptunes, the ubiquitous midsize "bridge" planets that our solar system lacks, and whose composition, habitability, and formation history are unknown. Assuming that, over the next few months, everything unfolds as it should and the James Webb Space Telescope finds its focus, it will point at eleven of these planets on behalf of Natasha Batalha and her team. When she awoke to the good news, first she called Teske. Then she called her mom.

Bloomberg Green with *Bloomberg Businessweek*

"The Methane Hunters," by Zachary R. Mider, was one of three articles—the others were "An Empire of Dying Wells," by Mider and Rachel Adams-Heard, and "Turkmenistan's Dirty Secret," by Aaron Clark and Matthew Campbell—that earned Bloomberg Green *and* Bloomberg Businessweek *a joint nomination in Public Interest. Based on scientific research as well as old-fashioned fieldwork, these stories took readers on what the ASME judges described as "a fascinating though disturbing hunt for methane leaks" (disturbing because, as Mider explains, methane is "thought to be responsible for about a quarter of the increase in global temperatures caused by humans"). Mider won the Pulitzer Prize for Explanatory Reporting in 2015.* Bloomberg Green *is a web vertical focusing on climate change;* Bloomberg Businessweek *is a frequent National Magazine Award finalist, last year winning an Ellie for coverage of the pandemic.*

Zachary R. Mider

The Methane Hunters

Five hundred miles above the Earth's surface, the Copernicus Sentinel-5 Precursor, a satellite about the size of a pickup truck, has been circling the planet for four years, taking pictures of the atmosphere below. The satellite's infrared sensor can see things humans can't, and in 2019, Yuzhong Zhang, a postdoctoral fellow at Harvard, got a look at some of its first readings.

Zhang was interested in methane, an invisible, odorless gas. Although carbon dioxide from burning fossil fuels is the principal cause of global warming, methane has many times carbon's warming power and is thought to be responsible for about a quarter of the increase in global temperatures caused by humans. When Zhang laid the satellite readings over a map of the United States, the biggest concentration of the gas showed up as a red splotch over a 150-mile-wide swath of Texas and New Mexico.

The postdoc loaded the readings into a supercomputer to calculate what it would take to form that pattern. A few days later he had an answer. Beneath the splotch, Zhang discovered, 2.9 million metric tons of methane were pouring into the sky each year. By one measure, that cloud of gas is contributing as much to global warming as Florida—every power plant, motorboat, and minivan in the state.

Zhang, now at Westlake University in Hangzhou, China, calls it the "Permian methane anomaly." The anomaly lies directly atop the Permian Basin, one of the most bountiful oil-producing regions in the world. Wells there churn out less-profitable natural gas alongside petroleum, and natural gas is mostly methane. Zhang's research demonstrated that a surprising amount of that gas, more than twice what the U.S. government has estimated, is just spilling into the air unburned. Imagine that someone turned all the knobs on a stove without lighting a flame. Now imagine 400,000 stoves scattered across the Southwest, hissing day and night, cooking nothing but the planet itself.

Identifying and plugging these leaks could do more to slow climate change than almost any other single measure. Unlike carbon, methane breaks down relatively quickly in the atmosphere. That means efforts to curtail it can pay off within a generation. According to one recent estimate, almost one-third of the warming expected in the next few decades could be avoided by reducing human-caused methane emissions, without having to invent new technology or cut consumption. Some of that would come from cleaning up other sources, such as landfills and cattle feedlots. (Cow burps are full of methane.) But oil and gas fields are the most obvious places to start, because they offer the biggest potential reductions at the cheapest cost.

Only in the past few years has the urgency of the methane problem come into focus, partly because of new technology and scientific research that's uncovering leaks from pipelines in Russia to old wells in West Virginia. The latest assessment, published on August 9, 2021, by United Nations–backed scientists, says "strong, rapid, and sustained reductions" in these emissions are key to meeting climate goals. In the United States, regulation hasn't kept up. In many cases, energy producers and pipeline operators are free to spew methane into the air without running afoul of any law.

In lieu of regulation, nonprofit groups and activists are acting as self-appointed private eyes, running their own Permian monitoring programs and pressuring companies directly. Gas markets are responding, too. Last year a $7 billion contract to send Permian liquefied natural gas to France collapsed over concerns about the greenhouse gas footprint. Lenders and investors are also pushing for action. Now oil companies are launching their own drones, airplanes, and satellites in the service of mostly voluntary efforts to find the spills and stop them.

It's unclear how far private and voluntary actions will go. One obstacle is the sheer size of the Permian, a sparsely populated scrubland where spills from open hatches, equipment malfunctions, and the like can continue for days before anyone notices. Another is the jumble of companies and wells. Even the Sentinel-5P's powerful sensor has trouble identifying individual leaks. Spills are so large and numerous that, seen from space, they merge into one indistinguishable mass.

• • •

Up close, the Permian is flat and dry. Cows wander across lonely plains of mesquite, and rusting pump jacks dot the horizon. Wildcatters have been chasing oil here for a century, but nothing in the past compares to the frenzy that gripped the region about six years ago.

Advances in extraction techniques, including horizontal drilling and fracking, had opened up reserves in previously inaccessible shale rock, helping to drive down global energy prices. That set off a hunt for prospects that could be profitable even if oil stayed cheap, and the Permian's unusual geology stood out. Meanwhile, Congress ended a longtime ban on oil exports, benefiting basins that produce light sweet crude, which foreign refineries are better-equipped to handle. Money poured in from oil majors and private equity funds. More than half the nation's drill rigs were mobilized. Drilling rights neared $100,000 an acre, and hotels in Midland, Texas, the commercial hub of the oil patch, started charging Manhattan prices.

The landscape was transformed. Clusters of cylindrical oil tanks appeared everywhere, along with rectangular ponds as big as football fields holding the water needed for fracking. Camps for thousands of itinerant workers were laid out with military precision.

A few days after the ban was lifted, on Christmas Eve 2015, drillers broke ground on a new well whose story is a microcosm of the Permian. State Pacific 55-T2-8X17, as the site is known, sits on a stretch of rangeland near the Pecos River in Texas's Loving County (population 169). Two months later, it was complete: a wellhead and six storage tanks squatting on a rectangle of bare earth.

The money behind State Pacific came from BHP Group, an Australian mining colossus that spent big to drill faster than rivals. State Pacific alone brought forth 166,000 barrels of oil and other hydrocarbon liquids in its first year, as well as 620 million cubic feet of gas.

As companies such as BHP started chasing Permian crude, there wasn't much of a plan for the gas that came up with it. Gas is difficult to store, and getting it to market requires a complex system of pipelines, compressors, and cryogenic processing plants. In the most lucrative parts of the field, including Loving County, that infrastructure was inadequate or nonexistent. With gas fetching so little that the price sometimes went negative, companies could save money by just burning it off rather than waiting for pipelines to be built. Across the region, hundreds of flares began to light up the sky each night. From space, the desert looked as bright as Albuquerque.

Even when producers could hook up to a pipeline, these lines were often congested and prone to interruptions. At BHP wells such as State Pacific, the problems were compounded by frequent breakdowns of the diesel compressors required to push gas into pipelines at about 1,000 pounds per square inch. The machines tended to fail if the temperature or system pressure rose too high. Since the sites were unmanned, outages would stretch for days. According to readings from a U.S. satellite that can spot individual flares at night, BHP burned gas frequently at State Pacific during its first three years in operation, torching off at least one-fourth of the gas produced.

Theoretically, flaring shouldn't contribute much to the methane problem, because burning methane converts it to carbon dioxide—still a greenhouse gas, but a far less potent one. Of course, that's only true if the flare works as intended.

·　　·　　·

Long before Zhang tallied the scale of the damage in the Permian, Sharon Wilson, an activist from Dallas, was driving across Texas with a $100,000 camera, hunting for leaks. Wilson works for the environmental advocacy group Earthworks, and her hardware makes methane show up inky black in photos.

If a satellite offers a godlike view of the region, Wilson can track individual plumes right to the source. In May, during one of her regular trips to West Texas, she was in the back of a rented GMC Yukon as an Earthworks colleague steered down a highway past freshly plowed cotton fields. In her lap, the camera, a FLIR GF320, was whirring softly, the sound of a cooling mechanism that keeps its guts colder than dry ice.

"Your faucet drips, that's a leak," Wilson said, her graying blond hair tucked under a baseball cap. "I hardly ever see a leak out here. I see a garden hose. A fire hose. A volcano."

After each trip, Wilson uploads the most dramatic pictures to YouTube and emails them to state regulators—methane clouds pouring from broken valves, malfunctioning engines, and open hatches—hoping to pressure companies and government officials to clean things up.

Wilson, sixty-eight, didn't think much about the environment when she worked for an oil marketing company. That changed, she says, when she lived in the prairie country north of Fort Worth and saw fracking ruin the place. Now she calls company executives "gasholes" on Twitter and enjoys recounting stories of her run-ins with hostile oilfield workers, whom she always nicknames Jethro.

Some of the most common culprits Wilson has found are flare stacks. These are tall pipes crowned with burners designed to torch off unwanted gas. Wilson says they frequently malfunction—the flames go out, allowing a stream of invisible gas to jet into the air. To the naked eye, it's impossible to tell anything's amiss.

David Lyon had seen Wilson's videos of misbehaving flare stacks, but he wasn't sure what to make of them. Lyon, an Arkansas native, is the lead scientist for a massive Environmental Defense Fund research project in the Permian charting the pollution in unprecedented detail. Do flares really get snuffed out all that often, he wondered? He dispatched a contractor to fly over hundreds of randomly selected flare stacks in a helicopter to find out.

State Pacific was one of the first sites on the list. One sunny February day in 2020, the twenty-foot-tall flare stack on the south end of the facility looked inert, with no flame visible. When the contractor pointed at it an infrared camera like the one Wilson uses, he saw a huge plume of black gas spewing from the stack and drifting off into the distance.

State Pacific wasn't the only one. Lyon found that 5 percent of stacks with gas flowing through them were unlit, and an additional 6 percent were only partially burning. If those rates are typical of the entire Permian, Lyon estimates, that alone could explain the origin of 300,000 metric tons of methane a year. "I'll admit I was skeptical," he says. "But then we get out there and see, yeah, it actually is that bad."

• • •

Lyon's work is the latest chapter in EDF's decade-long effort to unlock the secrets of methane. In 2011, Steven Hamburg, the group's chief scientist, took note of how cheap, abundant shale gas was reshaping the country's energy mix, overtaking coal as the workhorse of the electric power industry. Since burning gas produces about half the carbon dioxide of burning coal, carbon emissions in the United States were dropping for the first time in a generation. That seemed, at first glance, like a lucky break for the environment.

But Hamburg wondered how much of that progress was an illusion. Release a ton of methane today, and over the next two decades it will warm the planet as much as about 80 tons of carbon. Only a small fraction of natural gas would have to spill from wellheads, plants, and pipelines to make it worse for the planet than coal, especially in the short term. Hamburg quizzed industry and government experts: How much was leaking? He concluded that no one really knew and that official U.S. Environmental Protection Agency estimates were little more than guesses. So in 2012, EDF undertook the biggest research project in its history. If the government wouldn't figure out how much methane is leaking, Hamburg reasoned, let's do it for them.

Six years, $18 million, and several dozen peer-reviewed papers later, Hamburg had his answer: the U.S. oil and gas industry was losing about 13 million metric tons a year, or 2.3 percent of gas production—60 percent more than the EPA was estimating. (The EPA has acknowledged that studies such as EDF's can reveal flaws in its estimates, but it hasn't yet adopted the group's numbers.) That rate erases most of natural gas's climate advantage over coal, especially in the short term, and highlights the urgency of getting methane under control. The bigger the leak, the bigger the payoff for plugging it.

With Lyon's Permian Methane Analysis Project, EDF is moving beyond just counting molecules. The goal is to reveal whose equipment is leaking, and how much, and publish the findings to compel companies and regulators to take action. University researchers and contractors do the fieldwork, with sensor-laden vans and airplanes carrying methane detectors and stationary monitors mounted on mobile-phone towers. Think of the project as a thousand Sharon Wilsons, armed with the scientific method and more money.

Lyon found his biggest spill last September. An airplane working for EDF picked up a large concentration of methane near a gas compression station south of Midland and circled back for a look. It found a huge cloud of gas jetting from a tank. EDF later calculated the size of the release at 12 tons of methane per hour. That's about the same climate impact you would create if you started up every car in the state of Maine and left them all idling.

The plant's owner, Targa Resources Corp., declined to comment to *Bloomberg Businessweek*, but it told state officials in an email that a wiring problem had caused one of the plant's compressors to shut down. Pressure built up to dangerous levels, triggering a safety valve to release the gas. The company called it "not a foreseeable or avoidable occurrence" and said such mishaps are not uncommon across the Permian because pipelines are frequently running at capacity.

•   •   •

Given the scale of the Permian, the thousands of wells, tanks, flares, hatches, separators, compressors, and plants in use, unforeseeable and unavoidable things are happening all the time. "Things won't work like they're supposed to work on paper," Lyon says. "It takes sometimes a while for people to realize that. There may even be disincentives for them to work. If they get bonuses based on how much oil they pump, then yeah, they're incentivized to go as fast as possible and not worry about emissions."

The contractor who found Lyon's unlit flares is a sixty-six-year-old former oilman named David Furry. Years ago, he pioneered the use of infrared cameras to find gas leaks, and he runs a small detection business catering mostly to oil and gas companies. Furry doesn't consider himself an environmentalist, but he's realistic about the scale of the pollution he's documented. He estimates that about one in five sites he checks has some kind of emission.

One afternoon in May, in his office behind a shuttered gun shop in Early, Texas, Furry tucked a wad of Copenhagen Long Cut tobacco behind his lip and reflected on the future of the Permian. He'd recently gotten a call from a gas exporter wondering how much it would cost to check suppliers' wells for leaks. That way the exporter could market "low-emissions" gas, akin to a fair-trade label on coffee.

"I was raised out there," Furry said. "And you know, in the old days, when you had an oil spill, you'd throw a little dirt over it. Cover it up. Nowadays, things are different. But the thing about emissions is people can't see 'em. They're not thinking about emissions." Furry tapped a finger to his temple. "The industry as a whole is going to have to be retrained to think emissions. And some are already starting. But not all."

BP Plc, the former British Petroleum, has long positioned itself as more climate-conscious than its rivals, and it's been at pains to improve its image in the United States since it caused a gargantuan oil spill in the Gulf of Mexico in 2010. BP acquired BHP's assets in the Permian in 2018. When it assumed control the following year, the wells were flaring about 16 percent of the gas they produced, one of the highest rates in the basin. "We asked ourselves one question," said David Lawler, the head of BP's U.S. operations, in a blog post in April. "How can we do this differently?"

Some changes came right away. BP began disclosing its flaring activity at State Pacific to the state and sought permits to flare there and at dozens of other wells—steps that BHP, like many operators in Texas, hadn't bothered with. BHP said in a statement that it strove to limit flaring and emissions in the Permian and that it "sought appropriate permits."

At the same time, BP began replumbing the operation to eliminate the need to flare. Rather than rely on those touchy machines at each well site, it started building centralized compression stations with more reliable electric motors. BP estimates that the project will cost more than $1 billion and will eventually pay for itself through the sale of gas that would otherwise be wasted. The effort has already reduced its flaring in the basin to less than 2 percent of production. In his blog post, Lawler said BP would end routine flaring at onshore U.S. operations completely by 2025.

Last October the company began installing devices across its Permian facilities that alert off-site employees if a flare isn't working properly, according to Megan Baldino, a spokesperson. Such a device went in at State Pacific late last year.

While BP's efforts in the Permian may be the most high-profile, almost every company of any size is announcing a plan to lower emissions and cut flaring. Some have renounced the practice of bringing wells online before a gas-gathering pipeline is in place and are rolling out costly monitoring programs. After testing eight technologies, Exxon Mobil Corp. said this year that it's hiring a company that shoots lasers from an airplane to spot methane leaks.

In another era, oil producers could have safely ignored environmental critics such as Wilson and Lyon. But just a few months after the French gas deal was canceled, something even more shocking hit executive boardrooms: Exxon's shareholders voted to replace three board members, handing a victory to critics who said the company wasn't doing enough to prepare for a low-carbon future. Lyon talks frequently to Wall Street investors. They always ask the same question these days, he says: Who has their emissions under control, and who doesn't?

Lyon's answer is usually some version of "it depends." He says the mess in the Permian can't be blamed on a few bad actors, and for all the money EDF has spent there, it still doesn't have a comprehensive picture. But one is coming into focus. A few weeks ago, Lyon dispatched an airplane with even fancier gear, a NASA-designed instrument that can snap pictures of methane plumes over a broad swath of the region with enough precision to identify the source. In 2022, EDF will launch its own $88 million satellite, capable of peering into oil fields around the world with hundreds of times the resolution of the Sentinel-5P.

Regulation is starting to catch up, though unevenly. While Texas hasn't taken significant action on either flaring or methane, the New Mexico Environment Department, after consultation with EDF, is phasing in limits on both. A federal methane rule, which applied to a limited number of oil facilities, was restored this year after being gutted by the Trump administration. Now the EPA is crafting a rule that would apply to more wells.

Wilson has heard the companies' promises, and she doesn't buy them. She met Lyon once, at a congressional hearing in New Mexico in 2019 after he testified about how oil producers could tackle methane with frequent inspections and better equipment. "Incremental changes and all that," she says. "I was like, 'David, David. That shit doesn't work. It does not work.'"

Oil companies have been promising to clean up their act for decades, she says, and in that time they just drilled more and polluted more. The only way to clean up the Permian, she says, is to stop drilling. "As long as oil and gas keeps expanding, methane and CO2 is going to go higher."

Even taking the company pledges at face value, it's hard to know how long they'll last. Right now, producers are retrenching after years of frenzied drilling ended in a COVID-fueled slump. In this go-slow environment, it's not so much of a sacrifice to try to end flaring or cut emissions. The question is what the industry will do when the next boom gets going, in the Permian or somewhere else, and there's money to be made by moving fast. And while Wall Street is forcing large, publicly traded companies to take action on emissions, many private operators are still doing whatever they please. Some of the majors have found themselves in the curious position of calling for more aggressive regulation so their voluntary pledges don't put them at a disadvantage.

In May, Lyon's team published the latest findings from that network of sensors installed on mobile-phone towers throughout the basin. Methane emissions plunged in April 2020 as the pandemic put the world economy on ice. But by the end of last summer, levels were already as high as they were when the year began. The stoves in the desert had switched back on.

Women's Health

FINALIST—SERVICE
JOURNALISM

Let the ASME judges explain the importance of this article: "As American women faced the biggest threat to abortion rights in decades, Women's Health *took on the urgent task of showing its readers what abortion really looks like today—dispelling myths, highlighting new research, and ultimately destigmatizing the process. The writer weaves together expert advice and plentiful statistics with rich, emotional, personal stories, attempting to accomplish exactly what the headline of the story promises: change the conversation." Kristin Canning is the features director at* Women's Health. *She got her start in magazine journalism as a college student in the Magazine Internship Program, which ASME has sponsored since 1966. The nomination in Service Journalism for "We Need to Change How We Talk About Abortion" was* Women's Health's *third in the category in the last five years.*

Kristin Canning

We Need to Change How We Talk About Abortion

When Larada Lee, twenty, found out she was pregnant at the end of March 2020, her home state of Ohio had just gone into COVID-19 lockdown. Even though Lee had discovered she was pregnant early enough to have a medication abortion that in several states wouldn't require an office visit, Ohio laws and a new statewide ban on telemedicine abortions made the process unnecessarily complicated and dangerous. She had to go into a clinic at the peak of the pandemic, when anxieties about spreading and catching COVID were higher than ever. "I was terrified to go into an office," says Lee. "But at the time, Ohio legislators were pushing to close abortion clinics completely, so I felt like my opportunity could be taken away at any moment. I was frantic to get an appointment as soon as I could."

As Lee looked into her options, she realized that if she couldn't get into a nearby clinic fast, she'd have to drive two and a half hours to the next available one for the care she needed. Thankfully, she was able to get scheduled last-minute at a local facility but had to have three appointments days apart (one for a mandatory consultation in which her providers were required by law to give her information to discourage her from having an abortion, one to receive medication, and one to follow up). "I had to visit the clinic in-person each time, and I had to risk my health at the height of COVID to access safe medication that can easily be prescribed via telemedicine. It was inhumane and isolating."

Unfortunately, the difficulty Lee had in accessing completely legal care is all too familiar for people who've had abortions. But despite the upsetting and dangerous barriers, she's confident in her decision and feels positively about it and the future it's afforded her. "Since my abortion, I made a cross-country move to California and got a job that I love, helping young people. If I hadn't had my abortion, I wouldn't have been able to take that leap of faith and pursue my dreams. I am certain of that," says Lee. "That single decision, that I am so affirmed in and empowered by, allowed me to alter the course of my life! Abortions aren't something to be ashamed of, and they shouldn't be framed as a last resort only—abortion is a completely normal and healthy option for anyone. I wish people understood that everyone loves someone who has had an abortion, and the way we talk about abortion should reflect that."

The freedom that Lee experienced as a result of her choice has historically been left out of the media portrayal of abortion, though it's not rare at all. Unfortunately, the exclusion of these kinds of stories isn't the only issue with the cultural conversation around abortion: Most of what we do hear about the procedure is actually just inaccurate. A few examples: Abortion isn't uncommon. Nearly one in four people with a womb will have one before they're forty-five, per the Guttmacher Institute, and that number may be even higher when you take into account unreported abortions. Second, abortion isn't dangerous. In fact, it's safer than childbirth, found a study in the journal *Obstetrics & Gynecology*. Abortions aren't just for young women. While most of the TV shows and movies that depicted abortions last year featured white, childless teens seeking care, the majority of people who get abortions are already parents, per Guttmacher.

Another hugely important fact: Abortion is almost never regretted. Ninety-nine percent of people with unwanted pregnancies who are able to get an abortion still feel it was the right decision five years out, per the Turnaway Study, the largest study of experiences with abortion in the United States. When looking back on the procedure, relief is the most common emotion people who have abortions feel over those five years, a study in *Social Science & Medicine* found. Those who have abortions also have no increase in their risk for mental health issues over time and initially following the procedure, are less likely to experience anxiety and low self-esteem than those who are denied abortions. They also have six times higher odds of having positive one-year plans and are more likely to achieve them, just like Lee.

Despite this evidence (and the fact that the majority of the country supports keeping abortion legal), more than 561 new abortion restrictions have been introduced across state legislatures in 2021. Of those, at least 83 have been enacted, putting 2021 on track to be the most damaging state legislative session for abortion in decades. And just this month, a Texas law went into effect that will ban abortions after six weeks of pregnancy—before many people even know they are pregnant—cutting off services to millions of people in the state. This is now the most restrictive abortion legislation in the country, denying care to an estimated 85 percent of patients seeking abortion in Texas—and deputizing citizens to sue anyone who helps someone get an abortion, like doctors and ride-share drivers. Eight other U.S. states have enacted similar six-week bans, too. Thankfully, those have been blocked by courts, but the presence of these bills still creates even more obstacles, fear, and danger around accessing care and increases stigma.

"Not only is abortion a standard part of health care, like any procedure you'd go to your gynecologist for, but considering it's something that a quarter of women will have, it's also *essential* health care," says Alexis McGill Johnson, president and CEO of Planned Parenthood. "We need to normalize abortion as the safe, common experience that it is."

It's almost a certainty that you or someone you care about will need abortion care at some point in their life, and the silence surrounding it doesn't help anyone make informed decisions about their reproductive health. And with laws around access constantly changing and the pandemic impacting how people receive care, it's more important than ever to have a comprehensive understanding of what abortion is like in our country today, and the options available.

So how do you navigate this complex topic? Familiarize yourself with these misunderstood truths about abortion, get clear on what the best care out there looks like and the biggest hurdles to access, and listen to people who've experienced it. Start here.

All Kinds of People Have Abortions for All Kinds of Reasons

When you picture an abortion patient, you're likely to imagine a high schooler, secretly saving up money and asking her friend or boyfriend for a ride to the clinic, a la *Fast Times at Ridgemont High* or, more recently, *Unpregnant*. But, while young women do have abortions, that's not what the typical patient or abortion story looks like. (Fact: The majority of people who have abortions are in their twenties and already have children!)

Reasons for having an abortion vary, but most people cite that they're not ready for another child or can't financially support one. Sixty-five percent of abortions occur in the first eight weeks of gestation, and only 1.4 percent occur at or after twenty-one weeks, according to the Centers for Disease Control and Prevention (CDC). Even though they're uncommon, there's heightened stigma surrounding abortions that occur later in pregnancy, despite the fact that many of them happen because barriers to abortion access have pushed the pregnant person further into gestation before they can have the procedure (fetal anomalies that make the pregnancy incompatible with life or put the pregnant person's health in danger are other causes).

It's unhelpful to judge when or why an abortion occurs, says Meera Shah, MD, chief medical officer for Planned Parenthood Hudson Peconic and author of *You're The Only One I've Told: The Stories Behind Abortion*, because each situation is so unique and one abortion can't be compared to another. Dr. Shah shares a story of a patient who had chronic medical conditions that made her unable to tell that she was pregnant until later into gestation, who needed an abortion. "She was ill and disabled and said the pregnancy would destroy her life. I didn't question that assessment and decision," she says. "As her doctor, I only know a fraction of her life, and I trust that she can make the best choice for her circumstances."

State Abortion Restrictions Harm Communities of Color the Most

Depending on who you are and where you live, abortion services can be relatively easy or incredibly difficult to access. "Abortion isn't available to everyone in every ZIP code," says Johnson, whether due to a lack of clinics (there are six states that have only one) or state laws that ban abortions after certain dates or force patients to jump through hoops to receive care, like requiring they pay for additional services, wait twenty-four hours after an initial appointment to have the procedure, or receive prior counseling about unfounded psychological effects of abortions.

There's no clear pattern linking abortion restrictions to abortion rates, but they may lead to unsafe or delayed abortions. "Sometimes people have to go to extraordinary means to access what is a legal and safe procedure in our country," Johnson says. "In the early days of the pandemic, when several state governments forced the closure of abortion clinics, inquiries about self-managed abortions increased, and states that still offered services saw a major increase in patients." In the three weeks after Governor Greg Abbott issued an executive order pausing abortion services in Texas during the pandemic, Planned Parenthood clinics in Colorado, New Mexico, and Nevada saw a 706-percent increase in patients from Texas, compared to the month before.

Because the majority of those who have abortions are people of color, these laws effect them the most. In particular, data shows that abortion restrictions disproportionately affect people of color in rural communities with little income, who may have more difficulty taking off time from work or securing childcare to get an abortion far from home. People of color are also more likely to face financial consequences and live below the Federal Poverty Line after being denied an abortion. (If you're interested in supporting efforts to protect and increase abortion access, Black Women's Health Imperative, National Asian Pacific American Women's Forum, National Latina Institute For Reproductive Justice, Sister Song, and Unite for Reproductive & Gender Equity are organizations that center the needs of people of color.)

Abortion Stigma Itself Actually Harms Your Health

People who live in communities that strongly oppose abortion are more likely to suffer negative mental health effects from it, even though they personally feel confident they made the right decision for them, per the Turnaway Study. And the more stigma a patient felt when they got their abortion, the more psychological distress they had as a result five years out. "This speaks to the negative power of shame surrounding abortion," says Dr. Shah. "We need to normalize abortion as a common part of people's reproductive lifespan, like miscarriage, infertility, and adoption."

Unfortunately, stigma can come from even well-meaning people and self-described supporters of abortion, too (say, a friend who says, "I'm prochoice but *I'd* never get an abortion"). Stigma exists in the medical community, too, especially against people who have had multiple abortions or are nearing the end of their reproductive years, adds Dr. Shah. "I had a patient, who was forty-one, come to me crying, telling me another doctor had told her she should continue the pregnancy because this could be her last chance. Not once did her doctor ask her how *she* felt about it," says Dr. Shah.

For a lot of patients, their doctor is the only person they feel they can talk to about their abortion, so that conversation can have a deep and lasting impact on the patient's perception of it, says Dr. Shah. "I tell people it's really common and that they're not alone and their shoulders always drop in relief. I used to be afraid to tell people I was an abortion provider, but once I started slowly coming out about it, I was met with a lot of compassion.

Sometimes we hide because we think we're the only ones, but the reality is that everyone has an experience with abortion."

You Can Now Get Abortion Pills Safely in the Mail

Not everyone has an abortion in a clinic; some choose to have a medication abortion (available to people who are up to ten weeks pregnant) at home. Medication abortion involves taking the pills mifepristone (to stop a pregnancy from growing) and then misoprostol (to cause cramping that empties the uterus).

In the past, you had to get these pills from your doctor in an office. But since April 2021, when the Biden administration temporarily lifted the FDA requirement that the first of the two abortion pills must be administered in a doctor's office, in certain states, there's no longer a need to visit a doctor (or even a pharmacy) to get these pills.

Enter Abortion-on-Demand (AOD), the first large-scale teleabortion provider in the United States, which can help people get abortion pills in the mail. When patients visit abortionondemand .org, they can fill out a questionnaire, have a video consult with a doctor, then have pills shipped to them overnight. This means safe, at-home medication abortions will be much more accessible—a total gamechanger for people who live far from a provider or may have difficulty securing time off from work, travel, and childcare to get to a facility. These pills are also cheaper—the service is $239, about $300 less than a typical medication abortion involving a clinic visit. More good news? Sixty percent of all profits from the service will go to the Abortion Care Network (ACN), an organization that supports independent, in-person clinics. While teleabortion access means fewer people will need to visit clinics, the AOD founder, Jamie Phifer, MD, didn't want the service to lead to the shutdown of clinics that people who need later abortions depend on.

Currently, AOD is available in twenty states, with plans to expand to seven more states soon. "Making medication abortion easier to access is critical to advancing health equity and ensuring all people can access time-sensitive abortion care," says Johnson. While this access is still a temporary measure, Johnson hopes the FDA will conduct a review of the full set of restrictions on mifepristone "to ensure all patients can access medication abortion without an in-person visit—during the pandemic and beyond."

For those who don't live in a state with AOD and who can't have an in-clinic abortion because it's inaccessible for distance and/or monetary reasons—or because having an abortion openly could put them in danger of abusive people around them—there are still options available. In these cases, some people perform what's known as a self-managed abortion.

Basically, self-managed abortions work the same as having a medication abortion at home, but you're acquiring the pills without a prescription or consultation with a doctor before taking them. While this method can be safe when patients are armed with proper information, says Dr. Gabriela Aguilar, MD, an ob-gyn and fellow and clinical instructor of family planning at Yale School of Medicine, there are potential health risks (you don't have a doctor you can turn to for guidance if something goes wrong) as well as legal ramifications to self-managed abortions.

You can learn about self-managed abortion options at aidaccess.org, as well as plancpills.org, which outlines how people facilitate safe, self-managed abortions in different locations where laws vary, says Dr. Aguilar. You can also take advantage of a chatbot called Ally on WhatsApp (833-221-ALLY) to answer your medical abortion questions in real time. It was launched in April by Women First Digital (WFD), a collection of online platforms that provides information and counseling services on safe abortion, contraception, and sexual and reproductive health, with the goal of being the world's first abortion virtual assistant.

It's Not Always Simple to Find an Abortion-Friendly Provider

For those seeking an abortion, finding an affirming provider and welcoming, safe clinic can be unnecessarily complicated. There are facilities known as crisis pregnancy centers and pregnancy resource centers that masquerade as abortion facilities but actually try to persuade patients from having abortions. They're often run by people who aren't health care professionals, and they typically advertise free pregnancy tests, baby formula and clothes, diapers, and prenatal care services, aimed at bringing in low-income and under-resourced patients, says Dr. Aguilar. Take these steps to ensure the clinic you're going to can provide the care you need, as well as a positive experience.

Your Positive Provider Checklist

- *Search for a clinic using trusted sources.* Look up legit providers near you via Abortion Finder, Planned Parenthood, or National Abortion Federation.
- *Don't tolerate pressure.* Even in seemingly abortion-friendly settings, misinformation and thinly veiled shaming abound. Maybe because you've struggled with fertility in the past, your doctor is nudging you to continue your pregnancy, or they're assuming you want to because you're in a relationship. "In any health-care encounter, if you feel like you're being pressured or persuaded into something or you're not actively participating in the decision making, that should give you pause," says Dr. Aguilar. "All decisions should be made between each patient and their provider, with the patient leading." If you feel uncomfortable or like you're not being heard, it's perfectly okay to leave and search for care elsewhere.
- Vet the clinic. Read the facility's website carefully, as abortion-friendly ones will explicitly state that they provide these services; you can also call ahead and ask them outright. Search reviews on Google or Yelp to ensure the providers are LGBTQ-friendly and offer a stigma-free experience.

Help Is Available for Any Hurdle You're Facing

There are resources that offer assistance—financial, logistical, or emotional—no matter your circumstance. The answer to common obstacles:

- "I need help paying." Abortion can cost anywhere from $0 to $1,500. It's a wide range that depends on whether you have a medication or in-clinic abortion, how far along in your pregnancy you are, whether your insurance offers any coverage, whether your clinic offers a sliding scale for payment, and where you're located. If you can't afford the process you need, abortion funds—organizations that raise money to help people pay for the costs—can help. You can find one near you through the National Network of Abortion Funds.
- "I need help getting to a clinic." Whether you need childcare while you get your abortion or need assistance traveling to a clinic, volunteer orgs like the Brigid Alliance and Haven Coalition can help by offering rides, travel funding, and places to stay before and after an abortion. Local abortion funds can also be a helpful resource or point you in the direction of groups that can lend a hand.
- "I need emotional support." You're not alone in your experience, and if you want to talk to someone about your abortion, that's totally normal. Exhale is a judgment-free after-abortion textline (617-749-2948), and you can find affirming abortion stories or submit your own on sites like Shout Your Abortion and We Testify, as well as *The Abortion Diary* podcast. Ending a Wanted Pregnancy offers support for those who had to end a pregnancy due to a prenatal or maternal medical diagnosis, and 2 Plus Abortions provides a stigma-free story-sharing space for those who have had multiple abortions.

AARP the Magazine

FINALIST—LIFESTYLE
JOURNALISM

When the 2022 National Magazine Award finalists were announced at the beginning of the year, one writer tweeted with a mixture of excitement and chagrin that he had at last been nominated for an Ellie—only to discover his competition included Kareem Abdul-Jabbar. The nomination of "The Games We Play" was of course based not on Abdul-Jabbar's fearsome status as a basketball legend but on the quality of his writing. The centerpiece of a memorable package about the legacy of Black athletes, "The Games We Play" is, said the ASME judges, "a powerful essay in which Abdul-Jabbar explores the history of racial progress in sports while also recounting his own pursuit of social justice on and off the court." Abdul-Jabbar now writes his own Substack newsletter—"about sports, politics, and popular culture and how they define America"—at https://kareem.substack.com/.

Kareem Abdul-Jabbar

The Games
We Play

In 1675, Sir Isaac Newton explained his remarkable achievements in physics by saying, "If I have seen further, it is by standing on the shoulders of giants." That expression of humility and gratitude resonated with me so much that I titled my book about the literary, political, musical, and sports giants of the Harlem Renaissance *On the Shoulders of Giants*.

In the thirty-two years since I retired from the NBA, I have been writing books, articles, documentaries and movies about many of the overlooked giants of color throughout American history. No group has had more influence on society—and on me—than athletes. Because of the courageous men and women who played games for a living, I have not only seen further but been able to achieve more in a profession and a country that for so long routinely resisted people of color. And, sadly, still does.

Now it's almost time for the Olympics, and the best athletes in the world will gather to prove once again that human beings are capable of more than we thought possible. People will jump higher, run faster, and leap farther than ever before. And the rest of us will watch in awe, fervently believing that the human body is an unstoppable vehicle of the imagination, rather than a thick tether of aging flesh. To watch Olympic athletes soar is to feel, if even for a few moments, untethered.

In 1968, I was asked to join the Olympic men's basketball team, but I refused, as a protest against the police violence and brutal racism bubbling up throughout the country. Martin Luther

King Jr. had been assassinated in April of that year, and there was an anger and hopelessness permeating the Black community. I didn't feel comfortable being an envoy of the American way to the rest of the world, as if everything was OK.

It was an act of defiance that probably hurt me more than it did the country, but after watching Muhammad Ali sacrifice his heavyweight-championship title, endure three years of being banned from boxing (worth millions of dollars), and face imprisonment simply because he was a conscientious objector to the Vietnam War, I had to heed my conscience as well. I couldn't forget his story of coming home after winning an Olympic gold medal in boxing, only to be refused service at a restaurant in his hometown. He was one of the giants who hoisted me up.

For the past hundred years, sports has been both a litmus test and a spearhead for racial progress. In some cases, Black athletes trying to break through the color barriers were like canaries sent into a coal mine to choke on the poisonous racism. In other cases, they endured the foul air and kept getting up, each time proving their worth as athletes. Like many pioneers, they were attacked, abused, vilified, excluded, jailed, and sometimes beaten or worse. For Black athletes, trying to break into white sports was like climbing a rope that stretched up into the clouds—while someone set the bottom on fire.

My own climb up that rope has not been without feeling the heat from below. But the greats who came before me were like thick knots in the rope, each helping us all climb just a little faster and just a little higher.

Paul Robeson, Jackie Robinson, Jim Brown, Muhammad Ali, Bill Russell, and Arthur Ashe are only a few of the giants on whose shoulders I ascended. More important than how to be a winning athlete, they taught me how to be a significant athlete. They taught me that winning wasn't just about trophies and rings but about using those things as currency to lift up the rest of the community. They taught me that every time I spoke out about injustice, I was providing strong shoulders from which the next generation could climb higher.

When I was young, sports seemed like a welcome oasis from the open racism around me. I had been shaken by reading about the brutal slaying years earlier of fourteen-year-old Emmett Till, whose murderers were acquitted by an all-white jury and who, once released, bragged to *Look* magazine that they'd killed him. Then, when I was seventeen, I accidentally got caught up in the Harlem riot of 1964, which broke out after a white cop killed a fifteen-year-old Black kid, James Powell. How was I to feel safe in a country where that could happen to me, simply because of the color of my skin?

But with basketball, the ball didn't care who put it through the hoop. The game was based only on ability. If you had better skills, people wanted you on their team. No one cared who your parents were or how many friends you had. It was a pure, sweaty meritocracy. For me, it was a glimpse, however temporary, of the way the world should be. When I played, the world outside the gym doors, with all its irrational prejudices and enraged injustices, was silenced. There was the sound of the ball being dribbled, the squeal of sneakers on wood, and the cheers of the crowd when the ball slapped through the net.

Of course, all paradises eventually fall. The more successful my high school team became, the bigger the crowds and the more I would hear the racial slurs and taunts. Even my beloved coach used the n-word, in a misguided attempt to fire me up. It did, but not in the way he'd anticipated. I began to realize that there really was no safe haven from racism. This inspired me to learn more about American history, and especially African American history, to understand why things were still this way a hundred years after the Civil War. I met Martin Luther King Jr. I read the words of Malcolm X. I stopped hiding in the gym.

Even while playing at UCLA, I heard the same slurs and even threats. But it wasn't just the overt racism that polluted the purity of the sport. I started playing for UCLA in 1966, and a year later, the NCAA banned the slam dunk. The ban, which lasted until 1976, was popularly known as the Lew Alcindor rule, because I had made liberal use of the slam dunk. In fact, many of the frequent slam dunkers were Black, and there was a definite feeling that the rule had been invoked to keep Black players from dominating.

We all knew it was no coincidence that the rule was laid down less than a year after the all-Black players from Texas Western College defeated an all-white team from the University of Kentucky and won the national championship. Even that historic victory was tainted with racism: The custom was to bring out a ladder and ceremonially cut down the net. No ladder was brought out. Traditionally, the winners appeared on *The Ed Sullivan Show* to celebrate their victory. Not this time.

As I graduated from college to the NBA and as more Black players were slowly integrating professional sports, a popular theory being tossed around was called Black athletic superiority, which credited the rise of the Black athlete to genetics. The gist was that white athletes earned their athletic success through hard work and grit while Black athletes were just born that way. In 2003, the *Journal of Blacks in Higher Education* addressed this claim: "If there is a 'black gene' that leads to athletic prowess, why then do African Americans, 90 percent of whom have at least one white ancestor, outperform blacks from African nations in every sport except long-distance running?"

Some would say, "Easy there, Kareem. That was all a long time ago. We've come a long way." Yes, we have. But not as long a way as many white people think. There's been plenty of publicity about how COVID-19 is having a much greater effect on the Black and Latino communities, both in the death rates and the economic devastation. Late last spring, an estimated 15 million to 26 million people marched to protest police brutality against Blacks, in the largest protest movement in U.S. history.

The headlines are also filled with the current aggressive attempts of states across the country to pass 361 laws to restrict access to voting, which will mostly impact minority and poor voters. The definition of democracy is being rewritten to be exclusive rather than inclusive. And most of those being excluded have dark skin.

How much have times changed? Amanda Gorman, the twenty-three-year-old Black poet who read at President Biden's inauguration and then read again at the Super Bowl, is now one of the most recognizable Black people in the country. Yet, in March, she tweeted that she was followed home by a security guard who said she "looked suspicious" and demanded to know if she lived there. He did not leave until she showed him her keys and let herself in.

Add that to the white woman, walking her dog in New York City's Central Park, who called the police simply because a Black man reminded her that her dog needed to be on a leash. Or the Black graduate student at Yale, napping in her dorm's common area, being questioned by police because another student thought she was not supposed to be there. And the two Black men, waiting for a friend at a Starbucks in Philadelphia, whom the manager called the police on because they were not paying customers.

Where do we belong?

That's what Black athletes have been asking for decades. Unfortunately, they are forced to keep asking that question. Because Black athletes can't just perform for fans and forget that while they're being cheered, their own children are in danger when they're just walking in the park, napping at college, waiting in Starbucks. When these athletes speak out against injustice, they aren't just virtue signaling; they are fighting for survival.

The great Black athletes I mentioned earlier all had a profound influence on me and thousands of other young Black athletes. They are all international superstars whose accomplishments in sports and effect on society have been well documented. Less well known are those like baseball player Moses Fleetwood Walker, whose life in some ways mirrors my own.

Moses played in the 1880s, nearly ninety years before me. He was the first Black man to regularly play big league baseball. (William Edward White was technically the first, having played one game in 1879, but he was biracial and passed himself off as white. Moses was also biracial but proclaimed himself Black.) Teams would protest his inclusion in the lineup, sometimes leaving the field until he was pulled. He faced relentless abuse from fans, newspapers, and players. Two of his own teammates constantly tried to sabotage his play.

The team released him a few weeks after receiving a threat that a mob was preparing to attack Moses if he played in Richmond, Virginia. At the time, he was the third-best hitter on the team. He was the last Black major league player until Jackie Robinson, sixty-three years later. For many ordinary people, to be so passionate about baseball and then lose their dream would drive them into a dark descent. Not Moses.

He used his baseball earnings to buy a theater. He became the coeditor of the Black newspaper *The Equator*; he wrote a 1908 book, *Our Home Colony*, which his biographer called "the most learned book a professional athlete ever wrote"; and he held four patents for inventions—from artillery shells to motion picture reels. Those are some mighty shoulders to stand on.

"Show me a hero and I'll write you a tragedy," wrote F. Scott Fitzgerald. But the heroism of Black athletes is also a story of resilience. For many African American athletes—and the Black fans watching them—winning isn't just crossing the finish line. It's a symbol of every Black American hurdling and dodging the multitude of cultural, economic, educational, health, and other obstacles launched like grenades in their lane, meant to stop them.

Athletes always wonder what their legacy will be. But they can make choices during and after their career to ensure their legacy reflects their values and their cultural history. We just have to remember that sports records come and go, but social justice can change lives forever.

Texas Highways

FINALIST—LIFESTYLE
JOURNALISM

This is the story of the vaqueros, the Mexican cattle workers who pioneered the ranching industry in south Texas but whose legacy has been largely ignored, even by Texans. "The Original Cowboys" was part of a series of articles—the others were "The Evolution of the Texas Cowgirl," by Sarah Hepola, and "Fight or Flight," by W. K. Stratton—that brought Texas Highways *its second National Magazine Award nomination in the last two years. The ASME judges described these pieces as "deeply reported stories devoted to classic cowboy culture" and praised the series for "the resonant prose that characterizes this celebration of a defining and perhaps misunderstood aspect of Texas life." Katie Gutierrez's debut novel,* More Than You'll Ever Know, *was published in June 2022.* Texas Highways *is published monthly by the Texas Department of Transportation.*

Katie Gutierrez

The Original Cowboys

amuel Buentello was fourteen years old when he left the
Rancho Nuevo in South Texas, the only home he'd ever
known. In 1945, the road to nearby Hebbronville, a
ranching hub fifty-six miles southeast of Laredo, wasn't much
more than dirt. All Buentello had was a paper sack of belongings
and his mother's tearful blessing. He had no money and no sense
of what might come next, except work. Work was what he knew.
Work was in his blood.

Buentello was a vaquero, a cattle worker whose horseback
livestock-herding tradition was developed in Spain and perfected
in Mexico before arriving in what would become south Texas in
the 1700s. Vaqueros often lived with their families on the ranches
they worked and were responsible for feeding, gathering, brand-
ing, castrating, and readying for market tens of thousands of cattle a year. Vaqueros were driving up to 20,000 head of cattle per
year from Texas to Louisiana and Mississippi a century before
Richard King of King Ranch began his legendary trail drives and
the mythology of the American cowboy was born, according to
historian Jim Hoy, who cowrote the book *Vaqueros, Cowboys, and
Buckaroos* with Lawrence Clayton and Jerald Underwood.

"The American cowboy, our great national folk hero, is recognized around the world as a symbol of our country," Hoy says.
"Cowboys as we know them, however, would never have come
into existence without the vaquero. They were the original
cowboys."

Buentello learned every aspect of cattle work from his father, Pedro Buentello, who had learned from his own father in the hardscrabble late 1800s. A tall, imposing man, Pedro Buentello worked for various ranches and Rodeo Hall of Fame calf roper Juan Salinas before becoming a caporal, or foreman, at the Rancho Nuevo.

Pedro Buentello was a strict father and mentor. When Buentello was nine and a powerful horse threw him in the corral, Pedro Buentello ordered, "Vengase—p'arriba." *Come here—get up.* Buentello struggled off the dirt, mounting the horse again. For the second time, the horse lowered its head and arched its back, kicking its hind legs until Buentello flew off. "P'arriba," his father commanded. The third time the horse bucked him, Buentello couldn't get up. His pelvis was shattered, and he spent the next nine months in bed.

"Así fue el trabajo más antes," Buentello says, reflecting on his childhood. *That was the work back then.*

In those days, a day in the life of a vaquero began early and often ended in pain. In this part of South Texas the Spanish once called el Desierto de los Muertos, or the Desert of the Dead, the summer heat is like a blowtorch, and the land, thick with mesquite and cactus, can rip a rider's legs apart without the right protection. Yet if you ask any vaquero about his way of life—especially if he is old enough to remember rounding up cattle without the help of trucks or trailers or helicopters, without cell phones or GPS, when the men slept for months beneath saddle blankets underneath the stars—he'll tell you he wouldn't have it any other way.

·   ·   ·

The roots of the vaquero tradition are long and tangled within complex histories of colonialism. They extend from Northern Africa with the Muslim conquests in the mid-seventh century to the sixteenth century, when Hernán Cortés brought the first horses to what would become Mexico and Gregorio de Villalobos followed with the first cattle. To the Mayans, the mounted Spaniards were a terrifying sight: half man, half beast. After the conquests, the Spanish maintained their dominance by decreeing that any Native American caught riding a horse would be put to death.

But the livestock multiplied quickly and needed keepers. At first, Cortés and the conquistadores, who considered themselves above such labor, assigned the work to their Moorish slaves. According to *Vaqueros, Cowboys, and Buckaroos*, these enslaved Black Muslim men were the first true vaqueros—a term that translates to "cow men"—in North America. As the need for vaqueros grew, the Spanish law changed to allow Native Americans to ride horses, but only for work and only without saddles, which were the mark of gentlemen. Unwittingly, the Spanish ensured that Native Americans became superior horsemen.

By the seventeenth century, descendants of the Spanish and Native Americans (and, one can speculate, the Moors) were working cattle using Spanish methods. This was the first generation of Mexican vaqueros—men who had first ridden horses on cradles strapped to their mothers' backs, learning as children how to snare small game using ropes made from native fibers such as maguey, *lechuguilla*, and horsehair. Later, they made *lazos* out of cowhide, a tedious process of drying the skins, cutting them into strings, and weaving a rope of six strands up to sixty feet.

They adopted sombreros for shade and leather *chaparreras* (later abbreviated as chaps) to protect their legs from thorny brush. They could throw *la reata* (later Anglicized as "lariat") to catch the front feet or heels of an animal. They developed the technique called *dar la vuelta* ("dallying") in which they wrapped the rope around the saddle horn instead of tying it off hard and fast. Both methods required immense skill to avoid getting dragged or maimed when roping wild cattle from the back of a horse galloping through the open frontier.

By the early eighteenth century, vaqueros were driving herds of cattle, horses, and sheep alongside Spanish missionaries to settle beyond the Rio Grande. But Texas—then still a part of Mexico—was harsh and unforgiving, marred by violence, heat, and drought.

In the 1830s, to increase population, the Mexican government encouraged migration from the United States, setting the stage for Texas's battle for independence and eventual annexation.

Enter Richard King and Mifflin Kenedy, friends and business partners who had served together in the U.S.-Mexico War and saw an opportunity in Texas's herds of wild longhorns, descended from the original Spanish breeds. Together and separately, they began to acquire huge swaths of South Texas acreage in the 1850s and '60s, which would become the venerable King and Kenedy ranches, according to *Voices from the Wild Horse Desert* by Jane Clements Monday and Betty Bailey Colley.

At the time, though, King and Kenedy had no livestock experience. While Kenedy eventually hired vaqueros from the Rio Grande area, King traveled to Cruillas, Tamaulipas, in northern Mexico, offering the entire impoverished town housing and jobs for life if they would move back with him to his ranch. About one hundred families accepted. Over time, they adopted the moniker of Kineños, or King's men. (On the Kenedy Ranch, they were Kenedeños.)

The Mexican vaqueros taught King and Kenedy everything: how to work cattle and train horses, how to cull and keep the best stock, how to build a ranch. King and Kenedy trusted the vaqueros implicitly and took paternalistic responsibility for their well-being, and the vaqueros rewarded that trust with their loyalty. With his Kineños, King went on to drive tens of thousands of head of cattle to northern markets, helping establish the American ranching industry and building the most successful beef-producing operation in the United States.

• • •

Even after breaking his pelvis at nine, Buentello loved riding and roping. By fourteen he was a highly skilled vaquero. But after a falling out with one of the Rancho Nuevo's *patrones*, Buentello left. He hitched a ride to Hebbronville, once ranked as the largest cattle-shipping area in the country, where he was let out on a corner in front of the Texas Theater. Across the street, a Bruni rancher named Floyd Billings was pumping gas into his big black car when he saw the boy. "Do you need money?" he called. No, Buentello said. He only needed work.

Billings drove Buentello fifty miles to King Ranch. By the mid-1940s, the ranch totaled 825,000 acres and more than 20,000 head of cattle. It had advanced methods of clearing brush, perfected the American quarter horse, and bred a line of thoroughbreds. King Ranch had become legendary, and the Kineños were the vaquero elite.

Two Kineños in crisp blue uniforms and cowboy hats greeted Buentello as the July sun beat down on his dusty khaki shirt and narrow-brimmed felt hat. The men looked at him skeptically. He was small and skinny for his age, more like a child than a man.

"A ver si pasas un test," they said. *Let's see if you pass a test.*

They took him to a corral, inspecting Buentello as he saddled and bridled a sleek dark stallion. "Ten cuidado," they warned. *Be careful.* "He's fast." Buentello slipped his feet into the stirrups, knees high as he guided the horse to a trot, then a full gallop. "Suéltalo!" the men shouted. *Let it go!* Buentello loosened the reins while retaining complete control, land and sky blurring as the horse flew at full speed. The Kineños told him he'd start work in the morning.

Each day, Buentello rose when the sky was still pierced with stars. His job was to exercise fifteen horses before noon. He didn't realize it, but these were King Ranch's thoroughbreds, including Assault. The horse would, the very next year, in 1946, become the seventh Triple Crown racing champion in U.S. history. To date, Assault is the only Texas-bred horse to accomplish this feat.

·   ·   ·

The best vaqueros have "cow sense," the innate understanding of the way cattle think and move. They are masters of the lasso and ride as one with a horse. But one of the most important qualities of a good vaquero is the willingness to teach his skills.

In 1968, Samuel Torres Sr. was a caporal at Alta Vista, the head-quarters of the original Jones family ranches that once spanned more than 300,000 acres between the Rio Grande and the Nueces River. His sons, Samuel Torres Jr. (Sammy) and Gerardo Torres (Jerry), lived for the days he would take them to roundups. They'd pick out their clothes and put their spurs on their boots, and by three a.m. they'd be heading to the camp house a mile or two from the main ranch. The cook had coffee going, plus beans, *pan de campo*, and tortillas. While they ate, they could hear the distant thundering of horses. The *remuda* was coming in, up to 300 horses being brought from the pasture by two *remuderos*, brothers Felipe and Miguel Piñon. By five-thirty, the men—and boys—were sad-dling up.

On most large ranches, roundups happened twice a year, once in the spring to brand, vaccinate, and castrate calves and colts and once in the fall to cull cattle for market. Torres Sr. was a patient teacher, not just to his sons but to other young vaqueros, includ-ing Jose "Red" García Jr. García was used to learning on the job. The first time he castrated a horse, a vaquero had told him, "You've seen enough—now do it." But Torres Sr. took eighteen-year-old García under his wing, explaining which two vaqueros to keep in sight and which landmarks to look out for to maintain his posi-tion when driving cattle.

Marty Alegria, who was born on King Ranch in 1966, also benefited from mentorship by legendary vaqueros. Chief among them were Kineños Alberto "Lolo" Treviño, whose ancestry goes back to the de la Garza family who owned the land before King purchased it, and Martín Mendietta, a fifth-generation Kineño and caporal. Alegria grew up in a Kineño colony of about one hundred brick houses and spent weekends and school holidays alongside old vaqueros who would teach the children how to rope, ride, and break horses as well as how to read cows and people. Eventually, Alegria graduated to working big corridas with thirty other vaqueros, gathering thousands of head of cattle on pastures up to 10,000 acres.

The best thing Alegria learned in his forty-one-year career at King Ranch, he says, is how to palpate cattle to check for pregnancy and ensure high-percentage calf crops each year. With intricate knowledge of the cow's reproductive system, Alegria can tell whether the animal is pregnant as early as thirty-five days after conception, when the embryo is only nine to ten millimeters long. Over the course of his career, he has palpated upwards of 280,000 head of cattle. Alegria's eagerness to pass his knowledge on to fellow vaqueros is how he measures his success. "I ain't gonna take this to my grave," he says.

· · ·

Any conversation about the legacy of Texas vaqueros must contend with difficult truths. The first is vaqueros' general erasure from cowboy mythology. In her introduction to *Voices from the Wild Horse Desert*, Ana Carolina Castillo Crimm notes that a history of King Ranch published in the *Corpus Christi Caller-Times* in 1953, which describes the lives of the Anglo foremen in detail, neglects to mention the Kineños at all.

This isn't a coincidence. The Mexican Revolution, between 1910 and 1919, led to a spell of deadly anti-Mexican sentiment. The border became militarized, and the Texas Rangers grew from a small militia group to an official law enforcement agency that targeted "both the 'Indian warrior' and the Mexican vaquero as enemies of white supremacy," the historian Monica Muñoz Martinez writes in her book *The Injustice Never Leaves You*. National political cartoons portrayed Mexicans as revolutionaries and bandits, and this is how they came to be depicted in most Western literature and film, opposite the noble white American cowboy. Notable exceptions are the 1972 photo book *Vaquero: Genesis of the Texas Cowboy* by Bill Wittliff, founder of the Wittliff Collections at Texas State University, and the 1958 book *With His Pistol in His Hand: A Border Ballad and Its Hero* by the Texas folklorist Américo Paredes.

"Mexican vaqueros have largely been erased from Texas popular memory because they provide a picture of a Mexican that contrasts with racist depictions of them as unskilled, uneducated, dangerous, and a threat," Muñoz Martinez says. "To tell the history of the vaquero you also have to tell the history of a long effort to displace Mexicans from economic, cultural, and political power in South Texas."

To Muñoz Martinez's point, vaqueros have never been paid commensurate with their skill or the importance of their contributions to the cattle industry. "It's not going to make you rich," Alegria says. Indeed, in the 1940s, Pedro Buentello made $25 a month, one-eighth the median U.S. income. In the 1970s, García made $175 per month, one-fifth the median U.S. income, per the U.S. Census Bureau. The most Buentello ever made was $1,200 a month in the 1980s. Until recently, there was no pension or retirement plan for vaqueros. They simply worked until the work changed. At King Ranch, when a vaquero got too old to ride horses, he would inspect fences or fill water barrels, chop wood or teach the children, like Alegria, and pass the tradition forward. Stories abound about vaqueros whose hearts gave out the day they could no longer work, as if broken by the loss of life on the range.

The model of lifelong work on a ranch began to change in the mid-1970s when helicopters started being used for roundups. Pilots were paired with old vaqueros and, without headphones to communicate, would rely on their body language for clues: if the vaquero winced or turned, the helicopter was getting too close or pushing too hard. Once the pilots learned how to herd cattle from the sky, they became known as helicopter cowboys. For $200 to $350 an hour, a helicopter might take half a day to gather a pasture that would take thirty vaqueros two days.

Mechanizing any process takes a human toll. Helicopters were one reason King Ranch eventually laid off or offered early retirement to more than half of its Kineños in the 1970s and '80s. Many of them had been born there and expected to die there. Across Texas, as helicopters, trucks, and trailers became the norm and younger men were drawn to an education or better pay in the oil fields, the number of vaqueros dwindled.

Today, ranches that once employed two dozen or so vaqueros might only have a half dozen. Knowledge of the old ways is disappearing along with them. Torres Jr. has tried to remedy that by founding the Vaqueros of South Texas, a Facebook group 9,000 members strong that posts pictures and stories of vaqueros who have long since passed. "My dad's skills never diminished," Torres Jr. says, "but his skills were no longer needed. There were very few ranchers who might have come and pat him on the back and said he did a good job. So, I figured now's a good time to recognize vaqueros for all the work they did and still do."

•   •   •

South Texas is usually sepia-tone and sunburned, but on the May day I visit Santa Fe Ranch, just north of Linn near Edinburg, everything is luxuriantly green after a recent rainfall. Scarlet-throated wild turkeys strut around, and cream- and tan-colored Charolais cattle graze the pasture alongside the mile of road leading to Mike East's home.

The East family is descended from the Kings, and Santa Fe Ranch used to be a part of King Ranch. East's story begins with Moto Alegria, the accomplished vaquero (and Marty Alegria's great-great-uncle) who helped raise two generations of East children. Moto Alegria was a constant, protective presence who intervened if East's mother went to spank them. Once, Moto Alegria rigged up a harness for a tortoise out of a string and tied an empty shoebox for it to pull, a playful memory East treasures.

Black and white photos of vaqueros line East's hallway. There is Tiburcio Rodriguez, standing beside East's grandfather, father, aunt, and uncle, who crouch with their arms around dogs. Many years later, as an old man, Rodriguez still rode horseback to check on fences and windmills every day. East's grandmother would pour tequila into a cup and tell East, "Take this out to Tiburcio."

There is also Juan Molina, dust kicking up from his boots as he helps a young East and his father rope a horse they're about to castrate. And there, in a place of honor on the mantel, sits a plaque of gratitude from the family of Paublino "Polín" Silguero, who insisted on working until he took a fall in his nineties. Years later, when East visited him in the nursing home, Silguero's first question was how many vaqueros East still employed. (That answer, today, is seven.)

East tells me about Buentello—the boy who left home at fourteen with only his shopping bag of belongings. After exercising King Ranch thoroughbreds for several years, Buentello worked for East's father before going on to train Arabian horses in Corpus Christi and eventually managing a ranch in the Rio Grande Valley. Now, at ninety, Buentello might be the oldest living vaquero in South Texas.

When Buentello arrives for lunch, he is wearing a black plaid shirt, tooled leather belt, and jeans with a crisp iron crease. It's been more than sixty-five years since Buentello worked for East's father, but the warmth between the men transcends time.

"You were kicking rocks because you didn't want to go to school," Buentello tells East in Spanish, reminiscing about the year they met. "And Motito would tell you, 'You *have* to go to school, Mikey.'"

East smiles at the mention of Moto Alegria. "I wanted to be with the vaqueros," he says.

For the next two hours, Buentello and East talk about their tough upbringings and the men they knew—their escapades and heroics and deaths. Buentello's daughter, Magda Buentello-Vergara, has hired a videographer for the occasion. Buentello is the last of an age, and after all, it's always been up to vaqueros to pass down their own tales.

In a space between stories, Buentello reflects silently. "El tiempo se pasa," he says. *The time passes.*

New York

"How do you know a soul?" asks E. Alex Jung in this profile of Anthony Veasna So, a writer who was on the cusp of stardom when he died of a drug overdose, age twenty-eight. Jung answered that question by interviewing So's family and friends, studying his stories and essays, and reading his Twitter account. "The tensions and ambiguities that Jung highlights here," wrote the ASME judges, *"seem especially significant in a story about a queer, bipolar writer of color who strove to emerge from an immigrant community and claim his place in the American pantheon." Jung is a senior editor at* New York, *where he writes for the* Vulture *web vertical. The recognition of "Infinite Self" as a Profile Writing finalist was one of a pacesetting eight National Magazine Award nominations* New York *received in 2022.*

E. Alex Jung

Infinite Self

I. The Next Literary Superstar (Yes, He Knew He Was the Shit)

Here's something everyone can agree on. For the occasion of his first book, *Afterparties*, Anthony Veasna So would have loved it all: the interviews, book tour, readings, attention, praise, pans, mythmaking, the opportunity to opine on the treacly queer writers he hates (or at least shade them) and the insufficiency of Asian American identity. He might talk about how he identified as Cambodian American before Asian American and, for that matter, Californian before American, which would have been a way of making space for himself as well as others. Some writers might be tentative about the limelight, but not him. His parents survived the Khmer Rouge genocide, and he survived Stockton, California, so you can be damned sure he'd make every second count.

Everyone could agree, too, that he was ambitious. Anthony was twenty-eight with a plan. He graduated from Stanford and then got his MFA at Syracuse, where he was adored by his teachers: Dana Spiotta and Jonathan Dee and Mary Karr, who would all write glowing blurbs for the back of his book. During his third year, he got a $300,000 two-book deal with Ecco, and he made the bold move of hiring a personal publicist to promote the first. Most important, he had a (roughly) five-book plan: Following *Afterparties*, a short-story collection that draws from his Khmer American universe in Stockton, would come his debut novel, *Straight Thru Cambotown*. Then an essay collection called *Dreadful Places* and two more books, including a novel about the Cambodian singer Pan Ron, whom he had tattooed on his right arm from a sketch he drew himself, paired with a quote from *Slaughterhouse-Five*: "And I asked myself about the present: how wide it was, how deep it was, how much was mine to keep."

But instead of that agreed-upon future, in the early hours of December 8, 2020, Anthony died of a drug overdose. His partner of seven years, Alex Torres, whom he had met as a student at Stanford, found him in the morning. It's a bittersweet irony that Anthony is now enjoying a literary debut he could have only dreamed of. His death changed the narrative but not the goal— instead perhaps adding to the specter of other young, brilliant artists who passed too soon. After his death, his publicist, Michael Taeckens, contacted national media desks to let them know Anthony had died suddenly. The AP, the *L.A. Times*, the *San Francisco Chronicle*, and the *New York Times* ran obituaries describing an author "on the brink of stardom"—his potentiality cut off at the point when it was limitless.

Since Anthony didn't have a will, California law dictated that his estate be split between his parents, Ravy and Sienghay So, and Alex, with whom he had entered a domestic partnership two months prior. While handling the estate, the tombstone, and the matter of the unfinished second book in the contract, tension has grown among those who knew him best. The family did not learn the official cause of death until just last month. Instead, they've had to rely on Alex's vague and ever-shifting account of that night and what exactly led to the overdose. It has created a rift between Alex and many of Anthony's family and friends, who were forced to question how well they really knew Anthony. Memories blurred and diverged. He was a bundle of frenetic energy, a silent observer; a hard worker, a hard partyer. His friends would say he was sharply funny, generous, and confident in his awkwardness. If you ask Alex, his partner was many of those things but cast in a garish light toward the end of his life: bossy, cocky, self-centered, manic, boundaryless, a creative supernova and an addict. If you ask Anthony's mother, Alex lies. His parents think of him as their wise, quiet angel who could tell the story of their family. Each person has their own conception of Anthony, dependent both on who he was when he was with them and also, perhaps, on how they wish to remember him.

Anthony's death left the bereaved acutely aware of the parts of the self that will always be closed off, private, unknowable. Dark corners that can never be fully legible. How do you know a soul? "As time goes on, I'm learning new stuff about him," says Danny Thanh Nguyen, a fellow Southeast Asian Bay Area writer who became friends with Anthony after they both taught poetry classes in 2019. "He was good at code switching and hiding certain things from certain people. The person who I taught with was a different person than the one who texted me at three o'clock in the morning doing Adderall to finish up his edits. When I reflect upon that, I'm sensitive to this idea of—I knew him and, also, I didn't know him."

II. The Quiet One

Let's see . . . in the extended-family universe, Anthony is number seven out of eleven, right between Christina and Kevin. His older sister Samantha Lamb is giving me the rundown as various aunts, uncles, and cousins gather at her parents' house in an upper middle-class gated enclave in West Stockton, situated in the ample plenitude of California suburbia. The cousins she's referring to are on their father Sienghay's side of the family, including his three sisters, Somaly, Serey, and Chavy. Unlike their mother Ravy's branch of the family tree, the dad's side is as thick as thieves: Somaly lives next door to Sam and Anthony's parents, with a gate connecting their back yards, and Serey is just down the street. (Chavy died in a car accident in 1999.) The sheer number and proximity of family members means that holidays, birthdays, and special events can all get rolled up into one big party, like *Happybi rthdaymerrychristmasit'saboy!*

"Oh, we *numbered* each other?" breaks in Christina (number six), when I ask whether David, the baby of the bunch, is number eleven. "Now we're ranking behind the scenes. I see how it is."

"I wasn't ranking!" replies Sam. "It was literal birth order."

"I know how the cousins roll," Christina says, laughing. "We're assholes."

"Christina," commands Ravy from across the kitchen island. "Can you make a pot of rice?"

"Yes, in a bit."

My visit has occasioned this gathering to remember their son, cousin, nephew, and grandson. In the family dynamic, Anthony was the quiet one reading in the corner. He was smart but lacked common sense. Clumsy. One of their favorite stories is how he once tripped and sent that night's dinner, salmon, splattering on the ground. He had been sickly since childhood: asthma, chronic ear infections, allergic to everything—pollen, grass, dogs, cats, Stockton. Like his mom, he had a nervous twitch around his eye. He got straight A's in high school (okay, except for that B in Spanish that cost him valedictorian), 5s across the board on his AP exams. He was their shy, sweet, awkward boy who went—can you believe it?—to Stanford.

"When he first graduated from Stanford, I didn't know he was gonna become a writer or anything," says Ravy. "He told me that he majored in English. I'm like, *Oh my God. I paid this much money for you to major in English?* My husband was disappointed, and Anthony knew he was disappointed."

"But for me, I saw what Stanford instilled in him. He understood the generational differences," she continues, referencing the title of one of his short stories, written from her perspective. "I always have a problem with my daughter. Always fight with her. *Ay-yi-yi*. But Anthony was different. He understood me. He was very wise. He's my little professor."

"He was just listening and soaking it all in," says Christina.

"Every story we told since he was five," says his mom. "I'm surprised that he remember."

To read Anthony's work, most of which his family didn't see until after his death, is to see the place memories specific to Stockton reflected back at them: the auto shop Sienghay owns and runs; the Cambodian supermarket Super King; the duplexes his father rents out; the carne asada burritos packed with french fries from Adalberto's; his sister's badminton practices. But *Afterparties*, which has the warm intimacy of a sleeping body, is gathered here around the iron-wrought patio table crowded with food and people and stories. Anthony was interested in writing archetypes— the roles you either take on or that are foisted upon you—in part because that's how his family operated. His short story "We Would've Been Princes!" declines to name secondary characters and instead typecasts them: FAMOUS SINGER, FUN COUSIN, LOCAL ACCOUNTANT. Maybe limiting but maybe true; the accountant cousin *could* give tax advice. (That would be Melissa, cousin number nine.)

Anthony's parents had wanted him to become a doctor or a pharmacist. Most of his cousins got stable jobs with 401(k)s: Sam works as the dean of students at a charter school in Richmond; the "all-star" cousin, Leana (number five), is a lawyer; Sopheap (number one!!) works at Social Security like his mother and aunts before him; Brian (number three) works in IT. Anthony picked the thing so many Asian immigrant parents fear: a life of creativity and fellowship applications. The older he got, the further his adult life spun away from his family's. Feeling uncomfortable as a queer man with his conservative family was a part of it. Another was the mutual language barrier; Anthony's Khmer wasn't that good, in part by design. He was raised on a steady diet of encyclopedias and American sitcoms like *Frasier*, *Arrested Development*, and *It's Always Sunny in Philadelphia*. He didn't watch the Khmer-dubbed Thai Lakorns like his sister did, so as good as Ravy and Sienghay's English is, they felt the barrier between everyday conversation and the intellectual world he aspired to be a part of. The American Dream for immigrant children means entering rooms their parents cannot.

Still, he couldn't always keep his worlds separate. Before he switched to English, Anthony majored in computer science at

Stanford. He was put on academic probation for plagiarizing code and suspended for one quarter. He spiraled. He was diagnosed as bipolar and began taking Seroquel. For once, he was in the family hot seat, and he let it all out: not only was he failing a class for a major that he hated, he was gay and bipolar, too. "I was like, 'So you got suspended and you tell your parents [that you're gay]?'" remembers Christina. "He was like, 'Yeah, I opened Pandora's box.' And we started laughing."

"I feel like a bomb just dropped on top of me," says Ravy. "My beautiful child, I thought he was healthy. He's very brave because his dad still did not accept."

"Tell you the truth?" his dad replies. "I don't want to know about it. Whatever you do, don't need to tell me. That simple."

"He only hid from me his relationship with Alex," says Ravy of Anthony's partner.

"Actually, he hide everything from us," says his father.

They learned much more about Anthony's life after his death: that he and Alex had gotten a domestic partnership and that he had a virtual graduation ceremony at Syracuse during the pandemic. He kept his literary ambition on the down low, as though his parents would only be able to take it seriously once he could hand them a physical copy of his book, which opens with the dedication: "For everyone who underestimated me, including myself."

"I think he really blossomed more once he left [home]," says Christina.

"If you meet him, you do not know that he has the funny thing," says Ravy.

"*They* don't think he's funny," corrects Christine. "He's very witty. The last Christmas we were all together, we did a family trip to Tahoe. We were in a restaurant, and I started laughing hysterically because we were stealing the salt and pepper shakers as we were bashing Caucasians. And Anthony tweeted, 'we can't be screaming about white people AND trying to steal their condiments.' That was a typical conversation."

"I'm just looking at his tweets," Sam says, checking her phone. "I never looked at them before."

"Where do you find this app?" asks his mother.

"Mother," replies Sam. "Don't look at the tweets. I don't even wanna look at the tweets."

III. A Twitter Break

#TFW your home address is literally in the center of the Folsom Street Fair. pic.twitter.com/yxzqeBInDf

> —tall and tan ocean vuong (aka anthony veasna so)
> (@fakemaddoxjolie) September 25, 2016

im a gen z top, millennial bottom cusp, the pisces boy of your dreams. there is not one fire sign in my whole damn chart.

> —tall and tan ocean vuong (aka anthony veasna so)
> (@fakemaddoxjolie) July 29, 2020

had a horrible joke about my bottom prowess coming from my tight hole that's kept tight from my inherited trauma but that when I get loosened up by a top it's like the haunting of my life is alleviated, temporarily, and im so inspired that it fuels the sex, makes it transcendent.

> —tall and tan ocean vuong (aka anthony veasna so)
> (@fakemaddoxjolie) August 3, 2020

i cant believe people ARENT using covid as an excuse to avoid family, like me, i guess everyone truly isnt gay

> — tall and tan ocean vuong (aka anthony veasna so)
> (@fakemaddoxjolie) November 23, 2020

IV. The Artist As He Saw Himself (for Others)

Anthony's artist's statement from his time at Stanford:

I am a gay first-generation Cambodian-American diagnosed with manic depression—an absurdly overdramatic amalgamation of identities. On top of that I am a stand up comedian, creative typist, drawing man, painting boy, video guy, world class amateur, failed computer scientist, sketchy animator, self-loathing narcissist, average beauty, obsessive compulsive lover, and anything else that is worldly and self-indulgent.

As an artist, I'm interested in the idea that even the most simple concepts are made complex by the mind, whether done consciously or subconsciously, and because of this the human psyche is an everlasting web of intricacies. Thus, my artistic process is an effort to unravel so much of myself that I hit an universal core of complex thoughts, emotions and instincts. This is conveyed mostly through projects combining prose, drawing, print transfers, photography, and animation. All with a splash of laughter and tears.

Currently, I'm the editor-in-chief of The Stanford Chaparral, Stanford's humor magazine. I'm also preparing a writing and art portfolio to send to MFA programs and trying to finish that damn Computer Science minor. Follow me on instagram @antvso or watch my funny animations and performances at https://vimeo.com/user13978309.

V. The Consummate Performer

As his friends tell it, Anthony was a magnetic presence on campus. He was awkward and gangly, with an endearing cackle. He had a generosity and immediacy that could make you feel as though you were instantly his best friend. He talked fast and loved to perform. Sometimes it felt sincere, and other times it was a bit "amplified," as Nguyen puts it. You could tell when he was testing out a joke to see how you reacted or when his self-confidence tipped into arrogance. But it was all rooted in his ability to make 'em laugh. Anthony loved to gossip, critique, shit-talk, swap stories, and maybe mine yours for his own. "He had this bravado about him that was charming," says Nguyen. "I loved hearing him read a bitch, because his comments would be hilarious."

Socially, he identified as Erin from *Derry Girls*, which is another way of saying he liked to concoct schemes. Out in the world, he was an extension of his family: loving, opinionated, wanting the absolute best for you, and a momager about getting you there. "He was always pushing a ridiculous agenda," says Sharon Bade Shrestha, a classmate of Anthony's from Stanford. He held endless convictions about the world, which ranged from the serious to the seriously silly—impact matters more than intent; humans shouldn't eat dairy; tops shouldn't be mad about poop dick. "You had to be careful with Anthony, because often he would be like, 'You're being dumb. This is clearly what you should do,'" says Gaby Quintana, who knew him since their first year of undergrad. "And he was right like 70 percent of the time, but then there was that 30 percent when he wasn't." His prescriptiveness could be applied to anything—he would try to get his friends to apply to fellowships or eat more vegetables or stop drinking milk. (He was very "anti-milk," says Shrestha.) "His love language was to help bolster people's careers," says Zeynep Özakat, who lived with Anthony in Syracuse for the first two years of their MFA, starting in 2017. "I would text him randomly throughout the day, and he'd be like, 'Did you get your writing done today?' before he kept talking to me. Or just planning my whole future." As he saw it, what was this journey called life for if not to become hot and successful?

Anthony was suspicious of institutions of power but savvy about leveraging them. Immigrant know-how. "He was really good at making use of opportunities," says Quintana. "Networking, connecting with people, taking advantage of programs." He was constantly discovering new artistic mediums, which he would obsessively pursue for a while: cartoons, stand-up, painting, photography, animation, film. Because he kept this all close to the vest, it was hard to know exactly what he was up to. It wasn't until he applied for a Levinthal Tutorial at Stanford, where undergraduates are paired with Stegner fellows, that his friends realized writing fiction was one of those pursuits. "He wouldn't tell you about everything he was doing," remembers Quintana. "Then you would suddenly go to an art show of his and be like, 'Oh my gosh, when were you doing all this?'"

For college graduation, Anthony's friend Soo Ji Lee gave him a copy of Chang-rae Lee's *Native Speaker*. It contained a line that tickled them—the soon-to-be ex-wife of the protagonist calls him a "B+ student of life." Great on a Raya profile but lacking a certain zest. When Anthony began naming characters for his short story "Human Development"—the only one of the book that pointedly skewers San Francisco tech culture—he gave two characters *A* and *B* names. The latter goes to Ben, an earnest older Cambodian man who unironically believes in tech-utopia and states that one of his life goals is to "disrupt the Khmer food industry with organic modifications." Technically, Ben might be successful, but he is also boring at life. He reserves the *A* name for his sharp-tongued narrator, Anthony.

VI. The One Who Knew Him Best—or Worst

Everyone grieves differently, but even Alex would say he's further along in the process. "Anthony and I took a really philosophical approach to living," he says. "That's why I'm handling my grief very well." He tells me he feels great, and I believe him. He is buoyant as we walk around San Francisco, pointing out the exterior of their old apartment in the industrial no-man's-land of Soma. He may be the co-executor of Anthony's estate, but he says that Anthony feels more like an ex-boyfriend to him now, and that perhaps they would have been better off as friends anyway. Anthony's family has found his detachment cruel and perplexing. "He really surprise me when he didn't show that much love when my son died," says Ravy. "I thought he would be heartbroken like me."

Alex didn't have much of a relationship with the Sos when Anthony was alive, which may have been by Anthony's design. The versions of Anthony they experienced were worlds apart. Alex depicts him as a libertine—together, he says, they lived a "very queer, Bohemian, underground" lifestyle. "There's just things they wouldn't know," he says of Anthony's family. "His art wasn't just fueled by sitting in the classroom and being a straight-A student. It was fueled by somewhat chaotic living."

As modern lovers do, Alex and Anthony met on Grindr. It was Alex's second quarter at Stanford; he was a nineteen-year-old first year, and Anthony was a super-senior at twenty-two. Their first date took place at the Philz Coffee on Alma Street. Anthony asked him to guess what kind of Asian he was, and he guessed the fancy Asians—Chinese, Japanese, Korean. Wrong! He was a jungle Asian, as Ali Wong, whom Anthony admired, would say. He got up off the couch right there in the coffee shop and asked Alex if he wanted to hear some of his stand-up material. *Sure . . . ?* He told the one about how he wished he could tell people he had Tourette's because of his facial tics. "I'd rather just have Tourette's than try to stop eye twitching," he said with a performative slouch.

Alex thought he was a dick, and it wasn't until the second date, when he went to Anthony's dorm room, that he could see past the shtick: He looked at Anthony's photographs, print transfers, and sketches. He was taken by a self-portrait with text that read, "I have food, I have shelter, I have water." Things clicked into place; he understood that even the jokes were Anthony's way of telling you about himself. "We had a real powerful ability to be moved by aesthetic experiences. All of a sudden I felt like I understood something about him that other people didn't get," he says. "We instantly fell in love. It was effortless."

From that point on, Anthony and Alex became the kind of couple that shared everything. "They did enter into this world where you knew they were a package deal," says Quintana. They wore the same clothing, shoes, underwear even. Alex thought they were like Gertrude Stein and Alice B. Toklas or Robert Mapplethorpe and Patti Smith. They read each other's work voraciously: When Alex was writing about Emily Dickinson for his undergraduate thesis, Anthony would recite poems like "Wild Nights—Wild Nights!" aloud. When Anthony began writing fiction in earnest, Alex became his first reader and executioner, axing pieces he thought weren't worth it. "There would be no book without Alex," Anthony writes in the acknowledgments. "Thank you for showing me that a queer Cambo from Stockton, California, could find a wealth of commonality with a queer half-Mexican kid from rural Illinois.

I don't think I could've finished this book without knowing that. I love you. You wrote these stories with me."

Alex still wears Anthony's clothes, including the dotted T-shirt and brown Doc Martens he has on when I meet him at his one-bedroom apartment in the Mission. His new place is just a couple of blocks away from the one they shared, and it is filled with Anthony's personal effects: a glass cupboard arranged with photographs and *Afterparties* like a miniature shrine; a cracked mug he loved; a hospital-blue bookshelf Anthony insisted on taking from California to New York and back again; all manner of notes and marginalia; old issues of *The Stanford Chaparral*. Anthony drew one cover in the style of the *New Yorker* as a way of declaring that he would one day be in its pages. "Everyone's like, 'Shut up, Anthony, you're not going to be in the *New Yorker*. You're a computer-science major,'" says Alex. When the magazine published his short story "Three Women of Chuck's Donuts" in February 2020, he remembers Anthony said "'I told you I was right.'" He adds, "Anthony had this sort of arrogance about him that was usually accurate."

Alex's version of Anthony is spikier than others', with more effervescent highs and crushing lows. From the time they met, he says, Anthony loved to party; he was a social ringleader, loud, outlandish. He polarized the girlies; people loved him or hated him, but at least they felt something. He did what you'd classify as circuit gay drugs: coke, ketamine, molly. "He didn't have a sense of boundaries and restrictions, like hooking up with somebody he shouldn't hook up with or pressuring people to do drugs," says Alex. "He had that ethos about him, picking anybody to do a drug. I think he was toxic in certain ways. The problem is people thought he was funny. People liked having him around."

Alex speaks quickly, volubly, and incessantly; the way he talks about Anthony feels like a way to talk about himself. After Anthony died, he began pitching himself to his publicist and agent as someone who could help editorially. He has been a little aimless anyway—he dropped out of his Ph.D. program in English at

Berkeley—and this gave him purpose. Now he's getting assignments. He wrote the foreword for a posthumous piece by Anthony about never finishing books for *The Millions*; he wrote another about Anthony's creative process for *Poets & Writers*; he published one about their relationship in *BuzzFeed* that he's "super-excited about." He asks me if I can get him a job—"just kidding." "I didn't have any Twitter followers before this. Now, I have over a thousand. I had my first tweet go viral," he says, referencing one in which he says that holding galleys of *Afterparties* was like "meeting our child for the first time."

"I tell people it felt like I woke up when he passed," Alex continues. "I was in a spinoff in my old life in a way, rather than the main character now, which I didn't really want." Despite what he saw as his partner's flaws, he also saw him as a mentor, and I get the distinct sensation he is trying to become his own version of Anthony. Alex tells me he thinks he could be the one to finish Anthony's novel, *Straight Thru Cambotown*, because he knew him so well—"but there's a lot of the politics and ethics around me not being Cambodian American writing that book."

The closer we get to discussing the night of Anthony's death, the vaguer Alex becomes. He says that in the months prior, their partnership was fracturing. Anthony's single-minded focus on completing the book was so all-consuming it was burning up all the oxygen in their relationship. He says that Anthony would have nightmares about the genocide and talk about it. "You don't always want to be thinking about Pol Pot," he says. "Being in his creative space was very difficult. I needed a break from it." He was starting to feel like a muse trapped in amber. "Sometimes I feel like he was Hades, and I was Persephone," he continues. "Like if I left him, he would do something bad. There was a lot of concern there." He alludes to horrific things—things he told the family and their mutual friends that have caused rifts in those relationships—but he won't elaborate on them.

He does say that he "started to sever [him]self from him creatively" and that as he did, Anthony grew more dependent on drugs to get work done. Anthony was anxious about finishing *Afterparties*, he says, and living off nonprescription Adderall and fumes. "I think he was probably up sixteen, seventeen hours a day, going nonstop on his edits," says Alex. "And he couldn't let go of the work. He was very fixated on it. He had OCD, and I think that was not always a good thing for his art. I would tell him, 'You're at an A-plus. You don't need an A-plus-plus-plus-plus-plus-plus.'"

Anthony's friends remember this time in a different light. They were more concerned about Alex's partying and drug usage. "Anthony didn't have the space and time to focus on his work because Alex was demanding a lot of attention," Quintana recalls Anthony saying. She and Shrestha were in a quarantine pod with Anthony and Alex, and they would see each other regularly. "He would put his headphones in and be like, 'Okay, this is my work time,' but Alex would keep talking while his headphones were in," Shrestha adds. "And then he would have to listen for extended amounts of time and that would disrupt his schedule." They recalled discussing whether it would be a good idea for Anthony to apply for a fellowship to get a separate studio space to write.

Alex can't or won't explain exactly what happened the night of Anthony's death; he's more evasive in conversation than he was with the police. "I don't remember a lot of it . . . I can't really get there," he says. "'He made cocktails, and he spiked it, I think. I think he was on so much Adderall and caffeine." When told that the medical examiner said there was no evidence of alcohol in Anthony's system, he backtracked and said that he may have had a hard kombucha while Anthony had an orange juice. "I think he just took a lot of something, and I don't know what," he continues. "I woke up the next day feeling tired. I showered, I logged onto Slack, and then I realized he wasn't moving." To Alex, his partner's death was in line with the Anthony he knew: drug-dependent, impulsive, self-destructive. "I'll leave you with this thought," he says after our first conversation in May. "I was not surprised by his death in ways that other people were. Anthony was a very complex, beautiful person. It's very difficult for me to watch other people talk about him in ways that they do. And it's not that they're wrong. It's just that they're not seeing the full story."

VII. The Cause of Death, According to the State

According to the police report, at approximately 8:28 a.m. on December 8, two members of the SFPD were dispatched to Anthony and Alex's apartment. A medic was on the scene and had pronounced him dead four minutes prior. The official police report gave the following statement from the incident:

> On 12/8/2020 at approximately 0030 hours, he and So were celebrating that So had just finished writing a book. [Torres] stated he and So used GHB, Adderall, and ate an edible marijuana induced pastry. So and [Torres] went to sleep at approximately 0200 hours. So fell asleep in the bedroom and [Torres] fell asleep in the living room of the apartment. On 12/8/2020 at approximately 0800 hours,
>
> [Torres] woke up and checked on So. [Torres] saw that So was lying face down on the bed . . . [Torres] attempted to wake So up to no avail. When [Torres] touched So, he noticed that So was cold and stiff. [Torres] called 911.
>
> [Torres] stated he and So had been domestic partners for the past 7 years and that So had been a drug user since they met 7 years ago. [Torres] stated that to his knowledge, So used GHB, Marijuana, Cocaine, Molly, Ketamine, and Adderall. [Torres] stated that So was writer and had been writing a book for the past several months. [Torres] noticed that since So began writing the book, So had been using Adderall more than usual and had hardly been sleeping. [Torres] also stated that So had Asthma.

On July 1, 2021, the medical examiner's office of San Francisco released the official autopsy report determining that the cause of death was the "toxic effects of gamma-hydroxybutyric acid (GHB), methamphetamine, and 3,4-methylenedioxymethamphet amine (MDMA)." There is no evidence of alcohol ingestion. The manner was determined as accidental.

VIII. Afterlifes

In "Maly, Maly, Maly," the third story in *Afterparties*, two cousins, named Ves and Maly, get stoned before a family gathering to celebrate the reincarnation of Maly's dead mother as their second cousin's baby. Both find the presumption from the elders ridiculous. The story is drawn from So family lore. When Anthony's aunt Chavy died suddenly in a car accident, his grandma's cousin's wife believed she was reincarnated in her granddaughter. The cousins' real-life reaction was similarly incredulous. "Like, 'Who the fuck are you to say my aunt is a reincarnation of your granddaughter?'" remembers Sam. Still, after harboring hostility toward the idea, at the end of the story, Maly caresses the baby and says, "I've changed my mind. She's actually pretty cute." In that moment of quiet, Ves realizes, "Of course Maly would want to be with her mom, no matter how."

After Anthony's death, Sam started dreaming that he was following her around. "I felt like Anthony was haunting me in the sense of like, *Hey, I need your womb so I can be reincarnated.* Like, *Get pregnant already,*" she says. Then, on what would have been Anthony's twenty-ninth birthday—February 20—Sam told her mother she was pregnant again. "When she found out, she was like, *Oh good, Anthony has come back,*" she says. Ravy explains that she wouldn't want her grandchild to necessarily *be* Anthony. In Buddhism, reincarnation is a way for the soul to grieve, understand, and, eventually, let go. Over time, the body they inhabit becomes their own, and the deceased becomes a faint memory. More than anything, Ravy has been searching for closure and understanding. Anthony's death unmoored her. "I talked to him in the coffin all day long, telling him to come back," Ravy recalls. She thought he was her perfect son, but then he caused her the greatest injury by dying. "It's like I lost my soul," says Ravy.

In March, the family gathered for a one-hundred-day ceremony, traditionally held after the funeral to let the soul go. They put together a slideshow of photos. The event was light-filled, communal, personal. Shrestha and Quintana were there. Alex did not attend. "That felt like the first time somebody created a space for us to just focus on Anthony," says Quintana, "because everything else had been distracting us from our friend." For seven arduous months, the family waited for the medical examiner's report. A delay with the city had dragged out a very basic question—what happened? They had to rely on Alex, who had left them with gaps in their understanding of Anthony and the events of the night he died. "The hardest part for my family is not having a clear picture of why," says Sam. "And how. Because there's only one person with him on that night. And for whatever reason, they don't feel they can trust that person's story."

The family continues to find ways to remember Anthony. Sienghay is planning on getting a tattoo of his son's Khmer name, Veasna. Anthony and his father always liked the name, which means "destiny." (His mother hates it.) For the release of *Afterparties*, they have been thinking about having their own book party. "We felt like we should have a celebration and invite all his friends to come," Ravy says. "I still don't know what his writing means to the world." Sam begins to say the preorders are good, but her mother interrupts her. "No, no, no, no, no, nothing money with me. I don't really care. I just want . . . I want his dream to come true."

IX. The Mythmaker

When Mark Krotov accepted "Superking Son Scores Again" for *n+1*'s spring 2018 issue, he remembers Anthony telling him he was particularly proud of that moment—it was one of the stories his MFA workshop had liked least. "No, that's not true," says Dana Spiotta, his first-year workshop instructor. "I think that was a bit of self-mythologizing." Indeed, Spiotta dug out her notes at the time—she had called it "brilliant" and summed up her observations thusly: "This is a terrific story and wonderfully original and funny." "Anthony was a deviser of his own apocrypha," says Spiotta. "He exaggerates for comic effect or for drama."

Anthony was a performer; he had a sense of himself as a writer not just on the page but in the world. The publication of "Superking" got him an introduction to his agent, Rob McQuilkin, who wanted to build up what the latter called a "war chest" of stories and essays they could use to promote the book. The original auction had been timed with the release of "Chuck's Donuts" in the *New Yorker*, when interest would be at its peak. "So much of it is going just as he had planned," says McQuilkin. "He didn't care about riches much. He did care about renown. He did want to be a well-regarded famous writer."

The machine Anthony devised has continued apace, and without him here to subvert his public persona—or just enjoy himself as a hot boy writer—his death has ascribed a different myth to him. There has been no dearth of coverage since Anthony's passing: *Afterparties* continues to grace summer reading lists; the *New Yorker* and the *New York Times* have run multiple pieces about him ahead of the book's publication. The *Paris Review*, where Anthony had long wanted to be published, accepted "Maly, Maly, Maly" posthumously. *n+1* has dedicated an annual fiction prize in his name, "to a writer whose work, like Anthony's, brings new and neglected worlds onto the page with great care and boundless imagination." The *New York Times Book Review* likened *Afterparties* to the works of Bryan Washington and Ocean Vuong, despite there being few stylistic similarities between So and those authors; the comparison makes more sense in terms of the career trajectory that would have opened up to him. Anthony was talking to TV producers about potentially adapting *Straight Thru Cambotown*. He wanted to go to Hollywood.

The initial interest in Anthony undeniably had to do with the pathway that brought his parents to the United States as survivors of the Khmer Rouge genocide. Individual talent and historical circumstance had convened to create someone singular, someone they had never seen before. "I sadly had not read fiction set in a Cambodian American community before," says Helen Atsma, the editor of *Afterparties* at Ecco. "As an editor, what's always exciting is feeling like you're reading something new and alive and invigorating."

Anthony might have raised an eyebrow at all of it but would ultimately have taken it in stride—after all, talking about the white gaze is "boring," as he put it in a posthumously released interview in Soft Punk. He was good at intellectualizing his work, grafting theory onto craft. "I don't think people are actually that interesting," he said in the same interview. "They're not that complex—they're very much created by the institutions and the forces around them. If you think that I'm interesting, it's probably because you never met someone that's come from my particular context."

X. Anthony as Described by Himself

Here's how it should have gone down: I would have flown to San Francisco, where Anthony might have shown me his favorite haunts around Soma and the Mission. We would have grabbed food at Tartine or gotten drinks at El Rio. Our exchange would have existed within the parameters of a conventional profile: the tension of mutual seduction. He would have been charming and engaging. Someone as well versed in critical theory as in Pokémon types. We might have rehashed a discussion around autofiction or cruel optimism and the American Dream. I would have asked about his chaotic bottom tweets, his family, his queerness, the collisions between them. I would have wanted him to dish, no *really*, and maybe asked to go to Stockton; he might have said no to the fancy Asian reporter, which, fair. Either way, I probably would've liked him.

Like almost everyone else, I got to know Anthony through his language: the specific worlds he inhabited and the humorous incongruities he created. He could see through cool postures for the protective mechanisms they were—the devastation that hides under humor—possibly because he was adept at using them himself. Many of the stories in *Afterparties* end with a vision of what's to come, through the lens of what has come before. The present moment is wedged between damned pasts and possible futures. In "Maly, Maly, Maly," as Ves packs for college, he pictures Maly becoming the same mother in "all her reincarnated selves." In "The Shop," after all the sacrifice and heartache and hardship to keep the family auto shop alive, the son looks at his father's worry-worn wrinkles and thinks to himself, "'But what,' I was ready to ask, for every life Dad and I had lived and lost, 'will we do after?'"

During one of his last public appearances, a Zoom reading of the Steinbeck fellows in December, Anthony reads pages from *Cambotown*. He sports a mustache; he looks healthy. During the audience Q&A, his answers are concise but inviting—perfect for the rigmarole of a book tour. At the end of the event, one of the audience members asks, "Is there a particular emotion or feeling that you want to try and evoke in your readers?" He replies, "I got really drunk one time and just, like, started screaming—it was, like, in my MFA—and I just started screaming to everyone about how all I ever wanted my work to be was to communicate an exuberant grief."

ESPN.com

FINALIST—PROFILE WRITING

"In this illuminating profile of Jake Paul," reads the judges' citation for "Is Jake Paul Bad for Boxing? Next Question," "Dotun Akintoye finds his subject at a crossroads. One of YouTube's most successful content creators, the twenty-four-year-old Paul is already rich and famous, but he's desperate for a more credible kind of celebrity. Much more than a study of Paul's quest to become a boxer, this stylishly written story explains Paul's appeal to a generation of media consumers while also capturing the flavor of our current cultural moment. This is how a new kind of fame monster is born." Akintoye is a staff writer at ESPN and a 2023 Nieman Foundation fellow. ESPN was also nominated for the Profile Writing award last year, for "The Remarkable Life (and Near Death) of Boxer Christy Martin," by Allison Glock.

Dotun Akintoye

Is Jake Paul Bad for Boxing?

Next Question

Jake Paul has taken to scrawling poster board messages in the living room of his home in Dorado Beach, Puerto Rico. Consider the writing on the wall: "Make History." "Inner Athlete." "Win." "Win!!" "Give Back." "What Would Jordan Do?" "Secretary Bird," "Orca Energy," "Box Jellyfish—no heart, deadliest animal."

On the other side of sliding glass doors that lead outside to his pool, Paul shudders through his daily ice bath in what looks like a toppled refrigerator. Paul's assistant, Marcos Guerrero, has invited me to sit with Paul while he makes a few business calls. There's more on the posters, goals for each week heading toward Paul's bout against former UFC welterweight champion Tyron Woodley on Sunday. Next to each agenda item are circles to color in when the task is completed.

"6 Ice baths"—colored in. "3 sparring sessions"—colored in. "Troll UFC"—colored in. "Meet Trump"—colored in.

Paul walks inside and sits down at the head of his dining table. His ramen noodle hair flops on his head and his nose veers off-center. He's wearing a white T bearing the blue block font of his new charity, Boxing Bullies. Mounted on the wall behind him is a painting of Paul screaming on the turnbuckle after his KO of Ben Askren in April. Paul's chef, who told me Paul and his team go through about two eighteen-egg cartons a day, brings him an omelet. Paul lays out several ivory sheets of lined paper with lists of things to do each day, what he's doing wrong in sparring and "Moves 2 Make."

Move 2 Make—"I need to step my style game up."

Guerrero, who turns twenty-two the next day but who one team member describes as "really about forty-five," sits nearby in an oversized T-shirt and shorts, looking up from his phone or laptop to speak in short, quiet bursts of Sorkinesque hypercompetence. He reminds Paul when his next meeting is, with whom he'll be speaking, and what about. Paul picks up his pen and scribbles a new note after almost every conversation he has on the phone or with Guerrero. A new bubble needs filling, a new action item appears. It turns out Paul, one of the savants of our online visual culture, is scripturient.

I ask what the secretary bird, orca, and box jellyfish stuff is about. He says he studies a new deadly animal each week to remind himself that boxing is ruthless. He picks up his phone to take a call with Tyler Winklevoss, one half of the bitcoin billionaire twins who didn't invent Facebook.

Paul loves talking to billionaires because he has wanted to be one since he left his childhood home in Ohio at seventeen and moved to Los Angeles with his brother, Logan, to pursue social media fame. If you know Jake Paul's name now you either hate him or know you're supposed to. Some of his transgressions are trivial: His song, "It's Everyday Bro," is the sixteenth-most disliked video in the history of YouTube. He's not welcome in Beverly Grove or Calabasas. There is the air of the scammer about him: if the pay-per-view numbers from his April KO of former MMA champion Askren are at all proximate to fact, Paul, at 3–0, is one of the most lucrative boxers on earth, despite never having boxed a trained boxer. Critics say he duped young fans eager for social media success into purchasing a bogus how-to-become-an-influencer program called Edfluence. But more than that, he also has been accused of crimes: Last summer, the FBI raided his California mansion in connection with looting in a Scottsdale, Arizona, mall in the aftermath of a protest (the FBI has since declined to press charges). Former employees and friends have called their

211

Is Jake Paul Bad for Boxing? Next Question

tenures with him abusive and exploitative. And earlier this year, Justine Paradise, a prominent TikToker, posted a twenty-minute video on YouTube in which she said she was sexually assaulted by Paul, a charge he has denied.

He has been recording himself for the internet since he was ten. He has lived several child-star adolescences already: fired by Disney (the parting was described as mutual at the time), recorded using the N-word in a freestyle rap, sued for the reckless stunts that made him famous. None of it has halted his accumulation of followers, subscribers, and money. He has learned he can run headlong over the cliff, that waiting in the chasm is a thermal that will float him blithely up, high into the troposphere of notoriety.

He specializes in the boom-and-bust moral cycles of the internet, violation then contrition, contrition then a promise to change, a brief respite and then the next violation, this time followed by defiance, perhaps—one can't let the audience get bored. The offense is just an investment after all, a growth stock in the capital markets of attention. "It's Everyday Bro" went platinum. Its remix features rapper Gucci Mane.

At first glance, Paul's money and fame confound. Scrutiny reveals a shrewd, ambitious young man bent on winning on the impoverished terms the culture has supplied him. He allowed follower attention and brand-sponsorship money to decide his life for him as a teenager and hasn't stopped wondering since who he is supposed to be. Now his attempted flight from his own gnawing emptiness, from one kind of illusory celebrity to a purportedly more secure one, casts him upon the narrow, perilous shoal of professional boxing. "I'm an entertainer. Period. That's who Jake Paul is," he says. "My means of entertaining are just evolving as I get older." Boxing is his latest bit, and he is committed enough to its rigors to fool himself, maybe even enough to change.

·　　·　　·

Paul meets the Winklevoss twins in June at Bitcoin 2021, the annual cryptocurrency festival, held in Miami this year. Paul is scheduled to appear on the last panel of the day with the twins and the comedian Tim Dillon. Outside the festival's geodome-shaped tents, the grounds are strewn with Venezuelan fifty-bolivares notes, a jape about the destiny of fiat currency. Jack Mallers, a crypto evangelist and CEO, openly weeps onstage. "I will die on this hill," he shouts between sobs. "You are improving humanity and don't let anyone tell you otherwise."

A young man wearing a red "Make Bitcoin Great Again" hat holds a sign over his head that reads, "Take Me Down Get One Bitcoin." I ask him how it's going. He pulls up his white T to flaunt wine-colored abrasions along his back and rib cage.

Bewildered by the whole thing, Paul tells me later it felt like walking into an "army or cult."

Backstage, where the assembled cool kids have no green rooms, there is a different kind of excess. The feeling is that of a house party on the verge of running too long. One of the Winklevii wears a shirt adorned with the iconic Corinthian columns of the New York Stock Exchange, underneath which is written, "Rage Against The Machine." Here are rich kids and scenesters, specula-tors and confidence men and earnest seers, losers, YouTubers and TikTokers, the clueless and those who should know better, all cosplaying as exiles from the old consensus, all clamoring for the brave new world, a windfall.

Weeks later on their FaceTime call, Paul and Tyler Winklevoss exchange jargon ("metaverses" and "NFT marketplaces" and "a crypto credit card," series Bs and Cs) and talk potential collabo-rations. Paul invites Winklevoss to the Woodley fight and a brunch that's meant to bring together Hollywood with tech and crypto types.

In Paul's mind, Hollywood stands for the entire edifice of what he sees as unchallengeable and legitimate fame and wealth and access. It is his long game. Boxing is his exit strategy from the kind of celebrity he has enjoyed thus far, that of the influencer.

Part of what Paul hates about his social media career is its cir-cular quality. "It's a bottomless pit. Imagine someone eating and the food just goes right through them. Social media, you have to

213

Is Jake Paul Bad for Boxing? Next Question

keep posting. You have to keep creating. You have to keep on coming up with new ideas and be hustling all the time. All the time, if you want to be the best in that category. But as soon as you stop, then there's nothing left to show for it.

"The money stops. The merchandise sales slow down. No one wants to sponsor you anymore because you're not putting out that content. So, it's like you're working every single day to have nothing if you stop working, which to me is a dead end."

I ask Paul the difference between where he wants to go and where he has been, between a celebrity and an influencer.

"An influencer, take away their Instagram, take away their TikTok, take away their YouTube, they're f——ed," he says. "What are they going to do? That's an influencer. If you could take away all their social media profiles and they can still do whatever it is that they do, they're not an influencer then. They're a celebrity."

I ask him later if a loss to Woodley jeopardizes his plans. Hesitating, he says yes, before confessing that losing on August 29 is his biggest fear.

"If I play my cards right over the next couple of fights and win and win and win a couple more times, then I could walk away from this sport having made $250 [million] to $500 million. That would suck to not do that.

"One of my earliest goals was to become a billionaire. Just to see if I could do it honestly. And so now, it's there. And I think regardless of winning fights or not, I think I will become a billionaire just as a challenge to myself. I don't even know what I would do with all that money. I don't even really even do anything with my money now, but just as a challenge. I like a challenge more so than anything. And having that get cut short because of a loss would just suck, first and foremost."

Guerrero tries to explain the new status Paul wants: "All these big outlets that people see in a normal household, on a day-to-day basis when they go to a store, when they're watching TV and so forth, versus these smaller outlets where it's like YouTube based and blog based, that's the difference right there. Influencers, you don't really see them too much in the mainstream media. You don't see them on *Good Morning America*. You don't see them on *SNL*. You don't see them on the Conan show. You don't see them appearing on ESPN."

In other words, they think I'm here to help.

.　　.　　.

After Paul departs the festival, he attends a late private dinner in a downtown Miami restaurant. Seated around a long banquet table are a clutch of billionaires; crypto financiers; venture capitalists; self-styled founders and creators; the DJ 3LAU; Chris Kelly, a part owner of the Sacramento Kings, former first general counsel for Facebook, and one-time runner-up to Vice President Kamala Harris in the democratic primary for state attorney general of California, who patiently answers my questions about "Whales," "SPACs" and "Elon Musk"; and the singer Trey Songz.

Dinner begins with an icebreaker. One by one the attendees stand and introduce themselves. When Paul's turn arrives, he stands, casually working his right fist into his left palm. Paul wears two watches, a ring on each ring finger, two bracelets and three chains. There is no message in the bling, it doesn't catch the room's apricot light or make noise. He's just twenty-four years old and rich.

"My name is Jake Paul. How we doing . . ." he begins in his customarily downtempo speech. Not thoughtful per se, though he is capable of clear-eyed self-assessment, but extruded at a rate and in a manner that's vaguely hypnagogic. Even when he's staring at and addressing you it can be like he's returning to himself from a daydream.

He continues: "I run a venture fund with Geoff Woo," and gestures to his business partner and cofounder of Anti Fund, their new VC company, at the other end of the table. "We got crypto stuff, business stuff, consumer products. Oh, and I box people and knock them out." This to peals and applause.

Minutes later, a dinner table shuffle finds the host, Nikil Viswanathan, CEO and cofounder of Alchemy, a startup that received a

215

Is Jake Paul Bad for Boxing? Next Question

half-billion-dollar valuation this spring, seated next to Paul and urging the latter to tell the room his "original hustle story."

Paul ventures into a childhood memory about the origins of his competitiveness with his older brother. Soon after they started posting videos on the now-shuttered app Vine, the two teenagers were standing in the kitchen, with their father, a friend of Paul, and Logan's girlfriend when Logan tried to give his younger brother some advice on a clip he was working on. "Why would I do that?" Paul retorted. "What do you know? I have more followers than you." Paul's friend and father laughed, so did Logan's girlfriend. Logan went quiet.

"I was like damn, he's right. My younger brother does have more followers than me," Logan recalls. "F—— this guy. I went out and started making Vines with the intent of becoming famous on the internet."

Over the next few days Paul noticed a difference in his brother's videos: they were funnier. Logan's views went up. Their long-running competition began there, says Paul, who is in Miami this weekend for the absurd spectacle of his older brother's fight against Floyd Mayweather the following night.

Paul was born in January 1997, which makes him one of the very earliest members of his cohort, Generation Z. He grew up in Westlake, Ohio, an affluent Cleveland suburb some thirty minutes west of downtown. His parents divorced when he was a child. He says his first real memory is of police entering his home to quash an explosive domestic dispute between his parents. "It was a very normal bubbled suburban kind of childhood," Paul's mother, Pam Stepnick, says.

Their family roles are so fixed it's like listening to people recount a sitcom. Stepnick was loving, indulgent. Her ex-husband Greg Paul cast himself as the drill sergeant. The meagerness of his Christmas gifts—wood-cutting knives, socks, bar soap, pop tarts, all wrapped in newspaper—are the stuff of family lore.

Both brothers credit their father with their work ethic (they are convinced of nothing so much as the belief they've earned their money and notoriety), but he also imparted to them a reckless attitude to the world around them. Greg recorded my conversation with him because he's wary of journalists "twisting" his words.

About his own manhood: "I'm a savage. I'm an alpha male. When everybody else runs away from the burning plane, I'm running to the burning plane."

About alimony, unprompted: "I've heard women say I've been married to him for this long and I deserve this. Really? You don't deserve s——. What makes you think you deserve something?"

About Logan's infamous video of a hanging man in Japan's Aokigahara forest, known as the Sea of Trees, a place where people go to kill themselves: "For me personally, quite frankly I didn't give a—I could care less if he filmed a dead person that had already hung himself. . . . I said, 'What bothers me is that you put a dead fish on somebody's taxi. That you hung a squid on a restaurant owner's window. That you went into a store and you broke something.'"

A true suburbanite, nothing disquiets his mind like property damage. His feats of moral jiu-jitsu displace, with a flick of the tongue, his children's responsibility for their lapses, continually reducing them to the meme of large adult sons. He's a disciplinarian without a conscience.

"If I had all the success and money and stuff that Jake and Logan have achieved at their young age, if I had all that when I was nineteen back in the day when there weren't cameras around and blah, blah, blah, I don't know that I would have lived to make it to twenty-three or twenty-four," he says.

At the end of our phone call, perhaps stricken with the uneasiness of having been found howling at the moon, he says, "Please don't be one of the people who twist the story for content or to get more views or more reading. Know what I'm saying?"

Logan was a golden boy, his younger brother a barely lovable knucklehead. One the type of bright-faced, dead-eyed achiever adored by coaches and teachers; the other more sensitive, wounded by his parent's divorce, acting out in unpredictable ways.

217

Is Jake Paul Bad for Boxing? Next Question

In ninth grade, Paul participated in a small ring of boys stealing iPhones from their classmates for resale. When the boys were caught, they were suspended and ended up in court, where they received community service. His parents were humiliated. He didn't want for anything—what was this about?

His brother was coming to the creeping realization he didn't know or like his sibling. "I remember thinking, who is this person? Who is my brother? I thought I knew this kid, but he's a little bit of a s——head," Logan says.

"I didn't think anything of it. I was just like, I saw the dollar signs," Paul says, recalling the time with visible embarrassment. "I didn't even know what I was planning to spend the money on."

Logan went to Ohio University on a full scholarship for engineering. By that time, he had amassed enough of a social media following on Vine that he began to imagine pursuing a career in entertainment. At the end of his freshman year, he came home and told his parents he planned to drop out and move to Los Angeles. His growing brand sponsorships would finance the move. His brother decided to come with him.

Besides insisting that Paul eventually get his diploma online, Pam and Greg didn't resist the move at all. "I just knew they would be OK," Stepnick says. "I was less sure about Jake, but I was pretty sure Logan would be OK." In June 2014, at ages seventeen and nineteen, the brothers left Ohio for L.A. Stepnick disenrolled Paul from high school and called OU to relinquish Logan's scholarship on the same day.

By early 2016, Paul had been cast in Disney Channel's (the Walt Disney Company is majority owner of ESPN) comedy *Bizaardvark*. He played a version of himself named Dirk Mann, a character who takes on dares from fans on the internet. And that summer he moved into a $17,000-per-month mansion in the Beverly Grove neighborhood of Los Angeles and brought other influencers in with him to start a content collective called Team 10, so named because there are ten digits in a billion. It wasn't the first "collab house," as they're now called, but it was the most prominent, pioneering a method that has been replicated throughout the social media industry. The Hollywood Hills are now dotted with TikTok and gaming houses.

Over the next eighteen months, Paul's talent for creating controversy began to appear. The Beverly Grove address was leaked, causing a daily swarm of fans to the street in front of the house. The pranks that made him famous started to get out of hand. Firefighters had to come extinguish a mattress in an empty pool. The local news station, KTLA, showed up to the street the neighbors had started referring to as a "war zone," and Paul responded by climbing onto the news van. Disney kicked him off *Bizaardvark* in response. His follower count went up anyway. He and his brother engaged in an ugly public feud involving one of Paul's ex-girlfriends and unlistenable but startlingly personal diss tracks. Their mother, somewhere on vacation, wept.

In October 2017, Paul bought and moved into a new mansion in Calabasas and brought the members of Team 10 with him. But something was happening inside him, an attrition of self: "I used to have so much anxiety and was very lonely I think in life. And I had a lot of anger and resentment towards people because of all the things I went through from accusations, my friends falling out, business managers stealing money from me, the media just constantly tormenting me. That can create a monster. It was starting to create a kid who just was like . . . I mean to be blunt it's like why do you see so many stars kill themselves."

At the end of the year Logan uploaded his video from the "suicide forest" in Aokigahara, Japan. Sponsors withdrew, YouTube demonetized his account temporarily. As 2018 began, Logan looked like he might be deplatformed, and Jake's life was imploding from the inside. Boxing, when it came along, was not their idea.

When YouTuber KSI called out the brothers in February 2018 after winning the first influencer boxing match over YouTuber Joe Weller in London, he could not have known the favor he was doing the Pauls. The August event, matching KSI against Logan and Paul against KSI's younger brother, Deji Olatunji, made the

219

Is Jake Paul Bad for Boxing? Next Question

siblings the talk of the internet. Logan lost; it didn't matter. Jake won, it did.

In front of a sold-out crowd at the Manchester Arena, an exhausted Olatunji's corner threw in the towel in the fifth round of a six-round bout. "When I won that fight, I jumped upon the ropes in front of [21,000] people who were wanting to see me lose. And I roar like a lion and flex. Like, 'Ahhhh.' It was one of the best feelings in my life," Paul says. "I was like, 'I proved all of you wrong. Ha Ha. I get the last laugh.'"

Returning to the Team 10 mansion was a devastating comedown. He started to fantasize about smashing his phone against a wall, wordlessly getting into his truck, and slipping away to the woods. One morning he woke up alone and hung over in his Calabasas mansion with a shattering feeling of emptiness.

"We were just lost f——ing kids in Los Angeles, just drinking their problems away. And I was just like, 'Who are these people around me?' And I feel like I was [seventeen] years old, moved to Los Angeles, and it's almost like I blinked and woke up here."

He didn't want to live this way anymore. In truth, social media pioneer that he is, he says he has never truly loved it. "I started to become famous and see money, and that's what motivated me, " Paul says. "I didn't wake up every single day with a burning desire to do social media." I'm stunned to hear that a person with 20.4 million YouTube subscribers, 16.9 million Instagram followers, who's generated 70 billion YouTube views, has never had a poster's heart, has never wanted to be there.

His pivot to boxing comes down to being in better shape than Olatunji was that August night. That's the truth of it. It's more accident than he is probably capable of admitting to himself. When you want salvation bad enough, every penny on the street will glow with the aura of providence.

•   •   •

"For your Jake Paul profile, could you just write, 'He's scum' 3,000 times?" An email from a former colleague.

"ESPN is really going to give this dude clout?" A text from a family member.

"Come the f—— on. That garbage human deserves NONE OF OUR ATTENTION." A text from a friend.

Everyone who asked what I was working on had this reaction when they heard it was Paul. Any serious consideration of Paul must deal with it—the idea that Paul is an illegitimate subject and that to give him any attention is to fall for his gimmick. It's not just that Paul is disliked for potentially being a bad person; it's that his success is considered illegitimate. He's perceived as being famous for being famous, as being a nonboxer making money fighting nonboxers while stealing money from real boxers and having a laugh at the sport.

Paul is merely another media creature, rescued from banality only because he has so deeply internalized the incentives of engagement, of self as billboard. There's nothing alien in his motivations. What sets him apart, rather, is the degree to which he has taken them. Any media person who has ever spent an entire day online reposting and responding to every positive comment they receive knows intimately what neuroses pursue and drive Paul.

On my first day in Miami, I watch Paul record a podcast episode at the South Beach mansion of Dave Portnoy, the founder of Barstool Sports. When Paul arrives for the interview, he's hunching over his phone in the passenger seat of his white Lincoln SUV while the rest of his entourage disembarks. His bodyguard opens the door and Paul says to his manager, Nakisa Bidarian, without looking up, "Posting posting posting."

"What's up?" Bidarian asks, stopping short of the lecture about tardiness he had been warming up while he and I waited for Paul to arrive.

Paul looks up for a second before returning to the phone, alternating between smiling at the screen and a blank, more concentrated look—mouth slightly open, thumbs working quickly.

"I'm shutting down the internet right now," he says. "I'm getting into beef right now."

221

Is Jake Paul Bad for Boxing? Next Question

He is accusing his erstwhile friend and fellow YouTuber turned boxer, Austin McBroom, of being a serial adulterer.

After the interview, we hear McBroom is outside Portnoy's house waiting for his own podcast appearance. Here now is one of Paul's greatest tricks, the ability to conjure via prestidigitation on his phone, the irreality of the internet into flesh-and-blood happenings of almost no consequence whatsoever. The two men confront each other outside as security steps between them. I count at least three videographers and several smartphones. No one looks very concerned this will grow violent.

I stand just beyond the group. As the two parties separate and McBroom goes inside for his interview, a line of pink neon script hanging in Portnoy's dining room pops into my head: "It doesn't get any better."

• • •

A few weeks later I arrive in front of Paul's Dorado Beach house just in time to hop into the back of one of two departing golf carts. As we speed toward the fitness center, Jacob Chavez, one of Paul's trainers, gives me a brief history of the resort.

"A Rockefeller built this," he says. "And that woman who flew around the world, she took off from here the last time. What was her name?" He swivels slightly to look over his shoulder at BJ Flores, Paul's head trainer, who cannot hear us over the breeze or the toy rattle of the cart.

"Amelia Earhart?" I say.

"Yeah."

"Who lives here?"

"Bunch of tech guys, millionaires . . ." I lose his voice for a second as we take a slight downhill bend too hard. I squeeze the seat's guard rail.

"Because of Act 20 and 22 there's like no personal income tax if you live here 183 days a year. And you never really have to leave and go outside it. There's a grocery, movie theater, everything."

We drive past an expensive and dreary waterpark. It's in the high eighties and clear. Across the way, groups of workers clear dead palm fronds from front yards.

"There's the waterpark. If you don't live here, you can't use it."

We pull up to the gym behind Paul's cart, and the eight of us head into the sleek fitness center with vaulted wood beams and floor-to-ceiling glass. Paul wears a gray sleeveless shirt and a backward cap, and begins to warm up on the treadmill. There are a handful of teen and early-twenties boys in the gym. A couple of them eye him furtively, a few ignore him histrionically. He puts on a YouTube clip of Anthony Joshua vs. Wladimir Klitschko. I ask what he's looking for.

"I actually fight like Klitschko," he says.

"What do you mean?" I ask.

He stabs his right fist into his left hand with a loud slap. "I use the jab to control distance, I got the brute power in the right hand and I use the check hook." Flores, standing beside the treadmill, nods along to his pupil's appraisal.

His third trainer and occasional sparring partner, J'Leon Love, is a student of the late Emanuel Steward's revered Kronk gym in Detroit. It was from Steward that Klitschko acquired the late style that allowed him to dominate the heavyweight division for a decade.

I watch him shadow box and rehearse his footwork under the exacting eyes of Flores, Chavez, and Love, who are always prodding, adding details, harping on his fundamentals. It's obvious within minutes that his fledgling boxing career is no scam. As it was obvious when I watched him at Evander Holyfield's gym in Miami weeks before. Paul and his team spent the morning before I arrived in Dorado Beach studying footage of the previous day's sparring session. If his self-defined style sounds rudimentary, it's consciously so. Someone who picks up boxing in their early twenties is unlikely to develop the intricate technical mastery purists admire. Flores has developed a style in which Paul makes up for his lack of amateur background by perfecting the basics.

Out back, where tennis courts sit against a tropical backdrop as pristine and shimmering as a Thomas Kinkade, Paul and his

223

Is Jake Paul Bad for Boxing? Next Question

strength and conditioning coach, Dejuan Butler, who goes by DCut, go through reflex and core-strength work. Paul removes his shirt to reveal cupping circles on his back. DCut stands in front of Paul and drops tennis balls that Paul has to rescue before they hit the ground.

Later, Paul groans as the last abdominal exercises take their toll. DCut yells, "They not working hard as we do and if they are, they not working as smart and if they are, they don't got a team behind them and if they do, they not in Puerto Rico and if they are, they not eliminating distractions! Nobody doing what we do, bro!"

Assuming Paul was moonlighting as an influencer fighter instead of transforming himself into a professional was the mistake his first three opponents made. In the fall of 2019 Paul traveled to Big Bear, California, a two hour drive from L.A., to train with Hall of Fame boxer "Sugar" Shane Mosley. Two years before, Paul and Mosley had become acquainted because the Hall of Famer's kids were fans of Paul's and dragged their father to the Team 10 house. Paul recognized Mosley and had his security let them inside for a visit, even showing up sometime later to Mosley's daughter's sixteenth birthday as a favor.

By the time he arrived in Big Bear the idea that he was going to transition to boxing full time was already forming in his mind. He surprised and pleased Mosley with his teachability and effort. Mosley sparred with him and put him in against some pros whom he cautioned to harry Paul but not hurt him, trying to preserve his confidence. When Mosley noticed Paul was getting a little too confident, he took him down the road to Abel Sanchez's gym and let a smaller fighter beat him up, bring him back down to earth. Paul got the message and doubled down. They worked through the holidays.

In January, Paul won his first pro fight when he stopped YouTuber AnEsonGib in the first round in Miami. Because the opposition was hapless, no one noticed that Paul was developing basic competency.

Flores, an experienced pro who developed a rapport with Paul at the Big Bear camp when he sparred with him and then took the time to tell Paul how to improve, took over for Mosley after the Gib fight. In February, Paul asked him to move into the Calabasas house and work with him full time. They worked throughout that spring with no next fight scheduled.

At Flores' urging, Paul started to live more and more like a professional. He loved what he was doing, loved waking up every morning with a purpose. He had built a ring at his mansion, shocking friends when he'd emerge from sparring sessions bloodied and smiling. Paul started pruning his gaggle of friends. Alcohol and partying were banned in the house. An eleven-p.m. quiet hours was enforced. People like DCut and Ibok Ibok, Paul's Yoga coach and longevity instructor, had joined the entourage.

Paul's focus began to shift away from the churn of online content. "I could see him changing so quickly and it's hard to represent that in your content going out, because people are used to a certain type of content," Ibok says. "There was a level of stress in that gap between who he had to be and who he was becoming. . . . He felt like a slave to YouTube. He's created all this success, and everybody's expecting him to keep going. But he's different than Logan. You could see that there was something bothering him."

In May, Flores sat Paul down and told him it was time to go to Las Vegas. Flores's plan was to have Paul spar with professionals for three to four months straight, attempting to accumulate as many as fifty sessions. If Paul was serious, then he had to make up for not having an amateur career.

Paul rented a house outside the city, sparred, trained, and watched sparring films all summer. Fighting primarily out of Clarence "Bones" Adams's gym, Paul took on all comers: heavyweights, welterweights, MMA fighters, anyone who would get in the ring. Adams won't reveal any names, honoring the omertà that typically governs sparring, but describes many of Paul's opponents as fighters who "have been on TV."

Surprised at what they encountered in the ring, some of Paul's opponents continued their combativeness outside of it. Adams remembers one super middleweight who was jawing with Paul in between rounds.

225

Is Jake Paul Bad for Boxing? Next Question

"You ain't hit me with nothing clean," Paul shouted after the last round.

"I was taking it easy on you," the other man said.

"No one said take it easy on me."

Adams doesn't remember the next part of the exchange, but he does remember Paul finally shouting, "Listen, son, I made half a million dollars today, what the f—— did you do?" The gym erupted in laughter.

"Sometimes I wish my fighters would want it as much as he does," Adams says. On Paul's off days he would come to the gym and watch sparring. "He's a living-eating-drinking-smoking every-thing, whatever it is everything boxing."

The Gib scenario replayed itself with Nate Robinson, an oppo-nent with no experience who figured he was fighting Jake Paul, YouTube enfant terrible, not someone who had been fighting pros every week for months and running Red Rock in ninety-plus-degree heat screaming, "I, Jake Paul will knock out, defeat, and embarrass Nate Robinson."

He annihilated Robinson in less than ninety seconds last November, turning Robinson's prone and rigid body into a meme. It was a crossover moment of sorts, and one that had sharp-eyed observers noticing Paul's development. But five months later, one final opponent, the MMA champion Ben Askren, would wager that Paul still wasn't the real thing.

Paul took three weeks off after the Robinson fight and then put his L.A. house on sale and relocated to Coral Gables, Florida, to leave behind his old reputation and avoid state income taxes. He replicated the Las Vegas process, sparring talented prospects like Ulysses Diaz and Daniele Scardina, championship-level fighters like Andrew Tabiti, and former lineal light heavyweight cham-pion Jean Pascal.

In April, Askren lasted just under two minutes.

Backstage before the fight, Love and Tyron Woodley, former UFC welterweight champion and longtime friend of Askren, had a tense exchange that was captured on Triller's stream of the fight. After some more back-and-forth on social media after the event,

Woodley emerged as the next logical opponent. He will be Paul's first serious test, and the first opponent to take Paul seriously. For the first time, Paul will have to fight without the element of surprise.

•　　•　　•

One night we drive to the Casa De La Juventud, a winsomely run-down gym just down the road. The night is windy and damp, rain on the way. Paul is building his own gym nearby, but for now this place is at the heart of his whole project.

The place has a bracing physicality. Outside, the sea wind breaks against the squat walls; while the trees overhead nod obligingly, tires from the car bringing his sparring partners turn slowly on the asphalt, the same sound as unrolling athletic tape for his hands. The gym lights glow sulfur in the threshold, from which petrichor seeps inside, volatiles perking up in response to the wet air, what you never remember insisting on itself again, the fibrous, dense tension of things, you can nearly draw your finger against it—real life.

No wonder he's given himself over to the sport—its rituals are a direct repudiation of everything he thinks of already at the age of twenty-four as his old life. Here he records only for himself; here every action is purposeful, significant, every mistake punished.

An industrial fan in the back doorway growls on, fails to allay the dank heat but instead covers all other sounds in a maternal way—a mollifying drone sharply repealed when the action starts. Watching Paul spar his diminutive opponents emphasizes a fact he has used to his advantage in his three previous bouts: he has yet to fight anyone his own size. Up close Paul is broad, thick limbed and, at around six feet, deceptively tall. Flores says he will come down from just over 200 pounds to make the fight's 190-pound catchweight limit against Woodley, who is five-nine and has fought at the 170-pound welterweight limit in the UFC for years. Flores envisions Paul competing against cruiserweights at the 200-pound limit eventually.

227

Is Jake Paul Bad for Boxing? Next Question

Paul goes six rounds—it is late in the week and early in camp, so the workload is moderate—against two different fighters, one an experienced journeyman useful for keeping Paul technically honest and the other young, energetic Anthony Taylor, who will face off against Tommy Fury on Paul's Showtime undercard in Cleveland.

Bidarian reached out to Showtime Sports EVP Stephen Espinoza after Paul vs. Askren's reported 1.4 million PPV buys, no matter how disputed, proved that Paul was a lucrative talent. Espinoza and his staff went to work, doing their homework on Paul's history, and Espinoza had several long conversations with him via Zoom. He was impressed with Paul's boxing knowledge, his commitment to training and improvement, and his marketing acumen. The obvious thing happened—money won.

Espinoza is one of the headiest entertainment executives in the world. Seeing the influx of influencer boxing, legacy exhibitions, and boxing-MMA crossovers, which he helped pioneer with the towering financial returns of Mayweather vs. McGregor, he sees his business as now existing in three genres: "We've got the championship-level fights. We've got ShoBox, the developmental series, and this is sort of a separate element of the business that is obviously still within the same sport but different from what we've been doing. . . . I've struggled for a name. I have to be very clear. These are competitive fights. They're not exhibitions. They're not influencer events. These are legitimate competitive sanctioned boxing events where there's going to be a winner or loser. The difference is it's neither fish nor fowl."

Whether Paul's union with Showtime signals the immanent or imminent death of boxing is beyond my ken. I have heard and read boxing declared dead so many times it can come to feel like a zombie sport, sometimes near the pulsing heart of the culture and sometimes enfeebled and at the margins.

I ask Espinoza if the April sexual assault accusation against Paul played a role in his decision. "There certainly were some candid conversations about everything, about things that have been reported and things that haven't," Espinoza says, adding that Paul categorically denied the allegation. "If we were not convinced that Jake was mature enough and committed to being a positive representation of our boxing program, then we wouldn't be in business with him."

On April 9, Paradise accused Paul, in detail, of forced oral sex. A follow-up *New York Times* story said Paradise told three friends immediately what had happened, and they corroborated her story and that she plans to file charges. Paul insists he has never made any sexual contact with Paradise and further that the screen grabs of text messages between them are fake. I was unable to reach Paradise for further comment for this story. Paul declines to answer whether he will pursue charges of defamation he threatened in his statement denying the accusation.

Panic spread through Paul's camp in the aftermath of the allegations. His parents and manager and lawyer and PR reps called incessantly. Logan pulled him aside and asked him to deny the accusation to his face; so did his business partner Geoff Woo. Sponsors withdrew from the Triller fight. Everyone wanted to handle the response in a different way. Finally, Paul grew so frustrated that he told everyone to back off so he could think. Four days after the video posted, he released a statement he had written himself denying the accusation.

It reads in part: "Sexual assault accusations aren't something that I, or anyone should ever take lightly, but to be crystal clear, this claim made against me is 100% false. . . . At the time of her story, I was in a relationship, and as someone who was a momma's boy growing up, I respect women and mothers more than anything. I most certainly have never laid a finger on a girl without their consent."

Whatever happened between Paul and Paradise has left her the object of scorn and abuse from his followers online and left him right where he was before the accusation—hated and rich and progressing toward his meaningless ambitions.

"As long as they're [the audience] consuming, that's my main goal," Paul says. "The media and the public made me the villain . . . after a couple of years, I was like, 'I don't know why I'm fighting this

229

Is Jake Paul Bad for Boxing? Next Question

anymore. I'm just going to lean into it.' And I think it was freeing because that's when I stopped being at the mercy of others. . . . Because I was like, 'Oh, now, I'm in control. I'm not the media's puppet anymore.' . . . I've always said that my favorite role to be in a movie would be the Joker."

•   •   •

"You gotta learn to say 'Viva Puerto Rico,'" Flores says to Paul. "The only Spanish Don King ever knew was viva someplace, it worked for years. Yo soy Jake Paul, viva Puerto Rico."

Paul is taking pictures one by one with the roughly ninety kids who are attending the inaugural event of his new charity, Boxing Bullies, held in a San Juan sports facility. In the center of the gym is a boxing ring where young amateurs will fight in exhibition matches as the final part of the event.

One boy says he thought Paul would be taller. Paul laughs and stands on his toes and says, "You should see Woodley though."

He has a natural rapport with teenagers, his original audience. Suddenly the vlog kid shouting soon-to-be-outdated slang into a shaky cam reappears. "Let's get it!" he says. And, "I don't want that smoke." And, "Flex on 'em." And, "I like that fit, bro."

Paul's mother is here, as is a Showtime crew, as is Tydus Talbott and his family. Tydus is known on the internet as Mini Jake Paul. He has 1.3 million followers and he's seven years old. He first went viral when a video of him snowboarding at seventeen months was reposted by Shaun White.

Talbott's father, Travis, invented the Mini Jake character when he recorded a video of his son imitating Paul in various skits. Paul liked the video enough to fly the family out to California, and Tydus has since been featured in Paul's content and attends his fights. The Talbotts have become family friends.

I catch glimpses of Tydus throughout the afternoon. A small drama unfolds in fragments. Travis nudges the boy to go stand at Paul's side and "help Jake." Tydus smiles like a seasoned professional for a fan picture. Paul and Tydus briefly huddle together on folding chairs, Paul leaning down to whisper something to his protégé. Travis nudges Tydus to climb into the ring while Paul leads the children through stretches, lifting his son onto the ring apron like a package. Tydus, anxious and unsure, stands outside the ropes for an unbearable fifteen seconds before Paul notices him out of the corner of his eye and beckons him in. The satisfied smile on Travis's face as he picks up his camera, the way it dissolves into blank concentration as he begins to record.

It's true that Paul is here to launder his reputation, to extirpate what Logan calls "the stigma of being a YouTuber" and behave like a normal celebrity. It's also true that the assembled young people have enjoyed themselves and that the president of the Puerto Rican Boxing Federation, Jose Laureano, says Paul has agreed to help sponsor amateur boxing events throughout the island. In as much as Boxing Bullies does anything (there's minimal antibullying messaging), that's what it does.

• • •

For all the talk that boxing has saved his life, Paul and everyone in his circle insist he plans to fight for only about three more years. Paul's content chief, Jon Marianek, and principal videographer, Gustavo Noah, told me they're at work on a documentary meant to capture the five planned years of Paul's boxing career. Even when he's found religion, it comes with a five-year plan.

The only dissenter is Flores, who suspects Paul might become addicted to the routine of boxing, the way it gives you a direction to walk in when you wake in the morning. Perhaps. Paul knew the emptiness once, and one day, when boxing ends, he will wake up in a mansion somewhere and know it again.

The final time we speak, Paul is eager to correct the record about why a loss to Woodley would be damaging. He fears he came off as too materialistic. "It's just much deeper than that, it's missing out on the opportunity I have to change the world with the impact that I could create. . . . I can take these superpowers of

231

Is Jake Paul Bad for Boxing? Next Question

media attention and all this stuff and give back and do good and change the sport and make an everlasting impact.

"This is like a story. I think that if I go out 10-and-0, become a world champion, and do so much for the sport, I think it's something that will go down as one of the greatest boxing stories ever. And again, that's my goal is to simply make history with everything that I'm doing."

People are always feeding you the cover-up after they've confessed the truth. Buried somewhere in that palaver, Paul thinks, is a desire to serve something besides himself. What am I supposed to take from this, that his fame has some kind of civilizing mission?

Logan tells me that his dream as a teenager was to become an engineer and invent something that would "make meaningful change in the world."

"Ironically," he says, "I just became that product. . . . I believe I have inspired a significant amount of people."

Inspired them to do what? I asked.

"Believe in themselves."

Their understanding of fame, of success in the moment they are living through, is the purest I've ever encountered—their gift to us is themselves. What's shocking is how received it is, how common. The endless self-promotion and vicious careerist streak, the cynical posturing that what redounds to one's personal advantage does anything more than precisely that, the self-medicating delusions, the abuse of words like "story."

I ask Paul, given his contentious relationship with the press, why he agreed to do this story.

"I think it's cool to see how someone interprets my life. So I honestly am genuinely excited to see the article that you write," he says. "And I also think what I'm doing is different, special, sort of a once-in-a-century narrative for this sport specifically. And I think it's cool to maybe get my message out there more."

I ask what his message is. He says he didn't mean "message;" he meant his "story." He tells me Muhammad Ali is actually his biggest inspiration. I bite my tongue.

What he has never considered, what his life has likely taught him is impossible, is that disclosure of any kind can diminish his stardom. He has watched every viral video. Since at least ninth grade he has understood that money's true purpose is to allow the holder to continually perform the victory of having it. He is still struggling to understand what the performance of that victory means. He sees himself as a "simple person." He wants to get his message out. The message is there is no message. He thinks I'm here to help. Maybe he's right.

For if Paul's final talent is transforming attention into money, then writing about him is another way of paying him; then writing about him makes us both media creatures. By which I mean our gimmicks aren't so different—he wants you to read this. So do I.

Yale Review

FINALIST—LIFESTYLE
JOURNALISM

*When "The Wrong Daddy" ran in
the* Yale Review, *it bore the subtitle
"Morrissey and the Cult of the
Wounded White Male." For those
of you who missed the late
twentieth century, Morrissey was
the lead singer of a band called the
Smiths that played something
called alternative rock. This
pop-culture tutorial is, however,
entirely unnecessary to an
appreciation of "The Wrong
Daddy," for the real subject of this
essay is not a rock star but the
story of his hold on the psyche of
one of his now rueful fans. The
ASME judges called Atherton Lin's
essay "culturally astute and artfully
executed" and said it "offered
insights into racial identity,
alternative subcultures, and the rise
of the alt-right movement." More
than 200 years old, the* Yale
Review *received its first National
Magazine Award nomination for
"The Wrong Daddy."*

Jeremy Atherton Lin

The Wrong Daddy

1. Commonplace

I first saw the object in someone else's hands. She was a teenager at Vallco, the most comprehensive shopping mall in the Silicon Valley. This was 1986 or so, when I was not yet teenaged myself. I watched her pull the twelve-inch square out of her Rainbow Records bag. Roughly half the plane, though it seemed like more, was occupied by one man's face. Even in severe close-up, cropping out cues like hairstyle or shirt collar, he had the look of a chap from decades before—from back when the world was safe, watched over by strong-jawed fathers.

The man conveyed a respectable anonymity. (Much later I'd learn that he was Richard Bradford, an American actor known for his role as a private eye on the British TV series *Man in a Suitcase*.) His angle is one of reverence, forty-five faithful degrees. He could have been a priest or Joan of Arc in the silent film. He could have been on his knees about to pray—or give head. Maybe he was just filled with ennui. In front of him, electric blue letters, italicized and sideways, spelled out "*SMITHS*."

The ascetic design seemed far more sophisticated than what I'd hitherto known. I'd started out buying records by Duran Duran and the Go-Go's, bands with recursive names and album artwork crowded with ancient palimpsests and party bunting. But here a process of extraction had occurred, and what was left was stripped so bare it was almost embarrassing to see. The cover also depicted a specific kind of manhood—generic, taciturn, self-contained. In this man's presence, I'd be clumsy, unintentionally speak too loudly. The stoic became an object of desire. Though the cover did not state the name of the single, "Panic," it elicited in me that febrile state of being.

By thirteen, I'd become devoted to the band. In the suburbs of northern California, I felt adrift. The sunshine and manicured lawns that surrounded me could not be my natural habitat; I belonged somewhere more historical, and gloomier. I found my place through the Smiths. The band, a product of postindustrialism, formed in 1982 in Manchester, England, where, under Margaret Thatcher, manufacturing was in decline and unemployment on the rise. Fronted by the beguilingly maudlin, lizardy, weird-sexy lead singer Morrissey, the Smiths had little truck with the New Wave flourishes—teased hair, pirate blouses—of acts like Dead or Alive and Adam Ant; instead, their look was more akin to a style dubbed "hard times" in the September 1982 issue of *The Face*—distressed, rockabilly-tinged, Dust Bowl–ish, evincing downbeat economic realities.

•   •   •

Morrissey, born in 1959 to Irish immigrants in a Lancashire town outside Manchester, came to embody a caustic and erudite distillation of northern English working-class sensibilities. His lyrics, wrapped around Johnny Marr's distinctively jangly guitar lines, tackled economic disparity ("England is mine, it owes me a living"), and his public comments cut straight to the mendacity of powerful politicians.

Morrissey constructed himself as an unlikely bard of the common people. In place of Thatcher or the queen, his national treasures were the saturnine playwright Shelagh Delaney and the bouffanted Viv Nicholson, who flamboyantly squandered the small fortune her husband won gambling. Morrissey's spotlighting of working-class figures could be vital and productive. But he tended to fix his gaze on a certain point in history, some time in the era of his youth. He made icons of a photogenic few while dismissing the rest as hoi polloi. "Birds abstain from song in postwar industrial Manchester, where the 1960s will not swing, and where the locals are the opposite of worldly," he wrote in his autobiography. Rendering a subtly camp vernacular from this provincialism, Morrissey aestheticized a partial, and mostly whitewashed, image of the working class. I was yet to grasp all this consciously: I came into an aesthetic the way young people do, in a conundrum of longing and envy.

2. Shirtlifter

I was compelled, too, by the post-Warhol sameness and replication of Morrissey's art direction. The Smiths' cover artwork comprised a procession of faces: when they weren't brash working-class women, they were statuesque white men in banal clothing. It was a *homo* that was distanced from the *sexual*. "I hate this 'festive faggot' thing," Morrissey proclaimed of gay culture in 1984. People said he was celibate, which made him attractively hard to get. He was a pinup for the closet, expert in imperious denial: "I'm not embarrassed about the word 'gay,' but it's not in the least bit relevant. I'm beyond that frankly," he said in an interview in 1985. (Weirdly, few seemed to talk about the significance of a sexually abstinent pop star rising to fame at the time of the spread of AIDS.)

The band's sparkling second single, "This Charming Man," tells of a lad who gets into the car of a flirtatious gentleman. The song was as chaste and coded as Frankie Goes to Hollywood's "Relax" (released a week earlier) was smutty and overt. Words like *charming* and *handsome* gleamed like polished antiques; the syntax of *hillside desolate* was archaic. Even when Morrissey's lyrics were forthright, as in the song "Miserable Lie," the sex remained awkward: "I know that windswept, mystical air / It means: I'd like to see your underwear." This was reassuring to someone like me, as desperate to be corrupted as I was terrified by penetration. We Smiths fans kept our undies on.

In place of copulation, the Smiths extolled stalking, hesitation, repulsion, disavowal. This provided me with a model for deflection: instead of being gay, I could be what the critic Richard Dyer identifies as "the sad young man"—as Dyer points out, generally meaning "sad young *white* man"—a paradoxically impermanent archetype in literature, "moving between normal and queer worlds, always caught at the moment of exploration and discovery."

I was enthralled by an older Smiths fan named Aaron. He worked the lightboard at the theater where I ushered. He had a serious, sensuous face, with hair lying close to his scalp in golden waves. He passed close by me in the lobby once, wearing a necktie as a belt, its length dangling along his thigh. I was deeply impressed. Not long after that, Aaron shot himself in the head. It was said he did so in his bedroom beneath a giant poster for the Smiths' single "Shoplifters of the World Unite." I fought against imagining his shattered brains on the wall.

A lot of kids kill themselves in the aspirational county where I was raised. But Aaron's suicide seemed to me specifically homosexual. Only recently did I learn that *shirtlifter* was once a British slur for gay men; the phrase "Shoplifters of the World Unite" may be Morrissey's play on words. I can't imagine that Aaron would have been any more alert to this reference than I was; we had no way of learning about that kind of history. We had only our intuition about the atmosphere around such codes.

3. The Sun and the Air

After moving to London in my thirties, I rediscovered that "Panic" twelve-inch in a basement record shop. I purchased it, finally, and marveled that the dour cover had captured the attention of my very young self. I then set out to write a memoir about growing up *out of place*—a Smiths fan in the California suburbs. I titled the manuscript "The Sun and the Air"—a mondegreen of "the son and the heir" from the Smiths song "How Soon Is Now." My homophonic misapprehension goes some way toward demonstrating how I construed in the band something elemental, transcendent. The actual verse is, "I am the son / And the heir / Of nothing in particular," a culturally specific reference to bloodlines, to the lack of title or entitlement. But I had taken Morrissey's postindustrial landscape of iron bridges and grim side streets as poetic invention and the spiritual home for my own awkward puberty.

In *Saint Morrissey: A Portrait of This Charming Man by an Alarming Fan* (2003), the critic Mark Simpson coined the portmanteau *melanalgia* (combining *melancholy* with *nostalgia*) to describe how Morrissey's lyrics pine for the England of a gritty yet spectral past. To Simpson, who actually grew up in England, melanalgia meant wearing secondhand clothes and checking foxed books out of the library, pointedly reacting against the slick 1980s status quo. To the sect of American teens to which I belonged, it meant identifying ourselves as *alternative*. The term wasn't futuristic or utopian; instead, we donned makeshift signifiers of authenticity from eras past. At Savers, a sprawling thrift store, I sought out the hand-me-downs of strangers. I particularly loved a scratchy green cardigan the hue of an artificial Christmas tree. We traded optimistic, aggressive Americana (cheerleading, drinking from kegs, weight machines, jeeps) for the chalky terroir of old England. Though I had near-perfect vision, I was always looking out for a pair of bulky spectacles like the ones Brits got for free from the National Health Service. Morrissey wore a pair like that. He adorned himself in meretricious stigmas such as Band-Aids and hearing aids to accentuate his alluring vulnerability. Like him, we wanted to look wounded.

Morrissey emboldened my sense of disaffection through songs like "What Difference Does It Make?" and humored my persecution complex in songs like "Unloveable." I responded to his historicized English landscape because I saw myself in it—a romantically anemic, damp, pitiable, somehow *justified* version of myself. I wanted to be, as the press called Morrissey, "pale and interesting."

4. Common Name

When fans talk about the Smiths, they talk about themselves. They testify that Morrissey's lyrics *seemed to speak just to me*. I knew as much but remained convinced that my own elision of fandom and autobiography was somehow idiosyncratic enough to merit pursuing at book length. I got down tens of thousands of yearning, impetuous words. What I didn't grasp was that a meaningful study of my connection to the band would require me to expose a rupture.

As a boy, I had been told that Smith was *the most common name*. I saw commonness as an honor. I envied every Smith I knew, all of them blonds; I failed to note the many Smiths of color. In a 1984 interview on *Good Morning Britain*, Morrissey said of the band name: "It really had to be as basic as humanly possible. . . . It's the most popular name in the universe, nearly." The host interjected: "Outside of a couple of Chinese ones, which wouldn't have gone down too well in this market." Morrissey demurred with a grimace. For my part, I tried to take consolation when my father informed me that Lin was a Mandarin equivalent of Smith—a ubiquitous name in China, meaning "forest." But it did not have the trustworthiness of the Old English patronym, as derived from *blacksmith*—a reliable, hardworking appellation.

In my inchoate memoir, I fixated on my compulsion to blend in, be undetectable. I was the son of a Chinese immigrant writing about the urge to achieve anonymity through manifesting an essential Englishness. I invoked Gilles Deleuze and Félix Guattari: "To go unnoticed is by no means easy. To be a stranger, even to one's doorman or neighbours. . . . This requires much asceticism, much sobriety, much creative involution: an English elegance, an English fabric, blend in with the walls, eliminate the too-perceived, the too-much-to-be-perceived." My proclivity for white Englishness wasn't totally extrinsic—I'm of Anglo matrilineage. In Morrissey (and in his stand-in on the cover of "Panic" or in his other heroes/surrogates, like James Dean and Little Joe from Warhol's Factory), I sought compensation for what I took to be the disapproval of white males in my extended family. I latched onto Morrissey's perpetual ambivalence. I didn't have to impress Morrissey; I could imagine his affection as a remote possibility. *Morrissey loves you, we all love you*, a friend wrote in my yearbook. (The icon was ours to ventriloquize like that.) Yet I wasn't obsessed with Morrissey in order to *feel seen* but because he looked the other way.

In 1991, my junior year in high school, Morrissey, by then a solo artist, released the song "Asian Rut," about three white lads beating a druggy, vengeful Asian boy. The narrative was ostensibly a nuanced condemnation of racial conflict, but it was told in a manner at once fetishistic and phlegmatic. My Asian American friends and I giggled uncomfortably over the title. We understood that in Britain, *Asian* referred to the subcontinent, to Pakistan and Bangladesh; our ancestors were from China and Korea. Still, it felt personal. We detected a vague chauvinism cast over Morrissey's perspective, as in his 1988 song "Bengali in Platforms," with its vexing line "Life is hard enough when you belong here." I *felt seen*, but in a creepy way, as in sussed out.

But Smiths fandom proved hard to outgrow. After moving to New York City, Ben, my Korean American friend, magnetic and as "out" as could be in high school, began to cohost a night inspired by the band at a club called Sway. The weekly event had no name, so people referred to it however they wanted, keeping its image low-key and cool. Soon enough "It began to draw crowds, first of downtown scene-making types, later of celebrities." That line was from Ben's 2017 obituary in the *New York Times*, headlined "Death of a Downtown Icon" to chime with the Smiths song "Death of a Disco Dancer." At his funeral, a gospel choir performed another, "There Is a Light That Never Goes Out," and those words were illuminated in LED.

When we were in our twenties, Ben regaled us with the tale of spotting Morrissey at a restaurant in Los Angeles. He'd been in the presence of *big papa*, as he put it. Or would he have spelled it like the Notorious B.I.G.: "Big Poppa"? Either way, it put in mind the Indian American girl at the high school next to ours who legally changed her surname to Morrissey at sixteen. This idol worship seemed tongue in cheek and yet obviously committed and strangely devoid of any introspection about why we all yearned for a grumpy white daddy. Maybe on some level we thought our purchase on Morrissey and his doppelgangers—the ordinary aesthetic, classic grooming tics, regular fit jeans—was empowering. There was nobody to enlighten us as to how *ordinary*, *classic*, and *regular*, like *neutral*, had been constructed by a culture dominated by whiteness. What's more, *alternative* may have been just a different shade: even whiter.

5. Big Papa

I figured Ben's funny, slightly icky nickname for Morrissey had been spontaneously put, a one-off. Recently, my brother-in-law Euan was strolling in a park in Los Angeles when a Chicano man approached, calling "Hey, big papa!" and offering him a protracted handshake. At some point, Euan realized he was being mistaken for Morrissey.

By now, it's well known that the singer has a lot of Latinx fans. In a 2017 TEDx Talk, Gabriel Avalos, an earnest Mexican American teenager, wearing a blazer over his Smiths T-shirt, almost tripping as he walks onto the stage, advances the theory that while artists typically define the fans, in this case the fans have redefined the artist. Other devotees wear T-shirts that transpose Morrissey's song "Irish Blood, English Heart" to "Mexican Blood, American Heart." The symbol riffs on Mexico's coat of arms, adding an American bald eagle to the Mexican golden eagle devouring a rattlesnake while perched on a prickly pear cactus.

Morrissey has professed his fondness for Mexico, donned a Chivas jersey, and written a song called "Mexico" to lambast inequality across the border: "If you're rich and you're white / You think you're so right / I just don't see why this should be so." Writing in *The Guardian*, Raf Noboa y Rivera describes a shared "sense of estrangement and longing" that links the lyrics of Morrissey's ballads and those of Ranchera, a northern Mexican folk-music tradition. "My family has myriad tales of living in a golden Mexico during the 1940s and 1950s," he writes. "Those stories helped foster a deep-seated melancholy within me about where I truly belong. Not quite American; not wholly Latino, living in all the spaces in between."

The etymology of the word *nostalgia* combines Greek *nostos* (a return to home or native land) with *algos* (pain or suffering). It was once a medical term for homesickness, considered to be a physical disease. The historian David Lowenthal explains that by the seventeenth century, immigrants who had languished or perished were considered to have been enfeebled by dislocation from their homeland; bodies that succumbed to meningitis or tuberculosis or malnutrition were said to be *nostalgic*. "Today," the critic Carol Mavor wrote in 2007, "nostalgia is a disease of longing, sociocultural and not medical."

That year, Morrissey lamented the impact of immigration on his homeland: "England is a memory now," he said. Curry and reggae had come to be considered national heritage, evidence of a pluralistic society. I had my own part in spoiling the English identity, I guess: I relocated there a few months before he made that comment. Morrissey himself had done the reverse, moving to Los Angeles in 1995. "The England that I have loved, and I have sung about and whose death I have sung about, I felt had finally slipped away," he said about his expatriation. With that statement, he laid bare how he—the son of immigrants—*authored* his own England, a willful confabulation. Even in his most miserable depictions of Britain, Morrissey helped mythologize it as a place to be cherished as waves of foreigners erode it. Long before he left, Morrissey dwelled in *the old country*.

6. Apologist

Morrissey is not a racist. So stated, with whatever amount of sincerity, the editors of *NME* in a 2012 apology after Morrissey sued the magazine for suggesting otherwise. Then in 2019, the singer proclaimed the word *racist* meaningless. "If you call someone racist in modern Britain you are telling them you have run out of words," he said. "You are shutting the debate down and running off. The word is meaningless now. Everyone ultimately prefers their own race—does this make everyone racist?"

As I toiled over my prose about being his fan, Morrissey would periodically pass remarks like that. He spoke of how the Chinese could be a "subspecies," considering their record on animal welfare, and how London has been debased by a British Pakistani mayor who "cannot talk properly." On late-night TV, Morrissey wore the badge of a far-right UK political party whose leader has focused on quashing Muslim immigration. I tried to take his outbursts in stride, to fix my narrative in the past, as if the past is fixed. But revisiting his lyrics, I began to find them more vituperative, less empathetic than I'd recalled. A song's narrator would be woefully misunderstood, but that was because he was surrounded by the dim-witted and distinctly othered: women bucktoothed and monstrous; gay pederasts; Bengalis who don't belong. Whereas I'd once positioned the singer in a coalition of outcasts, I began to see him as sneering at the rest.

In his essay "The White to Be Angry," the critic José Esteban Muñoz revisits the lyrics of X, his favorite band as a teenager. Their anthemic song "Los Angeles" describes a resident of the city who finds herself hating Blacks, Jews, Mexicans, and gays. It's an allegory about white flight, but listeners may suspect the message is as collusive as critical. Muñoz, a Cuban American, writes:

> Though queerness was already a powerful polarity in my life, and the hissing pronunciation of "Mexican" that the song produced felt very much like the epithet "spic," with which I had a great deal of experience, I somehow found a way to resist these identifications. The luxury of hindsight lets me understand that I needed X and the possibility of subculture it promised at that moment to withstand the identity-eroding effects of normativity. I was able to enact a certain misrecognition that let me imagine myself as something other than queer or racialized. But such a misrecognition demands a certain toll . . . to find self within the dominant public sphere, we need to deny self.

Self-denial is a tricky position from which to write memoir. Ultimately, I was relieved to abandon "The Sun and the Air."

You'd have been brought onto the radio, a friend laughed, and introduced as a Morrissey apologist.

7. Weirdos and Misfits

In early 2020, Dominic Cummings—then chief special adviser to Prime Minister Boris Johnson and architect of the victorious Brexit campaign—posted a job recruitment notice for "weirdos and misfits with odd skills." This jargon and the jobseekers it attracted came under scrutiny after one new hire was forced to resign; comments he'd made in support of eugenics had surfaced. The "weirdos and misfits" line struck me as in accord with the way *alternative* was now being bandied about—as in *alt*-right or *alternative* facts.

In my youth, "alternative" connoted, or so I thought, not only a position on the social margins but the open-border policy there. At some point, the word flipped to mean angry white people with abandonment issues, the far-right fringe. I'm forced to consider that the subculture I'd participated in, by centering the narrative of wounded white men, might have laid foundations for this consequential turn. Looking back, what was alternative without bitterness, pasty complexions, hatred of the contemporary, feelings of ostracization, moping? The alternative scene *was* basically angry white people with abandonment issues. Morrissey's England was depressing yet glorious, an island in the doldrums, yet halcyon, *white*—the very place members of today's alt-right want to paddle back to.

Mid- to late-period Morrissey, paunchy, remote-eyed, spouts off a rose-tinted jeremiad about the loss of identity. He's pretty zeitgeisty that way. Just recently a poll showed that nearly a third of England's adult residents, hot off leaving the European Union, would also vote in favor of independence from the United Kingdom, despite London being the center of power and seat of government. The academic Alex Niven responded in *The Guardian*: "One of the major problems with contemporary debates about 'Englishness' is that England does not really exist as either a coherent or a concrete political reality." Niven cites the historian Benedict Anderson's concept of "imagined communities," which are drummed up to foster a sense of shared belonging. "England," Niven proposes, being scarce of political institutions that differentiate it from Britain as a whole, "can mean pretty much whatever people want it to mean." England, to amend Morrissey, is now a *false* memory.

"Why did you call yourselves the Smiths?" a schoolboy asked the band on a children's TV show in 1984. "Because it was the most ordinary name," replies Morrissey, almost teacherly, "and I think it's time that the ordinary folk of the world showed their faces." I admired that class consciousness. It took much longer to recognize that Morrissey saw *ordinariness* in his own image, a perspective that can slide into "Make _____ great again" politics. I'm not sure there's a place for (mixed-race, faggoty) me in that mythical past.

When I was an alternative teenager, uneasy in the present, I sought refuge in the retro. The fashion statement of my anachronistic green cardigan was, basically, *History is worth repeating*. In truth, against my skin, it wasn't a great look. But I was *a Smiths fan*, charmingly old-fashioned, thriving in disjunction from my surroundings. Today, having forsaken my idol, I've also exited the illusory country he inhabits. I can never go back to the house of the wrong daddy again.

New Yorker

WINNER—PROFILE WRITING

The ASME judges described this profile of the psychologist Elizabeth Loftus as "a deeply reported, deceptively complicated piece of writing that probes the definition of memory." A professor at the University of California, Irvine, Loftus is an influential albeit controversial figure who has assisted in the defense of several celebrities charged with crimes, including Bill Cosby and Harvey Weinstein. The ASME judges concluded their praise of "Past Imperfect" simply with this: "You'll want to read this story more than once." This was one of two pieces by Rachel Aviv nominated for National Magazine Awards this year. Her story "The Kentler Experiment," about a German program that placed foster children with pedophiles, was nominated in Feature Writing. Another of her stories, "Punishment by Pandemic," about the impact of the coronavirus on the incarcerated, was nominated just last year in Public Interest.

Rachel Aviv

Past Imperfect

E lizabeth Loftus was in Argentina giving talks about the malleability of memory in October 2018 when she learned that Harvey Weinstein, who had recently been indicted for rape and sexual assault, wanted to speak with her. She couldn't figure out how to receive international calls in her hotel room, so she asked if they could talk in three days, once she was home in California. In response, she got a series of frantic e-mails saying that the conversation couldn't wait. But, when Weinstein finally got through, she said, "basically he just wanted to ask, 'How can something that seems so consensual be turned into something so wrong?'"

Loftus, a professor at the University of California, Irvine, is the most influential female psychologist of the twentieth century, according to a list compiled by the *Review of General Psychology*. Her work helped usher in a paradigm shift, rendering obsolete the archival model of memory—the idea, dominant for much of the twentieth century, that our memories exist in some sort of mental library, as literal representations of past events. According to Loftus, who has published twenty-four books and more than six hundred papers, memories are reconstructed, not replayed. "Our representation of the past takes on a living, shifting reality," she has written. "It is not fixed and immutable, not a place way back there that is preserved in stone, but a living thing that changes shape, expands, shrinks, and expands again, an amoeba-like creature."

George A. Miller, one of the founders of cognitive psychology, once said in a speech to the American Psychological Association that the way to advance the field was "to give psychology away." Loftus, who is seventy-six, adopts a similar view, seizing any opportunity to elaborate on what she calls the "flimsy curtain that separates our imagination and our memory." In the past forty-five years, she has testified or consulted in more than three hundred cases, on behalf of people wrongly accused of robbery and murder, as well as for high-profile defendants like Bill Cosby, Jerry Sandusky, and the Duke lacrosse players accused of rape in 2006. "If the MeToo movement had an office, Beth's picture would be on the ten-most-wanted list," her brother Robert told me.

But after the conversation in Argentina and after reading more about the allegations, she referred Weinstein to a different memory researcher. Over the phone, she told his lawyers, "He's a bully, and I've experienced that bullying myself." She didn't realize that Weinstein was on the line until he piped up: "I'm sorry if you felt I was bullying you."

She resisted the job for about four months, but Weinstein and his lawyers eventually prevailed, persuading her to fly to New York and testify on his behalf, in exchange for fourteen thousand dollars, only ten thousand of which was ever paid. "I realized I was wanting to back out for selfish reasons, and I didn't want to live with that feeling about myself," she told me. (The only time she has ever turned down a case for reasons of repugnance was when she refused to testify for a man accused of operating the gas chambers at Treblinka.)

On February 6, 2020, the day before she testified, she received an e-mail from the chair of the psychology department at New York University, where she was scheduled to give a lecture. Her plane tickets had already been purchased. "Unfortunately, due to circumstances beyond our control it is necessary to cancel your talk," the professor wrote. Loftus asked whether the cancelation was because of the Weinstein trial; the professor never responded.

Loftus can't remember the last time that she bought something she considered unnecessary. At Weinstein's trial, she wore a red jacket that she bought at Nordstrom Rack for about eighty-five dollars and a thin necklace with a golden feather that she has worn every day for the past forty years. As she walked through the courthouse, she looked as if she were struggling to appear somber. "I have to admit," she told me later, "that it is fascinating to be, you know, in the trenches with the trial of the century."

She testified for roughly an hour, presenting basic psychological research that might lead a jury to think that neutral or disappointing sexual encounters with Weinstein could have taken on new weight in light of revelations about his predatory history. "If you are being urged to remember more," Loftus said at the trial, "you may produce, you know, something like a guess or a thought, and that then can start to feel like it's a memory."

"Can an event that was not traumatic at the time be considered traumatic later?" Weinstein's lawyer asked.

"If you label something in a particular way, you can distort memory of that item," Loftus said. "You can plant entire events into the minds of otherwise ordinary, healthy people." She explained that in one experiment, her most famous study, she had convinced adults that, as young children, they had been lost in a mall, crying. "The emotion is no guarantee that you are dealing with an authentic memory," she said.

The assistant district attorney, Joan Illuzzi, challenged the idea that experiments done in a "pretend situation"—free of context, stripped of gender and power dynamics—are relevant to understandings of trauma.

"You do not treat victims of traumatic events, is that right?" Illuzzi said.

"I may study them," Loftus said, "but I do not treat anyone officially."

Illuzzi went on, "And isn't it true, in 1991, that the name of your book was *Witness for the Defense*?"

"One of my books is called *Witness for the Defense*," Loftus answered.

"Do you have a book called *Witness for the Prosecution*?" Illuzzi asked. A few people in the courtroom laughed.

"No," Loftus said, calmly.

The next week, at the UC Irvine law school, where Loftus teaches classes, she passed by a colleague who specializes in feminist theory. "Harvey Weinstein—how could you?" the professor said. "How could you!" (Loftus remembers that the conversation occurred at the buffet table at a faculty meeting, but the colleague told me, "I know that it didn't because I would not have stood next to her in a buffet line.") Loftus said, "I was reeling. How about the presumption of innocence? How about 'the unpopular deserve to have a defense'?"

Not long afterward, the dean of the law school received a letter from a group of law students who demanded that the administration "address the acute problem of Elizabeth F. Loftus." "We are terrified that she is a professor for future psychologists and lawyers and is training them to further traumatize and disenfranchise survivors," they wrote. The students asked that Loftus be removed from the faculty, but she continues to teach.

Her friends and family were also skeptical of her decision to testify for Weinstein. Her ex-husband, Geoff Loftus (whom she calls her "wasband" because they still treat each other like family), an emeritus professor of psychology at the University of Washington, said that he thought, "Oh, God, Beth, really? Come on." Her brother David told me, "Here these women are blossoming into a world in which people are finally going to listen to them, and then they're going to have some professor on the stand— someone they've never met before—tell the jury that they can't be believed."

.　　　.　　　.

"I'm completely satisfied with my life," Loftus wrote in a leatherbound journal, in 1958, when she was thirteen. "I have a pretty good personality (not dull or anything), my family is one of the happiest." She grew up in Bel Air, in Los Angeles, and spent weekends at the beach or at friends' pools. For six years, she wrote in her journal every day, marking whether the weather was clear, cloudy, or rainy; recording compliments (in a middle-school poll, she won "best figure," "lovable," "most comical," and "irresistible"); and describing the expanding circle of boys with whom she chatted on the phone. "Life is really my best friend," she wrote.

She almost never mentioned her parents, whom she outlined in impersonal terms—"the family." When I asked Loftus to describe her mother, Rebecca, she could come up with only one vivid memory, of shopping for a skirt with her. Loftus's brother Robert said that he also faced an "empty canvas." He told me, "I can't grab an adjective or noun to describe my mother. There's nothing that will allow me to say, 'This is who she was as a person.' There is no coagulation, no coherence." He does have one memory, from when he was seven or eight, of standing by the front door of their house and misbehaving: "I was waiting for her to counter my disobedience with enforcement, and she just couldn't pull herself together. I remember thinking, oh, my God, she can't even parent me. I pitied her."

One evening, when Loftus was a young teenager, she and her father, a doctor, who was barbed and aloof, were driving through Los Angeles. They stopped at a red light and watched a couple, laughing, cross the street. "See those people having fun?" Loftus's father said. "Your mother can't have fun anymore."

Loftus's diaries read like an exercise in proving that she existed on a different emotional register from that of her mother. She summarized her mood with descriptions like "happyville," "I'm so happy!" and "Everything's GREAT!" It's as if she were continually trying to outdo herself. "I can honestly say that this was one of the happiest days I've ever lived through," she wrote in eighth grade. A few days later, she reached new heights: "I've never been so happy. I love the world & everyone."

Loftus and her brothers didn't have language to describe what ailed their mother. Their father seemed annoyed by her vulnerability. Eventually, Rebecca's siblings intervened and sent her to a private psychiatric hospital in Pennsylvania, near her brother's home, where she was treated for depression. "My mother's family blamed my father for being so emotionally flatlined and unavailable that he drove her to madness," Robert said. In her journal, Loftus, who was then fourteen, never mentioned her mother's absence. "Life's wonderful!!" she wrote after Rebecca had been away for four months. "When I'm old and lonely at least I'll know once I wasn't!"

After nearly half a year, Rebecca was discharged from the hospital, and Loftus and her aunt Pearl, along with her daughter, Debbi, drove to Pennsylvania to pick her up. They planned to spend time together at a vacation lodge in the woods, fifty miles south of Pittsburgh, that Loftus's uncle owned. But five days after arriving, Loftus drew an arrow in her diary that pointed to a smudge on the page. "A tear," she explained. "Today, July 10, 1959, was the most tragic day of my life," she wrote. "We woke up this morning and found her gone, and an hour later we found her in the swimming pool. Only God knows what had happened."

The coroner ruled the death an accident. "She apparently fell in unnoticed," a front-page article in the Uniontown, Pennsylvania, *Evening Standard* reported. But when Loftus returned to California and described the death as accidental, Robert said, "our father tried to overrule her in his fatherly way, to give his realistic stamp on what had happened. He told her, 'Beth, it was suicide.'" For decades, Loftus and her brothers didn't discuss with one another what had happened, but they all individually decided to ignore their father's interpretation.

Within a week of her mother's death, Loftus's journal had returned to its usual jaunty tone. "I'm a happy teenager!" she wrote in December. "It's sort of sad to leave this year behind—it was such a wonderful year for me." But on some pages of her journal, she used a paper clip to attach scraps of paper, where she shared private thoughts that she called "removable truths." She could pull them out if anyone ever demanded to read her journals. In one "removable truth," she blamed herself for her mother's suffering. "She would be watching T.V. and ask me to come sit by her," she wrote. "'I'm busy now,' was my usual reply." She labeled the memory, written in elegant cursive, "My Greatest Regret."

•   •   •

When Loftus discussed her mother's death, Maryanne Garry, a former postdoctoral researcher in Loftus's lab, was reminded of the passage in John Knowles's novel *A Separate Peace*, from 1959, in which the narrator "jounced the limb" of a tree, causing his best friend to fall and eventually die. The language in the passage is vague enough that it's unclear if the act was intentional. "I was always struck by something similar in Beth's ambiguous framing of her mother's death," Garry told me. "It was as if the death existed without causality or agency."

Loftus's career has been defined by her recognition that the language we use to describe an event will change the way we remember it. She received her Ph.D. from Stanford in 1970, writing a dissertation, on mathematical word problems, that she found boring. She wished to study a topic more relevant to people's lives. In 1973, around the time that she accepted a job at the University of Washington, she borrowed recordings of car crashes from police departments and began examining the participants' recollections. When she asked people to estimate the speed of the cars when they "smashed," they remembered the cars going faster than when she used the word "hit." She went on to publish dozens of studies showing that she could manipulate people's recollections of the past in predictable and systematic ways. "Does the malleable human memory interfere with legal justice?" she titled one article, in 1975. She said, "I remember my father saying to me, 'I don't like the word "malleable."'" She doesn't recall why. She stuck with the term, which became closely associated with her body of research and gave energy to an emerging innocence movement. (Her father died not long after the conversation.)

Defense lawyers began calling on her to testify about the ways that memories are distorted by leading questions, sloppy police lineups, and cross-racial identification of faces. (The chance of misidentification is greatest when the witness is white and the defendant is Black.) James Doyle, a former head of Massachusetts's Public Defender Division, who cowrote a book with Loftus, said that she "obliterated the idea that there is a permanent, stable memory capacity in humans." He told me, "Her work changed the whole story of what an eyewitness case was about and destabilized a solid and routine part of the criminal caseload."

Beginning in the early nineties, Loftus began getting questions about a new kind of case. Incest had entered the American consciousness, and women in therapy were uncovering memories of being abused by their fathers. The discovery was reminiscent of a similar one, a century earlier, when Freud realized that his patients had suppressed memories of being sexually abused as children. Within a few years, Freud had changed his mind, arguing that his patients were afflicted by fears and fantasies surrounding sex abuse, not by memories of the actual thing. In doing so, Freud walked away from a revelation—that sexual abuse of children was prevalent—but also proposed a more complex theory of the mind.

A new generation of therapists was careful not to repeat Freud's mistake. "If you think you were abused and your life shows the symptoms, then you were," Ellen Bass, a leader in the recovered-memory movement, wrote, in 1988. The movement challenged the foundation of family life—the home, it turned out, was the site of cruelty and betrayal—as well as the authority of experimental psychology. Trauma was described as an extraordinary and idiosyncratic experience that could not be simulated in a lab or even expressed by the rules of science. "Trauma sets up new rules for memory," the psychiatrist Lenore Terr wrote in 1994.

Loftus emerged as perhaps the most prominent defender of her field. She could find little experimental evidence to support the idea that memories of trauma, after remaining dormant for a decade or more, could abruptly spring to life, and she worried that therapists, through hypnosis and other suggestive techniques, were coaxing memories into being. As she began testifying on behalf of men who she believed may have been wrongly accused, she came to be seen as an expert who was complicit with, rather than challenging, institutions of power.

Phoebe Ellsworth, a social psychologist at the University of Michigan, said that when Loftus was invited to speak at her school in 1989, "the chair would not allow her to set foot in the psychology department. I was furious, and I went to the chair and said, 'Look, here you have a woman who is becoming one of the most famous psychological scientists there is.' But her rationale was that Beth was setting back the progress of women irrevocably." Ellsworth and Loftus, who are friends from graduate school, had started their careers at a time when female research psychologists were so rare that the two of them were treated "like dogs walking on hind legs," Ellsworth said. Loftus identified with an earlier generation's feminism—she wanted to be treated as equal to men, but she preferred not to draw attention to her particular experiences as a woman. "I've trained myself to be wary of emotions, which can distort and twist reality," she has written.

Loftus rose to prominence at a time when the computer was becoming the dominant metaphor for the mind. Social and cultural forces were treated as variables that compromised memory processes, turning people into unreliable narrators of their own experiences. "That's the frightening part—the truly horrifying idea that what we think we know, what we believe with all our hearts, is not necessarily the truth," Loftus wrote in *Psychology Today* in 1996.

But social influences on memory, however transformative, need not lead to a "horrifying" result. Janice Haaken, a professor emeritus of psychology at Portland State University who has written several books about memory, told me, "Scholars who look at the history of trauma understand the importance of groups—often created by political or social movements—in holding on to memories. There is always a contest over versions of truth in history, and if you don't have other people to help you hold on to your memories, you are going to be disqualified or seen as crazy."

Haaken, who has been deeply involved in feminist activism for forty years, added that she is cautious of slogans, popularized by the MeToo movement, urging people to "believe women." She said, "I think, in some areas of the women's movement, white feminists have not dealt with our country's history of putting people in prison, usually those of color, based on eyewitness testimony that is wrong." Few psychologists have been more influential than

Loftus in revealing how standard police procedures can contaminate memory. Haaken said, "We have enough history behind us as a movement to demand more than the principle 'believe women,' which reduces us to children and denies us the complexity and nuances of everyday remembering."

•   •   •

Loftus talks about her personal history candidly, yet there's a sense in which it is also deadwood. Her openness does not translate into reflectiveness, though she welcomes personal questions. Garry, her former researcher, described her as a "disarmingly friendly, fuzzy Muppet." She seems genuinely curious about other people's experiences and a little tired of her own. The first time we talked, she warned me that because of the pandemic, "I'm feeling a little bored and boring."

She has lived alone for thirty years. She and Geoff tried to have a child in the mideighties, but, Loftus said, "it was many years of seeing blood at the end of the month and saying, 'Oh, shit.'" When her gynecologist recommended that she have surgery to remove a fibroid from her uterus, she was so annoyed by the idea of missing days of work that she turned her surgery into an experiment. Her anesthesiologist read her a hundred words while she was unconscious, to see if she could recall them later. "We here report the results of a rigorous experimental test conducted on a patient who was undergoing an abdominal myomectomy under general anesthesia," Loftus wrote in the journal *Acta Psychologica* in 1985. "The patient was an experimental psychologist with a keen interest in human memory."

The fibroid was removed, but she couldn't get pregnant. Six years later, she and Geoff divorced, in large part because of the intensity of her work ethic. "When I let up to do something that seems frivolous I feel guilty," she told a friend in an e-mail. Loftus had asked Geoff how many vacations she had to take per year to save the marriage. But he said that relaxation quotas wouldn't work: even if she consented to theoretically pleasurable activities, she wouldn't enjoy them.

For decades during cross-examinations, lawyers have accused Loftus, a childless scientist, of being unable to comprehend the pain of victims. "You really don't know anything about five-year-old children who have been sexually abused, do you?" a prosecutor asked her in 1985 at the trial of a camp counselor accused of molesting his campers.

"Well, yes, I do," Loftus responded. "I do know something about this subject because I was abused when I was six," by a babysitter. At that moment, she later wrote, "the memory flew out at me, out of the blackness of the past, hitting me full force."

The defense attorney at the trial, Marc Kurzman, recalled a "stunned silence." He said, "That was supposed to be the big finale of the cross-examination, and it pretty much shut the whole thing down."

Some scholars have proposed that Loftus has her own repressed memories. "She has not been able to integrate her own experience into her research," two literary critics wrote in 2001. "There is something split off in Loftus," the psychologist Lauren Slater asserted in her book *Opening Skinner's Box* from 2004. "She is the survivor who questions the validity of survivorship. That's one way out of a bind."

The criticisms seem to suggest that there is only one kind of story that women can tell about sexual abuse. But Loftus never forgot what happened. She had shared the memory with Geoff shortly after they married. "It wasn't 'Oh, my God, I was abused,'" he said. "It was more like 'What's more, I myself was abused.'" He went on, "I have a very poor recollection of the conversation, which means that I probably wasn't shocked by either the act itself or the casualness with which she described it."

Loftus's babysitter used to sit on the sofa with her, gently scratching her arm with the tips of his nails—"a sweet touch, soft, comforting, lulling," as she writes in *Witness for the Defense*, a memoir focused on her work in court. One night, after her brothers had gone to bed, the babysitter led her into her parents' bedroom, lifted her dress over her head, took off her underpants, and pulled her on top of him. Their pelvises were touching and she felt him pushing against her, until she squirmed off the bed and ran out of the room.

Loftus was under the impression that all girls start menstruating at the age of thirteen. But, when her thirteenth birthday passed and she hadn't got her period, "I wondered if he did something that made me turn pregnant," she told me. Loftus imagined that she had somehow been in a state of latent pregnancy for seven years. Eventually, she got her period, but she was distressed when she couldn't figure out how to use a tampon. "I actually went to my father and said, 'I'm worried there's something wrong with me, because I can't get this in,'" she told me. "And he drew me the hymen and explained that I was still a virgin, and then I felt better."

"That actually does sound traumatic," I told her, in one of our many conversations on Zoom. "Seven years later, it was still in your mind that you might have been raped."

She paused for a few seconds and ran her hand through her hair, which is the color of frost, and spread it like a fan. "I'm not sure," she said. "I know you think that. But somehow, you know, somehow when your mother gets depressed and goes away and drowns in a swimming pool—I mean, I had a lot more on my mind."

She explained that in *Witness for the Defense*, to avoid liability, she gave her babysitter a pseudonym. "I don't know why I named him Howard," she said.

When reading her diary, I noticed that Howard was the name of Loftus's first boyfriend—an important and ambiguous figure who "serenaded me on the phone" ("Wow! Blast!") and also dumped her for another girl, causing her to cry in front of her mother.

Loftus dismissed the idea that the name had any significance. She'd had many boyfriends as an adolescent, so, she said, "whatever name I gave the babysitter might have been, at some point, the name of a boyfriend."

Her brother David said that he had once encouraged Loftus to go to therapy, but she told him, "I can't because the next time I take the witness stand they'd grill me with questions." (Loftus doesn't remember the conversation.) He said, "I'm not sure if that's why or if the wounds are so deep and her habit all her life has been to avoid them."

•   •   •

At court appearances in the late nineties, Loftus was often asked about a landmark case that seemed to provide concrete evidence of repression. In 1984, a child forensic psychiatrist, David L. Corwin, recorded an interview with a six-year-old named Nicole, whose parents were fighting for custody of her. Nicole seemed sad and subdued. She said that her mother was "rotten" and had put her finger up her vagina, an allegation that her father also made in court. Corwin found the story of sex abuse credible, and, as a result, Nicole's mother lost custody.

Ten years later, when Nicole was sixteen, her father died, and she was placed in a foster home. She couldn't remember why she and her mother were estranged, and she asked Corwin if she could see the video from when she was a child. Corwin agreed, but by the time they met to watch the video, nearly a year later, Nicole had reunited with her mother. She had begun to wonder if, to get custody of her, her father had made up a story about abuse and coached her to say it. "I want her to be my mom," Nicole told Corwin. "I don't want to deny her a part of my life, so I've chosen to say, 'Well, if my dad did lie, it was just because he wanted me so badly.'"

"Do you remember anything about the concerns about possible sex abuse?" Corwin, who recorded the conversation, asked her.

"No," she said, closing her eyes. "I mean, I remember that was part of the accusation, but I don't remember anything." She inhaled deeply. "Wait a minute, yeah, I do."

"What do you remember?" he asked her.

"Oh, my gosh, that's really, really weird," she said. "I remember it happening, that she hurt me." She started crying. "I was getting a bath, and I don't remember anything specific until I felt that pain." She went on, "It's like I took a picture, like a few seconds long, a picture of the pain. . . . That's all the memory consists of." With Nicole's consent, Corwin published a paper in *Child Maltreatment* in 1997 that described how a forgotten memory of sexual abuse had resurfaced eleven years later. He also played the set of videos of Nicole at professional conferences. Nicole cut off contact with her mother again.

Loftus watched the videos and was skeptical of the conclusions that psychologists had drawn from them. She decided to embark on what she called "my own little innocence project." Although Nicole's name wasn't used in the paper, there were biographical clues in the videos. With the help of two private detectives, Loftus discovered Nicole's identity and obtained sealed court records, which revealed that child-protective services had originally dismissed the allegations brought by Nicole's father. Loftus interviewed Nicole's foster mother, stepmother, and mother, Joan Blackwell, who shared with Loftus poetry that she had written about the pain of being separated from her daughter. Blackwell told me that she felt at ease with Loftus. "It had been a long time since I had felt anyone believed me," she said, adding that the family-court system had seemed sexist. "The attitude was 'He wouldn't lie.'"

Not long afterward, an administrator from the University of Washington's Office of Scholarly Integrity told Loftus that she had fifteen minutes to hand over all her notes and files on Nicole's case. Nicole had accused Loftus of invading her privacy. The university forbade Loftus to research Nicole's case or even to speak about it, an experience that Loftus described as an "Orwellian nightmare." "Who, after all, benefits from my silence?" she said in 2001, in her acceptance speech for the William James Award, one of the most prestigious honors in the field of psychology.

After an investigation that lasted nearly two years, the university cleared Loftus of scholarly misconduct, but she felt so betrayed that she took a job at UC Irvine. In 2002, she published the results of her research in the *Skeptical Inquirer*, arguing that Nicole's mother had likely been wrongly accused. Loftus called her report a "case study of a case study—a cautionary tale." Her friend Jacqueline Spector, a lecturer at the University of Washington, said that Loftus's psychological motivations were clear. "Beth didn't have her mother long enough, and here was this mother that, clearly—from Beth's perspective—had been robbed of her daughter."

Loftus told me, "I think I had this fantasy—maybe I could bring the mother and daughter back together."

Instead, Nicole sued Loftus for defamation. Reading Loftus's article, she told me, was like "taking a very coarse piece of sandpaper and rubbing it over my entire life."

· · ·

In Nicole's interview with Corwin when she was seventeen, she told him that she hoped to become a psychologist. "I'm prepared to give my life, devote my life, to helping other kids who have gone through what I've gone through," she said. After ten years in the navy working as a helicopter pilot, she fulfilled her goal, getting a Ph.D. in clinical psychology and writing her dissertation on how trauma affects memory and identity. By then her case was so well known—in the lawsuit against Loftus (which she ended up losing), she disclosed her full name—that one of her professors likened her to H.M., the famous patient with an unusual form of amnesia who was studied from 1957 until his death. "I was appalled," Nicole told me. "My professor was making the point that Loftus had the right to do what she did because my case has now become one of these 'for the good of science' kind of situations."

As part of her psychological training, Nicole led a therapy group for adult survivors of sexual abuse. As she listened to the other women's stories, she felt, for the first time, that she was part of a collective. Her suffering no longer seemed like a character flaw. She wasn't an object in someone else's story—she could tell it in her own words. Being a survivor soon became the defining fact of her life, the scaffolding on which she rebuilt her identity.

Yet there were days when she asked herself, What if it didn't happen? She tried to ignore the question. But occasionally, when a

friend asked about her case against Loftus or when she was cleaning her office and came across her old copy of the *Skeptical
Inquirer,* she would revisit the article. She was disturbed to see
that Loftus had made compelling points.

Some days, Nicole believed that her mother had been wrongly
accused, and then she'd wake up the next morning having changed
her mind. In a conversation with the philosopher Eleanor Gordon-
Smith, who interviewed Nicole for her book *Stop Being Reasonable*
from 2019, Nicole said that her uncertainty "affected every *single*
relationship, in every possible way. It requires me to have a sense of
self that is not dependent on whether I was sexually assaulted by
my mother. It's a really big ask." She tried to step away from her
identity as a survivor, a process that she compared to dieting: "You
start, and then you lose your motivation and you go back to the
way you used to eat. I would start, and then I would revert back to
my old way of thinking."

Nicole, who is forty-two, spoke to me from her home office in
San Diego, where she now sees patients remotely. She sat in a
swivel desk chair and wore a T-shirt that quoted Desmond Tutu:
"If you are neutral in situations of injustice, you have chosen the
side of the oppressor." When I asked if she knew of psychological
literature about the effects of having one's memories doubted, she
told me, "Oh, no. There would not be literature on that because
clinical psychologists are trained to believe."

I was interested in what it meant to "cross the bridge," as she'd
described it, from victim to survivor. I asked if it was similar to
what Susan Brison, a philosopher who has written about her
experience of rape, had characterized in her book, *Aftermath,* as a
process of taking control of one's narrative. "That control, repeatedly exercised," Brison wrote, "leads to greater control over the
memories themselves, making them less intrusive and giving
them the kind of meaning that permits them to be integrated into
the rest of life."

Nicole was silent for a few seconds. "You know, I realized something," she said. A few weeks earlier, she had exchanged e-mails
with a woman whose memories of abuse Loftus had cast doubt on

at a civil trial. "We kind of realized together that we are survivors of Elizabeth Loftus," Nicole said. For years, she'd had intrusive thoughts. "I'm not sure if there is a greater sense of outrage than that of having your own memories challenged," she said. She had felt terror at the idea of seeing Loftus at psychology conferences. Recently, though, "I stopped wanting to hide under a chair every time I thought she might be at a conference and decided, no, I'm going to stand here and let her see me," she said.

Nicole has entered a new phase in sorting out whether her mother abused her. "Instead of waking up and wondering where I'm going to land today," she told me, "I just know that I don't know and that I'm probably not going to know in my lifetime." She has found herself in a position not dissimilar to that of Freud's female patients whose memories of abuse were believed and then, a few years later, discredited. But she doesn't feel commandeered into someone else's theory anymore. "On the face of it, I look like a sexual-trauma survivor," she told me, referring to problems that she had with trust. But she wondered if the conflict between her parents or her time in foster care were traumas that could hold similar explanatory power. In recent years, she has drifted in and out of a relationship with her mother. "I realized that I could just never give her what she wants from me, which is to go back in time and be allowed to mother me again," she said.

I told her of Loftus's hope that her work might have inspired Nicole and her mother to reunite. "It's transference," Nicole said of Loftus's preoccupation with her case. "To act out this darkness from her own past." In her clinical practice, Nicole is cautious whenever she faces patients whose struggles remind her of her own. "It is paramount that I say to myself, 'Nicole, it is not your job to save this person. You can't go back and save yourself by saving this person.'"

· · ·

"I unraveled it," Loftus's brother David, a seventy-four-year-old lawyer and the president of a Buddhist meditation center, told me in our first conversation. One night, when he was in his late thirties, he was in a hot tub and began to feel sleepy. "It was part of some drug experience, and as I was beginning to submerge, something woke me up," he said. "I thought, wow, this is what happened to our mom. It became so clear to me that there was nothing intentional about her death."

His younger brother, Robert, a property manager in Garberville, a small town near the northern tip of California, had pieced together a different explanation. In the years after their mother's death, he was in "grief free fall," he told me. "It's like somebody jumping out of a plane who hasn't figured out to pull the cord on their parachute—and that's where I came up with the idea of 'accidental suicide.' The fact that it is an oxymoron doesn't bother me at all." He theorized that his mother might have taken sleeping pills and then had some sort of panic attack—perhaps she felt that her skin was on fire—and jumped into the water. He went on, "But David tries to big-brother me and outmaneuver me, and the other night he was trying to get me to walk back the 'accidental suicide' label and say, Why not 'accidental drowning'?"

Since the pandemic began, Loftus and Robert have spoken on the phone daily. David joins their calls most weekends. Recently, on a Saturday evening, we all talked together on Zoom. "I'm pretending it's happy hour," Loftus said. She sat in her home office, in her three-bedroom condominium in University Hills, a residential complex for faculty at UC Irvine. "So, hey—cheers," she said. She took a sip of white wine.

A few days earlier, I had interviewed their cousin Debbi. "Oh, it was suicide," she told me when I asked about Rebecca's death. That I had framed this as a question seemed absurd to her. "We found her, my mother and I," she said. "We found her in a cold spring. I remember it like it was yesterday." Debbi had been twelve at the time. Later, her father showed her a suit of his with a bullet hole through one sleeve and explained that Rebecca had initially attempted to kill herself with a gun that he kept in his bedroom closet. "She must have fired it too early," Debbi told me. "The bullet went through my father's suit. It was at that point that my parents knew she needed to be institutionalized."

Debbi hadn't seen her cousins for years. Loftus asked me what I had learned. "We all would like our memories stimulated, if they can be," she said, at the beginning of our call.

I warned them that Debbi did not think there was any ambiguity about their mother's death. "Maybe there's a reason you've not asked her these questions," I said. "I don't want to mess around with your—"

"Denial system?" Loftus asked.

"With the way that you've made peace with things that happened a long time ago," I said.

"I understand that completely," Loftus said. "In Linda Meyer Williams's paper"—a 1994 study in the *Journal of Consulting and Clinical Psychology*—"she did not want to tell people, 'I have records from the hospital that you were abused,' because, if they were in denial and living with that, maybe it would do something bad to them. But I think we are giving you permission."

"You have to tell us, or you're not in our circle of trust anymore," David joked. He was sitting at his desk in a two-bedroom wooden geodesic dome in Northern California.

"Yeah, our memories are already polluted to the saturation point," Robert said.

I explained that Debbi had been with their aunt Pearl when she found Rebecca's body—in a cold-water spring, not a pool. I was about to continue when Loftus interrupted, "The swimming pool was a little lake-ish, so I'm not sure I trust that. I mean, if it were in an urban area you would know the difference between a lake and a pool, but in this summer place—what is a pool?"

"Sounds to me, from the country-property point of view, that our idea of a pool is much different," Robert said. He had been a math prodigy, the most brilliant of the three children, Loftus had told me. Now his speech had the cadence of someone who had spent his formative years socializing with stoners. He does not have an internet connection, so he was sitting in the trailer of his adult son, Abe, who lives on his property, and was sharing his hot spot. Abe sat next to him, staring out the trailer window.

"What else did Debbi remember?" Loftus asked.

I said that Debbi seemed surprised that anyone believed Rebecca's death was an accident. "She sort of acted like it was a no-brainer," I said.

"If she believes that . . ." Loftus paused for a few seconds. "I'm not sure she believes it from her own observation or what she would have learned afterward. Debbi was living in the world of the relatives who hated our father, so I don't think Debbi's age-twelve observations are—I mean, Debbi's great, but." She stopped midsentence.

The sun was setting in California, and there were few working light bulbs in Abe's trailer. Robert wore a flannel shirt, unbuttoned, and his image was so dim and grainy that he somehow looked like he was twenty again. He said, "When Beth did the Weinstein case, she was saying that after one of the gals went through the interrogation it sort of massaged her memory in a way to get it to migrate."

"You don't need to bring in Weinstein right now, Robert," Loftus said, amiably.

"I was sort of thinking of this in terms of how Debbi viewed what happened to Mom," Robert continued, "and how the general attitude in her home might have affected Debbi's memory."

"Leave Weinstein out of it," Loftus said. "You know, because honestly—I was a blind witness. I didn't even talk about any specific people. It was just stuff about memory."

When I had first spoken with David, he mentioned hearing a story about his mother getting hold of his uncle's gun. I told him that Debbi had heard about a similar incident.

"That is total news," Loftus said.

"Not to me," David said.

"How did you know?" Loftus asked him.

Beyond interactions on social media, David hadn't had a conversation with Debbi in several decades, and even as children they were not close. "I bet she posted something," he said. "That's my only guess. On Instagram. Or Facebook."

"Debbi wouldn't have posted about this on Facebook," Loftus said.

"I know—that doesn't make sense," David said. "That's so interesting: when you have such a clear memory and then you go, well, how did I come to know what I believe? And you can't think of any way in which you could have acquired that knowledge." David spent five years studying Tibetan Buddhism in a Himalayan village in India, and he seemed well suited to this line of pondering. "Did something happen in a dream and I remembered it as true?" he said.

Earlier that day, Loftus had forwarded a scan of her 1959 diary to David. It was the first time he had read her journal, and he was curious about the entry she had written the night before their mother's death. "Should I read it?" he asked.

Loftus, who hadn't read the journal for years, nodded.

"My mother and I had a long talk until midnight all about her childhood and many other things," he read. "I was really happy because we'd never been too close before, and now we were talking like we really were."

David looked up from the page he was reading. "Beth, are you crying?" he said, tenderly.

She was. "It's OK," she said, nodding quickly and pursing her lips. She had never paid close attention to the timeline. "But if I really was with her until midnight the night before," she said, "it is a little bit weird that we're having this really wonderful night and she dies the next day." The timing had struck me, too. Sometimes, once people resolve to commit suicide, they become uncharacteristically lucid and emotionally expansive, perhaps because the end of their suffering feels near.

"Was she apprehensive about going back to California—to an intolerable household reality, to the responsibilities of motherhood and parenting?" Robert asked. "I mean, where did I get that infusion of images?"

"I said that to you because I do believe that," Loftus said. "But I don't know where I got that. I have no idea."

"If Debbi is sure it is suicide," Robert said, "it might be that some people come into their experience of mental illness with a baseline rigidity. They can't relate to mental illness and see these people as extraterrestrial."

Robert's son, Abe, who has had psychiatric treatment, suddenly chimed in: "The first question they ask is 'Have you had any suicidal thoughts?' They shame you right off the bat. The minute you get in their office. How can you answer something like that? And then they say you're depressed because you can't answer it correctly. That's just me, though—sorry."

"No, it's OK," Loftus said. "Abe, is this weird for you?"

Abe said that he didn't realize he had relatives who lived in Pennsylvania. Then they reflected on what a child in the 1950s would have understood about mental illness. "We could not fathom it," Robert said. "We had no metrics."

I proposed that maybe there was some truth to the theory of "accidental suicide"; their mother may have been in so much pain that it wasn't possible to speak of her as having full volition.

Loftus said that she had a friend, a mother, who had tried to kill herself. "And when I said to her, 'I can't believe you did this—do you realize your kids will be still talking about this years later?' she said, 'I honestly thought they would be better off without me.'" She told her brothers, "Mom could have had that thinking."

David recalled a memory of their mother standing at the top of the stairs in a slip when their father came home from work. "Dad yelled at her," David said. "He said, 'How can you run around the house naked in front of the children?' And she cried and ran back into the bedroom."

"Oh, wow," Loftus said. "I never knew you had that." She had a poorer memory of childhood than her brothers, and she treated their memories as possessions they'd been gifted unfairly.

Robert, who was now barely visible in the darkness, recalled that Debbi's father, Harrold, a former marine, had a den where he kept all his paraphernalia from both World Wars. "It's plausible that Mom would be rummaging around in there, and maybe Har-rold had a sidearm in a holster that was draped over one of his uniform jackets, and this could have been what set the stage for this alleged event," he said. "I don't buy the fact that she attempted suicide with one of Harrold's sidearms."

David was building a fire, and we could see only his legs. He came back to the screen and said, "Well, the interesting thing is I had this idea, which I never really evaluated, that Dad had thought it was suicide and Mom's family thought it was some accidental thing. But I think everybody knew it was suicide."

"Nope," Loftus said. "Not everybody."

"I'm getting more comfortable with the idea of accidental sui-cide," David said.

"Why?" Loftus said. "I thought you were rejecting Robert's label."

"If somebody dies like that, then you go, 'Well, I don't know—I can really think whatever I want,'" David said. "But if you then hear there was a previous suicide attempt—"

"*If* there was," Loftus said.

"Yeah, if there was," he repeated. "You think Debbi may have misrecollected that?"

"I think Debbi was twelve years old and what Debbi knows she learned from adults who had their own ideas," she said. "It's all these different memories." Her voice rose in pitch. "And the idea that here we are, in our seventies, trying to sort this out!" She said this like it was funny, but she looked upset. Loftus's approach to the conversation was so studious that it occurred to me that this call, like the surgery that she turned into a memory experi-ment in a peer-reviewed journal, might be another way of chan-neling life events into publishable work.

I told Loftus that it seemed hard to avoid the thought that her career had been shaped by the slipperiness of this foundational memory. "No," she said, shaking her head. "No way. No way. It was purely, got a chance to work with a professor in graduate school on a memory project, got a chance to—no. None of all this." She asked her brothers, "Would you guys agree?"

"You're kind of like Forrest Gump," David said. "You're the Forrest Gump of psychology because you just tumble into these situations."

"Oh, my God," Loftus said, laughing, perhaps harder than necessary, because it was such a relief no longer to be talking about her mother. "You know—it is a little Forrest Gump–y. I step into it and suddenly there is Phil Spector, and suddenly there's Harvey Weinstein and there's Martha Stewart, you know, and Michael Jackson"—she had assisted with the defense of all four—"and I don't even know why I'm here. You're right."

"All the people you mention are corrupt," David said, to no one in particular.

She said that Spector, who was convicted of murder in 2009, had sent her a beautiful card before he died. It was on the bookshelf behind her.

David asked if she'd like to read it aloud, but she said no. We'd been on Zoom for three hours, and Robert's dog, which had spent the conversation in a parked car nearby, needed to be let out. Loftus said she still believed that her mother's death was either an accident or "accidental suicide." Nothing in the past three hours had changed her view. "We should not use a twelve-year-old's memory," she repeated. She suggested that they find some sort of concrete evidence, perhaps a map of her uncle's vacation property. "I don't know why, but I don't like it being a spring," she said. She shrugged. "I've always said it was a pool and remembered it was a pool, and I don't know why that's important to me—to not even challenge that fact."

The next evening, Loftus e-mailed me saying that she and David had just spoken with Debbi. "We caught Debbi in two major memory errors tonight!" she wrote. Debbi had forgotten that she'd driven, rather than flown, to Pennsylvania. She also claimed that Loftus's father had never once called to check on Rebecca—a memory that Debbi had to retract once David read aloud a passage in Loftus's diary showing that her father had, indeed, called. The tone of Loftus's e-mail seemed somewhat disciplinary, but when we talked on the phone it was clear that she saw nothing shameful about Debbi's errors. Instead, she expressed a sense of camaraderie; they were fellows in misremembering—her cousin was just as human as she. "Thank goodness for independent corroboration," Loftus told me. "Especially when you have somebody who expresses their memory with such confidence that you're tempted to just capitulate to it."

Every week, Loftus receives letters from prisoners, and she (or her research assistant) always responds. "We empathize with you," she recently wrote to a man convicted of murdering another inmate while in federal prison. "We wish you the best and welcome updates," she wrote to a man convicted of shooting someone multiple times. "I received your letter and request for information on 'my theory,'" she wrote to Jerry Sandusky, who in 2012 was convicted of sexually abusing children while a football coach at Penn State. "It must be terribly difficult for you and your family, and I hope you have the legal help needed to resolve your situation justly."

David joked that maybe Loftus experienced some sort of Stockholm syndrome. "Because who would pick that side?" he said. "Now, I'm not totally attached to this view—because it seems like something I've contrived as an explanation—but it's possible that she never got appreciation from our father so she's now trying to win that approval by representing the other rich white guys who have been accused of doing bad things." (Loftus has testified for numerous poor defendants of color, too, in cases that tend to get less attention.)

But there are rarely just two sides. A larger cast of characters, embedded in different institutions of power, determine what kinds of stories get believed. Even Loftus's study about being lost in the mall, which has assumed an iconic status, becoming one of the most famous experiments of the century, has lent itself to conflicting interpretations over time. (Its reputation is discordant with its size—there were only twenty-four subjects.) In the study, subjects came to believe the story about getting lost in a mall because older relatives falsely told them that it was true. Loftus and others have described the study as a kind of parable for skepticism. But Steven Brown, a social psychologist at England's Nottingham Trent University who studies memory, told me, "For those of us differently positioned, the parable is entirely about power." The study reveals the ease with which children can be betrayed by adults, who lie to them, rewriting their stories.

In an interview on a Dutch television station, Loftus once said that if she had wanted to do experimental research that emerged from her own childhood experiences she would not have studied memory errors and distortions. "I would have designed my experiments to answer different questions," she said. After the conversation with her and her brothers, I asked Loftus what those research questions would be. "You know, I'm not sure," she said. She paused for a long time and then teared up. "It's the M-word," she said, referring to "mother." Her brothers told me that they have a saying: "Don't say the M-word, or Beth will break down." She waved her hand in front of her face, as if to cool the emotional temperature. "Maybe it would be about, you know, how come this never goes away?" she said, crying. "And is that true for other people?"

BuzzFeed News

FINALIST—PUBLIC INTEREST

This is the first in a series of three articles by Heidi Blake and Katie J. M. Baker—"They Both Fought to Break Free from Guardianship. Only One Escaped" and " 'My Human Rights Are Being Violated': Fighting a Family Conservatorship" are the others— that investigated what the writers describe as "an opaque, overgrown, and malfunctioning system wielding vast and frightening power in the dark." The ASME judges said that "this series, based on thousands of documents, hundreds of interviews and fifty statewide legal reviews, paints a devastating portrait of a failing legal framework." Blake and Baker are investigative reporters for Buzzfeed News, *both based in London.* Buzzfeed News *won the National Magazine Award for Public Interest in 2016 for two stories, "The New American Slavery" and "All You Americans Are Fired," about our abusive guest-worker program.*

Heidi Blake and
Katie J. M. Baker

Beyond Britney

Abuse, Exploitation,
and Death Inside
America's Guardianship
Industry

They can isolate you: A teenager with cerebral palsy was snatched from the school gates and hidden from his parents.

They can bleed you dry: A successful rheumatologist was declared incapacitated after a bout of depression and lost her million-dollar waterfront home.

And they can leave you to die: A forty-six-year-old man died under a do-not-resuscitate order that went against the desperate pleas of his wife.

All three nightmares share a common cause: These people had been placed under the care—and control—of legal guardians. America's guardianship system was designed as a last resort to be used only in the rare and drastic event that someone is totally incapacitated by mental or physical disability. In those cases, conscientious guardians can provide vital support, often in complex and distressing circumstances. But an investigation by BuzzFeed News has found that the system has grown into a vast, lucrative, and poorly regulated industry that has subsumed more than a million people, many of whom insist they are capable of making their own decisions, and placed them at risk of abuse, theft, and even death.

The #FreeBritney movement has drawn international attention to the case of Britney Spears, and wrongdoing by individual guardians has surfaced in the past, but our investigation reveals the systemic failings behind these isolated stories.

In local courts across the country—often woefully unfit for the sweeping power they command—guardians, lawyers, and expert witnesses appear frequently before the same judges in an established network of overlapping financial and professional interests. They are often paid from the estate of the person whose freedom is on the line, creating powerful incentives to form guardianships and keep them in place.

"The judge knows the lawyers, the lawyers know each other," said J. Ronald Denman, a former state prosecutor and Florida lawyer who has contested dozens of guardianships over the past decade. "The amount of abuse is crazy. You're going against a rigged system."

Without being convicted of any crime, those declared incapacitated face some of the most severe measures that the courts can take against any U.S. citizen. Most freedoms articulated in the UN Universal Declaration of Human Rights are denied to people under full guardianship: they can lose their rights to vote, marry, start a family, decide where they live, consent to medical treatment, spend their money, seek employment, or own property.

Thousands of professional guardians, lawyers, and corporations now hold sway over assets totaling tens of billions of dollars. Some guardians have hundreds of people under their control. And despite the public perception that guardianship is a protective measure for older adults nearing death, the system traps huge numbers of young people.

BuzzFeed News has scoured hundreds of thousands of court documents, obtained confidential mental health filings and financial records, examined hundreds of guardianship cases, gathered exclusive data from extensive public records requests, conducted hundreds of interviews, and carried out a detailed review of guardianship laws in all fifty states. Our investigation reveals an opaque, overgrown, and malfunctioning system wielding vast and frightening power in the dark.

- People have been abused, neglected, and killed while living under guardianship. *BuzzFeed News* identified twenty cases in which young or middle-aged people died under questionable circumstances, including murder, severe neglect, or malnourishment. A thirty-one-year-old man was abused by care home staff and buried in concrete for months before his guardian realized he was missing. No charges were brought against her, and she is still in charge of 130 people.
- People under guardianship—commonly referred to as wards—have been locked up and isolated from their families and friends, with guardians obtaining restraining orders to keep loved ones at bay. One professional guardian who concealed the whereabouts of a woman's teenage son declared, "I'm mom now," and said she had no problem "taking the noose around" the mother's "neck and tightening it" to keep them apart, a nurse alleged in court filings.
- In many states, guardians can force wards to undergo invasive medical procedures, including the implantation of contraceptive devices—and in several cases, wards were permanently sterilized.
- Court clerks have failed to perform vital checks in hundreds of cases, and lax vetting has left vulnerable people in troubling hands. The owner of one major guardianship corporation was given control of hundreds of wards—including young people—despite having been repeatedly accused of domestic abuse and assault involving children.
- Guardians have had scores of younger people placed under do-not-resuscitate orders (DNRs)—including some who have a mental illness but are physically healthy—blocking their access to potentially lifesaving treatment if they fall seriously ill. Several middle-aged people, including a former space shuttle scientist, have died under these orders, sometimes without the courts being informed.
- Professional guardians have stolen tens of millions of dollars from hundreds of people and exploited obscure trust

fund laws to conceal their financial activity from the courts. One guardianship nonprofit drained the accounts of more than 800 people while another professional guardian transferred money from several of her wards' accounts into a trust controlled by her husband.

- Other wards say they have been trapped under the guardianship of controlling relatives who strangled their ability to have social or romantic relationships, choose where they live, or express their true gender identity.

The public rarely hears from people who have been stripped of their rights given the significant restrictions they live under, but in an ongoing series, *BuzzFeed News* will report on the cases of wards who endured harrowing ordeals while under the control of private, public, and family guardians.

BuzzFeed News reviewed details of more than 200 guardianships involving young and middle-aged people across more than thirty states. In 130 of those cases—gleaned from court documents, interviews, first-person testimony, and local news reports—we found evidence suggesting that wards were exposed to financial exploitation, and 110 may have suffered abuse or neglect. There were nearly fifty claims that people had been isolated from friends and family, and dozens of reports that people were confined against their will. In scores of cases, people were put under guardianship based on a questionable finding of incapacity. Many cases indicated that wards had experienced several of these alleged harms at once.

No comprehensive data exist on the guardianship system, and courts in many states keep case documents under seal, making it impossible to say for sure how many people are under its control. Estimates have put the number of adult guardianship cases at more than one million—a figure that experts say is rising. *BuzzFeed News* filed public records requests to all fifty states and the District of Columbia to create an unprecedented dataset on the number of cases being opened across the country each year. Fewer than half of the states had fully usable data, but *BuzzFeed News* consulted statisticians to develop a national estimate based on the figures provided. Our analysis suggests that as many as 200,000 adult guardianship cases are filed per year.

People whose capacity is in question are often struggling with physical and mental conditions that make caring for them unquestionably difficult. But guardianship is such an extreme measure that in most states, judges are required by law not to impose it unless no other options are available. Too often, however, they opt for full guardianship in hearings that can last just minutes, without considering any alternatives. Many state laws allow hearings that determine if someone is incapacitated to be held without notifying the person in question, meaning someone can be placed under emergency guardianship without having an opportunity to fight back. Some people are placed under guardianship without even undergoing a medical examination. And people who have been declared incapacitated generally lose the right to appoint their own lawyers or represent themselves, which means that once guardianships are in place, they are often impossible to escape.

The loss of liberty is particularly consequential for people who have not yet had a chance at adult life. Many young Americans with disabilities are funneled into guardianship as soon as they turn eighteen as part of what the National Council on Disability calls a "school-to-guardianship pipeline." Most eighteen- to twenty-two-year-olds who receive publicly funded services for intellectual and developmental disabilities have guardians.

Others have been declared incapacitated because of conditions that can often be managed, such as depression, PTSD, autism, physical disability, or addiction.

And for professionals who are unscrupulous, younger wards with access to large inheritances or personal injury payments can represent the most lucrative cases of all because they have decades ahead during which the guardian can keep billing.

With no federal laws to govern guardians, the powers given to them can vary dramatically: In more than ten states, the law grants full guardians the same powers over a ward as a parent has over an "unemancipated minor child." Illinois judges may give guardians "custody of the ward's minor and adult dependent children." Guardians in Arkansas can put wards in the county jail "for safekeeping," and in Texas, they can lock wards in psychiatric hospitals before asking for court approval.

Many professional guardians work hard to care for clients who genuinely can't care for themselves. Others are committed family members looking after vulnerable loved ones in exceptionally difficult situations.

But Shannon Butler, a "master guardian" and board member with the National Guardianship Association, said judges are too quick to put people under full guardianship because "it's just easier for them, and honestly, it's easier for us too."

The association has clear standards that guardianship should only be considered as a last option. "We should only be using those powers that are absolutely necessary," she said. "A good guardian is actually working towards getting their wards out of guardianship."

Yet flaws in the system leave "room for abuse," Butler said. "If you're somebody that's predatory and you get into this business," she added, "it's scary."

When No One Is Watching

Elizabeth Hensley was stripped of her rights and put under guardianship by a judge while she was receiving treatment for depression in a Florida hospital.

The fifty-nine-year-old acknowledged she had autism and mental health difficulties but begged the judge not to take away her rights. "I really do not need a guardian!" she wrote to the court, pleading to be allowed to return to her home where her partner, "precious cats and the garden" were waiting for her. But her pleas were denied.

Hensley was assigned a professional guardian who was meant to help her. Instead, she complained, she was kept under "lockdown" while court filings show the guardian paid herself from Hensley's accounts without court permission.

Florida's guardianship industry is among the most bloated outgrowths of the system, with more than 500 professional guardians and hundreds more lawyers who draw their income from vulnerable people across the state. Hensley had fallen into the hands of one of the most notorious.

Rebecca Fierle made millions while controlling the lives and finances of more than 500 people before she was charged last year with abuse and neglect of an older adult ward who died after she had him placed under a DNR and allegedly told doctors to cap his feeding tube. When police raided her office, they found urns containing the cremated remains of nine former wards on display. An analysis of thousands of court records by *BuzzFeed News* sheds new light on her practices.

Though Fierle marketed herself as a specialist in care for older adults, around a third of her wards at the time of her arrest had been placed under her guardianship in their youth or middle age. She sold people's homes, cars, and belongings to pay her bills and moved hundreds of thousands of dollars from their accounts into opaque trust funds that shielded her from court scrutiny. More than $660,000 of Hensley's money was moved into a trust that a 2019 audit found Fierle used to pay herself without court approval. Court auditors were able to track several thousand dollars Fierle had directed to herself and her business from Hensley's accounts, but they noted that she had failed to provide records for numerous other transactions.

Fierle declined to respond to detailed questions from *BuzzFeed News* but has previously denied any wrongdoing and pleaded not guilty to the abuse and neglect charges. She told court auditors who flagged multiple concerns about her use of Hensley's funds that all her spending was "for the ward's benefit," but she couldn't prove it because her paperwork had been seized by law enforcement.

Like Hensley, many of Fierle's wards were diagnosed with mental rather than physical ailments, including depression, bipolar disorder, and alcohol addiction. But records reveal she had dozens of young and middle-aged people placed under DNRs and diverted thousands of dollars from their estates to buy prepaid burial plans from two favored local funeral homes—in one case for an eighteen-year-old with bipolar disorder and ADHD.

Judges eventually revoked nearly one hundred DNRs in Fierle's cases—but records show it was too late to free at least two of those wards from those orders. Unbeknown to the courts, Penny Pilkington, a fifty-six-year-old woman with developmental disabilities, and Drazen Premate, a sixty-three-year-old former space shuttle scientist who had schizophrenia, were already dead.

Other professions that yield such large financial rewards and power over the lives of vulnerable people—like law or medicine— typically require years of intensive training and extensive vetting. But guardianship generally demands neither.

In some states, guardians (sometimes referred to as conservators) control both a ward's personal life and their money while others assign a separate person to manage financial matters. These roles can be assumed without a degree in law, social work, or accounting—and some states require no more than a few hours of education before guardians are empowered to assume control of people's lives.

Guardians are required to file annual reports on their wards' well-being and financial affairs, often reviewed by low-paid, overstretched court clerks who lack formal training in spotting fraud. Many clerks are also charged with vetting people seeking to become professional guardians—but troubling cases can slip through.

In Minnesota, records reveal the owner of a major guardianship corporation was placed in charge of hundreds of vulnerable people despite pleading guilty to domestic assault in 2004 after her son told police she threw him on the floor, slammed him against the wall, and called him a "shit head." Rebecca Reich, who owns the firm Guardian and Conservator Services, had also been arrested the previous year for allegedly telling another child to get a knife from the drawer and kill her then-boyfriend, though no charges were brought. Court filings detail other allegations of domestic abuse involving her son.

The Minnesota Judicial Branch declined to comment on Reich's case but said background checks are run every two years and provided to judges who use them to decide on a case-by-case basis whether to appoint guardians.

Reich's father, a retired local judge who now represents her guardianship firm, responded to questions from *BuzzFeed News* on her behalf. He said she had pleaded guilty to assault only to spare her son the distress of testifying in court and the case was dismissed without an adjudication of guilt after she met her parole conditions. Reich's father said she disputed all the allegations, which arose during a messy divorce, and reiterated that no charges had been brought against her. She had been fully vetted, he said, and currently serves on the statute committee of the Minnesota Association for Guardianship and Conservatorship. "The background concerns that you raise are incomplete, contested, and do not reflect years of subsequent competent and compassionate service," he wrote.

In Florida, Fierle's wrongdoing went unchecked for more than a decade. Court clerks had failed to raise warning signs, and regulators did not respond in a timely manner to reports about Fierle's suspect practices. After her arrest, the head of the Florida Department of Elder Affairs said that the Office of Public and Professional Guardians—whose four employees were tasked with overseeing the conduct of hundreds of guardians across the state—had a backlog of eighty open investigations.

This spring, the comptroller of Orange County, where Fierle controlled the lives of more than one hundred people, issued a damning eighty-six-page report warning that overworked and ill-qualified court clerks were failing to subject guardians to basic scrutiny, such as criminal records checks. Some guardians had failed to report on the well-being of their wards for years without the clerks raising any concerns. Guardians had paid themselves from wards' estates without court approval and moved money into trusts without filing mandatory paperwork. The Orange County Clerk of Courts told *BuzzFeed News* she disagreed with many of the report's findings but had made recent improvements including adding more deputy clerks to the guardianship team and providing training in general accounting principles and reviewing internal procedures.

BuzzFeed News identified more than 130 cases across the country in which evidence suggested young or middle-aged wards were exposed to financial malpractice, including fifty cases involving trust funds, which can be used to shield guardians from court scrutiny.

One professional guardian moved money belonging to several of her wards into Florida trusts before successfully petitioning the courts to release her of any obligation to account for future spending because she said the money was no longer under her control. But in three of those cases, the funds had been moved into a trust controlled by her husband. The conflict of interest was highlighted in the report by Orange County investigators this spring, without naming the guardian concerned. *BuzzFeed News* has identified her as Theresa Barton, a professional who has controlled the lives of wards in Florida for twenty-five years. Her husband, Nick Barton, runs a nonprofit that controls a pooled special needs trust used by guardians across the state to store wards' funds. The Bartons did not respond to repeated requests for comment.

Another Florida guardian, Teri St. Hilaire, has faced scrutiny over alleged financial irregularities involving more than sixty of her wards—including a twenty-nine-year-old man with funds of more than $2 million following a personal injury settlement. Records show St. Hilaire established a trust with his money and charged fees of more than $70,000 by the time regulators launched an investigation into the "wellbeing and financial affairs" of scores of people in her care last year. The probe concluded in May, and a report was sent to the Office of Public and Professional Guardians, but its findings have been designated confidential. Meanwhile, St. Hilaire continues to wield power over the wards who remain in her control. She did not respond to requests for comment from *BuzzFeed News*.

Guardians are often legally empowered to liquidate wards' assets to pay their own bills—and *BuzzFeed News* identified cases where people lost almost everything they owned. Among them was a rheumatologist in her fifties who was placed under guardianship after experiencing a bout of depression during acrimonious divorce proceedings in 2019. Her professional guardian had her placed against her will in a lockdown facility while arranging the sale of her $1 million waterfront home and other belongings. By the time she was released from guardianship eight months later, the guardian and her lawyers had charged more than $100,000 in fees and expenses. The guardian refused to comment.

In New Mexico, the owners of the nonprofit Ayudando Guardians embezzled around $10 million from more than 800 clients, spending the stolen funds on expensive cars, luxury homes, Las Vegas shopping sprees, and exotic holidays to the Caribbean and Hawaii. Court clerks had spotted no red flags in any of the firm's financial filings, leaving the abuse to continue unchecked for more than a decade until junior employees blew the whistle. The firm's president was finally sentenced to prison in July, but by then there was almost nothing left in the accounts of any of Ayudando's wards.

As well as serving as guardian, conservator, or trustee for hundreds of "private pay" clients, Ayudando was paid millions of dollars by New Mexico's Office of Guardianship to take over the lives and finances of people living in poverty.

The Poor Can Vanish

Private guardians can profit from wards with access to large amounts of cash and valuable assets, but people with little money who get sucked into the state-run guardianship system are also vulnerable to abuse—and may be more easily overlooked.

Carl DeBrodie was a happy and high-spirited child with multiple developmental disabilities when he was first placed under the guardianship of Mary Martin, who said she raised him in a loving home with his own pet horse. But she didn't realize she and her husband had to apply to be his guardians after he became an adult, she told *BuzzFeed News*, so DeBrodie eventually came under the control of a public guardian named Karen Digh Allen.

In Missouri, elected public administrators handle the cases of incapacitated people without financial resources or anyone else to care for them. Allen has overseen hundreds of wards in Callaway County since 1997. As DeBrodie's guardian, she was responsible for ensuring he received proper medical care and lived in a safe and comfortable setting.

Debrodie was placed in a group home named Second Chance. While he lived there, Martin reported seeing him covered in cuts and bruises. After she reported the alleged injuries, she was banned from seeing DeBrodie, according to her testimony in confidential court records obtained by *BuzzFeed News*. Martin applied to adopt him as an adult, but Allen filed an objection.

A law professor named Mary Beck who was appointed by the court to determine DeBrodie's best interests in the adoption case concluded that he wanted to live with Martin and her husband, whom he knew as "Mom" and "Dad." In the confidential report, she also noted what she saw as a "conflict of interest": Allen's long-time deputy had a second job working for Second Chance. Allen later said that homes like Second Chance had a financial incentive to hold on to clients, according to the *Fulton Sun*: "The amount of money paid almost creates a scenario that invites deception if you don't have good people in there."

The judge ruled against the adoption, and the Martins said they never saw DeBrodie again.

"Why keep him from a home where he was loved, where he wanted to be?" Beck said to *BuzzFeed News* regarding Allen's objections.

DeBrodie had been missing for around seven months when his remains were found encased in concrete in a storage unit in April 2017. He had been made to sleep in a staffer's basement and denied medical care when his health deteriorated. He died just two blocks from Allen's office. Second Chance staffers hid his body and then falsified medical documents describing him enjoying snacks and dancing to music in order to keep collecting over $100,000 from Medicaid for his care.

Multiple Second Chance staffers went on to plead guilty in connection to DeBrodie's death in what a judge called "one of the most deplorable, depraved and disturbing" cases he'd ever heard.

Allen refused to answer questions about her role in DeBrodie's case. "In 25 years, I've always been neutral," she said, adding that it was the judge's decision to deny the adoption she contested, not hers. She said she was involved in efforts to strengthen guardianship policy both state and nationwide. She was originally named in the civil lawsuit but was dismissed as part of a settlement agreement with the county. Her lawyer argued she could not have known about DeBrodie's abuse or death given Second Chance's elaborate cover-up.

She still holds her elected office and currently oversees 130 people. In May this year, Allen was named Missouri's public administrator of the year as well as Callaway County's April employee of the month. "Allen is a great example of an employee who goes above and beyond every day," the announcement said.

Public guardianships for people who have little or no money form a significant part of the industry. Across America, young people in group homes, specialist schools, or foster placements have been pushed straight into guardianships as soon as they turn eighteen.

"In a lot of cases, it's just reflexive," said disability rights attorney Viviana Bonilla López. Parents of children with disabilities turning eighteen are often told by doctors, teachers, or lawyers that they will lose any say in their care unless they get a guardianship. What they don't know is that, as soon as they're in the system, the judge can push the parents aside and appoint a professional—even a stranger—in their place. "Parents say, 'I don't know how this happened. I didn't mean to do this. Help me get them out,'" Bonilla López said. But by then, it's often too late.

Public guardians are typically paid by the state to take on wards only if no one else is willing to do so. In such cases, judges frequently favor the total removal of the ward's rights. Young adults who enter guardianship can find that they are in it for life.

BuzzFeed News reviewed details of nineteen cases in which wards were allegedly abused, neglected, isolated from friends or family, wrongly stripped of their rights, or killed while under the control of public guardians.

In one case, a twenty-four-year-old autistic man in California died with a blood clot in his lungs after being assaulted by staffers at the care home where his public guardian had placed him, according to a claim filed by his father. In another, a forty-seven-year-old man with an intellectual disability suffocated in Michigan after a care home worker wrestled him to the ground and knelt on his back. His family said they learned of his death through a notice in the local paper.

Shutting wards off from their loved ones is a feature of many guardianships—public and private—a *BuzzFeed News* analysis shows. In scores of cases, wards were allegedly forcibly separated from their partners, close friends, or family and sometimes held against their will in facilities where they were cut off from the outside world.

A guardian from a Texas nonprofit called Family Eldercare agreed with a hospital's decision to instate a DNR for Michael Hickson, a forty-six-year-old man with quadriplegia, even though his wife, Melissa, begged her not to. She was blocked from seeing her husband or getting information about his condition, according to a lawsuit she filed. By the time she found out he was dead, she said, his remains had already been sent to a funeral home. The lawsuit states Hickson's guardian had only a provisional guardianship certificate and less than a year of experience.

Family Eldercare said it was responding in court to the ongoing lawsuit, which it called inaccurate, and that it "consulted medical professionals on the care decisions" for Hickson "after carefully considering the information available."

Omar Rojas has severe cerebral palsy caused by a hospital accident that resulted in a large payout. His mother, Ruthelyn, applied to become his guardian when he turned eighteen, but her ex-husband contested it, so the court appointed a professional Florida guardian named Susan Whitney, who has been placed in control of more than fifty wards. Soon after, Ruthelyn said, she arrived at Omar's school to find Whitney had removed him. For weeks, court filings show, the guardian refused to tell his parents where he had been taken. Records show she told his caregivers to remove a Spanish-speaking staffer from the case and "give instructions not to talk to mom." Ruthelyn, who speaks Spanish, says she was left in the dark. In the meantime, Whitney moved Omar's money into a new trust and charged almost $30,000 in the first five months of the guardianship.

Whitney had acted in a "very unethical, aggressive and inappropriate manner," according to a statement from a nurse in charge of Omar's care, filed in court by his father. The nurse recalled that Whitney called Ruthelyn a "bitch who was fucking out of her mind who would never be Omar's mother ever again."

"I'm mom now," the nurse said Whitney told her. "I make the decisions. I call the shots. Not her. Me."

Whitney denied any wrongdoing in a letter from her lawyer. "Had those allegations been proven to be true, Susan Whitney would no longer be Omar's guardian," the letter said. "Susan Whitney remains Omar's guardian."

Velvet Sommer, an elected public guardian in Missouri, placed a young man with multiple disabilities in a group home and restricted his parents from seeing him, changing his Facebook password and monitoring his contact with family and friends, his mother told *BuzzFeed News*. Sommer did not answer repeated and detailed questions about this case.

When the man messaged his father, Sommer intervened and shut down the conversation, screenshots show. She also moved him eight hours away from his family to a poorly rated nursing home.

His parents said they haven't seen him since April. In an August recording obtained by *BuzzFeed News*, Sommer said she was protecting the man and told his cousin: "I can actually keep them from seeing him for the rest of his life."

Experts for Hire

BuzzFeed News found gaping holes in safeguards designed to ensure that only people who are completely incapacitated end up in guardianship.

In some states, people can be placed under guardianship without even being examined while in others courts can appoint experts with no medical training. In many cases, examiners can be nominated by the guardian or the person petitioning for guardianship, creating the potential for perilous conflicts of interest.

In Florida, the Orange County comptroller's report noted this spring that investigators had identified "several conflicts of interest" among lawyers, guardians, and medical professionals tasked with examining allegedly incapacitated people.

BuzzFeed News has identified one of those physicians as Dr. Thomas Sawyer, a radiation oncologist who is regularly appointed by the Florida probate courts to assess people facing guardianship. Sawyer occupies an extraordinary double role: he also founded a law firm that specializes in representing professional guardians. His son-in-law Thomas Moss, a partner at the firm, represented Rebecca Fierle—the guardian who displayed the ashes of nine wards in her office—in hundreds of cases. Fierle was known to the Sawyer family and mingled at the firm's Christmas parties. Yet court records show Sawyer examined several people for whom she was guardian.

Examination reports are sealed, making it impossible to tally up an examiner's overall track record. But *BuzzFeed News* has obtained documents from one case in which a woman's efforts to free herself from guardianship were rejected on the basis of a report by Sawyer: Elizabeth Hensley, the fifty-nine-year-old woman who complained of being held in a lockdown facility while Rebecca Fierle paid out thousands of dollars from her accounts without court approval. Fierle was later removed from her case, but Hensley remains under the control of another guardian.

Moss told *BuzzFeed News* that his relationship with his father-in-law was "well known by those in Central Florida's guardianship court system" and had never been hidden. "Throughout the hundreds of cases our firm has handled in this area, Dr. Sawyer has only been appointed in a very small number of cases. His appointment in these matters is the very rare exception, not the rule, and never as a result of the firm's request." Though

Dr. Sawyer cofounded the firm and retains the title "of counsel," Moss said he is no longer involved with its affairs and does not receive any financial gain from its work. Sawyer did not respond to requests for comment.

Other cases reviewed by *BuzzFeed News* reveal the influence that professional guardians can wield over supposedly independent experts—especially when large amounts of money are at stake. When court-appointed examiners don't provide the desired answers, guardians can simply look for others.

In 2020, a twenty-five-year-old woman named Megan Smoot wrote to a Florida judge to claim that her guardian, Marie Bambi Nikolakis-Williams, was controlling her life "to an extent that is abusive," isolating her from family and friends and misusing her money. Williams was driving Smoot's Cadillac, the letter said, and had claimed to be giving Smoot hundreds of dollars more each week for food and clothes than she was actually receiving.

Smoot had a near million-dollar settlement from her mother's wrongful death and suffered from a drug addiction in the wake of the tragedy. But guardianship was making her situation worse, she told the judge. "In recovery communication is vital and essential," she wrote. "A lack of outside communication and isolation I don't believe is good for my mental health or continued growth."

Smoot's brother had filed a petition to restore some of her freedoms, but Williams fought it. Although a court-appointed examiner found that Smoot should have her rights partially restored, Williams presented two additional reports as part of a lengthy dossier arguing for continued control.

Williams denied Smoot's claims against her but resigned after it came to light that she had lied on several guardianship applications about past bankruptcy. Smoot was transferred to a large guardianship corporation. She told *BuzzFeed News* that she had relapsed this spring, under the strain of continued guardianship. In June, days after Britney Spears spoke publicly against her own predicament, a judge finally gave Smoot back her freedom. She continued to spiral and died in September of unknown causes.

Williams did not respond to repeated and detailed requests for comment via phone, text message, email, and social media, nor did the attorney who represented her.

The Office of Public and Professional Guardians found that Williams had indeed made false statements on her applications, which she signed under penalty of perjury. The only consequence was three hours of training on guardianship ethics.

Intimate Control

The powers that guardians wield over their wards extend into the most intimate areas of their lives. When Britney Spears spoke out against her guardianship in June, her testimony that she had been banned from removing an IUD even though she wanted to have more children sent shockwaves across America. Lawyers for her father denied the claim—but many commentators questioned whether the practice would be legal and drew comparisons with the forced sterilization of women with low incomes, people of color, and people who are incarcerated.

But guardians in many states can put people on long-term birth control without even seeking a court order first, since the decision can fall under their sweeping powers to make medical decisions on behalf of their wards. Guardians can also move to have wards permanently sterilized, and while some states require court approval, others have no clear law on the topic.

Without any requirement for court filings, there's no way to track how often guardians have forced wards to get IUDs, Depo-Provera shots, or other contraceptive measures. But *BuzzFeed News* found cases in which wards said they were put on long-term contraception and even sterilized against their will.

One public guardian in Nevada, for example, forced a young woman to receive Depo-Provera shots, records show, on the basis that she had borderline personality disorder and wasn't competent to make her own medical decisions. A few years later, the public guardian petitioned the court for permission to sterilize the woman permanently, arguing that it was what she now wanted. The court granted the request.

In Colorado, a woman with a developmental disability claimed in a lawsuit that her mother, who was her guardian, had convinced a hospital to sterilize her without her consent immediately after she gave birth to a son. She "wanted to have more children, and continues to want more children," the lawsuit said, arguing that if it wasn't for her intellectual disability, the hospital would not have sterilized her "upon the behest of a third party." She did not win the case.

In Minnesota, a young man's guardians "unconscionably and untruthfully" persuaded him to consent to a vasectomy by telling him it was the only way he could continue seeing his girlfriend, according to court documents filed by his attorney. The man, who has fetal alcohol syndrome and bipolar disorder, said he did not understand the consequences of the procedure—and his guardians did not seek approval beforehand, even though that's the law in the state.

Fixing the System

Advocates say there are clear fixes that could make the guardianship system fairer: more federal oversight, better data collection, stronger training for court clerks, higher education standards for guardians, caps on the number of wards someone can have under their care, mandatory legal representation for prospective wards, a ban on holding guardianship hearings without notifying the allegedly incapacitated person, increased use of alternatives to guardianship, and more effective checks on conflicts of interest among lawyers and expert witnesses.

Spurred by the Britney Spears case, lawmakers in both the House and Senate have been pushing for change. In July, Democratic Sens. Elizabeth Warren and Bob Casey Jr. urged the federal government to improve oversight by collecting national data related to guardianships, and a bipartisan bill was introduced in Congress that would establish more federal safeguards for wards.

States have enacted a number of reforms, too. A recent Minnesota statute, for example, mandates that people under the age of thirty cannot be put under guardianship for longer than six years. Florida has boosted funding to the Office of Public and Professional Guardians, the agency tasked with overseeing the conduct of professional guardians, and a new statewide task force has been established to recommend further improvements.

Thirteen states and DC have passed laws encouraging an alternative to guardianship known as "supported decision-making." Under this system, people with disabilities form trusted networks to help them make choices, instead of submitting to a guardian who makes every decision for them. A growing number of people nationwide have been released from their guardianships after their lawyers argued that supported decision-making would work instead. Other states have established new programs to address guardianship abuse and fraud and have adopted a uniform law that could help standardize such changes.

The biggest challenge, however, lies in turning law into practice, experts say. For example, most states already require judges to consider less restrictive alternatives before ordering guardianship, yet in practice this often does not happen.

Ultimately, advocates say, until public attitudes change, people with disabilities and mental health conditions will remain vulnerable to overreach and abuse.

"People with disabilities in our society are treated as if they were children, sometimes as if they were villains, when really they are just people," the disability rights lawyer Viviana Bonilla López said. "We all deserve to decide what happens with our own lives and our own bodies. That's fundamental."

Harper's

"Every other infliction can eventually be withstood or overcome, but not humiliation," writes Vivian Gornick in *"Put on the Diamonds"* (the words taken from an episode in George Eliot's novel Daniel Deronda). *"Humiliation lingers in the mind, the heart, the veins, the arteries forever. It allows people to brood for decades on end, often deforming their inner lives."* Subtitled *"Notes on Humiliation,"* this essay, said the ASME judges, *"skillfully interweaves examples drawn from literature, film, politics, the #MeToo movement, and Gornick's own experiences to evoke the 'derangement of the senses' that humiliation causes—in which, however, may lie a deep well of creative strength."* Gornick is *perhaps best known for her memoirs* Fierce Attachments *and* The Odd Woman and the City. *Her most recent book is a collection of essays,* Taking a Long Look, *published in 2021.*

Vivian Gornick

Put on the
Diamonds

Sheila and I were best friends from age ten to thirteen. I
lived four blocks from our grade school and she, two.
She'd wait for me to pass her house in the morning and
then we'd fall in step as we entered the building. From then until
five-thirty in the afternoon—when our mothers demanded our
presence at home—we were inseparable. After the summer we
turned thirteen, something unimaginable happened: Sheila was no
longer in front of her house in the morning when I passed; she
no longer saved a seat for me in class; and after school she simply
disappeared. At last it registered that whenever I spotted her, in
the hall or the schoolyard, she was in the company of a girl new to
the school. One day, I approached the two of them in the yard.

"Sheila," I said, my voice quivering, "aren't we best friends
anymore?"

"No," Sheila said, *her* voice strong and flat. "I'm best friends
now with Edna."

I stood there, mute and immobilized. A terrible coldness came
over me, as though the blood were draining from my body; then,
just as swiftly, a rush of heat, and I was feeling bleak, shabby, forlorn, born to be told I wouldn't do, not now, not ever.

It was my first taste of humiliation.

Fifty years later, I was walking up Broadway on a hot summer
afternoon when a woman I did not recognize blocked my path.
She spoke my name, and when I stared at her, puzzled, she
laughed. "It's Sheila," she said. The scene in the schoolyard flashed

before me, and I felt cold all over: cold, shabby, bleak. I wouldn't do then, I wouldn't do now. I would never do.

"Oh," I said, and could hear the dullness in my voice. "Hello," I said.

·   ·   ·

Anton Chekhov once observed that the worst thing life can do to human beings is to inflict humiliation. Nothing, nothing, nothing in the world can destroy the soul as much as outright humiliation. Every other infliction can eventually be withstood or overcome, but not humiliation. Humiliation lingers in the mind, the heart, the veins, the arteries forever. It allows people to brood for decades on end, often deforming their inner lives.

In *Jeanne Dielman*, the Belgian director Chantal Akerman demonstrates that exact proposition. The film is deliberately static, seeming to unfold in real time (it runs for three and a half hours). We are present during three days in the life of a thrifty widow with a teenage son. She cooks, cleans, shops for food, polishes her son's shoes, turns the lights on when she walks into a room and off when she leaves. And, oh yes, every afternoon she turns a trick. The trick is always some respectable-looking burgher whose coat she removes, brushes, and hangs up as though it were her husband's. Then one day we follow our protagonist and her client into the bedroom for the first time, where we see her lying submissively on the bed while the man on top of her humps away. The camera plays on her face: we see her eyes wandering aimlessly about, as we've seen the eyes of many women in the movies enduring unwanted sex. Then, suddenly, without a hint of what's coming, she picks up a pair of scissors and stabs the trick to death. The End.

I remember sitting glued to the seat when the screen went black, shocked but somehow not surprised. In an instant I realized: this is for all of them, including the dead husband. In or out of marriage she's been turning this trick all her life, lying beneath some man who pays the bills and for whom she has no reality. Why be surprised that such a deal, sooner or later, might produce the twist in the brain that only a stab in the chest can accommodate?

There are many things we can live without. Self-respect is not one of them. One would think the absence of self-respect would resemble much of a sameness, but the circumstances that can make people feel bereft of it are as variable as persons themselves. A psychiatrist who interviewed a group of men imprisoned for murder and other violent crimes asked each of them why he had done it. In almost all cases the answer was "He dissed me." On the other hand, I have a cousin, a doctor, who feels humiliated if he's shortchanged in a grocery store. His wife, too: if another woman is wearing the same dress at a party, she feels humiliated. I once had a mother-in-law whose critical observations amused me; my husband's next wife felt humiliated to the bone by them. She used to call me up and hiss into the phone, "Do you know what that bitch said to me this morning?" repeating sentences I had experienced as harmless. Then there is the testimony of Primo Levi in his concentration-camp memoir, *Survival in Auschwitz*. Levi tells us that given the massive amount of death and destruction going on all around him, it was somewhat remarkable that the humiliation of humiliations, the one that remained ever fresh in his mind for the rest of his life, was the moment when a *Kapo*, finding nothing to wipe his greasy hand on, turned to Levi and wiped it on his shoulder. That was the moment when Levi understood viscerally what it meant to be seen as a thing.

I believe the exaggerated response to humiliation is unique to our species. In feeling disrespected, each of these persons—Levi, the men in prison, my cousin, my ex-husband's wife—felt they had their right to exist not only challenged but very nearly obliterated. Their inclination then—each and every one—was to crawl out from under the rock that held their prodigious capacity for shame in place and stand up shooting. When we speak of ourselves as an animal among animals we misspeak. That is exactly what we are not. A four-footed animal may go berserk if attacked by another four-footed animal and not rest until it kills its attacker, but it will not experience the vengefulness that the walking wounded do when humiliated.

In a review by the critic David Runciman of a book written by the cricketer Shane Warne, I learned that Warne had wanted to be an Australian rules footballer but hadn't been good enough. When it turned out that he was brilliant at cricket—one of the great bowlers (pitchers) of all time—he took that path to fame and fortune. But he played the game "with a sliver of ice in his heart." He didn't necessarily hope to inflict injury on the batsman, but he definitely hoped to make him look a fool. "Deep down," Runciman writes, Warne wanted the batsman "to feel like shit, as bad as he once felt when he got the letter that told him he wasn't good enough."

What is remarkable here is how tenaciously Warne held on to the memory of having failed as a footballer. Every time he acted viciously on the cricket field he was reliving the moment when he imagined himself being discounted, holding the memory close to his heart, feeling warmed by its live fire, convinced that it energized his talent. Runciman does not say what Warne does with his outsized attachment to the wrong done him now that he's retired from cricket, but we have plentiful other examples of what happens to those who allow a sense of humiliation to hold them hostage all their lives.

When Harvey Weinstein was identified publicly as a sexual criminal, some wondered why he needed to force himself on nonconsenting women when surely there were many in Hollywood who would have slept with him without any struggle. The *New York Times* columnist Frank Bruni was right when he wrote that Weinstein's "hotel-room horror shows had as much to do with humiliation as with lust." The question then was: Whose humiliation did Bruni have in mind, Weinstein's or the women's? The answer is both. Think of all the taunting rejections Weinstein must have endured before he found himself in a position of power. How those memories must have traveled daily through his nervous system. How his skin must have crawled every time he looked in the mirror. What recourse did he have, primitive as he was, but to displace all that inner coruscation onto the women he felt free—legally (he thought) and culturally (he knew)—to strong-arm into servicing him? For such a creature no amount of reparations can ever be enough. The only thing that will do is to enact the crime of humiliation again and again in an emotional melo-drama wherein it matters not who is the principal and who the supporting actors.

The first time I understood humiliation as world-destroying was the morning I watched the World Trade Center evaporate from a street corner in Greenwich Village and found myself thinking, This is payback for a century of humiliation. I have sub-sequently discovered that a wealth of scholarly literature argues that a national sense of humiliation is, more often than not, a key motive in a country's decision to go to war. Evelin Gerda Lindner, a German Norwegian psychologist affiliated with the University of Oslo, has spent her professional life hypothesizing humilia-tion's central role in starting, maintaining, or stopping armed conflicts. A country understands itself (for whatever reason) to be discounted in the eyes of the world at large and passes down that sense of national insult, generation after generation, until a day arrives, however far in the future that day may be, when it requires retribution. Historians have observed that after its defeat in the Franco-Prussian War of 1870, an emotional sense of having been humiliated dominated the politics of France right up to the out-break of war in 1914; a similar humiliation, doled out to Germany after it lost World War I, led to the rise of Adolf Hitler and a level of vengefulness that nearly destroyed the Western world.

On the ground, that devotion to national insult is translated into what passes between the individual persons on either side. It is vital that the soldier refuse to see the man in enemy uniform as a fellow creature, otherwise he might not be able to pull the trig-ger; the best way to assure this refusal is to destroy the irreducible humanity all persons believe themselves to possess.

Primo Levi speaks often of the Nazi practice of "useless violence," by which he means that even though everyone in Auschwitz—guards, gatekeepers, commanders—knew that all the prisoners were headed either for the gas chamber or a bullet in the head, they were nonetheless beaten, screamed at, made to stand naked and to endure a roll call that kept them at attention for an hour or two several times a week, outside, in every kind of weather.

Before the wars in Afghanistan and Iraq, I thought Americans incapable of inflicting such horrors. After Abu Ghraib, I realized that Americans were as willing as the nationals of any other country to inflict the kind of humiliation that would make it a matter of indifference to the prisoner whether he lived or died.

In April 2011, the *New York Review of Books* published a letter written by two law professors, protesting the conditions under which the U.S. Army whistleblower Chelsea Manning was being held: in solitary confinement, asked every five minutes the question "Are you okay?" and the very week that the letter was written, forced to sleep naked and stand naked for inspection in front of her cell.

The law professors pronounced this treatment tantamount to a violation of the U.S. criminal statute against torture and defined the army's methods as, among other things, "procedures calculated to disrupt profoundly the senses or the personality." Indeed. I think if I were forced to stand naked in public it would definitely disrupt my personality—profoundly. The piece was headed "Private Manning's Humiliation."

•   •   •

Humiliation commands the shape and texture of the works in which the following characters appear: George Eliot's Gwendolen Harleth, Emily Brontë's Heathcliff, Alexandre Dumas's count of Monte Cristo, Nathaniel Hawthorne's Hester Prynne, Charlotte Brontë's Jane Eyre, Herman Melville's Bartleby, F. Scott Fitzgerald's Gatsby, Edith Wharton's Lily Bart, Richard Wright's Bigger Thomas. Many of these characters are made to suffer materially, but their material pain is as nothing next to the immaterial pain they suffer simply by being in a position that inflames the disgust and anxiety of those who seem to hold all the cards but need the tormented inferior close by—just to make sure.

Of these characters, the one whose destiny always stops me in my tracks is Gwendolen Harleth, from Eliot's 1876 novel, *Daniel Deronda*. She could pose for a public statue dressed in Grecian robes on whose pedestal is written the single word "Humiliation."

Gwendolen is young, beautiful, marvelously selfish, and at the age of eighteen, already knows that marriage for a woman is slavery. But her widowed mother and sisters are on the brink of destitution, so marry she must—the richest man who will have her. Enter Henleigh Grandcourt, a character so broadly drawn he's a caricature of the evil Victorian aristocrat: remote, possessed of a scorn for humanity strong enough to cut through steel. While courting, Grandcourt is calculatedly patient, considerate, even generous, and Gwendolen is lulled into forsaking her fear of losing her independence, imagining that she will easily manipulate him to her own satisfaction. Once married, however, Grandcourt quickly displays the special contempt reserved for a prize that, now secured, is no longer valued. He never lays a hand on Gwendolen, hardly ever inflicts himself sexually, or even cares much about how she occupies herself. But she is constantly made to be aware (very much like Isabel Archer in *The Portrait of a Lady*) of the prison her husband's iron will (sanctioned by law and social custom) has constructed around her. Before a year has passed, Gwendolen realizes her marriage is a life sentence.

There is a moment in the book that I have always found to exemplify the derangement of the senses that everyday domestic humiliation can lead to. Grandcourt possesses a set of family diamonds meant to be worn in a woman's hair. Gwendolen hates the diamonds, as she now hates and fears her husband. One evening as the two are preparing to go out to a party, Gwendolen parades before Grandcourt in all her silk-and-satin beauty, hoping to put him in a good mood. She asks if her appearance pleases him. He looks appraisingly at her:

> "Put on the diamonds," said Grandcourt, looking straight at her with his narrow glance.
>
> Gwendolen paused in her turn, afraid of showing any emotion, and feeling that nevertheless there was some change in her eyes as they met his. But she was obliged to answer, and said as indifferently as she could, "Oh, please not. I don't think diamonds suit me."

"What you think has nothing to do with it," said Grand-court, his *sotto voce* imperiousness seeming to have an evening quietude and finish, like his toilet. "I wish you to wear the diamonds."

"Pray excuse me; I like these emeralds," said Gwendolen, frightened in spite of her preparation. That white hand of his which was touching his whisker was capable, she fancied, of clinging round her neck and threatening to throttle her; for her fear of him, mingling with the vague foreboding of some retributive calamity which hung about her life, had reached a superstitious point.

"Oblige me by telling me your reason for not wearing the diamonds when I desire it," said Grandcourt. His eyes were still fixed upon her, and she felt her own eyes narrowing under them as if to shut out an entering pain.

Gwendolen wears the diamonds, and from then on dreams daily of an escape from her life that can be achieved only through death, either hers or his; soon enough she cares not which. The problem is solved when Eliot has Grandcourt fall off a boat while on holiday and allows Gwendolen to watch, mesmerized, as he drowns, begging her to throw him a rope. She is twenty-two years old; her life is over.

Put on the diamonds. For years, I could hear the menace in Grandcourt's voice whenever I saw or felt a woman struggling to break free of a despotic husband or lover. The piteousness of her position—that of one born to sanctioned subordination—always seemed emblematic to me of all the sadism allowed to flourish in intimate relations, doomed to end one fine day with a twist in the brain that can no longer bow beneath the yoke.

The tales of harassment in the workplace that surfaced when the #MeToo movement erupted in 2017 made my head swim, so wide-ranging were the accusations. From an arm rub and com-ment about a sexy dress to physical assault, they revealed behaviors that were simultaneously condoned as acceptable and experienced as denigrating. Among these tales I found particularly haunting precisely the homeliest examples of the sort of sexual offenses that have been shrugged off for generations, those that typified the instrumental use men and women commonly make of one another.

I imagine a woman walking into her office every workday for years, her throat tight, her stomach in knots, ready to swallow the dose of medicine she has to down if she is to hold this job. She speaks of this vile ritual to no one because she knows the men would laugh and the women roll their eyes, so commonplace is her complaint, but day by day, month by year, it feels as though something vital in her is eroding: some sense of personhood she was becoming aware of at exactly the moment she felt she might be losing it. It is the helplessness of her position that gnaws at her—the shock of realizing she has no agency in a culture that accepts as normal that which she experiences as degrading.

In 2017, when such women were coming out of the woodwork, their faces contorted with rage, their voices hissing and spitting, sending out a tsunami of resentment that threatened to drown all of us—women and men alike—they were demonstrating that if the insults go too long unaddressed, they might one day bring down a civilization.

Why *does* it hurt so much, do so much damage, twist us so horribly out of shape? Why does life seem unbearable—yes, unbearable—if we feel discounted in our own eyes? Or perhaps a better way to pose the question is to turn it around and ask, as a wise woman I know once did, Why do we need to think well of ourselves? Ah yes, I thought, when she put it that way, why *is* it not enough to be fed, clothed, and sheltered, given freedom of speech and movement? Why do we also have to think well of ourselves?

The question haunts every culture: no matter who, no matter where, we crave an explanation for why we are as we are; we manufacture bodies of thought and faith, century after century, that hold out the promise of an explanation that will assuage if not our suffering, at least our brooding. Sigmund Freud, whose analytic thought concentrated on curing us of the inner divisions that make us vulnerable to self-hatred, hit upon an explanation that for the longest time offered the greatest hope; out of his empathic imagination arose the therapeutic culture, armed with its encyclopedia of theories designed to address the dilemma.

Psychoanalysis explains that from the moment we are born we crave recognition. We open our eyes and we want a response. We need to be warm and dry, yes, soothed and caressed, but even more we need to be looked upon with interest and affection, as though we are a thing of value. Routinely, we get only some small amount of what we need, and sometimes we don't get it at all. The emotional conviction that we are not worthy sets in. From this condition none of us ever wholly recovers. Mainly, our feelings go underground and we struggle on, in general doing to others no more harm than was done to us. Some of us, however—starting with those born into the wrong class or sex or race, or perhaps those whose physical appearance leads to mockery or rejection— are so damaged we obsess over being made to not think well of ourselves, and we become dangerously antisocial. The effort to overcome this primitive state of affairs is what preoccupies analysis, but all too often the endeavor drags on and on (and on!) while our demons refuse to relent; then therapy begins to feel like a romantic hope of salvation destined to fail.

In the 1940s, the social psychologist Erich Fromm asked the same question—in essence, why we succumb so readily to humiliation—and arrived at a place some distance, but not a great one, from that of Freud. Fromm's thesis in his great work, *Escape from Freedom*, was a simple one; like Freud before him, Fromm did not hesitate to use the convention of mythic storytelling to make his insight vivid for the common reader.

In Freud's case the story derived from the classics; in Fromm's, from Genesis. Human beings, he argued, were at one with nature until they ate from the Tree of Knowledge, whereupon they evolved into animals endowed with the ability to reason and to know that they felt. From then on, they were creatures apart, no longer at one with the universe they had long inhabited on an equal basis with other dumb animals. For the human race, the gift of thought and emotion created both the glory of independence and the punishment of isolation; on one hand, the dichotomy made us proud; on the other, lonely. It was the loneliness that proved our undoing. It became our punishment of punishments. It so perverted our instincts that we became strangers to ourselves—the true meaning of alienation—and thus unable to feel kinship with others. Which, of course, made us even lonelier. The inability to connect brought on guilt and shame: terrible guilt, outsized shame, shame that gradually developed into humiliation. If there was any stigma that survived the exile from paradise—that is, the womb—any proof that we were unfitted to make a success of life, it was this. How else to explain all the centuries in which human beings have been mortally ashamed of admitting they were lonely?

Where Fromm joins Freud is in asserting that the very development—consciousness—that brought about our rise and then our fall is the only one that can release us from this pervasive sense of aloneness. The problem is that the consciousness bestowed on us is just barely sufficient; if we are to achieve inner freedom, it is necessary that we become more (much more) conscious than we generally are. If men and women learn to occupy their own inspirited beings fully and freely, Fromm posited, they will gain self-knowledge and thus no longer be alone: they will have themselves for company. Once one has company one can feel benign toward oneself as well as others. Then, like a virus that had been stamped out, humiliating loneliness would surely begin to wane. This is a proposition we're required to take on faith.

The great Borges thought it best to look upon our broken inner state as one of life's great opportunities—to prove ourselves deserving of the blood pulsing through our veins. "Everything that happens," he wrote, "including humiliations, misfortunes, embarrassments, all is given like clay," so that we may "make from the miserable circumstances of our lives" something worthy of the gift of consciousness.

I'll leave it at that.

Audubon

FINALIST—ESSAYS
AND CRITICISM

"What do we do with a racist, slave-owning birding god almost 200 years dead?" asks J. Drew Lanham in "What Do We Do About John James Audubon?," written for the publication that bears Audubon's name. "In this clear-eyed and unflinching essay," wrote the ASME judges, "the Black ornithologist J. Drew Lanham offers a reassessment of a man whose work he admires yet who was nonetheless, and unforgivably, a white supremacist; traces the history of racism that besets even bird watching; and argues for a more inclusive approach to environmental justice." A professor of wildlife at Clemson University, Lanham is the author of The Home Place: Memoirs of a Colored Man's Love Affair with Nature. Audubon was nominated for the National Magazine Award for General Excellence for the fourth consecutive year in 2022, having won the award in 2021.

J. Drew Lanham

What Do We Do About John James Audubon?

My name is J. Drew Lanham, and I'm a Black American ornithologist. A Black birdwatcher. I confess here and declare now multiple identities—race and ethnicity, profession and passion. My love of birds lies at the intersection of these and renders me, and the minuscule percentage of others who would declare themselves the same, a rarity. Like the seldom-seen skulking sparrows so many of us seek, we are few and far between among an overwhelmingly white flock. I celebrate who I am, but like far too many of us "living while Black," I have also felt the frustration and pain of being discounted or disrespected.

Here we go again, some of you may be thinking, the race thing. Some are asking, "Wasn't Black Birders Week over months ago?" "That overblown Central Park thing was put to rest, right?" But just as I don't forget assaults with deadly words against friends, I must expand my Blackness and bird love beyond a week. Race is an issue in every aspect of American life, including birding, conservation, nature stewardship, and environmentalism writ large. For birders, it is an issue fledged from the nest of its "founding father," John James Audubon, and flies fully feathered now in present day.

John James Audubon *is* American birding; the name falls wistfully, almost like a mantra, from admirers' lips. Mention him, and like Edison and the light bulb or Zuckerberg and Facebook, more people than not will associate the name with a singular thing: birds. Though some would precede Audubon, and many come after, no one in ornithology is as revered. But what do we do when an origin story begins with a rancid "Once upon a time"? What do we do with a racist, slave-owning birding god almost 200 years dead? And what do we do with such a man who might have been in denial of his own identity?

You may have entered the realm of *Audubon* magazine to escape such a discussion. But it belongs here. The person whose name graces the publication, brands the national organization, and shapes how we perceive birds was more than most of his acolytes know—much less want to openly address. Questions about the bird man's own race, how he identified others, and how his soured, inhumane legacy carries forward will define the future course of the movement he inspired. They also hold truths about our ability to help birds, and ourselves.

So here I am, deconstructing—or perhaps more precisely, dissecting—John James. I'm also pushing beyond that exhumation to dig into current affairs. I'm concerned with how birding and bird conservation rest too comfortably in a homogenized stasis. I'd like to show what they can and should be.

•   •   •

I don't just love birds, I'm in love with birds. They are an obsession that first took hold at about eight years old when my designs on boy-powered flight fell hard to gravity. After an arduous migratory route from childhood dreams of being a red-tailed hawk through expectations of an engineering career, I finally flew. Today I'm a cultural and conservation ornithologist who spends most waking hours (and some sleeping ones) thinking about birds. Some of my thinking is about others similarly given over to chasing, naming, listing, saving, and in almost any way connecting to birds.

From my earliest day of bird envy, I understood the almost mythical power of Audubon. I read everything I could get my hands on. In every book, John James was woodsy and heroic, the kind of birdwatcher I wanted to be. While others on the playground pretended to be cowboys or astronauts, I imagined myself in buckskins with a telescope and shotgun. I wanted to be like Audubon, watching and collecting birds. I would kill the birds as he did and paint them. I just happened to be Black.

From the outside looking in, there was a lot to admire. Audubon roamed the continent in the early nineteenth century cataloging its avifauna in a way none of his contemporaries did (and no one really has since), bringing attention to its amazing diversity of birds and opening the door to North American ornithology. Audubon's idea was to paint every bird. He tried his damnedest and, in the end, produced *Birds of America*. It must have been shockingly beautiful to behold: life-size bird paintings, artfully observed and illustrated, in a series of three-foot-tall plates engraved on "double elephant folio" paper. (The price for a set was certainly shocking: about $30,000 in today's dollars.) These plates were later bound into enormous books, and now people visit the extremely rare copies in libraries and museums to reverently watch the pages turned by gloved docents. Audubon's work became canon, and John James himself akin to birders' Jesus. Like water to wine, anything the name "Audubon" touches is somehow imbued with ascendant conservation powers.

The litany of North American bird noticers/naturalists/conservationists have all belonged to the same storied club—Wilson, Bartram, Grinnell, Roosevelt, Pinchot, Thoreau, Muir, Darling, Leopold, Peterson, *etcetera ad infinitum*. It is a pantheon that speaks to the white patriarchy that drives nature study in the Western world. Rachel Carson and Rosalie Edge—two women who played a pivotal role in bird conservation—break the pattern, but Black, brown, or Indigenous figures are hardly ever acknowledged as contributors to the cause of "saving things." As important a role as George Washington Carver played in protecting the soil of the South and Majora Carter plays as a founder of the environmental justice movement, their contributions go mostly unnoticed outside of Black History Month, and barely then.

In my life as a conservation professional, I've been steeped in this white history, told from a white perspective. And I've seen firsthand how the organizations that grew from this foundation are likewise predominantly white, with a homogenized point of view. I was a board member of many, including the National Audubon Society. I was a rarity there, too. I resigned in 2020 because the essential work of diversity and inclusion remained siloed, at the highest levels, from priorities like climate change, habitat conservation, and community science. Audubon's policies and practices diverged from my own, and I had to remove any conflict of interest in order to maintain my personal agenda of connecting conservation and culture. Yes, environmentalism and conservation are inarguably worthy causes. But without consideration for human injustices, they are wildly unbalanced in ways that are coming home to roost like so many homeward-bound crows at dusk to the tall pines.

Now, in the midst of isolation and quarantine and a nearly yearlong, rending stretch of protests and debates, rioting and sedition, the nation faces an identity crisis of its own. The seemingly innocuous world of watchers who hold birds and birding as escapes hasn't itself escaped a glancing blow. Injustice and inequity don't have statutes of limitations and don't cease to exist where people sling binoculars. Racism doesn't stop at the borders of migratory hotspots.

Last summer, the Sierra Club denounced its first president, John Muir, as a racist unworthy of organizational adulation. Muir is a founding father of the American wilderness movement; he also characterized Blacks as lazy "sambos" and Native Americans as "dirty." The National Audubon Society followed suit, stating that Audubon, too, was a racist. He enslaved at least nine people. He mostly referred to them as "servants" and "hands," but never seemed especially concerned that the people helping him could be bought, sold, raped, whipped, or killed on a whim. Then again, relatively few men of his time did. Presidents did not. Why would he? Audubon's callous ignorance wouldn't have been unusual for a white man. It would have been de rigueur—an expectation of race and class that he enjoyed.

Both Muir and Audubon were "men of their time" and judged accordingly, but could have been men ahead of their time and judged otherwise. The stories of icons and heroes are critical, but what happens when truth rubs the shine off to reveal tarnished reality? As patriarchy, privilege, and the closely allied sin of racism persist, how many monuments to environmentalism and conservation need to come down—or at least be rigorously inspected? And as we consider how we treat past memory, do we need to rethink our current mission?

•   •   •

Playing Audubon or any other mostly white character as a ten-year-old, I never thought too deeply about race. Identity was suspended in fantasy. Growing into adulthood as a Black American, race is ever present and too frequently brought to my attention as bias or prejudice wrought by individuals and institutions. Bias plagues my life, including that portion of it dedicated to loving birds and bird-loving people. And so I am forced to think about it even when I'd rather be doing something else, like watching birds or thinking about the people I like watching birds with.

A simple question from my nonbirding wife, Janice, brought another facet of Audubon's identity to mind. She was in the New Orleans African American Museum of Art, Culture, and History and called to check in. "Hey, did you know that Audubon was Black?" she said. It was one of those questions to which she already knew the answer but took premature glee in knowing that I might not. "Ummmm . . . I knew there was a question about it." In fact, I didn't know for sure that Birding Jesus was possibly a person of color, but my ego pushed a slight lie forward. "Well," she said, "apparently they know it down here 'cause I'm standing here looking at James John Audubon" (she usually gets his name reversed for some reason) "and he's on the wall of the museum. They obviously know something y'all don't."

I bristled at the "y'all." After all, I am a birdwatcher, but I'm a Black man. I didn't have a problem with Audubon being Black-ish. "What do you mean 'y'all'?" I asked. "You bird people," she shot back. "Y'all need to get a clue."

We hung up, but it was clear that Audubon's identity was more fact to her than to me. Like many birders it was some sort of tangent I hadn't paid much attention to. Audubon's father was a French ship captain who traded slaves. Audubon's mother was French or Haitian Creole. By some definitions, a Creole is a person of mixed white and Black descent. Definitions of race and identity have morphed over time to both cover and expose truths, so we may never know who John James Audubon's mother was. But my wife saw his portrait hanging on the wall because there was a belief in his Blackness strong enough to ignore the biographers who say there was no doubt about Audubon's whiteness. Blackness in America is a function of perception by some, belief by others. Proof sometimes lies in what cannot be proven. The difference between white burden of proof and Black knowing is emblematic of our national cognitive dissonance on race.

Maybe I'd been blinded by the brilliance of Audubon's art and still stuck in the boyhood hero stories that didn't mention his parentage, or his thinking toward humanity. Maybe I'd been made myopic by a mutual love of birds. But that someone with no stake in the birding game could call him as others saw him brought home the glancing blow. That one drop of knowledge was enough for my wife to definitively ID him, but it opened a whole line of questioning for me.

Historians continue to debate Audubon's Blackness, but for the sake of current argument, let's just say the birding icon *wasn't who he appeared to be.* What if he was really just good at "passing"— being a Black man of passable whiteness such that he was able to travel around 1800s America without pause or fear. Look at paintings of Audubon (some of them selfie portraits—J. J. would have LOVED cell phone cameras) and he's as robust, courageous, and white as any wilderness explorer ever was. An aquiline nose and sun-flushed face always peering into whatever wild place he would next venture to watch, kill, paint, and eat birds. Audubon was a master at marketing his own image and by all accounts sought to distance himself from any ideas about his background that would taint his privileged skin.

Deconstructing holiness is hard work. As I made the speaking circuits over the next few years, talking bird science but also trying to connect dots between conservation and culture, I began to float the idea of Audubon's questionable heritage. "What about holding him up as a multiracial role model?" I asked. After all, there was a Black POTUS (half-white) and a "Cablinasian" (Tiger Woods's contrived name for Caucasian, Black, Indian, and Asian heritage) golfer who found widespread acceptance and acclaim. There seemed to be a different standard for John James, though. The first time I posed the question at a meeting in Arizona, I could almost hear squirms. There were plenty of other issues to dredge up that dealt more immediately with making birding more colorful; why this?

A couple of people got up and left. Maybe their parking meters were running out. But the tone in the room changed. I was amped up by it. I had no definitive answer to the question I asked. I dropped it as an exercise in heuristic exploration, one that might begin to open some binoculared eyes to larger questions of identity and inclusion. I asked again at talks all over the country, anywhere I had an audience. I wanted to gauge attitudes of acceptance, or at least open minds. The question isn't just about Audubon's identity but our own. Who are we as a culture, as a community?

For years I had assumed that all the hybrid cars at birding festivals with leftish-leaning bumper stickers meant I was in a world of allies who would understand "the struggle" of Black people. I know better now and cast those assumptions aside to understand more realistically who we are—a subset of the whole.

•   •   •

As we tear down monuments that deserve to be dismantled and hopefully melted down and cast into monuments of truly heroic—not perfect, but heroic—people, what difference would it make if an ancestry test revealed the "taint" of sub-Saharan African in John James Audubon? Would the great egret flying proudly white on the emblem of the national organization have to be changed to something . . . less white? Perhaps a common raven or sooty tern? Would those birders who left the room where I made such audacious mulatto claims come back in? And does the possibility that John James Audubon may have been a man of mixed race give him a pass on his racism?

Racists do not get passes because of identity confusion or historical context. None.

I do not believe perfection should ever be the standard, but I know we can do better. The public watches unarmed Black people being killed and assaulted daily in high def and the protests that ensue. Meanwhile there are counterprotests, riots, and attempts to deconstruct democracy by white people who'd just as soon have those Black people remain in a certain space. Almost all of this is rooted in a history that Audubon witnessed near the apex of its horrific turn. He chose to watch birds and be inhumane. What choices will be made now by conservation organizations? Will there be excuses of context to brush over with paint the truths that need to be revealed? Seeing beauty and advocating for justice are not mutually exclusive acts. I would argue that one can feed the other powerfully. Perhaps that might appear in a mission statement somewhere.

Whoever Audubon was, he haunts my world. I own a budget reprint of *Birds of America*, a treasured gift from my older brother Jock. I've picked up a palm-size version I keep in my writing shack, as well as a compressed copy of *The Viviparous Quadrupeds of North America*, John James's go at mammals; several biographies; and a few replica prints bought from consignment and thrift stores. Audubon's art is a monument. I look at his portraits of "southern birds"—my birds, the ones I know best from my South Carolina home: loggerhead shrikes, yellow-breasted chats, northern mockingbirds, swallow-tailed kites. The beauty of the work is undeniable. The birds would seem to fly or flush from painted page into present time.

But then there's something behind what was portrayed, and I'd like to know more about what we can't see. One of my favorite portraits is of Carolina parakeets (*Carolina Parrot*, plate 26), the way the now extinct Psittacids poked their dexterous feet outward and looked beyond two dimensions into a world they would disappear from forever. Perhaps it was the final look before Audubon laid waste to them. Maybe in their superintelligent parrot minds they knew something we didn't. I'm wondering how many of the Black people Audubon encountered saw what he seemed to work so hard to hide.

I venture deep into Google to try and shake loose some definitive answer as to who he was. I talk to knowledgeable sources who volley identity back and forth with me. Audubon, in any form, seems to have been an arrogant, sometimes prickish birder who had little regard for anything other than himself or the birds he sought. I know some birders like that. Hell, some would probably describe me that way. But then, beyond that, John James Audubon had that elephantine blind spot that opened his eyes wide for birds and shut them tight to humanity.

Maya Angelou advised that when people show you who they are, believe them. Audubon showed his full hand in "The Runaway," a story he published in the five-volume companion to *Birds of America*. Whether Audubon was Black or not holds little sway to me considering his own account of a chance meeting in a Louisiana swamp, where the lord god birds still reigned and flocks of Carolina parakeets huddled in the hollows of thousand-year-old cypress trees.

I can see Audubon there in the glow of firelight, probably with a sack of dead birds he intended to skin, eat, and paint. I wonder if he shared that flesh with the likely hungry and exhausted family he encountered, a family that had been enslaved, separated, and sold until the father reunited them all for an attempt at a free life. They are all sitting around the fire. Their clothes have been torn and soiled, fleeing hounds and slave catchers. The children are frightened. Trembling. Crying. Cold. They tell a distracted John James of the cruelties they endured. Audubon barely hears them; he is probably preoccupied with the birds he's seen and wants to see. He needs to pose the empty skins and paint. But then there are these Negroes in the way. Their stories and pleas fall on ears tuned in to hear a barred owl calling. And then John James, who momentarily recognizes something human and perhaps even familial in the faces of the free Black people sitting with him, tells the family that he will return them to their owner. I imagine he's convinced it is the white thing to do, and here in Louisiana he must keep the story straight. Imagine, if you will, the horror of the moment of being Black and free but knowing you'd soon be re-chattled. I wonder in that moment what I would have done.

If his story is to be believed, the family was "gladly" imprisoned again. Audubon was prone to exaggeration, but even if he made it all up, the lie is almost worse than the truth. Whatever humanity rested in Audubon, it all leaked out into the murky waters that night—or into the story he concocted to double down on his own white supremacy.

· · ·

While America roils in plagues of politics, viruses, and a persistent reckoning with its racist past and present, few have paid attention to the perceived progressive bastion of environmentalism. If the Muir revelation might be likened to one of the giant redwoods he worshipped, rife with heart rot, falling hard in a forest where we can all see and hear it, then John James Audubon's racism is the albatross rotting around the necks of those who would hold him in reverence. It is past smelling foul and beginning to reek.

Audubon enslaved people. He bought and sold humans like horses. That is evidence enough to recast the hero into a different role. The organizations bearing Audubon's name must press forward in this new light and decide who and what they want to be. Most of their members are white people with enough disposable income to dump into the coffers of overwhelmingly white-led organizations who have no need or desire for John James to be anyone other than the myth. No one willingly pays memberships for discomfort, but if "progress" is the end goal, then it's a likely partner.

Why muddy the ornithological water with race? Because racism pervades everything—even our love of birds. To see it blatantly codified in black and white is sad proof of a deeply ingrained bias. South Carolina Audubon Society reports from the early 1900s blame Black people for the decline in songbirds and waterfowl. Arthur T. Wayne, a luminary among South Carolina ornithologists, placed "negroes" among a litany of agents (alongside raccoons and house cats) deleterious to bobwhite quail in the book *Birds of South Carolina*. Racism even found its way into later ornithological texts. Sprunt and Chamberlain's seminal book, *South Carolina Birdlife*, published in 1949, cites the colloquial name of double-crested cormorants as "niggergeese"—a name for a bird perceived as deceptive and useless that's still being thrown around in duck blinds today. Perspective matters, and there is every reason to be concerned if institutions insist on not changing for the sake of tradition or donors easily offended.

Audubon may have passed as white, but most importantly, he passed on the chance to be a better human being. *That* is weight that should bear heaviest on all the preconceived notions, and I for one will have to tear down any monuments I've erected to him. Race and racism are immutable facts of my life. I am proudly a Black man. I am consistently punished for that identity, even among birders. I hold all these thoughts as I hold on to my Audubon books and prints. I won't burn them, but I'll see the Carolina parakeets and every other bird or animal he painted in a different kind of slanting light.

A few years ago I had a close encounter with an elephant folio myself. On a quick turnaround trip to Manhattan, my friend Jason Saul rushed me to the New-York Historical Society to lay eyes on a rare copy of Audubon's masterpiece. With time growing short, we got there only to find the gallery closed. I strained over the velvet ropes, trying my best to see the ornithological Holy Grail. No luck. As Jason cursed, then implored one staffer after another to let us in for "just a glance," I caught sight of an exhibit at the other end of the hall: *Black Citizenship in the Age of Jim Crow*. It was the worst kind of bird exhibit, but I was drawn in.

I wandered through a maze of misery, overcome. Blackness defined and then institutionally defiled. It was an American blind spot wrought over almost a century. I lost sight of the off-limits Audubon and immersed myself in the hard and heroic history of my people. As I neared the exhibit's end, Jason found me. He'd somehow gained entrance to the gallery. With my mind still lingering in the story of segregation, we entered—and there it was, looming even larger than I could've imagined. Beneath the glass, the folio's pages were opened to Baltimore orioles—two brilliant orange-and-black males and an equally beautiful, muted brown-and-ochre female perched on a pendulous nest.

Audubon's art lives like none other. That is fact. But that day, the facts of Jim Crow trumped his talent, a genius consumed by a system of bias he bought into. I later posted a photo of me staring at the black birds under glass, just down the hall from an exhibit on Black folks trapped under a ceiling that never let them see upwards. One was a history of which I had become a part, the other a history of which my ancestors had been a part. I made my train to Philly and thought about the irony all the way south.

· · ·

It's been a long haul from my early childhood flight-and-feather obsession to this complex thinking about just how the lives of birds can be "saved" even as we try to save ourselves from one another. Black lives matter now. They always have. Always will. It's critical to not just say the words or change some bird's colonialist name but also to change old mission to new, by persistent, sustainable acts to make the words live in policy and practice.

These days I sit in my side-yard writing shack, writing less than I should, Zooming more than I want, and thinking way too much. I'm spending hours pondering who I am in the context of who we are as a community of bird adorers, nature nurturers, and Americans divided into extreme factions. It's no easy feat watching birds without some echo of societal racism interrupting the songs of Carolina wrens. In one moment, I hope that evening grosbeaks will magically show up at my feeders in this finch irruption year; in the next, I think about the eruption of hate. I know it won't be magic that makes things better in America, but hard work and the people and organizations who say they care showing it.

I know that's possible. In the wake of racist encounters, I've been buoyed by an overwhelmingly positive and inclusive cadre of kindred spirits—good people who treat me with respect and love, people who want better for humans and birds. And, yes, there are organizations trying to do better. In this current call for awareness, they are digging deep and deserving of affirmation and support. But then, painful as it may be, we need to call truth to power—past and present—where it is stuck or regressive.

I look over my shoulder as I work on this essay, and there, on the shelf, is John James Audubon, memorialized on a book's dust jacket. His eagle eyes are fixed, it seems, on me. His vision of "my kind" is clear. And now, I see him more clearly, too. He was a despicable racist birder of his time, and now of this time. I'm hoping such an identification isn't one I have to make often. But I know many blind spots remain in the wake of a legacy that can either be ignored to a fate of stagnancy and decline or be learned from to move, with eyes wider open, toward a more equitable, just, and inclusive conservation future. I have a small, framed picture of George Washington Carver, the nature-loving Black man who saved the South's soil and was rumored to have loved birds as I do. I desire a better view and believe I've found just the spot for the Tuskegee professor, between me and John James. There. Blind spot gone.

New York Times Magazine

WINNER—REPORTING

This is what the ASME judges said about "The Collapse": "Drawing on a decade of experience in Afghanistan; a deep knowledge of its language, culture, and politics; and his own unfathomable courage, Matthieu Aikins provided readers with an astonishing portrait of the fall of Kabul. An end-of-days rooftop party. A bike ride through streets filling with Taliban. Freshly released prisoners running free while Afghans who supported the government hide. 'The Collapse' is reported literature that makes accessible a moment in history that we would be unwise to forget." Aikins's story for The Atlantic "Our Man in Kandahar" was a finalist in Reporting in 2012; his Rolling Stone story "Yemen's Hidden War" was nominated in Reporting in 2016. His first book, The Naked Don't Fear the Water: An Underground Journey with Afghan Refugees, was published earlier this year.

Matthieu Aikins

The Collapse

Part 1. The Withdrawal

After dark on a mild July evening, I made my way through a heavily fortified neighborhood in downtown Kabul. Over the years, the capital's elite had retreated deeper behind concrete walls topped with concertina wire; sometimes they even added a layer of Hesco barriers on the sidewalk, forcing me into the street as I passed. I buzzed at the home of a former government official, went inside, and climbed the marble stairs to a rooftop party. I'd been to a few of his gatherings over the years, some of them raucous with laughter and dancing, but this was a quiet affair, with a small group of Afghan men and women, mostly young and stylishly dressed, sitting in a circle under the lamplight.

The mood was grim. In recent weeks, large areas of the north, places that had not historically supported the Taliban, had suddenly fallen. A new assessment by the U.S. intelligence community predicted that the republic could collapse as soon as six months after the last American forces left. Yet President Biden was pressing ahead with the withdrawal. That very night, American troops were flying out of Bagram Air Field, the giant base north of the capital where the United States had built a prison to house detainees.

I greeted the guests in Persian, and when I was introduced by the host as a foreign journalist, they fell silent. "Tell us what you think is going to happen to Afghanistan," a young woman said, turning to me. She added sarcastically, "We've probably said the same things already, but we believe them when we hear them from a foreigner."

Like many people in Washington and Kabul, I thought six months was overly pessimistic. The government had a considerable advantage in men, weapons, and equipment, and it still held the cities. Surely, I said, Afghanistan's power brokers, fractious and corrupt as they were, would unite and rally their forces for their own survival.

As civilians, the guests at the party faced a stark question that summer, which they repeated to me: *Berim ya bashim?* Should we stay or should we go? Afghans had endured the agony of displacement and exile for forty years; the latest wave began in 2014 at the end of the U.S. troop surge, which was followed by an economic recession and the steady loss of territory to the Taliban. The following year, when Europe's borders collapsed and a million people crossed the Mediterranean in boats, Afghans were the second-largest group among them, after Syrians.

But the people at this party weren't likely to cross the mountains or sea with smugglers. Some had studied abroad and returned; others had no intention of leaving, like Zaki Daryabi, publisher of the scrappy independent paper *Etilaat-e Roz*, which had become known for exposing corruption within the administration of President Ashraf Ghani. Some were waiting for a chance to leave legally, with dignity, for work or school. Yet opportunities for Afghans were rare; they had the worst passports in the world when it came to travel without a visa. Now they were faced with the prospect of becoming refugees.

"I have seven visas in my passport—I can leave," an older Afghan businessman said. "What about the guy who has no chance, who just has a little house and a little shop?"

"One of them's me," Zaki said as he stood up for refreshments. He tapped himself on the chest and grinned ruefully. "One of them's me."

The Taliban were advancing on the capital, but the prospect of a peace deal frightened many of the guests as much as the continuation of the war, which had mostly afflicted the countryside.

At the insistence of the United States, negotiations between the government and the Taliban were underway in Doha, and a power-sharing agreement that would bring the Taliban to Kabul was seen as a disaster by the urban groups that had benefited from the republic's relative liberalism and international support, particularly working women.

At the insistence of the guests, a young poet, Ramin Mazhar, stood to read. Slender and stooped, Ramin had a gentle manner that belied his ferocious iconoclasm. Many of his poems, which he posted on Instagram, could be considered blasphemous by fundamentalists. I asked him earlier whether he had published any printed volumes. "No," he said, smiling. "They'd kill me."

He recited several of his poems; one, set to music by a singer named Ghawgha Taban, had become an anthem for Kabul's progressives. After Ramin was finished reading, someone put the song on the stereo, and the guests sang along from the rooftop, their voices growing louder:

You are pious, your kisses are your prayer.
You are different, your kisses are your protest.
You are not afraid of love, of hope, of tomorrow.
I kiss you amid the Taliban, you are not afraid!

•　　•　　•

The day before, I went to see Rangina Hamidi, Afghanistan's acting minister of education, at her home in Kabul. We were in the midst of the coronavirus pandemic's third wave, which had filled the hospitals with gasping patients, and the government had closed schools in response; Rangina herself was still recovering from an earlier bout with the virus. She coughed a little as she greeted me on the lawn, where her daughter's pet goat, Vinegar, stood watching us.

"I'm still having trouble with my memory," she told me. There were gaps in the lost year. Rangina had returned to work at the ministry, but she felt isolated, part of a political class confined to guarded compounds and armored cars.

In the living room, I embraced her husband, Abdullah, and marveled at how tall their daughter, Zara, who was in fifth grade, had gotten. She was just a baby when I met the family almost a decade ago in Kandahar, the Pashtun heartland that was the birthplace of the Taliban. I used to visit their home during my reporting trips there. I admired Rangina's ability to bridge two worlds as a driven entrepreneur who founded a handicraft collective and a woman enmeshed in the social life of Kandahar, one of the most gender-segregated cultures on the planet.

There were few women like Rangina in high office. She was born in Kandahar, but her family, escaping the communist regime, had gone to the United States as refugees in the 1980s, when Rangina was a child. She majored in women's studies and religion at the University of Virginia and considered herself a proud feminist; that was also when she chose to start wearing the hijab, which strengthened her connection to her faith.

Her father, Ghulam Haider, an accountant by trade, raised her to pursue the same opportunities in life as a man. He was her hero growing up. When she moved back in 2003 to help in the reconstruction of their country, he was inspired to follow her. At first, they were full of hope. She met Abdullah, an engineer, and founded the handicrafts cooperative; her father became Kandahar's mayor as the streets filled with American soldiers and the war intensified. In 2011, he was assassinated by a suicide bomber.

We sat down for dinner around a tablecloth spread on the carpet, and Rangina heaped my plate with samosas. "Thank you, Madam Minister," I teased, and we laughed. She told us the story of how she ended up in the cabinet. Four years earlier, she moved to Kabul after a friend recruited her as the first principal of Mezan, a coed private school that offered an international English curriculum. After a couple of years, the school's success had attracted the capital's elite. That, she believed, was why she received a call last year from the president. She thought Ghani wanted to know about Mezan's online learning programs for the pandemic; instead, he asked her to become his minister of education. Shocked, she asked for time to think.

Until then, Rangina had resisted joining the Afghan government; it was dominated by warlords who, she believed, were
responsible for killing her father, more so than the Taliban. Those
who took part became corrupt themselves or else were hounded
into leaving. But Rangina had long admired Ghani, who as minister of finance in the early years of the republic acquired a reputation as a brilliant technocrat, arrogant but personally incorrupt-
ible. When she met him in person at the palace, she was enthralled
by his intellect and his vision for reform—a true patriot, she
thought. Even his infamous temper reminded her of her father,
who didn't suffer fools.

Praising her work at Mezan, Ghani told her he wanted someone who could help him modernize Afghanistan's outdated curriculum. Rangina believed that the cultural gap that had grown
between the cities and the countryside could be bridged by mar-
rying a traditional version of Islam—one that drew on great
Afghan scholars like the poet Rumi—to contemporary teaching
practices. When she said yes, she became Afghanistan's first
female education minister since the communists, who brought
radical new opportunities for women to go to school and work in
the cities, gains that were wiped out after they were overthrown
by American-backed Islamists in 1992. The Taliban, who took
power four years later, instituted a ban on girls' education after
puberty. As a result of the American invasion in 2001, an entire
generation of Afghan girls had gone to schools and worked at
jobs that had been denied to their mothers—an entanglement
between the military presence and women's rights symbolized by
a mural outside the U.S. Embassy depicting the girls' robotics
team alongside the American flag.

With American troops finally leaving, that progress was now
at risk. In many areas controlled by the Taliban, which they
called the Islamic Emirate, girls were only allowed to attend
school until sixth grade, which Rangina's daughter would enter
next year.

•   •   •

The American withdrawal that had brought the republic to the brink of collapse began in February 2020. That month, the chief negotiator for the United States, Zalmay Khalilzad, dressed in a navy suit, sat at a table in Doha, Qatar, beside his turbaned Taliban counterpart, Mullah Abdul Ghani Baradar, signing copies of a document titled "The Agreement for Bringing Peace to Afghanistan." President Donald Trump, who came into office intent on ending the United States' longest war, had appointed Khalilzad, an Afghan-born, naturalized U.S. citizen who previously served as ambassador in Kabul.

Afghan government officials were notably absent from the table in Doha—the Taliban had long refused to negotiate with what they considered a puppet regime. But, as a result of the deal, in exchange for U.S. troops being out within fourteen months, the Taliban agreed to talks with the republic. Khalilzad and his team had hoped to make the final U.S. withdrawal conditional on peace between the Afghans, but Trump insisted on sticking to the timeline.

Now the vast gulf between republic and emirate had to be bridged. Khalilzad and his team, who believed that Baradar's side was genuinely interested in reaching a deal, proposed a power-sharing arrangement led by someone "acceptable to both sides"—a definition sure to exclude Ghani. "He hated that, because it means that he has to go," Khalilzad said of the Afghan president, whom he had known since they were boys. "I didn't see another way."

Ghani insisted that he would hand over power only to an elected successor. (He declined to respond to questions.) He proposed a caretaker government and new elections overseen by himself, a nonstarter for the Taliban. But Baradar and his team never offered a concrete counterproposal of their own, insisting instead on a prisoner exchange. Some believed that the Islamists were simply running out the clock until the U.S. forces left.

"The Taliban were not serious about peace," said Matin Bek, a senior official on the negotiating team. True power within the movement, he thought, resided not with Baradar's group in Doha but with the military commanders on the ground and the senior leadership hiding in Pakistan. It seemed clear to Bek that the rebels wanted to see if the government could survive on its own before they would accept anything short of outright victory. "If we could put up resistance and stand without the Americans, only then would they enter into real negotiations."

As the withdrawal progressed and the Taliban gained strength on the battlefield, Ghani grew isolated; allies deserted his government, some with an eye to Khalilzad's proposed power-sharing arrangement. And so the president came to rely on a shrinking core of trusted aides, who encouraged him to fight the Taliban. Foremost among them was Hamdullah Mohib, the president's right hand and heir apparent, who, as the national security adviser, controlled much of the information about the war that was presented to the president.

When Ghani selected Mohib to lead the office of the National Security Council in 2018, he had no military or security experience. He had studied computer systems engineering in Britain, where he emigrated as a teenager. In 2009, Mohib helped with Ghani's first, unsuccessful bid for president, running his website. Five years later, Mohib again volunteered for Ghani, who emerged as the improbable victor from a crowded field, though the disputed result had to be brokered by the United States amid evidence of fraud on all sides. In the West, Ghani was hailed by many as an educated reformer, coauthor of the book *Fixing Failed States*.

With Ghani in the palace, Mohib's rise to power began. The following year, at age thirty-two, he was sent to Washington as Ghani's ambassador. I got to know him in those days; easygoing and approachable, he seemed successful at the networking the job required, as he lobbied for U.S. support for the war effort. Three years later, Ghani brought him home to coordinate security policy, providing him a house next to his own on the palace grounds; their wives became close, and Mohib's young children played with the president, who was old enough to be their grandfather.

But Mohib quickly ran into trouble in his new role. As tensions grew between Kabul and Washington over Trump's plans for withdrawal, Mohib lashed out publicly against Khalilzad, accusing him of seeking personal power as a "viceroy." Outraged, the

Americans froze Mohib out of meetings for a year, and many expected him to lose his job, but the president stuck with him. Eventually, Khalilzad told me, he forgave Mohib at Ghani's personal request.

Mohib's team, like much of the Ghani administration, attracted a young cadre that reflected the president's technocratic values. Favoring tailored suits and speaking excellent English, many were raised or educated abroad, a type that some referred to as "Tommies," after the brand Tommy Hilfiger. "Young, educated, well-spoken, corrupt," said Sibghat Ghaznawi, a doctor who had been a Fulbright scholar in the United States with many of them. He said those who succeeded in the palace tended to excel in *chappalasi*, or brown-nosing, and telling their superiors what they wanted to hear. Last year, when Sibghat became a senior adviser to the office of the National Security Council, he said that Mohib warned him not to be too negative with the president. He already knows these things, Mohib told him, so you don't need to be reporting what he already knows.

•　　•　　•

In Afghanistan, the causes of state weakness preceded the Ghani administration and went deeper than any particular individuals: a forty-year civil war fueled by foreign superpowers, malignant corruption, and the Pakistani military's covert support for the Taliban. Above all, the U.S. occupation had created a state dependent on American troops and foreign money. As the republic entered a downward spiral, Ghani and his team struggled to consolidate their authority, alienating many who supported the republic. "They were always scared that if a potential deal happens between negotiators, they might be pushed out," Bek said.

Last year, for instance, Ghani ordered Mohib and the security council to review all district police chiefs and governors; ultimately, they replaced a majority, more than 200 of each, in what was seen as a damaging move in the middle of intensifying violence, one that sidelined local commanders. "The Taliban seized this moment and made peace with those people," Bek said.

The Islamic Emirate understood a basic lesson from Afghan history, which was that the nation's wars have often ended with individual commanders switching sides; that was how the Taliban rose to power in the 1990s and how they were defeated in just several weeks in 2001. After they signed a deal with the Americans in Doha, the Taliban promoted a policy of *afwa*, or amnesty, privately reaching out to power brokers with a clear message: The Americans are leaving, the republic is falling, but the emirate will forgive those who surrender.

In this battle for hearts and minds, the government's answer was its psychological-warfare program, overseen by Mohib and the security council. For years, the United States and its allies had funded psy-ops for the Afghan forces, spending heavily on advertising with the local news media. According to Afghan officials, the intelligence service, the National Directorate of Security, also made covert payments to Afghan journalists and civil society in exchange for their support. Another initiative was the creation of thousands of fake accounts on Facebook and Twitter dedicated to promoting the government and attacking its critics, work known by the Pashto term *Facebookchalawonky*.

But these messages did not spread much beyond the bubble world of the Kabul elite, where civil society had largely moved online, as demonstrations and events were targeted by terrorist attacks. Afghanistan's vibrant cyberspace must have been attractive to officials cloistered within blast walls and armored cars, but it failed to capture the reality of the countryside, where only a fraction of the population had access to the internet.

Sibghat, the adviser to the security council, told me that he was surprised how often social media was cited as evidence during meetings, where many made arguments that he considered demonstrably false: that the Taliban were militarily weak and it was simply that no one was taking proper action against them. That the insurgents could never act independently from Pakistan.

Above all, he said, many working for the council clung to the belief that the United States would never leave Afghanistan. There was simply too much at stake: counterterrorism, regional power, precious minerals. "They're not so stupid to have spent that money here and then leave," was how Sibghat characterized the prevailing view.

Bek and other officials also told me that there was a persistent belief within the government that the United States would remain, particularly after Biden defeated Trump. In fairness, there was hope within the U.S. establishment too; in February, a bipartisan group set up by Congress recommended making the withdrawal conditional on peace between Afghan parties—a move that the Taliban said they would react to by resuming attacks on U.S. forces.

Biden and his staff felt that they had been put in an untenable position by his predecessor; there were only 2,500 troops left in Afghanistan, so staying and fighting would have required a new surge. In April, Biden announced that U.S. troops would be out by September 11. "We will not conduct a hasty rush to the exit," the president said. "We'll do it responsibly, deliberately, and safely." Mohib, who answered written queries, told me he knew the Americans would leave: "We were planning for their departure." He said that what they consistently asked for was a "gradual and responsible withdrawal" that would allow Afghan forces to adjust. "We never got that."

• • •

On July 15, I went to the palace to see Mohib. Above the gate tower, a giant tricolor of the republic fluttered against a clear blue sky. After passing through security, I walked across the long, deserted lawn toward the building that held the Office of the National Security Council. I waited in the council's empty reception room until one of Mohib's staff members, a young woman who had studied in America, brought me upstairs to his office, where he sat behind his desk. Our conversation was mostly off the record. He seemed exhausted as we spoke about the desperate fighting in Kandahar City, which had been surrounded by the Taliban.

Only a few days before, there had been a farewell ceremony for Gen. Austin S. Miller, the long-serving U.S. commander. The military had completed 90 percent of its withdrawal, well ahead of Biden's deadline. This rapid pace was intended to reduce the risk of attack during the retreat, but it had a devastating impact on Afghan security forces. The U.S. military had spent billions to train and equip a force in its own image, heavily dependent on foreign contractors and air support. But the Afghan Army's notoriously corrupt generals stole their men's ammunition, food, and wages; while security forces were supposed to total 300,000, the real number was likely less than a third of that. Out in the districts, the army and the police were crumbling, handing over their arms to the Taliban, who now controlled a quarter of the country.

Ghani had repeatedly insisted that he would stand and fight. "This is my home and my grave," he thundered in a speech earlier in the spring. His vice president, Amrullah Saleh, and the security council were working on a post-American strategy called *Kaf*, a Dari word meaning "base" or "floor," which envisioned garrison cities connected by corridors held by the army and bolstered by militias, similar to how President Mohammad Najibullah clung to power for three years after the Soviet withdrawal. "It was very much the Russian model," said Bek, who returned to the government as the president's chief of staff that month. "They had a good plan on paper, but for this to work, you needed to be a military genius."

Earlier in July, Ghani was warned that only two out of seven army corps were still functional, according to a senior Afghan official. Desperate for forces to protect Kandahar City, the president pleaded with the CIA to use the paramilitary army formerly known as counterterrorism pursuit teams, according to Afghan officials. Trained for night raids and clandestine missions in the borderlands, the units had grown into capable light infantry, thousands strong. They were now officially part of the Afghan intelligence service and were known as Zero Units, after codes that corresponded to provinces: 01 was Kabul, 03 was Kandahar, and so forth. But according to the officials, the CIA still paid the salaries of these strike forces and had to consent to Ghani's request for them to defend Kandahar City that month. (A U.S. official stated that the units were under Afghan control; the CIA declined to comment on details of their deployment.) "They're very effective units, motivated, cheap," Mohib told me in his office, saying Kandahar would have fallen without them. "They don't need all sorts of heavy equipment. I wish we had more like them."

But the Zero Units had a reputation for ruthlessness in battle; both journalists and Human Rights Watch have referred to them as "death squads"—allegations that the CIA denied, saying they were the result of Taliban propaganda. I had been trying to track these shadowy units for years and was surprised to see them, in their distinctive tiger stripes, given glowing coverage on the government's social media accounts.

In Kabul, I met with Mohammad, an officer from one of the NDS units that operated around the capital, whom I had known for a few years. Mohammad had worked as an interpreter for the unit's American advisers and as an instructor for undercover teams that carried out arrests inside the cities. He said morale had plummeted among his men now that the Americans were leaving. According to Afghan officials, the station on Ariana Square was empty by late July. But Mohammad's team still received advice from the Americans. He showed me messages that he said were from the CIA, urging his unit to patrol areas around Kabul that had been infiltrated by the insurgents. "The airport is still in danger," one message said.

$\cdot \quad \cdot \quad \cdot$

The bubble world did not survive on psychological repression alone. At the end of June, I had visited an Afghan journalist named Shershah Nawabi at the office of his small news agency, Pasbanan. A group of young men and women sat at computers in the sparsely furnished office, guzzling energy drinks.

"Here, take this, I can't publish it," Nawabi said, handing me the draft of an article titled, in Persian, "Latest Report: 98 Percent of Government Officials' Families Live Outside Afghanistan."

The story listed the countries where the families of the Ghani administration were living, from the president—whose children grew up in the United States—on down. Out of twenty-seven cabinet ministers, it claimed, only two had families who resided in Afghanistan full time. "In the event of a crisis in the country," Shershah had written, "all government officials will consider fleeing."

He had been leaked the information by sources inside the government. "I made a mistake," he said. "I called them to try to verify the info." The NDS got wind, and one of his contacts at the intelligence service warned him not to endanger himself and his staff by publishing it.

It was clear that the consequences could be severe. There was growing concern in the international community that the Afghan republic was stepping up pressure on dissidents, especially after Waheed Muzhdah, a prominent commentator, was mysteriously assassinated at the end of 2019, an attack that many blamed on the government.

On July 11, Hedayatullah Pakteen, a young university professor who had been part of Muzhdah's circle, was arrested at his home by intelligence agents and held for seven nights. He said he was hung by his wrists and beaten repeatedly, in an attempt to get him to implicate several others who were accused of links with the Taliban. He was freed after a campaign from his friends in the media; he said he was forced to sign a document promising that he wouldn't give interviews anymore. His friend Abdul Ghafar Kamyab, a defense lawyer known for taking the cases of people accused of being Taliban, was snatched from the center of Kabul and was missing for more than forty days; he told me he was tortured severely, including with electric shocks.

According to Sibghat, the adviser to the office of the National Security Council, during the previous year he had participated in discussions about a group of lawyers and professors, former friends of Muzhdah, who called themselves peace activists. Sibghat told me that some officials had argued that they were Taliban sympathizers who should be arrested and "squeezed," which Sibghat understood as a euphemism for torture, until they agreed to stop speaking to the news media. Sibghat said he argued against it, pointing out that the communists had used such methods and failed; Mohib, as was his habit, remained aloof without saying anything definite.

Torture had long been common in the republic's prisons, as documented since 2011 by the United Nations. The UN's biannual reports cataloged a list of methods that included waterboarding and sexual assault, much of it carried out by the NDS, which was advised by the CIA and British intelligence (both agencies have denied any involvement with torture). That July, according to Afghan officials, the British had gone to the government to protest the existence of an NDS "hit list"; the Afghans fired two senior intelligence officials as a result. (The British government declined to comment.)

But as much as Kabul's journalists feared violence at the hands of the government, some worried that if the republic fell, worse would follow. At the end of July, I visited Zaki, the publisher I met at the rooftop party, to see how he was faring. We sat upstairs in the office of *Etilaat-e Roz*, cups of green tea and a packet of thin Esse cigarettes between us. "So what do you think is going to happen?" he asked with a smile.

Zaki was slight, with delicate features; he and most of his staff were Hazara, a historically oppressed Shia minority. He hadn't studied or lived abroad; he came from his village to Kabul for college and had founded his newspaper with a loan from friends. Over the last ten years, *Etilaat-e Roz* had slowly grown, scraping by with ad sales and subscriptions, resisting emoluments from powerful sponsors. It finally attracted foreign grants from places like the Open Society Foundations and had become known for its bold exposés of corruption in the government.

But with the system disintegrating, Zaki said that he had been thinking about the role of the gadfly differently. Criticism, like objectivity, made sense only within a shared set of values. "If we're talking political philosophy, and the question of a republic versus an emirate, well, that's different," he told me. "We're liberals. We believe in freedom and democracy."

The entire order had been dependent on foreign money, which created space for progressives like Zaki. But opposition to liberalism, or what was labeled "Westernization," was not confined to the Taliban. A broad streak of political Islamism cut across Afghan society; even among Hazaras, there were reactionary clerics who would have been happy to lash Zaki and the other men and women who hung out in the cafes near the office. Even under a power-sharing agreement, Zaki feared that freedom of the press and women's rights would be the first areas of compromise. But *Etilaat-e Roz* was his young life's work, his fourth child. Of course it was his other three children who made the choice to stay so difficult.

"Some of us have no choice but to keep doing this, because of what we believe," Zaki told me, with his rueful smile. He was going to remain as long as it was possible to do his work, as long as some foothold remained in the capital, however narrow, above the abyss that was opening. "We're working as if Kabul won't fall," he said. "If Kabul falls, *Etilaat-e Roz* will fall, too."

•　　•　　•

The republic's accelerating collapse, which had begun in the rural areas, soon reached the towns and district centers and finally the cities. On August 6, Zaranj, the capital of Nimruz, became the first provincial center to fall to the Taliban. Nader Nadery, a member of the republic's negotiating team from Nimruz, was called for a meeting with the president; he told Ghani that several of his relatives had been killed there. "I said that things are falling apart, the chain of command is broken, and people are not telling the truth to you," Nadery told me. "He answered, 'Yes, it will take another six months for us to turn it around.'" Stunned, Nadery left the palace wondering what kind of information the president was getting.

The day after Nimruz, a second capital, Sheberghan, fell. The next day, three capitals fell in the north: Sar-i-Pul, Takhar, and Kunduz.

That evening, I went to see Rangina. Zara's goat, Vinegar, which cried incessantly when left alone, had been taken into the guard shed for the night. I sat with Rangina and Abdullah, discussing the rumors of martial law circulating in the capital. Behind Rangina, I could see the reflection of the television in the window as the evening news played images of burning buildings, refugees, soldiers promising to die for their country. There were increasingly strident assertions about what a Taliban takeover would mean: stories about the forced marriage of young girls and widows to their fighters, even sex slavery. It would mean a return to the brutal days when men without beards were flogged in the streets, when women were not allowed to leave the home without a guardian, of public executions in soccer stadiums, of stoning and amputations, a massacre for everyone who had worked for the foreigners, a genocide for Afghanistan's Hazara minority.

In the past, these kinds of statements had always been followed by a "therefore": Therefore, America must not leave Afghanistan. Therefore, the war should continue. Now they were bleak predictions.

Rangina was frightened; the defense minister's home was blown up just a few days earlier. But she was also skeptical about some of the claims of Taliban savagery; she told me about how the staff at a local education ministry in a recently captured province had posed for a photo with their new Taliban boss, seemingly unharmed.

I had been planning to travel to the south for research, and I thought I might stay at the office of Rangina's cooperative, Kandahar Treasure. "Are you sure you want to go now?" she asked.

I didn't understand how quickly things were falling apart; maybe I was in denial, too. I went to Hamid Karzai International Airport three days later, on the morning of August 11. It was busier than I had ever seen it, a crush of passengers headed for the international terminal. The domestic side was quiet and tense. There were flights to the main cities of Herat and Mazar-i-Sharif, where, like Kandahar, battles were raging as the Taliban laid siege.

I went through security and sat in the boarding lounge, but I couldn't get in touch with the fixer who was supposed to pick me up in Kandahar. I couldn't get in touch with anyone there, in fact. Finally, a journalist friend called using the internet at the military base at the airport there. The Taliban had shut down the mobile networks in preparation for an all-out assault.

I got up and walked back out through security. The airline staff chased me down.

"I'm leaving," I said. "My trip has been canceled."

"Why?" They stared at me suspiciously.

"Because the phone networks are down. My office won't let me go."

I waited as they took a picture of my boarding pass and passport.

"He's the third person to cancel like this," one woman whispered anxiously.

When I got my documents back, I walked out against the flow of Afghans leaving their country. In the parking lot, there were groups of families, some crying and some silent, people in their Western outfits for travel, suits and T-shirts, girls with big up-dos and painted faces, matrons taking photos, men in turbans and karakul hats and prayer caps, the families embracing and then dividing, one part walking away, the others left watching.

The next day, Kandahar City fell.

Part 2. The Fall

For months, American leaders had been reassuring the Afghans that the military withdrawal did not the mean the end of U.S. engagement. Even after the last troops left on August 31, a 650-strong security force was supposed to remain behind to protect the massive embassy complex. And with the U.S. Embassy remaining, other Western organizations were more likely to stay, too, and supplies and financial aid would continue to flow to the republic.

But now the rebels were advancing as fast as their motorcycles could carry them. On Thursday, August 12, the city of Herat fell, and the Taliban captured Ghazni, seventy miles southwest of the capital. The Taliban had promised not to harm embassies and international groups, but the specter of the terrorist attack in Benghazi that killed U.S. diplomats in 2012 hung over the Biden administration. If even a single American was harmed, how could the Democrats defend having trusted the Taliban?

On Thursday, Biden ordered the embassy to shut down, and diplomats began destroying classified materials and shifting operations to the airport, where 3,000 U.S. soldiers and marines were being flown in to evacuate American citizens and their allies.

The Taliban would soon be at the gates. Could Kabul be defended? In theory, the capital boasted an impressive force: tens of thousands of soldiers and police officers, among them the country's most elite units. But even if Kabul could be held, Ghani seemed to have finally accepted that the war was lost and had opened secret talks with the Taliban. According to Afghan officials and U.S. diplomats, his envoy in Doha, Abdul Salam Rahimi, had been developing a back channel to the movement's leadership—not only to Baradar, the chief negotiator, but to the two powerful military deputies, Sirajuddin Haqqani and Mawlawi Yaqoub, son of the deceased leader Mullah Omar. The Taliban said they did not want to fight a bloody battle for Kabul, one that could mean the destruction of its banks and embassies and nongovernmental organizations, of its institutions, of the entire system.

On Thursday, the same day that Biden ordered the embassy to close, Rahimi, who had recently come back from Qatar, met with Ghani and Mohib and explained the proposal he had worked out with the Taliban, according to the officials. It was, in essence, a negotiated surrender; the Taliban would agree to a two-week cease-fire so that a delegation from Kabul could travel to Doha and work out the details of a transitional government. The Taliban would be in charge, but their rule would be "inclusive," which meant some republic officials might take part. Ghani would call a *loya jirga*, a gathering of notables, who would approve the deal. Then Ghani would resign and hand over power to the *jirga*, who would ask the Taliban to form a government.

Immediately after the meeting, Khalilzad's team in Doha, which had been in the loop about the back channel, received two calls. The first was from Rahimi, explaining that Ghani had agreed to the deal and was prepared to step down. (Rahimi did not respond to a request for comment.) The second was from Mohib. According to a U.S. diplomat involved in the negotiations, Mohib described the meeting in more conditional terms: Ghani would agree, but only if he was certain that his terms were being met. (Mohib denied this, claiming that he made "no reference" to Rahimi's discussions.)

That night, seeking clarity on Ghani's intentions, Antony Blinken, the U.S. secretary of state, spoke with him by video conference. According to the U.S. diplomat, Ghani said he would agree to the deal, to Blinken's relief. He was prepared to resign.

"It was closer to Rahimi's version than Mohib's," the diplomat said. Now the Afghans needed to carry out the peaceful transfer of power; they had, in theory, two weeks until the Americans left the airport, during which time the Taliban were supposed to remain outside the city.

The fate of the capital's millions of inhabitants hung in the balance.

•　　　•　　　•

On Friday, August 13, Kabul's residents awoke to news of the American evacuation. It was the Islamic day of rest. Though the Taliban were advancing, they still hadn't reached the nearest cities, and Kabul's streets were quiet as I drove to visit Rangina. She had invited me for lunch, and I found her in the hall by the kitchen, her sleeves rolled up, scraping out pumpkins alongside the cook. She cleaned up and joined her husband and me; she said she had just turned down a request from the National Security Council to turn the schools into shelters for refugees. "They just reopened the schools, and now you want me to close them?" she said. "If you want to do that, then declare martial law and do it."

People from neighboring districts were pouring into the capital, fleeing ahead of the Taliban, who the U.S. Embassy had warned were committing war crimes. Given Afghanistan's bloody history, they had reason to be fearful. In 1992, after the communist government collapsed, the mujahedeen tore the capital apart fighting one another. Four years later, the Taliban hanged the former president, Najibullah, and brandished whips against those who played music or shaved their beards. And in 2001, the United States and its warlord allies had hunted down the vanquished Taliban around the country; some were shipped off to detention centers and tortured. Now many were certain that despite their promise of amnesty, the Taliban would take revenge.

Rangina was getting calls from friends and relatives in the United States, telling her to flee before it was too late. "How many of us are you going to save?" she asked. "Thirty-five million? And then live with shame for the rest of my life? Because I had the American passport in my pocket, and I could just leave."

Her phone rang, and she answered on speaker. It was an employee from her cooperative in Kandahar City, who said that one of his relatives, a former police officer, had been pulled from his home by Taliban fighters and shot.

"Allah!" Rangina exclaimed.

"Be careful, be careful," Abdullah told him.

"We don't know what the hell is going to happen," Rangina said, after they hung up. We looked out the window, to where Zara was playing on the lawn with four other girls. Only one had an American passport. Rangina's mother, who is in the United States, had begged her to send Zara there, if she and Abdullah were too stubborn to leave. Rangina was considering it.

"This guy doesn't agree with me," she said, turning to her husband. "Unless he's changed his mind, I don't know. Have you?

You want her here? And if these wild animals come and, God forbid. . . ."

We looked at Abdullah, who was silent for a moment, as if some memory was stirring in him. He was older than Rangina. He had fought the Russians, lived through three regime changes, seen bodies in the streets and homes gutted by looting. And he knew how vicious the Taliban had been with their opponents in the 1990s. He was ready to give his life to protect his wife and daughter; he also knew that might not be enough. But he didn't want Rangina and Zara to be separated. "Then you leave, too," he said.

"I'm not leaving," Rangina replied.

.   .   .

That night, I went to a farewell party in the Green Zone, on the same blocked-off street as the Canadian and British Embassies. Many of the foreign nationals based in Kabul left the country during the pandemic to work remotely, but the few who remained had been as surprised as everyone by the sudden collapse of the government. As we gathered on the front lawn of an NGO guesthouse, gorging on hoarded wines and whiskey, some were in tears while others danced manically.

The decision of the U.S. Embassy to pull out meant that most other Western organizations were evacuating, too, although the embassies of Iran, Russia, and China—America's rivals—were going to remain. As a rumor spread at the party that the U.S. military would shut down commercial flights at the airport in a few days, people got on their phones and tried to rebook; most tickets were sold out.

Afterward, a friend persuaded me to go with him to another party at a senior Afghan official's house, someone close to Ghani. I'd been there a couple times. It was a blast-walled compound with AstroTurf in the yard, mirrors on the walls, exotic pets, and a bountiful liquor cabinet. Once we got past the guards, we found just a few people sitting around, glued to their phones. I sat next to the official, who liked to DJ at parties.

"Three thousand troops are coming, you think that will change anything?" he said. He showed me a message on his phone. "This is info from the TB side. They'll take seventeen provinces, in a power-sharing deal with the government."

That was roughly half of the country. "I don't think they'd settle for less than total control now," I said.

He shook his head angrily. "No, they'll realize if they take it all, the Americans might come with a hundred thousand troops," he said. He tapped his head. "They're rational. They have advisers from Pakistan, from China, from Russia. You think these guys with the long beards are making decisions?"

Ghani had banned senior officials from leaving the country, but the day after the party, my host made it out through the airport, accompanied by a relative of the president.

• • •

On Saturday, August 14, the start of the workweek, the streets of downtown Kabul were in a frenzy, crowded with people running desperate errands. Some were trying to obtain passports or plane tickets while others stood in long lines outside the banks. There was a shortage of cash. The value of the afghani had dropped suddenly; people wanted dollars.

Early that morning, I went for a jog in the park by my house and found it crowded with displaced families in tents, the air thick with cooking smoke and the stench of the outdoor toilets. Taxis and vans loaded with mattresses and a few household goods rolled up, and people piled out, seeking what free space was available.

I was busy that day with my own errands, like finding a satellite phone, even though for months I'd been making contingency plans with my housemate, Jim Huylebroek, a Belgian photographer. We'd talked through various scenarios for the fall of the capital, at first with the idle enthusiasm of preppers and then with growing earnestness. Would there be a breakdown in communications? Martial law, house-to-house fighting, abductions? Riots and looting?

The *New York Times*, like most Western media organizations, was preparing to evacuate its staff. But Jim and I were both free-lancers, so we could choose to stay. I had been watching what happened when the Taliban captured the cities of Herat and Kandahar. There was some violence, but there were no massacres, no executions of captured officials; the movement seemed to have control over its fighters. Now that they would govern, it was in the emirate's own interest, I thought, to stick to its promises, especially when it came to foreigners.

What I feared most was a chaotic interregnum before the Taliban could establish control, in a city filled with armed men. We might have to hole up in our house, which had solar power and was well fortified with bars on the windows; Jim and I stockpiled everything from canned goods to buckshot.

• • •

That afternoon, Ghani called a meeting at the palace, a gathering of the country's most powerful men. The former president, Hamid Karzai, sat in a semicircle with leaders of the mujahedeen, former communists, contracting barons—men who were handed power by the Americans in 2001, when their enemies, the Taliban, seemed utterly defeated. They had presided over two decades of plenty, when a rain of billions from abroad had enriched a minority, even as poverty among the people had grown. Now they faced the ruin of the republic.

Mohib was there, but the bellicose vice president, Saleh, wasn't—the daily Kabul security meeting he normally led had been canceled that morning because of his absence, one participant said, though no one made much of it at the time. Ghani asked the others what they had to say. Karzai spoke of his fears for families like his own, who, he pointedly noted, were still in Kabul. The time had come for painful sacrifices, Karzai said, but he did not explicitly call on Ghani to resign. His point seemed clear enough, and it was echoed by the others, who pleaded with the president to avoid bloodshed and destruction in the capital.

If Ghani had in fact agreed to a deal with the Taliban through Rahimi's back channel, then the meeting was mostly political theater. But Ghani didn't explain the details, whether out of caution or pride or because he still hadn't decided if he would go through with it. He simply told the others that a delegation should go to Qatar immediately; he would accept whatever agreement they made with the Taliban.

The president left the meeting, and afterward, a group stood outside in consternation. Some, unaware of the secret talks, wondered if the president understood he had to resign. There was confusion over who would go to Doha. Mohammad Akram Khpalwak, an adviser to the president, was sent to ask Ghani, who answered that he would decide after he talked with the Americans.

That evening, Ghani met with the commander of U.S. forces and the acting ambassador to discuss the security plan for Kabul. The Americans promised to provide air support and surveillance. Then Ghani spoke by videoconference with Blinken. Again, according to the U.S. diplomat, they discussed the back channel for an orderly transfer of power to the Taliban.

•　　•　　•

By that night, Mazar-i-Sharif in northern Afghanistan had fallen, and the Taliban continued their rapid advance on the capital. The republic's forces, utterly demoralized, were simply laying down their arms, allowing the rebels, after their long, lean years in the mountains, to take possession of billions of dollars worth of vehicles and weapons bought by the United States and its allies. The competition between commanders for booty and the prestige of being the first to conquer territory added momentum to the Taliban's advance—as did rivalries within the movement. The Taliban leadership was largely from the south, especially Kandahar, but most of the insurgency around Kabul had fallen under the command of the Haqqanis, a family-led network of fighters from eastern Afghanistan that was close to the Pakistani military. Several months earlier, a senior figure, Khalil Haqqani, began making contact with Afghan officials, his former aide told me, paving the way for a push on Kabul from the east. The Taliban's own psychological warfare was paying off: by now, cities were falling without a fight, surrendering after a mere phone call.

In the early hours of Sunday morning, the provincial governor of Nangarhar, the gateway to Kabul to the east, received his counterpart from the emirate. Taliban fighters entered the city without firing a shot. As the sun rose, Haqqani sent a voice message congratulating the governor for handing over power peacefully: "You will have a place in history, for protecting the people's lives and property."

Taliban forces from Kandahar, meanwhile, hurriedly advanced north, toward Wardak Province, whose capital, only ten miles from Kabul, fell around ten o'clock on Sunday morning.

The road was now open to Kabul, where the police and the army were starting to desert their posts. Saleh, the vice president who had run security meetings for the capital, had secretly escaped to his home province of Panjshir, which helped throw the chain of command in Kabul into disarray. Local criminal gangs—many of them connected to the police—were waiting for their chance to start looting. At nine that morning, when the police abandoned the station in District 7, near the king's old palace, local gangsters, some dressed as Taliban in turbans, began to loot the station of weapons and other valuables, according to residents; they were joined by passers-by, who carried off computers and furniture.

By noon on Sunday, August 15, Taliban fighters had reached the gates of the capital. The rebels gathered at the eastern and southern outskirts of the city on motorcycles and captured pickups, dusty and tired from the road, and waited.

•   •   •

Shortly before ten o'clock that morning, the president sat in the shade of a courtyard at the palace, reading a book. He had met with Rahimi, who updated him on the back-channel talks with the Taliban; that same morning, Khalilzad was meeting with Baradar in Doha to discuss the proposal for a peaceful transfer of power. Then Ghani met alone with Mohib, followed by a larger group including Bek, who said he suggested that the president call an emergency cabinet meeting in order to rally his officials. It was then that many learned that Saleh had escaped; the meeting never happened.

At ten a.m., Khpalwak, the adviser, arrived in the courtyard, in order to find out who was supposed to travel to Doha to negotiate the handover. Karzai was sitting in his house next door, ready to leave that evening or the next morning on an Afghan charter flight. Khpalwak told me that Ghani said that Mohib should go to Doha, as well.

Jawed Kootwal, Khpalwak's chief of staff, had snapped a photo of the president from his office window—Ghani's frequent reading breaks had become a joke between him and his friends. Now Kootwal watched as his boss left and Mohib arrived with a man wearing a white robe and an Arab headdress. Kootwal took another photo, which he would later publish online. The man, a United Arab Emirates official, was named Saif, an acquaintance of Mohib's who was well connected with Afghan power brokers. The meeting had not been listed on the president's schedule that day.

•   •   •

It was nearly eleven a.m. when I stepped out of my house, and the traffic jam in the city had grown even worse. The cars in the street were at a standstill. Jim and I had no idea what would happen next. We were too busy to dwell on it; the sight of an entire world dissolving produced a certain numbness. There was the relentless sound of helicopters while around us life continued as it had to—the shops and markets were open.

I had planned to meet two former translators from the U.S. military, who were desperately hoping to be evacuated with the departing forces. They got stuck in traffic and finally ended up walking the last mile; when they arrived, we decided to sit in the yard of a nearby restaurant and have an early lunch.

Over a pan of chicken karahi, the translators, Mahdi and Nadim, told me about the time they'd spent with the U.S. Special Forces. Each had extensive combat experience, and several Green Berets had written them recommendation letters, but they'd still been waiting for years to go to America under the Special Immigrant Visa program for local employees. There was a backlog of some 20,000 applications. According to a U.S. official, Ghani had resisted a mass airlift, arguing that it would spark panic, and charter flights didn't start until the end of July. In recent months, as the Taliban advanced on Kabul, their wait had turned to agony. Mahdi had reached the final stage and submitted his passport; in July, he was called to the embassy, where it was handed back to him, stamped "Canceled without prejudice"—most likely a paperwork snafu, he was told, but it would eventually be resolved.

"We don't have any more time," Nadim said, his voice rising. The two translators were certain the Taliban would behead them if they caught them. "If you don't hear from us, it means we're dead—so tell our story."

It was almost noon; my phone had been on silent the whole time. I looked up and saw my driver walking toward us, a look of shock on his face.

"People are saying the Taliban have entered Kabul," he told us. "They're inside the city."

•   •   •

Around eleven a.m., officials at the palace heard gunfire. Panic seized the NSC building as rumors spread that the Taliban were attacking the palace. From his window, Najib Motahari, Bek's chief of staff, could see some of Mohib's staff running across the lawn, fleeing toward the gate—*Tommies*, he thought contemptuously.

On social media, there was talk that the Taliban had arrived at the outskirts of the city. Were the Taliban breaking the agreement for a cease-fire? At the NSC building, Bek met with Rahimi, the president's envoy, and began making phone calls, trying to find out what was happening. They spoke with Baradar's team in Qatar, who insisted that their forces had not entered the city.

The Taliban were as surprised as everyone else by their lightning success; they weren't prepared to take control of the capital and feared a confrontation with the Americans at the airport. To confirm the cease-fire agreement they had made with Rahimi, the Taliban spokesman now posted a statement online: "Because Kabul is a big city with a large population, the mujahedeen of the Islamic Emirate do not intend to enter by force, and negotiations are underway with the other side for a peaceful transfer of power."

To the American team in Doha, the statement was validation that the back channel was in contact with the Taliban's military leadership, who could deliver a cease-fire on the ground. "To have them release a long statement like that about their fighters does not occur without Yaqoub and Siraj's blessing," the U.S. diplomat told me. According to several Taliban commanders I later spoke to, they had received orders not to enter the capital. And local residents said that the Taliban massed at the city's gates were in fact holding back at that point.

Bek, reassured, posted a message on Twitter at noon: "Don't panic! Kabul is safe!"

But while Khalilzad's team might have been optimistic about the cease-fire holding, the U.S. Embassy in Kabul had decided to get the last of its staff out immediately and haul down the flag. Twenty minutes after Bek's post, the embassy sent out an alert that prompted many of Kabul's foreigners to make a sudden dash to the airport. A security adviser at the embassy posted a WhatsApp message to a group of expats, giving a deadline of five-thirty that evening for helicopter evacuations from the Green Zone: "Urgent Update—the US Embassy advises that all foreign missions move to HKIA immediately."

•　　•　　•

Hearing the driver's news, I quickly paid for our meal and said farewell to the two interpreters. I told my driver to go home to his family and set out on foot. People were wild with fear, having heard that the Taliban were in the city. Some shouted into phones; others dashed heedlessly through traffic. The sound of helicopters and jets was loud in the sky. A motorcade of Land Cruisers, sirens blaring, forced its way through the intersection.

It was noon when I got home, and I found my housemate, Jim, with his camera in hand, already wearing a traditional robe. I donned mine; we both spoke Dari and could usually pass for locals. He wanted to take a walk and see what was happening in our neighborhood; it wasn't clear to us, from the rumors and official denials on Twitter, whether the Taliban had actually entered Kabul.

The last shopkeepers were locking their gates as we walked down Chicken Street. Workers were rushing out of their offices and heading home. Now and again, we could hear scattered gunshots. There was a police headquarters and ministry nearby; some guards were still in uniform, but others stood wearing robes, ready to run. Some checkpoints were deserted.

A police commander lived on our street, and when we got back, we found his guards milling outside his house, most of them in plainclothes already. I had a sudden sense of the fragility of the social contract that bound us; our shared reality was melting into air. I was as worried about being robbed or shot by them as I was about the Taliban.

"Our leaders sold us out," one of the police officers said. "If the Taliban come here, what can we do?"

We looked up. An American gunship was circling over the city, firing off shimmering flares.

•　　•　　•

After the panic that morning at the palace, Bek went to see Ghani and explained that the Taliban in Doha had announced that they would not enter the city. The president agreed to record a message to reassure the population of Kabul. It was filmed around one-thirty, with Ghani sitting at a desk in his office that once belonged to King Amanullah, who fled the country a century earlier in the face of an Islamist uprising. Afterward, Bek and Rahimi went for lunch together. The presidential guards had locked down the palace and sent most of the staff away; the place was quiet. To Bek, the situation seemed under control.

But Mohib was getting ready to escape. He had never trusted the Taliban and believed that they had already started to enter the city. Mohib later wrote to me that Khalil Haqqani called him and asked him to surrender. "I explored their desire for negotiations, but it was clear they were set on a military victory," he wrote. "They had not negotiated in good faith thus far, and they certainly were not in a position to have to do that on August 15." Haqqani's former aide disputed this, saying that Mohib asked to set up a meeting between their representatives and that Haqqani agreed and promised he wouldn't be harmed.

Motahari, Bek's aide, told me he saw Mohib's senior staff running around the NSC offices carrying bags and overheard them talking about the council's operational cash. (Mohib and his staff denied taking bags of money out of the country.)

The president's personal helicopters, on standby at the airport, were summoned to the palace. Three Mi-17s landed. Unusually, they were fully fueled, which meant they couldn't carry as many passengers. According to several people present, a group that included Mohib and Rula Ghani boarded first; then Mohib went back with the head of the palace guard and returned with the president. Several of the president's supporters later told me that Ghani had been reluctant to leave and had to be persuaded that his life was in danger.

As the president boarded, there was a fight between the remaining guards and staff over who would fit on board the last helicopter; Mohib's secretary was thrown to the tarmac.

The helicopters took off and headed north. They were not returning to the airport, where, according to one official present,

the UAE was going to send a plane to evacuate them. Instead—
whether it was because they feared the growing chaos at the airport or didn't want to face the Americans—the president and his
crew flew low through the mountains, trying to avoid detection by
the U.S. military, which still controlled Afghanistan's airspace.

By then it was around a quarter to three. Bek was walking
through the palace; he told me he didn't realize the president had
flown away in a helicopter. The sky was full of them that day. It
wasn't until he ran into an agitated Hanif Atmar, the foreign minister, who had been holding onto the president's passport, that
Bek learned what had happened, he said.

"Do you know where the president is?" asked Atmar, who had
arrived just as the choppers were taking off.

"The president went home," Bek answered.

"No. He ran away."

"I don't believe it. I just saw him."

"Look," Atmar said, pulling out the passport with the seal of
the republic on the cover. "He's gone."

•   •   •

When Jim and I got back from our walk, shortly before two p.m.,
I saw I had a message from Rangina: "Hi. Are you OK? What's
going on?"

I called her and we spoke briefly; she was at home, having left
the education ministry around noon, accompanied by her staff.
She didn't know any more than I did about what was going on at
the palace with Ghani. "I have no way of connecting with him, so
I have no idea where he is," Rangina said over the phone, sounding surprisingly calm. The Taliban's announcement that they
wouldn't enter the capital by force had eased her mind; she had
also heard a rumor that the Americans would take over security.

We said farewell. Jim and I decided to get on our bicycles and
go for a ride around the city. As we came outside, we saw the
police on our street fleeing in civilian vehicles as the neighbors
gaped.

The streets were almost empty of cars now, the shops shuttered. As we arrived at the traffic circle outside the U.S. Embassy, two Chinooks took off and roared overhead. We stopped and stared at the departing helicopters. "Remember, this is not Saigon," the secretary of state would say on television later that day.

Jim got off his bike and started snapping photos. It was hot and my mouth was dry, so I bought some water from a juice cart. We could see plumes of smoke rising from inside the Green Zone. A convoy of armored SUVs screeched through the roundabout, headed for the airport. Groups of ragged-looking men walked past, some carrying small bundles tied in scarves. "They're prisoners," the juice seller told us. "A big group of them came by earlier." Earlier that day, the guards at the main prison in the city had fled, and the prisoners had broken loose—the same thing happened at the detention center in Bagram, north of the capital.

The Taliban were still nowhere to be seen downtown. We headed home, passing the palace gates, where there were still some guards outside. Jim and I had looped the whole Green Zone: the ugly concrete maws of its compounds stood open, the barriers upraised. Across the city, soldiers and police officers took off their uniforms, laid down their weapons and walked off into the evening light.

•　　•　　•

At Karzai's house, a group of his advisers listened in dismay as the palace guards arrived and announced that Ghani and his entourage had fled. Karzai had planned to help negotiate the transfer of power; now the guards asked him to take charge of the palace. Abdul Karim Khurram, his former minister of information, was present and told me that Karzai declined, saying he had no legal basis to do so. They tried calling senior officials, including the minister of defense, but those they spoke to were in hiding or had already escaped to the airport. But Karzai chose to stay. He recorded a video, which they posted on Facebook that afternoon. In it, he stands with his three young daughters in front of him; the girls seem blissfully unaware, giggling as the littlest one tries to squirm away. "Citizens of Kabul, my family and I are here with you," Karzai said, straining to raise his voice over the roar of jets and helicopters. "I call on the security forces and the Taliban to ensure the security of the lives and property of the people."

Khurram said they were worried about what would happen once word of Ghani's escape became public. Already, the situation in the city was deteriorating rapidly. According to a police officer who was monitoring the radio network that day, by lunchtime many of Kabul's police stations had been abandoned, becoming targets of large, organized groups of looters. Around four p.m., the home of the deputy interior minister was visited by a convoy of armed men driving Rangers and Humvees they had taken from a nearby station. They were flying the Taliban flag, but the police officer who was present told me he recognized them—they were from a criminal gang from nearby Shakardara District. When he asked for a receipt for the vehicles and weapons they were seizing, they put a gun to his head.

· · ·

That afternoon, as the situation grew increasingly chaotic in Kabul, Khalilzad convened a meeting in Doha with the Taliban leadership and Gen. Frank McKenzie, head of Central Command, who had flown in to explain the American plan for evacuation to his former enemies. They met in Khalilzad's suite at the top of the Ritz Carlton; the two sides faced off across a table—on one, the craggy marine four-star general, an Alabama native; on the other, Mullah Baradar, dressed in a long robe.

According to two people who were present, McKenzie gave a presentation about his mission to evacuate U.S. citizens and their allies. He spread two maps out on the table. One showed a narrow corridor between the U.S. Embassy and the airport, where his forces would be active. The second had a thirty-kilometer radius drawn around the center of Kabul; any move by the Taliban into that zone, McKenzie warned them, would be interpreted as a hostile act. Baradar and the other Taliban leaned over the map, trying to find the names of the areas inside the thirty-kilometer circle, which extended well past the gates of Kabul.

We already have some people inside there, Baradar answered.

McKenzie told him to withdraw their forces.

Baradar replied that the Taliban had no intention of interfering with the American evacuation. But the situation on the ground had changed. They all knew by now that Ghani had fled and that the republic's forces were collapsing. Khalilzad and the Taliban had been getting messages from Afghan politicians in Kabul, begging for someone to take charge of security before the looting and violence got worse. Everyone feared what might happen come nightfall.

Who is going to take responsibility for Kabul—are you? Baradar asked.

Khalilzad and McKenzie looked at each other. My mission is what I described, the general said.

Baradar persisted, saying he wanted to know who would ensure security for the people of Kabul. He pointed a finger at McKenzie: Are you, general?

It was hard to know if the Taliban were serious in asking the United States to take over security in Kabul; according to the Biden administration, it would have required a massive troop deployment and was never considered as an option.

McKenzie repeated that he had his mission, and that was it.

In that case, Baradar asked, what if the Taliban went in and took over security?

There was a pause as the two sides conferred among themselves. Finally, McKenzie indicated the second map, with its narrow corridor. As long as there was no interference with his mission, the general said, he had "no opinion" on that.

•   •   •

It was nearly five p.m. when Jim and I returned home on our bicycles. Our driver, Akbar, was waiting for us; the streets were clear, so we decided to drive to the western outskirts of the city, where the main Taliban advance would be arriving from Wardak Province.

Traffic was light until we hit the main arterial road that runs west, where a stream of cars was leaving the city. As Akbar crept up the on-ramp, we got down and walked to the start of the driveway of the Intercontinental Hotel. The cops here had changed into robes as well, but still had their weapons. We introduced ourselves as journalists.

"The war's over!" one said. He laughed. "We've surrendered."

"You surrendered?" I asked "To whom?"

They smiled and pointed to a bearded man sitting in their midst; he had a black scarf over his head and was wearing white high tops. He carried a Kalashnikov and a radio. A Talib, the first we'd seen that day. He returned our greetings gruffly. Jim asked to take a photo, and he assented. He was from Wardak, and spoke a little Dari.

"How long have you been a mujahed?" I said.

"Eighteen years," he said.

I asked if he had anything to tell the public.

"Don't worry. We have no problem with ordinary people. All that's propaganda."

"What about the foreigners at the airport?"

"The foreigners should go. We don't have any need for them," he said. He'd assumed I was Afghan. "If you and I can make peace, then what do we need them for?"

The police had the giddiness of condemned men granted a reprieve; they crowded shyly around the Talib, who seemed annoyed by his duty but not in the least concerned about being surrounded by armed men who would have shot him a day ago. The cops wanted to pose for a photo with him. After Jim snapped it, the Talib waved us away. "Our leaders said we're not supposed to give interviews."

By now the car had made it up the on-ramp, and we got back in and headed to the western edge of the city, a predominantly Pashtun neighborhood called Company. The area drew rural migrants, many of whom were sympathetic to the insurgents. As we approached, we could see crowds gathered by the side of the road, cheering. A youth with a scarf wrapped around his face stood in the intersection, waving a white banner with handwritten Arabic script: THERE IS NO GOD BUT GOD AND MUHAMMAD IS HIS PROPHET.

A tan Ford Ranger drove by, with armed Taliban fighters sitting inside. Several more police and army vehicles followed, including Humvees and four-and-half-ton trucks; the Taliban on board were holding American rifles, M-16s and M-4s. They were carrying booty out of the city, back to their lines on the outskirts. The crowd of men, mostly young, was whistling and cheering; packs of little children ran after the trucks, trying to jump aboard the rear bumper. Jim had his camera out; the Taliban were happy to be photographed.

More fighters roared by on motorcycles, armed and blaring autotuned *taranas*, Islamic chants, from their cellphones. At the main Company roundabout, there was an immense crowd cheering: "Long live the Taliban."

•   •   •

After flying for more than an hour, the three presidential helicopters arrived at the Uzbekistan border and landed; confusion ensued at the Termez airport as they were surrounded by soldiers—the Uzbek government had apparently not been informed of their arrival. Eventually, the president, his wife, Mohib, and several aides were taken to the governor's guesthouse, but the rest of the fifty or so people on board spent a miserable night out in the open by the helicopters, relieving themselves on the tarmac. The next day, a charter flight arrived and took them all to Abu Dhabi.

The UAE, which had deep business ties with Kabul's elite, was a close ally of Ghani's; according to three sources within the administration, Abu Dhabi had secretly helped fund his election campaigns. (The UAE did not respond to a request for comment.) What exactly was discussed at that meeting between the UAE official, Ghani, and Mohib that morning remains a matter of speculation. Mohib told me that "we discussed an evacuation plan for the future, but not for that day."

For many Afghans, their president's flight from the country was a stunning act of cowardice and betrayal that plunged the capital into chaos. Days later, Ghani, in a statement posted to Twitter, promised to explain his actions in detail in the future and said he had left to avoid provoking a civil war. "Leaving Kabul was the most difficult decision of my life," he wrote, "but I believed it was the only way to keep the guns silent and save Kabul and her 6 million citizens."

Mohib made a similar argument to me, writing that the Afghan security forces were "no longer a consolidated force within our control at that point. Keeping security of the city without mobilizing militias and aerial bombardment was not possible, and we were not prepared to do that."

In retrospect, it's clear that the breakdown of Kabul's command and control, along with mass desertions by government forces, was already underway by the time Ghani fled. But it also seems obvious that the president was not in immediate danger. His guard force was intact, and the Taliban were still nowhere near the palace that afternoon.

"It was the safest place in Afghanistan," said Bek, his chief of staff.

Around six-thirty, the news of Ghani's escape finally broke. Around the same time, the Taliban published a second statement: "The Islamic Emirate has ordered its forces to enter the areas of Kabul that have been abandoned by the enemy, in order prevent thieves and looters from harming the people. . . . Mujahedeen are not allowed to enter anyone's home, or harass anyone."

The sudden fall of the city had caught the Taliban leadership without adequate forces on hand. Their men had been busy with capturing the neighboring provinces that same day; coordination was difficult, as many commanders avoided the use of phones and radio during daylight hours, for fear of airstrikes by the Afghan air force. The first Taliban units were scrambled into Kabul in the late afternoon and headed for key locations like the army and intelligence headquarters, where they were aided by sleeper cells and sympathizers that emerged from hiding. But it took until sunset to collect a force of several hundred men in Wardak, who did not make it into town until well after dark.

In all, according to one senior Taliban commander's estimate, the rebels took command of Kabul with well under a thousand men—less than the number of marines at the airport, let alone the tens of thousands of Afghan security forces who had deserted their posts.

•   •   •

That night, the street in front of the palace gate was dark and empty as a Taliban convoy arrived, followed by an Al Jazeera Arabic crew they had summoned to witness their entry. Hamdullah Mokhles, the commander in charge, was a deputy to a senior leader from Helmand—in the end, it was the southern forces, and not the Haqqanis, who had the honor of entering the palace. Accompanying him was Salahuddin Ayubi, the military chief for the central zone, who had captured Wardak that morning, and a former Guantánamo detainee, Gholam Ruhani.

They waited for one of the palace guards to arrive, a general named Mohammadullah Andar. He unlocked the gate for them shortly after ten p.m.; as they walked inside, Andar nervously told the journalists that he had been at the airport, hoping to escape, when one of Ghani's officials in Doha, Masoom Stanekzai, had called him and told him to hand over the palace to the Taliban, promising him he'd be safe.

They arrived at a locked gate, to which Andar didn't have a key. Hameedullah Shah, the Al Jazeera team's producer, told me he suggested they go a different route, through Ariana Square, past the evacuated embassy and CIA station. Ruhani replied that was a "red zone," using the English term, and that the Americans might bomb them if they did. Instead, Mokhles, the leader, pulled out a pistol and shot open the lock.

Andar led the group deeper into the palace, into Ghani's office. There they found the desk where, that same afternoon, the Afghan president had recorded his message to reassure the people. On it was a book of poems from an Afghan singer. As the cameras rolled, Mokhles and Ayubi sat down at the desk while a fighter recited a Victory Surah from the Quran:

Indeed, we have granted you a clear triumph, O Prophet.

Part 3. The Evacuation

In the days after the fall of Kabul, it sometimes felt as if we were living in two cities. In one, the streets were quiet, and people stayed home, afraid of the Taliban fighters with their turbans and long hair standing guard outside military compounds and shuttered embassies. In the other, the one the world was watching on TV, desperate crowds surged against the walls surrounding the airport as gunshots rang out.

I was receiving a constant stream of messages from Afghans asking for help escaping the country. Some were old friends; others, people I'd met once and interviewed. As a Westerner working in the developing world, I was used to my powerlessness in such matters. Usually, the most I could do was help people fill out the complex paperwork needed for programs like the Special Immigrant Visa. For years now, the West had been stepping up measures to keep Afghan asylum seekers out, making it almost impossible for them to get tourist visas, canceling study programs, paying countries like Turkey to build walls and even, in the case of Australia, detaining them on remote Pacific islands. Just ten days earlier, six EU countries, including Germany, had warned against halting deportations of Afghans, saying that it sent "the wrong signal." The evacuation—a collection of national efforts under the American military umbrella—was initially meant for countries' own citizens, green-card and visa holders, and a limited group of locals, mostly current and former employees.

That changed the night of August 15, when thousands of desperate Afghans overran the civilian terminal and spilled out onto the tarmac. On Monday morning, a U.S. Air Force C-17 was filmed taking off through the crowd. Several people were crushed under the wheels, while others, clinging to the underside of the jet, fell to their deaths as it lifted off. As these images played to a global audience riveted by the drama at the airport, the West, in a paroxysm of regret, opened its arms to Afghan refugees. Already, Canada had announced that it would take 20,000 people, a figure it would later double. Other countries followed suit, and the United States set up giant transit camps in Doha and other military bases overseas, to process Afghan evacuees for resettlement.

Although the West wanted to save Afghans from the Taliban, the evacuation could take place only with their tacit support. Their harried young fighters had taken over the southern, civilian side of the airport perimeter, where they used warning shots and whips to prevent the mob from overrunning the airfield, as they had on the first day. On the northern, military side, the line was held by marines and the Zero Units.

With each day, even as people were shot and trampled at the gates, the crowds grew larger and more frenzied, some arriving from distant provinces. A few petitioners already had resettlement cases, like the interpreters I'd met the day of the fall, but many more came bearing some piece of paper they hoped would qualify them for evacuation—a certificate given to them years ago by the marines in Helmand, a photograph from a conference for female activists, or a UN observer's card from a past, disputed election. There was a widespread belief that if you could only get inside the airport, you'd make it to Germany or Canada, and in fact, many had gotten out in the chaos of the first night, when, in order to clear the runway, people were bundled onto planes indiscriminately and flown to Doha.

For years, Afghans had been paying smugglers to cross deserts and mountains, risking their lives to reach Europe's hostile frontiers. The desperate scenes around the airport—families, half-dead from dehydration, being tear-gassed and beaten by men with guns—reminded me of what I witnessed when I traveled the smuggler's road five years earlier, during Europe's border crisis. Now the border was here in Kabul, manned by the Zero Units and the Taliban.

•   •   •

For many Westerners who had been involved with Afghanistan over the past twenty years and were watching this disaster from abroad, the only way to do something was to help the Afghans they knew to escape. They tried lobbying their home governments, but some turned to direct action. A group of my friends connected to Sayara, a research-and-communications company that contracted with the U.S. government, had gotten together to try to evacuate Sayara's local staff and others at risk. The list grew as they found donors who were willing to help get more people out—journalists, women's rights activists, and even members of the girls' robotics team, whose faces had been painted on the wall outside the U.S. Embassy.

Soon they had raised more than a million dollars from places like the Rockefeller Foundation, enough to fly their own charter plane in. They got permission from the Ugandan government to bring people there while they waited for resettlement. Then they tried to get access to the airport; they started with the State Department and the military, but in the end it was another friend of theirs, a writer and former CIA officer, who succeeded. He worked his contacts at the agency, whose paramilitary branch was playing a key role in the evacuation.

They needed someone on the ground in Kabul to get a convoy to the airport. They'd been in touch with me, asking for information; I'd been getting around through the crowds on my motorcycle and had a sense of what was going on there. Now one of my friends called and asked if I'd be willing to lead the buses in.

They explained who would be on the convoy: some local journalists I knew, some women from shelters that might be shut down by the Taliban. There would be four minibuses with more than a hundred people on board, many of them young children or elderly men and women. I knew that I was in a unique position to help them and that, in their desperation, they would go whether or not I did. So I said yes.

Two old friends had also volunteered, Andrew Quilty and Victor Blue, photojournalists who'd stayed behind in Kabul. The plan was to assemble the evacuees at the Serena Hotel downtown, and then drive to the airport. There was no way we could get through the crowds and traffic during the day, but if we left late enough at night, the roads might be clearer.

I'd ridden around the airport that afternoon to get a sense of the layout. On the north side, there was a road that ran along a wide sewage canal. Across the water, Hesco barriers and concrete walls were topped with guard towers, and on one I saw something I hadn't seen in days: the tricolor of the republic, fluttering in the breeze.

While the army and police had surrendered and deserted en masse around the country, the Zero Units had remained mostly intact. There was already a large force at Eagle Base, the CIA's paramilitary compound in northern Kabul, which the Taliban had agreed not to attack during the evacuation; the agency had helped rescue some of the units; others made their own way to the airport. One was the Orgun Strike Force from the southeastern border, which had participated in some of the United States' most secret missions, including covert operations inside Pakistan's tribal areas across the border. They were led by a longhaired, mustachioed commander whose operations that summer I'd been following on an Afghan government Facebook page. (A U.S. official requested that he not be identified by name, to protect his family.) The Orgun commander and his unit were given the ugly job of crowd control on the perimeter.

Coming around the north side of the airport, still a long way from the main military gate, I hit a traffic jam, and as I threaded the bike through I saw the reason. The Zero troopers, in their desert tiger camo, had taken over the road. They stood in front of a narrow passage formed by concrete blast walls. This new entrance, which some dubbed Glory Gate, was supposed to be a low-profile one for U.S. citizens and other priority cases, but large crowds were gathering there. When people pushed too close, the troopers fired shots in the air or brandished steel cables. A few days before, the crowd had gotten inside, and videos on social media showed the Zero troopers forcing them back, firing live ammunition overhead, women and kids screaming, a man bleeding in the dust.

Around seven that evening, Vic and Quilty came to pick me up in a taxi. On our way to the Serena, we discussed the latest news: There'd been a report that ISIS was planning to attack the airport. The threat was real, but who knew how imminent it actually was? In any case, it wasn't going away. We arrived at the luxury hotel, which had been targeted several times by the Taliban. In one attack in 2014, my friend Sardar Ahmad, an Afghan journalist, was killed along with his wife and two of his children. It was unsettling when the door opened to reveal several bearded men with Kalashnikovs: the hotel's new Taliban security. We were led in with a group of evacuees, where a Talib searched my bag, before letting me through to the scanner.

"Pretty funny, huh?" I muttered to Vic as we walked through the hotel's driveway, passing more fighters.

"This is insane," Vic replied.

In fact, the Serena was now one of the safest places in town, thanks to the Qatari Embassy, which had moved in earlier that year. The Qataris' strategy of hosting the Taliban's political office had paid off; they'd become a key intermediary between the West and the Islamists and were now running their own evacuation convoys through the Taliban-controlled civilian gate.

As we entered the lobby, we could see Qatari special forces in black polo shirts with pistols. They had a convoy going tonight, and among the evacuees, I spotted Bilal Sarwary, a former BBC reporter, standing by the reception desk. We embraced.

"How are you doing?" I asked.

"Not very good and not very bad—in between," he said, and laughed. "The time to process will come."

Sayara had rented a hall in the back where, over the next few hours, our own evacuees assembled, around 140 people. I was surprised at how many kids there were. I stood at the front and introduced myself and Vic and Quilty, explaining we were going to get them safely to the airport. Looking at the rows of anxious faces, I tried to smile back with a confidence I didn't feel.

Although I hadn't put anyone on the list myself, it turned out that I knew a few of the people in our convoy. One of them was Ramin, the poet who'd recited at the party two months ago, sitting with a young woman with pale skin and high cheekbones.

"This is my wife," he said, standing up to greet me.

When I met Ramin earlier that summer, they had already been engaged; when Kabul fell, the two got married so that they could escape together, in a tiny home ceremony where they played music on a mobile phone, with the volume turned down in case a Taliban patrol passed by.

"Are you planning to leave, too?" Ramin asked.

I explained that I was coming back with the buses, along with Quilty and Vic.

"Our friends have suffered a lot," Ramin said. "Please be careful." The previous day, he and his wife went to one of the gates controlled by the Zero Units, where the crowd had been teargassed and they were nearly trampled. He went home, hopeless, and tried to fall asleep; when he got up, he learned that a friend from France had put him on the list for this convoy.

I was wondering about him the day before and, on a whim, I'd left him a voice message and recited one of his poems. "Yesterday, when you sent me the message, I was in the crowd," he said. "You read it very well."

"Thank you. It's a beautiful poem," Before the fall, I had hoped to translate his work, but I'd only managed to commit one to memory, a love poem:

I'll stay with you like a scent on the body,
I'll stay with you like a half-forgotten song.

•   •   •

At two a.m., the scout car that we sent ahead reported back: there was still a traffic jam outside the main military entrance, but the road was clear in front of Glory Gate. Sayara was in touch with a CIA contact at the airport, and soon after, I got a call from someone who introduced himself as one of the Orgun commander's men, telling us to come.

It was shortly after three a.m. when we rolled out of Serena's gates. I chugged my third energy drink of the night and lit a cigarette. The city center was deserted. I was in the lead bus, and our driver decided to take a shortcut behind the old attorney general's office, where there was a height barrier intended to keep out trucks. As we passed under it, there was a crunch, and he slammed on the brakes. When he tried reversing, the metal roof began to shriek in protest. He'd wedged us under the barrier.

Twenty yards ahead, I saw a green laser sweep the road and fix on our bus. Three turbaned figures, carrying rifles, stepped out from the shadows and headed toward us.

"It's the Taliban," someone behind me whispered.

The other buses drove around us, where the barrier was higher, and sped off. Our driver was reversing back and forth, trying to get us unstuck, but the lead Talib broke into a jog and raised his hand for us to stop.

"*Salaam alaikum*," I called out the window, trying to smile.

"Where are you going?" he asked.

"The airport," I said.

He stared inside at the bus crammed full of families with their luggage. "*Mawlawi sahib!*" He called to his commander. "They're going to the airport." The other waved us away.

"Be careful you don't get shot," the Talib said.

We got out from under the barrier, made a U-turn and took another street, where we linked up with the other three buses and sped onward to the airport road. No more checkpoints. Soon we saw the neon lights of the gas station across from Glory Gate. I was worried about the trigger-happy troopers and the mob outside. I texted the group to remind them to lock the windows.

"We're close, slow down."

The road was clear, but there were still hundreds of people hanging around the dirt lots along the road. Clouds of dust whirled up as we approached; the floodlights from the gate cast the shadows of concertina wire through the murk. A Zero trooper came forward and leveled his rifle at my bus.

"Get out of here!" he screamed. "Go!"

"We're the Sayara convoy!" I shouted back. Leaning out the window, I recited the names we'd been given by the CIA

Hearing them, the trooper dropped his barrel, and motioned for us to wait. After a few minutes, another came forward and took my passport. They had us pull forward, out of the road. Then I saw a bearded figure come from the gate, his muscular calves apparent under his shorts—an unusual sight since Afghans don't wear shorts in public. He shone a flashlight on me, then on my passport.

"Hey, how are you?" he said in English. He asked about where we'd come from and who the passengers were.

"It's all civilians," I said.

"Well, you came to the right gate," he said and grinned.

He was an American operator, most likely with the CIA's paramilitary branch. He explained that we'd unload the buses, one at a time, so that the passengers could go through on foot to be searched. Then we'd load up again on the other side and head into the airport.

I stood to the side and watched as the passengers, many still terrified, filed off and went inside. With the floodlights behind me now, the Zero troopers seemed forlorn in the dust, the remnants of a once mighty army, now carrying out a final, grim duty. Occasionally, there was a crack of gunfire: more warning shots against the crowd. Seated in a plastic chair by the gate was a large man with a drooping mustache. He was looking down at his phone, listening to a voice message.

He looked familiar. I asked if he was the Orgun commander.

He turned his exhausted gaze up to me. "Yes," he said.

"I recognized you from your Facebook photos," I said. So this was the man who'd been the scourge of the borderlands.

He smiled sadly. "Thank you."

It took half an hour to get all four buses through the gate. As the last passengers were being checked, I walked over to where Vic was waiting. It was almost four-thirty, and the dawn prayer was being called. A chorus of barking dogs rose from the wastes around us.

The second operator led us in his truck as we drove through the concrete passageways, past a blasted-out armored vehicle, through an inner gate manned by U.S. Army soldiers, until we finally reached the edge of the tarmac. A vast panorama opened before us: the lights of distant planes, like ships on the open sea, and in the foreground, the hulking airframes of C-17s and C-130s, their ramps down, lines of refugees walking onboard. Far to the south, we could see the civilian terminal. The sound of jet engines was deafening.

Our buses followed the CIA truck to the military terminal, where there were U.S. Marines everywhere, some standing guard on the flight line, others crashed along a fence, sleeping against their rucksacks. There were soldiers from other NATO countries as well, sent to evacuate their nationals and local staff. Afghans sat together in groups, wherever they could find an open space to rest amid drifts of trash, empty water bottles, and rations.

Now we had to get our evacuees to their plane so that we could go home; I'd been told Sayara's charter flight was already on the tarmac. The buses pulled to a halt next to a disabled Afghan Air Force C-130, a few hundred yards from the terminal. The operator, a burly man in a baseball T-shirt, got down from his truck and came over to me.

"I would not take these people out of the bus," he said. He looked at the military planes around us. "Civilian charter.... I don't see a civilian charter."

As we walked toward the terminal, he explained that marines were kicking some people off who didn't have proper documents; we didn't want to get the Sayara group mixed up with the others. "There's around 20,000 people on this base right now, waiting for flights," he said.

At the terminal, the marine in charge, a harried lieutenant colonel, was polite but said he didn't know where to put our group, either. We were the CIA's responsibility; the operator suggested that he and I drive over to their compound to figure things out, so I got into his armored pickup.

Dawn was breaking on the tarmac. He blinked with fatigue as he explained that he arrived a couple of days before, part of a team rushed to help out with the evacuation. "Everybody thought that it was going to last longer," he said. "We knew it was gonna fall, but we thought months."

"Have you been here before?" I asked.

"Double-digit times, man. You lose count."

He said the CIA had been pulling people out all over the country: American citizens and important assets, often through touch-and-go missions into Taliban-held territory.

A CIA spokeswoman later told me, "The CIA worked closely with other U.S. government agencies to support in various ways the evacuation of thousands of American citizens, local embassy staff, and vulnerable Afghans."

We arrived at an area with several hangars that the CIA had taken over. Two C-17s were loading at its ramp, with a long line of men, women, and children behind each, carrying bags and bundles. The Zero Units were allowed to bring their immediate family members, and the operator said that given the large size of Afghan families, it would add up to thousands. Each C-17 could carry 400 people, and one had to get out every two hours. They were already behind.

The Sayara team had finally sent me the tail number for their charter plane, so we decided to go over to the civilian side of the airport and see if we could find it.

We drove around the west end of the runway. The operator stopped and looked both ways for jets before we crossed. "I don't know who's in some of these buildings," he said. The airport was a mess. The Taliban were supposed to stay on the outside of the civilian terminal, but the perimeter was worryingly porous.

"There's a Kam Air flight there," he said.

A jet with orange livery was parked on the tarmac. We got closer and read the tail number; it was the right plane, but it did not look as if it would be flying any time soon.

My phone buzzed again, and I read a message from my friend at Sayara aloud: "Hey I just talked to the plane people, and this charter is far from secured. It might be days."

We circled around in the truck.

"Huh," he finally said. We headed back to the CIA ramp, where the C-17s were still loading. Inside the hangars, I could see masses of bedding and garbage. "It's a humanitarian disaster," he sighed. He seemed bitter about the way the Zero Units had given up the fight, like the rest of the Afghan forces.

He was coming off his shift, so he handed me off to a colleague, another bearded operator, who dropped me off in a hangar to wait on instructions from above about what to do with Sayara evacuees. Three young marines sat at a folding table in front of laptops, registering Zero troopers and their families.

I poured myself some coffee and sat down, watching the scene. The contrast with the military's side of the airport, where there were marines everywhere, was revealing; here, around a dozen CIA paramilitary officers were handling thousands of locals, many of them armed but obedient. Their faithfulness was being rewarded with passage to America. And as the only Afghan forces who controlled part of the perimeter, they had the ability to bring their own people inside. I wondered how these men, who had been fighting a vicious battle in the borderlands with al-Qaeda and ISIS, would adjust to life in the United States.

The operator returned with a clamshell full of pancakes and sausage, which I wolfed down gratefully. We discussed what to do with the Sayara convoy; the best solution seemed to be to leave them with the marines, after all. We drove back over to the buses and pulled around to the entrance, where everyone got down with their bags. We still needed to find somewhere for them, for the long wait ahead; I spotted a marine sergeant and explained the situation, as we had to his colonel a few hours ago. He was a young guy with red hair and a raspy voice.

"Yeah, how about right there?" he said, pointing to a small outdoor waiting area next to the terminal. He grabbed a couple of his marines, and within a few minutes they had kicked out some others hanging around to make room for all 140 of Sayara's evacuees.

We said goodbye and wished them luck, and then Vic, Quilty, and I got back on the buses and rode back into the city. The sun was bright, and the crowds were already starting to gather—the few with papers to get inside and the many without them.

• • •

As August reached its end and America's self-imposed deadline for the evacuation neared, the violence at the airport grew more frenzied. Sayara asked us to lead another convoy two days later, this time with five buses. We made it to Glory Gate in the early hours of the morning, but this time Sayara's connection to the CIA failed. The operator on duty, one we had seen before, refused to let us through. Sitting outside in the buses, I watched a huge convoy arrive from nearby Eagle Base, which the CIA was getting ready to blow up.

The Orgun commander was gone, one of the troopers outside said. He seemed high on something; his pupils were enormous. He giggled and fluttered his hand. "He flew away."

Our friends at Sayara tried to work their contacts with the U.S. government, sending us to different gates as daylight broke and the crowds grew. One of our buses broke down; a mob tried to break inside; we made a last-ditch attempt at the Taliban-controlled gate, but when I got down to try to talk with them, a fighter started punching me in the head. In the end, we were lucky to get everyone back to the Serena alive.

On August 26, an ISIS suicide bomber made his way through the crowd to the marines at Abbey Gate and detonated his vest, killing thirteen American troops. Jim and I went down to the site and then to the emergency hospital, where they were bringing in bodies on stretchers. Almost 200 people were killed; it seemed like too many for a single bomber. Some might have been trampled or drowned in the sewage ditch; according to several witnesses I spoke to, the marines, who must have feared another bomber, also fired on those who panicked and tried to climb the walls. A doctor at a government hospital said that many of the casualties he saw had bullet wounds. (A spokesman said there was no evidence the marines shot anyone during the evacuation.)

Three days later, the United States carried out a drone strike inside the city, on what it said was another ISIS terrorist. The top U.S. general told the public it was a "righteous strike." We went to the house the next morning, where, in a courtyard strewn with a charred sedan and bits of flesh, a family and their neighbors wept in rage and grief. The drone's Hellfire had killed ten innocent people, seven of them children, as the military would later admit. That was the last known missile fired in what they once called the good war.

•   •   •

Nightfall brought an intensification of air traffic; I'd lie in bed and listen to the planes, trying to distinguish the roar of C-17s and fighter jets, the buzz of Reaper drones, the hum of a C-130's propellers as it climbed from the tarmac. The night of August 30 was the busiest we'd heard it yet, and then, shortly before midnight, it tapered off. Jim and I walked out into the yard and marveled at the quiet. Then we heard scattered gunshots, followed by more, until it sounded as if we were at the center of a raging gun battle. Every Talib in the city was firing into the air, celebrating the departure of the last American soldier. From our window, we could see red tracer fire crisscrossing above the city, deadly fireworks.

The next morning, the Taliban held a news conference at the airport. Their soldiers at the gate let us through; Jim and I walked down the long avenue, brass cartridges scattered underfoot. Heaps of suitcases, their contents emptied into piles, littered the median. The terminal parking lot was a snarl of abandoned vehicles left behind, ordinary cars, UN four-by-fours, and armored SUVs, some flipped on their sides or parked nose to nose as barricades:

one big GM, blocking the road sideways, had its plated window punched open by gunfire. The Taliban guards here were just waking up from last night's party; they had a big dog with them, probably one of the many left behind during the evacuation; the terminal was full of shattered glass, its furniture overturned, pallets of water bottles and MREs scattered around. It was like a hurricane-ravaged, abandoned coast.

The ceremony was on the military side, so the Taliban gave us a ride in the bed of a truck that had belonged to a Zero Unit, the kid at the wheel speeding recklessly across the tarmac, taking us to where the officials were giving a victory speech in front of a listing, disabled C-130. Their special forces were lined up, wearing helmets and uniforms. Suddenly, we heard a bang, and I turned to see two Rangers colliding out on the runway, one rolling and flipping high into the air before it crashed down. The ceremony went on.

Afterward, Jim and I walked back out through the gate and stood staring at the roundabout where traffic was flowing normally. Apart from a small group of onlookers, the crowds were gone. The spell was broken.

"There aren't any foreigners inside?" a street kid asked. He had a can of incense on a wire.

"No," I said. "They're gone."

Part 4. The Emirate

After the fall of the capital, it took time to get used to seeing Taliban at the checkpoint outside our house. In the days that followed, their scarce numbers in Kabul were bolstered by fighters from the provinces, arriving with the long hair and beards that would have gotten them profiled for arrest in the capital not long ago. Young, off-duty Taliban wandered around, clutching their weapons and staring at the bright lights and gaudy storefronts while the city dwellers looked back warily. Although the Taliban rank and file had been ordered not to harass residents, the men of Kabul swapped jeans for traditional garb while the women wore concealing clothes if they ventured out at all. Abandoned by their leaders and security forces, the capital's residents waited for what would befall them under the Islamic Emirate.

On August17, just two days after they captured Kabul, the Taliban held their first news conference. Jim and I rode down to the government media center, located inside the former Green Zone, where we found a line of local reporters waiting outside, their tailored suits traded for robes. Inside, we sat in front of a dais flanked by marble staircases, waiting for Zabihullah Mujahed, the longtime Taliban spokesman, whose voice we knew but whose face we'd never seen. After a moment, Mujahed and his aides descended stage left. He took his seat in front of the microphones. A diminutive, well-spoken man, he wore a turban in a tribal pattern from eastern Afghanistan. He announced that the Taliban would keep their promise of an *afwa*, the general amnesty.

"We have pardoned all those who had fought against us," he said. "The Islamic Emirate does not have any animosity with anyone. The fighting has come to an end, and we want to live in peace."

For a movement confident in its victory and in need of domestic and international support, the announcement made sense. And despite dire expectations, Kabul had fallen with remarkably little bloodshed. There were no massacres or roundups, and so far the few high-profile politicians who hadn't evacuated, like Karzai, had been left in peace. "You thought the Taliban were going to devour and kill everyone, but that didn't happen," Ayubi, one of the commanders who'd taken over the palace, told me. Afghans were tired of war, he said, and the emirate wanted to halt the cycle of killings and retribution that had raged for four decades.

But even if the leadership was sincere, could they control their fighters? I met a young commander named Mullah Sangin who, like many of the Taliban in the city, rushed here from a neighboring province after the fall. Sangin was from Wardak's Tangi Valley, and he told me he was one of a few survivors from a group that had shot down a helicopter carrying Navy SEALs there in 2011. Tall and gaunt, wearing a black turban, Sangin was only in his late twenties but now led a group of a couple of dozen men within the intelligence commission. Restaurants and other businesses had started to reopen in the capital, and we ate lunch at the same spot where I'd gone with the interpreters the day the city fell. The staff was surprised to see me arrive with the Talib commander and his Kalashnikov-toting driver. Sangin and I sat across from each other, smiling at how surreal it was to be meeting like this. I was the first non-Muslim he'd ever shared a meal with, he told me; he was used to thinking of foreigners as invaders. "But you're a guest in our country," he said.

This summer, as the prospect of victory began to seem real, the leadership had emphasized the order to spare the life and property of those who surrendered. During the Eid al-Adha celebration in July, the amir, Haibatullah Akhunzada, had disseminated a message over WhatsApp explaining that a general amnesty would be granted once the Taliban were victorious, just as the Prophet Muhammad had done after capturing Mecca fourteen centuries earlier. Sangin said it even included the Zero Units, his mortal enemies, who were still guarding the evacuation in progress at the airport.

"We were greatly wronged by them, but we will forgive them, because when the amir gives an order, we must obey," he told me. He referred to the religious concept of *eta'at*; disobedience to one's amir was a sin. But Haibatullah, a religious scholar from Kandahar, had yet to appear in public, and Sangin and his men, like the rest of the country, were waiting to see what kind of government the Taliban would institute. He was certain about one thing: It would be an emirate, not a republic. "Our constitution is the Quran and Islam," he told me.

•   •   •

When I showed up at Rangina's house, there were no guards outside anymore, and her government-issued armored SUV was gone from the driveway. When the Taliban had taken it, they'd assured her she would be safe. But she was getting ready to evacuate; there was only a week remaining until August 31, the deadline for the troops to leave, and she and Abdullah had decided to take Zara and get out.

The day before, Rangina had been invited to a meeting at the ministry with members of the Taliban's education commission. Schools were closed since the collapse of the republic, but Rangina had wondered if they might ask her to continue in a temporary capacity, like Waheed Majrooh, the minister of public health, who'd remained and helped keep the hospitals running through the violence at the airport. Rangina arrived with her deputy to find several older men in turbans sitting in her office. They were formal but polite; one turned out to be from a village in Kandahar next to her father's. Together, they went to speak to the ministry's senior staff. After thanking God for their victory, one of the Taliban officials gave a speech about placing Islam at the center of a new curriculum—now their fundamentalist vision would shape the next generation of Afghan children.

Afterward, the officials served her melon in the office. She wanted to know whether girls would be denied higher education as they were in the 1990s. The Taliban assured her that they would be allowed to study past sixth grade, but only after a system was worked out to keep men and women separate, in accordance with religious law.

"I don't know if their definition of Shariah has changed from twenty years ago or if it's the same Shariah—that's the big question," Rangina told me. "Shariah is not a book that you can pick up and say, 'Here's Shariah.' It's history and laws and regulations over 1,400 years, and it's open to interpretation."

The officials told her she no longer had a job at the ministry, but they asked her to stay in Afghanistan. They suggested she could help them by speaking to the media and telling the world they weren't the monsters they were made out to be. Rangina was offended. "They just want me as their female spokesperson," she said.

As a former minister and U.S. citizen, Rangina had been prioritized for evacuation. As we talked, her phone rang, and she answered it. It was a marine, calling from the military base in

Qatar. "If we can help you out, would you be willing to work with us to get through a gate in HKIA and get put on an airplane?"

The next day, her deputy, Attaullah Wahidyar, drove them in a truck to Glory Gate, with Zara sitting quietly beside her and Abdullah in the back seat. Rangina was racked with guilt over leaving; maybe if she stayed, the Taliban would be willing to listen to her. Wahidyar was certain she was making the right decision. "They would have used her," he told me later. "You can't say no to a Talib with a gun."

In the back of the pickup speeding toward the airport, Rangina wept as she remembered another journey she'd taken as a scared child more than thirty years ago. In the middle of the night, her father had taken the family and fled the communists in a truck like this one, and they'd become refugees. But now the little girl in the back seat was her own daughter, and she was sitting in her father's place. And Ghulam Haider was dead, murdered, a martyr for the lost republic and the country she was leaving behind.

•   •   •

A few days after the evacuation ended, I passed by the office of *Etilaat-e Roz* and was surprised to find Zaki still there. A couple of weeks earlier, he'd told me that he and his staff had decided to leave while they still had a chance to get out. But they hadn't been able to get through the crowds at the airport. Zaki had been offered a place on our Sayara convoy, but he wasn't willing to go without his colleagues.

The Qataris, who were helping the Taliban get the airport running again, were still flying out some evacuees, so Zaki was hopeful that they could leave as a group in the coming days. A few of Zaki's journalists were sitting around the office, looking depressed. They told me they hadn't been out reporting yet; they were afraid of the Taliban on the street. I tried to reassure them by recounting how Mujahed, the spokesman, had given me a letter of permission and that I'd been able to keep working, even interview Taliban officials.

Two days later, I got a message from Zaki saying that some of his staff had been arrested covering a protest by women's rights activists outside a police station. I rushed over, but by the time I got to his office, they had already been released. Two were beaten so badly that they had to be taken to the hospital, including Zaki's younger brother, Taqi. I went over and persuaded the nervous staff to let me in; the two reporters were just being wheeled out of the X-ray department.

"Hi, Matthieu," Nemat Naqdi whispered from his gurney. I peered at the gauze swaddling his face and realized, with a stab of guilt, that he was one of the young journalists I'd exhorted to get out and work. He and Taqi, who hadn't gotten permits from the Taliban, were arrested at the demonstration, taken into a room and whipped. Nemat was hit so hard that he lost partial vision in his right eye.

Taliban officials would later apologize for the incident, but no action was taken against the fighters who were now functioning as the police. According to the Taliban, public protests were illegal without a permit, and given the current emergency situation, permits would not be granted. Covering such protests was illegal, too. Although the Taliban claimed that free speech would be allowed "within the limits of Islam," they had never made any pretense to liberalism. When I sat for an interview with Mujahed, he told me that democracy and Islam were incompatible; in the former, the people were sovereign, but according to the latter, God and the Quran ruled. In a world where even dictators paid lip service to democracy, the Taliban offered a remarkably frank vision for a religious theocracy.

And yet, like Mullah Baradar, the chief negotiator in Doha, Mujahed was seen as representing a relatively moderate tendency within the Taliban, one that advocated a pragmatic engagement with the world. There was still hope for the "inclusive" approach that had been promised under the agreement scuttled by Ghani's escape, but the interim cabinet announced on September 7 was drawn from the movement's old guard—most were Pashtun, many were elderly clerics, and all were men. The Taliban's total military victory had strengthened its hard-liners. Baradar, who many in the West had expected to lead the new cabinet, was made a deputy.

Rangina's replacement as acting minister of education had previously run a madrasa in Pakistan. When high schools were reopened in September, only boys were given permission to return; while in some provinces girls were also quietly allowed, as the end of the year approached, most in the country were still being kept out of school.

•   •   •

The heat of the summer passed. The nights grew longer. On crisp mornings, the smell of wood smoke filled the air in Kabul. The city's residents and the Taliban fighters were adjusting to one another; some of the jeans reappeared while the Taliban donned a patchwork of uniforms that had belonged to the republic. When I had visited the remnants of the CIA's Eagle Base, the fighters who accompanied our group of journalists on a tour wore operator-style helmets and carried American-made weapons; some even wore the tiger stripes of the Zero Units.

In the end, nearly everyone who could leave left. Zaki and his team made it out to the transit camps in Doha to await resettlement in the United States, as did Mahdi and Nadim, the translators I interviewed the day the city fell. Ghani was in Abu Dhabi writing a book, a follow-up to *Fixing Failed States*, perhaps. Rangina moved to Arizona with Abdullah and Zara, where she was offered a teaching job at a university. The Orgun commander and the Zero Unit troopers were sent to military bases in America, where they would begin new lives as refugees. Ramin and his wife were given an artist's residency in a French farmhouse, where he was writing of his longing for his city, a Kabul that now lived on in the imagination of a new diaspora.

Although daily life had returned to the capital's streets, after dark they quickly emptied out, apart from the fighters standing at intersections. I stayed inside, too—my friends were gone from this city where the music had fallen silent. I was longing to get out, and finally, more than two months after the fall of Kabul, I headed south, toward Kandahar. Akbar and I took turns at the wheel; the valleys of Wardak stretched out, barren mountains behind them. We rolled down the windows and breathed the clear air, careful to turn down the stereo at checkpoints. Highway 1, which had been a battleground for more than a decade, was safe enough now to drive at night, although you had to watch for the craters from roadside bombs, which the emirate was slowly trying to patch. The farther we traveled from Kabul, the less nostalgia people seemed to have for the republic. In Panjwai, outside Kandahar City, the farmers had dug up the IEDs and were planting crops. Everywhere, white flags fluttered above the graves of young men.

"Not a day would go by without dozens of bodies coming back along this road," Akbar said. He was from a valley north of Kabul that had provided many recruits for the Afghan Army. He had never been to the south before; now he sat with farmers in pomegranate orchards, comparing their experiences on opposite sides of the war. "We thought the people here have been cruel to kill so many of our sons like that. Now I see they suffered just as much. Maybe more."

For ordinary people in the countryside, the fall of the republic had at least brought an end to the fighting. But the Taliban hounded former officials, searching their homes for weapons and government vehicles. In Kandahar, I was told about a quiet campaign of kidnappings and assassinations of former police and intelligence officers by Taliban fighters—which their leaders denied—some driven by local disputes, others by revenge.

Akbar and I drove westward to Helmand. Outside the cities, we saw few armed men. We passed the bases built with foreign money, many bearing the scars of final battles. Most were empty, with only a white flag fluttering above; some whose Hesco barriers had been raided of wire for scrap were now melting back into the earth. It felt as if the country, deprived of a constant input of dollars, was returning to a lower energy state. The economy was in free fall, the banks were out of cash; it had been a drought year; and everyone feared the hunger that winter would bring.

On the highway near Shurabak, we passed a series of concrete walls, which I recognized as the entry points for the enormous air base that had been run by the marines. I thought about my visits there, when the runway was crowded with jets, and tried to remember the brash generals who'd explained, year after year, how they were winning—they just needed more troops, more money, more time. Twenty years had passed, long enough for a child to be raised, to finish her studies and become a young woman. That was the life span of the republic. Now the dream was over, and America was gone, along with an elite that fled even before the last foreign soldier was out, leaving behind a country on the brink of starvation.

We kept driving to Nimruz and reached the Iranian border. Here the desert began. A great exodus was underway. We watched as the migrants crowded onto trucks, heading west.

The Atlantic

The ASME judges described Jennifer Senior's story about the family Bobby McIlvaine left behind when he died on 9/11 as "superlative, an affecting, complex meditation on grief that never once veers into the maudlin or treacly." Killed outside the Twin Towers, the twenty-six-year-old McIlvaine was, in Senior's words, "a sage and a sap— philosophical about disappointments, melancholy when the weather changed, moony over girlfriends." "Senior helps us grasp fully the healing power of words, even when those still in mourning stumble over what those words should be," the judges' citation continued. " 'Twenty Years Gone' is a perfect encapsulation of what magazine writing, at its finest, can do." The first story written by Senior for The Atlantic after joining the magazine as a staff writer, "Twenty Years Gone" also won the 2022 Pulitzer Prize for Feature Writing.

Jennifer Senior

Twenty Years Gone

W hen Bobby McIlvaine died on September 11, 2001, his desk at home was a study in plate tectonics, coated in shifting piles of leather-bound diaries and yellow legal pads. He'd kept the diaries since he was a teenager, and they were filled with the usual diary things—longings, observations, frustrations—while the legal pads were marbled with more variety: aphoristic musings, quotes that spoke to him, stabs at fiction.

The yellow pads appeared to have the earnest beginnings of two different novels. But the diaries told a different kind of story. To the outside world, Bobby, twenty-six, was a charmer, a striver, a furnace of ambition. But inside, the guy was a sage and a sap— philosophical about disappointments, melancholy when the weather changed, moony over girlfriends.

Less than a week after his death, Bobby's father had to contend with that pitiless still life of a desk. And so he began distributing the yellow legal pads, the perfect-bound diaries: to Bobby's friends, to Bobby's girlfriend, Jen, to whom he was about to propose. Maybe, he told them, there was material in there that they could use in their eulogies.

One object in that pile glowed with more meaning than all the others: Bobby's very last diary. Jen took one look and quickly realized that her name was all over it. Could she keep it?

Bobby's father didn't think. He simply said yes. It was a reflex that he almost instantly came to regret. "This was a decision we were supposed to make together," his wife, Helen, told him. Here was an opportunity to savor Bobby's company one last time, to hear his *voice*, likely saying something new. In that sense, the diary wasn't like a recovered photograph. It raised the prospect, however brief, of literary resurrection. How, Helen fumed, could her husband not want to know Bobby's final thoughts—ones he may have scribbled as recently as the evening of September 10? And how could he not share her impulse to take every last molecule of what was Bobby's and reconstruct him?

"One missing piece," she told me recently, "was like not having an arm."

Over and over, she asked Jen to see that final diary. Helen had plenty of chances to bring it up, because Jen lived with the McIlvaines for a time after September 11, unable to tolerate the emptiness of her own apartment. Helen was careful to explain that she didn't need the object itself. All she asked was that Jen selectively photocopy it.

Jen would say she'd consider it. Then nothing would happen. Helen began to plead. *I just want the words*, she'd say. *If Bobby's describing a tree, just give me the description of the tree.* Jen demurred.

The requests escalated, as did the rebuffs. They were having an argument now. Helen, Jen pointed out, already had Bobby's other belongings, other diaries, the legal pads.

When she finally left the McIlvaines' house for good, Jen slammed the door behind her, got into her car, and burst into tears. Shortly after, she wrote Helen a letter with her final answer: No, just no. If Helen wanted to discuss this matter any further, she'd have to do so in the presence of Jen's therapist.

Helen and her husband never saw Jen again. "She became a nonperson to me," Helen told me. Today, she can't so much as recall Jen's last name.

But for years, Helen thought about that diary. Her mind snagged on it like a nail; she needled her husband for giving it away; it became the subject of endless discussion in her "limping group," as she calls it, a circle of six mothers in suburban Philadelphia who'd also lost children, though not on September 11. They became indignant on her behalf. A number proposed, only half jokingly, that they break into Jen's apartment and liberate the diary. "You don't get any more memories," one of the women told me. "So anything written, any video, any card—you cling to that. That's all you're going to get for life."

The McIlvaines would have to make do with what they already had. Eventually, they did. Three words of Bobby's became the family motto: *Life loves on.* No one could quite figure out which diary or legal pad it came from, but no matter. Helen wears a silver bracelet engraved with this phrase, and her husband got it tattooed in curlicue script on his upper arm.

· · ·

Here I should note that I know and love the McIlvaine family. On my brother's first day of college, he was assigned to a seven-person suite, and because he arrived last, Bobby became his roommate. My brother often thinks about what a small miracle that was: if he'd arrived just thirty minutes earlier, the suite would have been an isomer of itself, with the kids all shuffled in an entirely different configuration. But thanks to a happy accident of timing, my brother got to spend his nights chattering away with this singular kid, an old soul with a snappity-popping mind.

Eight years later, almost to the day, a different accident of timing would take Bobby's life. He and my brother were still roommates, but this time in a two-bedroom apartment in Manhattan, trying to navigate young adulthood.

Back when Bobby was still alive, I would occasionally see the McIlvaines. They struck me as maybe the nicest people on the planet. Helen taught reading to kids who needed extra help with it, mainly in a trailer in the parking lot of a Catholic high school. Bob Sr. was a teacher who specialized in working with troubled adolescents; for a decade, he'd also owned a bar. Jeff, Bobby's younger brother, was just a kid in those days, but he was always unreasonably good-natured when he turned up.

And Bobby: my God. The boy was incandescent. When he smiled it looked for all the world like he'd swallowed the moon.

Then, on the morning of September 11, 2001, Bobby headed off to a conference at Windows on the World, a restaurant in a building to which he seldom had reason to go, for a media-relations job at Merrill Lynch he'd had only since July. My brother waited and waited. Bobby never came home. From that point forward, I watched as everyone in the blast radius of this horrible event tried to make sense of it, tried to cope.

Early on, the McIlvaines spoke to a therapist who warned them that each member of their family would grieve differently. *Imagine that you're all at the top of a mountain,* she told them, *but you all have broken bones, so you can't help each other. You each have to find your own way down.*

It was a helpful metaphor, one that may have saved the McIlvaines' marriage. But when I mentioned it to Roxane Cohen Silver, a psychology professor at UC Irvine who's spent a lifetime studying the effects of sudden, traumatic loss, she immediately spotted a problem with it: "That suggests everyone will *make it* down," she told me. "Some people never get down the mountain at all."

This is one of the many things you learn about mourning when examining it at close range: it's idiosyncratic, anarchic, polychrome. A lot of the theories you read about grief are great, beautiful even, but they have a way of erasing individual experiences. Every mourner has a very different story to tell.

That therapist was certainly right, however, in the most crucial sense: after September 11, those who had been close to Bobby all spun off in very different directions. Helen stifled her grief, avoiding the same supermarket she'd shopped in for years so that no one would ask how she was. Jeff, Bobby's lone sibling, had to force his way through the perdition of survivor's guilt. Bob Sr. treated his son's death as if it were an unsolved murder, a cover-up to be exposed. Something was fishy about 9/11.

And then there was Jen. She's married now, has two terrific kids, but she wonders sometimes, when she's quarreling with her husband or feeling exasperated with her life, what it would have been like if she'd been with Bobby all this time. I tracked her down in April, and of course she's nothing like the heartless villainess I had come to imagine her to be. That was just the story I'd told myself, the one I'd used to make sense of the senseless, to give shape to my own rage. Like I said: we all need our stories.

One thing I knew when I finally visited her, though: I wanted to see that diary. And I wanted the McIlvaines to see it too. "I'm not a saver," she said when we first met up for cocktails. My heart froze.

But she still had it, just so you know.

·　　·　　·

Tell me about your son.

Helen welcomed this invitation the first time she heard it, because it focused her thinking, gave her an outlet for her grief. But soon it filled her with dread, and she felt herself straining under the weight of it. How can you possibly convey who your firstborn was or what he meant to you?

Helen usually starts by telling people that Bobby went to Princeton, but that's hardly because she's status fixated. It's because she and Bob Sr. did not expect to have a child who went to an Ivy League school. They both went to state schools in Pennsylvania, not even particularly well-known ones. Both of their kids were sporty. But when Bobby was eight, his third-grade teacher said to them—and they both remember her exact words—"Start saving your pennies." This one's education might cost you.

"The amount of things that had to go right for my brother to go to Princeton were, like, astronomical," says Jeff, a high-school biology teacher and track coach in Somerdale, New Jersey. "To us, it was like someone from our family becoming the president."

This is how everyone in the family remembers Bobby: as a sui generis creature, exceptional and otherworldly, descended from the heavens through a basketball hoop.

He was an intense student. He was an even more intense athlete, competitive to the point of insolence. Writing in the *Philadelphia*

Inquirer last year, Mike Sielski, an old high-school classmate of Bobby's, described him as "all bones and acute angles and stiletto elbows" on the basketball court. It was a goose-pimpling story, one he had occasion to write because another classmate of theirs had unearthed thirty-six seconds of video from 1992, in which a teenage Bobby McIlvaine throws an immaculate pass that sets up an immaculate shot that flies right over the teenage head of . . .

Kobe Bryant.

Bobby scored sixteen points off Kobe and his team that day, in addition to setting up that floater.

When he arrived at college, Bobby retained a bit of that alpha-dog streak. He was still competitive, even while playing mindless, made-up dorm games. He wasn't bashful about ribbing friends. He was tall and handsome and had a high level of confidence in his sense of style, which may or may not have been justified. "There were times you wanted him to step back and not be so serious and intense," says Andre Parris, a former suitemate and one of Bobby's closest friends. "But it was part of who and what he was, and what he thought he had to do to get ahead."

What "getting ahead" meant to Bobby was complicated. Financial worries are all over his journals from those years (*I don't feel like a real person sitting here with no money*, reads one typical entry). Yet he was conflicted about what it might take to make money, flummoxed by all the kids who were beating a dutiful path to business school. (*Is youth really just a hobby?* he asked about them, with evident pique.) He wanted to be a writer. Which paid nothing, obviously.

This conflict continued into his brief adulthood. He spent two years in book publishing before realizing that it was no way to make a living and switched instead to corporate PR. He could still write his novels on the side.

But for all Bobby's hunger and swagger, what he mainly exuded, even during his college years, was warmth, decency, a corkscrew quirkiness. He doted on girlfriends. He gave careful advice. His senior year, he took a modern-dance class because, well, why not?

It would be fun. And different. His final project involved physically spelling out his girlfriend's name.

That was just a lark, though. Bobby's real intellectual passion was African American culture and history. After Bobby died, the McIlvaines got not one but two condolence notes from Toni Morrison, with whom he'd taken a class. The second came with the term paper he'd written for her. "It is certainly one of the more accomplished and insightful," she wrote, "as was he." His senior thesis received an honorable mention for the main prize in the department of African American studies.

At his funeral, Bobby's oldest friends spoke of what a role model he was to them. I was five years older than Bobby, which meant I mainly saw him as charming and adorable, intelligent and unstoppable.

But strangely, I wanted to impress him too. When I started my job at *New York* magazine, writing short features in the theater section each week, Bobby gave me grief about ending each one of them with a quote. At first I was annoyed, defensive—*the little shit*—but in hindsight, it's amazing that I cared so much about this twenty-two-year-old's opinion and even more amazing that he'd read me attentively enough to discover an incipient tic. To this day, I credit Bobby with teaching me a valuable lesson: if you're going to cede the power of the last word to someone else, you'd better be damn sure that person deserves it.

•　　•　　•

Bob McIlvaine Sr. cries easily and regularly when you speak to him. Everyone in the family knows this and has grown accustomed to it—his grief lives close to the surface, heaving up occasionally for air. He cried at our first lunch after the McIlvaines picked me up at the train station a few months ago; he cried again just minutes into our first chat when the two of us were alone; he cried in a recent interview with Spike Lee for a documentary series about 9/11 on HBO.

In talking with Bob Sr., something heartbreaking and rudely basic dawned on me: September 11 may be one of the most-documented calamities in history, but for all the spools of disaster footage we've watched, we still know practically nothing about the last moments of the individual dead. It's strange, when you think about it, that an event so public could still be such a punishing mystery. Yet it is, and it is awful—the living are left to perseverate, to let their imaginations run amok in their midnight corrals.

For Bob Sr., what that meant was wondering where Bobby was and what he was doing when the chaos began. For years, that was all he could think about. The idea of Bobby suffering tortured him. Was he incinerated? Was he asphyxiated? Or even worse? "I think Bobby jumped," he shouted up the stairs one day to his wife. The thought nearly drove Helen mad.

Over time, it became clear that Bobby didn't jump. Bobby's was one of fewer than one hundred civilian corpses recovered from the wreckage. But it haunted Bob Sr. that he never saw the body. At the morgue on September 13, the pathologist strongly advised him against viewing it. Only years later—four? five? he can no longer remember—did he finally screw up the courage to go to the medical examiner's office in New York City and get the official report.

That's when everything changed. "My whole thesis—everything I jump into now—is based upon his injuries," he tells me. "Looking at the body, I came to the conclusion that he was walking in and bombs went off."

A controlled demolition, he means. That is how he thinks Bobby died that day and how the towers eventually fell: from a controlled demolition. It was an inside job, planned by the U.S. government not to justify the war in Iraq—that was a bonus—but really, ultimately, to destroy the twenty-third floor, because that's where the FBI was investigating the use of gold that the United States had unlawfully requisitioned from the Japanese during World War II, which it then leveraged to bankrupt the Soviet Union. The planes were merely for show.

• • •

Does a man wake up on September 12, 2001, and believe such a thing? No. This belief takes shape over the span of years, many years.

That first year, Bob Sr. was numb. His sole objective was to get through each day. But he eventually got involved in a group called 9/11 Families for Peaceful Tomorrows, protesting the wars in Afghanistan and Iraq. "It opened up my life," he tells me. "I became very active. That's how I grieved. It was perfect."

Before Bobby went to Princeton, Bob Sr. had been indifferent to politics, voting sometimes for Democrats and sometimes for Republicans—including, he thinks, Ronald Reagan. "I was not a well-read person," he says. "I owned a bar in the city. If I even mentioned the word *progressive*, my customers probably would have shot me."

But then Bobby started taking classes with Princeton's glamorous tenured radicals. He started writing for the school's *Progressive Review*. His father devoured everything he wrote. Soon, he had Bob Sr. reading Howard Zinn's *A People's History of the United States* and *Z Magazine*, the radical monthly. Bob Sr. has been interested in politics ever since. "That's all because of Bobby."

So this antiwar activity? It *was* perfect—a natural outlet for him.

But as time wore on, Bob Sr. got impatient. In 2004, he went down to Washington to hear Condoleezza Rice speak to the 9/11 Commission, and her testimony—or lack thereof, he'd say—so enraged him that he left in a huff, cursing in the halls of Congress. "I wanted answers," he explains. Yet no answers were forthcoming. That's when he realized: the government was hiding something. "I became militant," he says. "To this day, I'm very militant."

Bob Sr. is a bespectacled, soft-spoken man, slender and slightly stooped. But his affect is deceptive. We're sitting in the upstairs den of the McIlvaines' three-bedroom home in Oreland, Pennsylvania, the same house where Bobby and Jeff grew up. It's sweet, modest, cluttered with family pictures. But this room has been transformed into a 9/11 research bunker, stuffed with books and carefully organized files—by event, subject, country. The largest piece of art on the wall is a world map freckled with pins marking every country that's invited Bob Sr. to tell his story.

"I speak out so much, the word just spreads," he tells me. "I'll show you Italy." Pictures and clippings from a Rome film festival, he means, because he appeared in the documentary *Zero: Inchiesta sull'11 Settembre*. He got to walk the red carpet. "The Russians came over. They spent two days here, wanted to hear what I had to say." Meaning Russian state news agencies. They parked themselves on the McIlvaines' back deck. "France came here, stayed a few days to talk." Same deal, though he doesn't remember which media outfit. ("My dad is practically a celebrity in that community," Jeff told me.)

Crucial to Bob Sr.'s understanding of September 11—that it was the cynical skullduggery of the U.S. government, not a grisly act of terrorism by jihadists using commercial planes filled with helpless civilians—is the work of Architects & Engineers for 9/11 Truth, which popularized the idea that jet fuel couldn't burn at a high enough temperature to melt beams into molten steel. This is, it should go without saying, contrary to all observable fact.

But this theory is what Bob Sr. is eager to illustrate for me. He has visuals prepared, lots of building diagrams. I tell him we'll get there; I just want to ask a few more questions about those early days—

He's disappointed. "Everything I've done in my life is based upon those seconds." This is something he very much wants to discuss.

And so we discuss it. Only a preplanned detonation, he argues, could bring down those towers, and only a lobby embroidered with explosives could explain the injuries to Bobby's body. He has the full medical examiner's report.

It is very upsetting to read. Most of Bobby's head—that beautiful face—was missing, as was most of his right arm. The details are rendered in generic diagrams and the dispassionate language of pathology ("Absent: R upper extremity, most of head"), as well as a chilling pair of responses on a standard checklist.

Hair color: None.
Eye color: None.

But a subtle thing made Bob Sr. think something was amiss. The report describes many lacerations and fractures, but they appear almost entirely on the front of Bobby's body. The back of his corpse is basically described as pristine, besides multiple fractures to what remained of his head.

The story we've told ourselves all these years is that Bobby had already left the building when the planes hit. Bobby didn't work in the World Trade Center; from what we could piece together, he'd gone to Windows on the World simply to help a new colleague set up for a morning presentation at an all-day conference, not to attend it. So Bobby did his part, was our assumption, then said his goodbyes and was making his way back to nearby Merrill Lynch when he was suddenly killed in the street by flying debris.

Bob Sr. doesn't buy it. If that were true—if Bobby were moving *away* from the World Trade Center—wouldn't he have fallen forward? Wouldn't there be injuries on his *back*? "If you're running away, it'd be more of a crushing type of thing," he tells me. "Probably every bone in his body would be breaking."

I tell him I'm not a pathologist, but it seems just as plausible to me that he heard the roaring sound of a plane flying too low and too fast, or maybe the sound of a hijacked aircraft hitting the North Tower itself, and turned around to see what had happened and never knew what hit him.

He rejects this explanation. "My theory is he was walking *into* the building at the time, because he had the conference up there."

"I thought his conference started at 8:30?" I ask. The first plane hit at 8:46 a.m. That would have meant Bobby was arriving late.

"I thought it started at 9," Bob Sr. says.

"Isn't there a way to find out?" I ask.

"You know, to tell you the truth, I never . . ."

He'd never checked.

        •   •   •

Breakfast and registration for the conference began at 8 o'clock. Opening remarks were scheduled for 8:30. Bobby's colleague was scheduled to speak at 8:40. The full brochure is available on the 9/11 Memorial & Museum's website.

When I eventually visit Jen—she of the purloined diary, the woman to whom Bobby was about to be engaged—she shows me the daily planner that was sitting on his desk at Merrill. It's cluttered with appointments. But the day of September 11 is blank. Whatever he was doing was not significant enough to merit its own entry.

My brother also tells me that he still has the note Bob Sr. left for him on his kitchen table on Thursday, September 13. It said that an investigator with the New York City Police Department, Joe Gagliardi, had just come by to drop off the wallet they'd pulled from Bobby's pocket. One line in particular stood out. *He was found on the perimeter.* Not near the lobby.

"Was he really?" Bob Sr. says when I phone him and ask him about the note. He'd completely forgotten that he'd written it. "If that's true, that's great." He thinks for a moment. "Though the perimeter—he still could have been ten feet away. He certainly wasn't one hundred feet from the building."

I then tell him about the conference schedule, which actually did leave open the possibility that he was one hundred feet from the building. If he'd left before his colleague started speaking—or the opening remarks—he could have been quite close to his office at Merrill Lynch, a five-minute walk away. Bob Sr. takes it all in. He repeats that he finds Bobby's injuries too extreme, too savage, to be caused by flying debris. "But you know what?" he finally says. "That's no longer relevant to me. My whole thing is who did it and why. It's been twenty years and I *still* can't get any answers."

·   ·   ·

It takes me some time, but eventually I summon the courage to ask Bob Sr. an obvious question: What makes his claims about the destruction of the World Trade Center more credible than the claims of, for instance, Donald Trump supporters who say the 2020 election was stolen?

"I can believe it was stolen!" he tells me. "But I'm not going to go around preaching that, because *I don't know*. Because I'm doing *my* homework." Bob Sr. is always reading. His latest is a biography of Allen Dulles. "Probably 99.9 percent of the people that you will find in those radical groups—the Oath Keepers, whatever—they really haven't done any research."

But then he adds that he sympathizes with Trump voters, as much as he despises Trump himself. "This country hasn't done anything for them in such a long time. So you can't blame them for voting for him."

· · ·

Bob Sr. asks if I would like to see Bobby's wallet. I didn't realize he had it, but he does, stuffed in a biohazard bag, itself entombed in a plastic box in the room that once belonged to Bobby. He carefully opens them for me.

"Helen and Jeff have never seen this," he tells me.

They haven't?

"No."

The wallet is covered in dust, still, and faintly redolent of that World Trade Center tang, a scent once so powerful that New Yorkers could smell it in their eyes. He starts pulling out a twenty-six-year-old's modest possessions: a Pennsylvania driver's license, a Visa card, some kind of work or building ID, a library card. The wallet still contains thirteen dollars in cash, but the money is disintegrating, almost completely rotted away.

"The only thing I do is 9/11 stuff," Bob Sr. says. "My whole basis of everything revolves around the day."

This is not, it should be said, anything like what Helen does with her days. A two-decade investigation into 9/11 was not part of her retirement plan. In one of our earliest conversations, she specifically told me that she'd walk across the United States to *not* discover some of the things that Bob Sr. has learned. So as he and I sit here, inspecting a wallet that she's never seen, I ask: Doesn't all this searching, this interrogating, have unhealthy consequences for his marriage?

He readily admits that it does: "We'd socialize and she'd catch me saying stuff, and she would go nuts. She'd say, 'Do not talk about 9/11.' But then someone would come up to me and say, 'Can I ask you about it?' And I'd start talking. Then she'd find out about it. She'd get so upset." They now tend to socialize separately. "I will talk 9/11 with anyone I see, if they want to talk about it," he says. "And I think that's why I don't have many friends. They're *afraid* I'm going to talk about it."

It may be hard to imagine why anyone would want to spend so much time immersed in the story, sensations, and forensics of his son's death. But for Bob Sr., that's precisely the point: to keep the grief close. "I don't want to get away from it," he tells me. He *wants* to stay at the top of the mountain. This is how he spends time in Bobby's company—by solving this crime, by exposing the truth about the abuses of American empire. "Doing what I'm doing, that's really helped me, because I think of him every day. Every time I talk, I talk about Bobby."

He's aware that there are other ways to spend time with Bobby that wouldn't be quite so excruciating. He could read his diaries, for example. To this day, he feels terrible that he handed that last one off to Jen. He felt so guilty about it for so long that he was still mentioning it in interviews in 2011. A British newspaper referred to it as "the journal episode."

"I'm just not that big on the journals," he tells me. "They don't mean that much to me."

So what means the most to you? I ask.

"That he was murdered," he says.

•   •   •

On the morning of September 11, Helen, the most stoic of the McIlvaines, was the only one who panicked. Jeff knew that his brother didn't work in the World Trade Center. Bob Sr., who was teaching that day in the adolescent psych unit of a local hospital, treated the macabre, smoldering towers like a news event and, along with everyone else, began watching the coverage on TV.

Helen, however, took one look at the television and needed to sit down. She knew it seemed ridiculous, superstitious, but she'd spoken with Bobby the night before and forgotten to end the conversation the way she always did: "Be careful." She'd later say those words to his casket as it was lowered into his grave.

By midday, when no one had heard from Bobby, everyone in the family felt like Helen. Yes, the cell towers were down in Lower Manhattan and the phones were working only sporadically, but surely Bobby, who could spend hours on the phone talking with his parents (*How do you guys find so much to talk about?* his friends always asked), would have found a way to call, and Jen had heard nothing, which *really* made no sense. Bobby had just asked her father for permission to marry her two days earlier.

In the late afternoon, Andre, his close friend and old suitemate, finally reached a woman at Merrill Lynch who awkwardly told him that Bobby and a colleague had been scheduled to attend a conference at Windows on the World that morning and no one had heard from them since. Andre called the McIlvaines.

"That first night was probably worse than after we found out for sure that he'd died," Jeff says, "because we had no idea what had happened. I couldn't get that out of my head—that he was *in* that, you know?"

They slept in the den, the three of them. Jen stayed in her own living room that night, glued to the TV.

On Wednesday morning, Jeff and Bob Sr. were too agitated to remain in Oreland. They took a train to New York and made a fruitless tour of the city's triage centers. Nothing. My brother stood on line at a missing-persons center; Andre ran a command center out of his apartment, working the phones and every lead he had; Jeff checked every website he could find. *Refresh, refresh, refresh.*

Jen sat and waited.

Bob Sr. spent Wednesday night in my brother and Bobby's apartment, sleeping in his son's bed.

The next day, Andre got a call from the NYPD, this time with grim news: everyone needed to go immediately to the armory on Lexington Avenue.

Once again, Andre had to tell the McIlvaines. Helen calmly did as she was told. She treated these instructions as if she were an astronaut, doing whatever step came next if one of the modules of the International Space Station caught on fire.

The armory was a seething mass of the desperate. Hundreds of families were lined up outside, carrying posters with faces of their loved ones. A minister escorted my brother, Jen, Andre, and the McIlvaine family inside. Helen gave him Bobby's name. A police officer approached her from across the room. "Are you the mother?"

Much of what followed was a blur. They were shown to a private room where grief counselors descended on them. Then something unusual happened: Rudy Giuliani walked in.

The mayor was unaccompanied. Without aides, without cameras, nothing. He looked genuinely relieved to have a family to console at that moment, with so many bereaved New Yorkers still twisting in limbo, posting flyers with pictures of the missing on lampposts, chain-link fences, hospital walls.

Giuliani embraced everyone. Then he took a seat opposite the McIlvaines. He uttered just five words: "Tell me about your son."

•   •   •

If Bob Sr. chose to feed his grief, Helen chose to starve hers. She spoke about it with her limping group because they understood. But she was determined not to be, as she puts it, "At-Least-I'm-Not-Helen." Living with the impossible was hard enough. But to be in the position of having to console others about her misfortune or to manage their discomfort or, worst of all, to smile politely through their pity—that was more than she could bear. Helen can still rattle off a list of all the well-meaning things people said that stung.

No parent should bury a child.

You will never be the same.

I was with my children last night and realized you'll never have something like that again.

Did people not realize that they were building a moat, not a bridge, when they said such things? That they were drawing attention to the pretty castles they lived in, their walls still lined with luck?

That first year was brutal. Once, while she was sitting in a diner with some friends, one of them started going on and on about the musical talents of her son. "I wanted to scream," Helen says. "I had to get out. I couldn't listen to somebody else talk about their child. For years. I couldn't."

The second year wasn't much better. She tried going to Italy on a tour with a friend. She says she came across as cold, distant, strange. She dreaded the most innocuous question: *Have any kids?*

Work helped. Her students needed her, and her colleagues were great. "Except I didn't want their help, because it was too soon," Helen says. "So afterwards, a few years down the road, I looked like I'd healed. And it wasn't true. I *wanted* to talk about it sometimes. But I had to find other means to do it, because I'd kind of shut that door."

I can't decide whether this corresponds with the Helen I've come to know. Maybe?

Helen: She wears little or no makeup. She is exceedingly good-humored. She is always brimming with questions about your life. She's the kind of person who goes along with any plan and can spend twenty minutes in a drugstore trying on funny pairs of reading glasses with you.

We actually did this together in Florida a couple of years ago. We both happened to be visiting my mom.

So the reserve she's describing is a little foreign to me. "I have a weird personality," she tells me. "I can cry over a blouse that I ruined in the laundry and then be stoic for something . . ." She trails off, but I believe the word she's looking for is *big.*

But with Bobby . . .! Bobby brought out her more emotional self because he was such a sensitive kid. "Once, after about half an hour of listening to his woe-is-me girlfriend stories," she tells me, "I said to him, 'You do understand I've been married to Dad for almost thirty years and I've never given him this much thought, right?'" But of course she loved every minute of it.

The last time she saw Bobby was two nights before he died. Not an hour before, he had asked Jen's father for permission to marry her; now the two families were having dinner at a restaurant in Lambertville, New Jersey, where Jen had an apartment. Helen took one look at her son and saw that his forehead was still shimmering with sweat. She reached under the table to find his hand. He locked his pinkie with hers. They stayed that way until the food came.

• • •

Around the tenth anniversary of September 11, Helen realized that she was not all right. She'd lost a child, so maybe this was what her new life was destined to be: not all right. But she wasn't convinced. Somewhere along the way, her toughness, her steadfast refusal to be a victim—it had backfired. "I found myself being petty. And bickering. I found myself being too gossipy sometimes."

I've never heard Helen say a cross word about anyone. Even when I mention that I'll soon be seeing Jen, she reacts with anxiety, not bitterness. She doesn't want to open old wounds. They were both suffering terribly back then; neither was her finest self.

Okay, but what if she lends me the diary? I ask.

"Oh my God. Would you marry me?"

But this is today's Helen. The Helen of a decade ago decided she wasn't who she wanted to be. Her therapy had stalled. She had trouble managing her anger. "My life just feels so amazingly off kilter," she wrote in a reminiscence marking the tenth anniversary.

She'd kept too much in, and she was fermenting in her own brine.

Not long after, she started seeing a different therapist. This one was spiritual. That new perspective changed everything. "She really believes that we don't see all."

Even before Bobby died, Helen was a big fan of self-help books. But after September 11, she bought them by the dozen, hoovering up everything she could about loss. She found Elisabeth Kübler-Ross indispensable—not so much for her writing about the five stages of grief, though that was fine, but for her writing about life after death.

Kübler-Ross once considered a belief in the afterlife a form of denial. But starting in the mid-1970s, she had a change of heart, compiling thousands of testimonies from those who'd had near-death experiences in order to show that our souls outlast us.

"I looked at life-after-death books, but they were too faith-based," Helen says. "I *wanted* to believe what I was taught in my Catholic upbringing. But what I liked about Kübler-Ross is that she had a science background."

It was precisely because she was a scientist, of course, that Kübler-Ross's fellow physicians were so dismayed by this strange turn in her interests. They thought it kooky and unrigorous, a stain on her legacy. I tell this to Helen. She laughs. "Bet they didn't sell millions of books."

Kübler-Ross used a hokey but intuitive metaphor to describe the body and soul: our bodies are our mortal coils, our "cocoons"; when we die, we shudder them off and our souls—our "butterflies"—are released into the wilds of the universe. Helen cherished this idea. It was a notion that could redeem a violently, capriciously abbreviated life. "One day I actually thought, *What if there's a hierarchy and Bobby's a part of that, and he just came down as a human for a bit?*"

She and Bob Sr. began watching *Supernatural* and *Buffy the Vampire Slayer*, shows they'd never have imagined watching before.

And here in this world, Helen came to understand that there was nothing to be gained by bottling up her grief. At age sixty, she took up running, not only because it felt good but because it allowed her to cry. She started expressing herself more. She noticed one day that the tempest of grievances she unloosed in her therapist's office were all so trivial, so petty, so *pointless*. What was she getting so worked up about?

Now she's doing the very thing the self-help books tell you to do: letting stuff go. She tells me about a friend whose towering self-involvement used to infuriate her. But recently, she chatted with her on the phone and decided just to enjoy the good bits.

Wow, I say. What makes you so forgiving?

"It wasn't serving me well."

• • •

You know what radical acceptance is? Living with a husband who has dedicated his life to spreading the word that the United States deliberately orchestrated the collapse of the World Trade Center and then conspired to cover it up. Forget all the chipper advice columns about how to get along with your Trump-loving uncle at Thanksgiving. How do you get on in your decades-long marriage after your son has died and your spouse wakes up each morning livid as an open wound and determined to expose the truth?

Helen would be lying if she said this didn't cause friction.

"There were many moments where I was like, *Oh, please*," she says. She was perfectly open to some of the things Bob Sr. said. "But a lot of it was emotional, and a lot of it, I couldn't trace to find out myself, and I'm not a go-on-a-website kind of person. I didn't want to burst his bubble by constantly saying, 'Well, did you check, is it a valid website?'"

Perhaps the more challenging issue, the nuts-and-bolts-of-living-in-a-marriage issue, was daily conversation. Bob Sr.'s single-minded focus meant that any conversation could segue without warning into September 11. She'd come downstairs and tell him she was thinking about buying a new sweater; he'd reply by asking if she knew that the government had lied about the actual date of Osama bin Laden's death.

"So has it gotten in the way?" she asks. "Yeah, many times. We'd be going somewhere, and I'd say to Bob, 'You *cannot* talk about 9/11.' And he'd say, 'Well, they ask me about it.' I fell for that for the first ninety-nine times until my therapist said, 'That's not good enough.' When we're out at a social event, we're out. I don't want to be always *victim, victim, victim.*"

How do you handle it now, I ask, if you feel another soliloquy coming on?

"Now I say, 'Bob, you have the I-won't-talk-about-anything-else-but-9/11 look on your face.' We've come to a point where we can actually joke about it."

Helen wants me to understand: There are some aspects of Bob Sr.'s obsessions that she doesn't merely tolerate; she actively supports them. Two years ago, she listened to a presentation by Architects & Engineers for 9/11 Truth and found it persuasive. It's the other parts of his narrative, which keep evolving, that leave her at loose ends. "If I were him, I'd just stick with the buildings," she says. I ask if she's up-to-date on his latest theory, involving Japanese gold. She shakes her head. "I don't even hear it," she says. "I'm defending the person, not the view."

Long ago, Helen realized that "9/11 truth," as Bob Sr. likes to call it, had sunk its hooks into her husband, and she's never thought it her place to pry them loose. "I'm very protective of him," she says. "If he decided to be a male stripper in an old people's home, it's okay with me. He has to be who he has to be, because damn it, this happened, you know? And if that's going to give him comfort—"

She interrupts herself, gives an embarrassed smile. "Get that visualization out of your head."

Helen would never dream of abandoning this dear man. He was Bobby's Little League coach. The one who organized races around the house when the kids were little, using a piece of tape for the finish line. Bob Sr. was her only suitor who ever suggested they play sports together—the others thought that was strictly for the fellas.

And now he's the only other person in the world who understands what it feels like to have raised Bobby McIlvaine and lost him.

She walks me over to the wall with a giant framed poster she had custom-made for her husband five years ago. It's a periodic table of Bob Sr., basically—dozens of images of him, all tidily laid out in a grid. Bob Sr. talking to Rosie O'Donnell. Bob Sr. giving an interview on French television. Bob Sr. speaking at a forum about the 9/11 Commission report, captured on C-SPAN. "I gave him that on his seventieth birthday," she says. She went online, punched his name into Google, and voilà. A hero's gallery. "I love looking at it." He's become the superstar, strangely, that his son never had the chance to be.

Bob Sr.'s crusade may look to the outside world like madness. Helen sees it as an act of love. "He's almost going to war for his son," she tells me. "He's being a father in the best way he knows how. How can I not allow that?"

• • •

Most theories of grief, particularly the ones involving stages, are more literary than literal. People don't mourn sequentially, and they certainly don't mourn logically. But there's an aspect of one of those models I keep circling back to whenever I think of the McIlvaines. It's the "yearning and searching" stage of grief, first described by the British psychiatrists Colin Murray Parkes and John Bowlby in the 1960s. "When searching," Parkes writes, "the bereaved person feels and acts as if the lost person were recoverable, although he knows intellectually that this is not so."

How Bob Sr. searches is obvious. But it occurs to me, after speaking with Helen, that perhaps her years-long preoccupation with Bobby's final diary is her equivalent of Bob Sr.'s obsessions. "Yes!" she says when I tentatively raise the possibility. "Yes, yes. It's 'If I can't have *this*, then I'll have *that*.'"

Yet here's what's curious. Helen has two earlier diaries of Bobby's. She also has stacks of legal pads of his writing, many with diarylike entries in them. But she's barely dipped into them at all.

One reason is practical: They're hard to decipher. Bobby's handwriting is neat but small and slightly peculiar. Another is instinctive: for a long time, Helen feared that reading them would be a violation of a sacred boundary, "like going into his room without knocking." Yet another is how much pain it causes her. "I tried today again," she wrote in another reminiscence on the tenth anniversary of Bobby's death. "I thought, 'If I don't tackle these before I'm dead, who will?'" She lasted ten minutes. Bob Sr. has never looked at them at all.

"But somewhere I did find the words *Life loves on*," Helen tells me.

I've been meaning to ask her about this because I'm now reading Bobby's diaries and legal pads, and I can't find the phrase anywhere. Does she still not know where it came from?

She doesn't. She thought he'd written it about a close family friend who'd died, but she was wrong. I tell her I'll keep looking.

I take one of the two diaries back to my hotel that night. And I realize, as I'm reading, that there's probably another reason Helen never dug too deep into either one of them. They're from his freshman and sophomore years of college, when he was still a proto-person, still essentially a kid. He was clearly older when he scribbled in some of those legal pads, but they're chaotic and undated. Only the diaries feel manageable and chronological, and they read like the musings of a boy in his late teens—florid, soulful, a little mushy. He doesn't sound at all like the Bobby of September 11, 2001, who was almost twenty-seven years old.

Yet I still get a kick out of them and those chaotic legal pads, especially the parts about writing. Even at nineteen, Bobby was trying to find his voice, sometimes shifting from the first person to the third to see if he liked it better (and then saying so in the margins—*third-person experiment!*). They're filled with exhortations and reminders to himself: *I need to stay true to my voice, whatever it is. I write horrible stuff in other people's voices.* And my favorite: *Hope is even more important than talent.*

There's also tons of beautiful stuff about his family. This may be what astonishes me most, given that Bobby was in late adolescence, a time when most kids morph into ruthless family vivisectionists. Yet he devotes page after page to how much he loves and admires Helen, Bob Sr., and Jeff. In May 1995, for instance, he wrote about discovering that Bob Sr.'s father had been an alcoholic. Bobby had had no inkling. *He made sure that he didn't give me the bullshit,* Bobby wrote of his own father:

> He made sure I had something better, and only asked that I do my best. That's all he asked. That's all my mom asked. And I want so badly to make them proud, even more proud than they already are. They deserve the pride. They deserve more than I can ever give them, and yet they will never ask for more than me. I love them so much.

You can hardly blame Helen for wanting to hear what he had to say once he'd become a young man.

•   •   •

Jen Cobb, now Middleton, wears her hair long, rather than in her old pixie cut, but her style and demeanor remain the same. She is still animated, still gracious, still beautiful to look at; when I walk up to her door in Washington, DC, she greets me with a long hug. There are rescue dogs, there are sunlit rooms, there is a kitchen straight from a Nancy Meyers film. (I half-expect Meryl Streep to come gliding up with a tray of unbaked croissants.)

Jen has made for herself what is, to all outward appearances, a lovely life. But she had to assemble that life brick by brick, and she works hard to keep the joints from coming apart.

When I spoke briefly with Helen about Jen, she made an astute observation: Jen came from a family with lots of money but little love while the McIlvaines had lots of love but little money. Jen says that yes, that's partly true, though her mother was a loving soul; she just didn't see enough of Jen's life. Susan E. Cobb died on April 20, 2001, less than five months before Bobby did, of a cancer that spread slowly, then fast.

Which is to say: On September 11, Jen was already a husk of herself.

Jen's father, her remaining parent, was highly successful but only narrowly rational, a bully and a screamer. This had predictable consequences in her romantic life: Jen always demanded complete control. She was done being bossed around.

Then along came Bobby, asking for more vulnerability and a shared say in both of their lives. Somehow, she trusted him. They first met a couple of years earlier, at the PR firm Burson-Marsteller, and around the office, he was known as the good guy who made everyone feel important. The inveterate romantic, he made *her* feel important, asking question after question about her family, writing her love notes for no reason. For her twenty-seventh birthday, on December 6, 2000, he asked my brother to scram and rearranged the furniture in their apartment to turn it into a restaurant, where he cooked her a three-course meal.

Jen would later learn that the dinner was a dry run for a proposal. She put a hold on the Ritz-Carlton in Philadelphia for October 20, 2002.

When her mother died, Jen could barely function. Her mother was the one who'd protected her from her father's storms of rage; she was the one who'd chatted with her late at night after Jen had spent a boisterous evening out with girlfriends. Yet Bobby remained steadfastly by her side, making the intolerable seem survivable. He would be with her every step of the way. She would still be loved.

Then Bobby died. The world became a mean, untrustworthy place. "There was not one thing I could control," she says. "Not one thing at all."

• • •

Jen keeps a steamer trunk of Bobby's things in the attic above her garage. In anticipation of my arrival, she's brought his belongings down in a turquoise canvas bag. She starts sifting through it. "There's the diary," she says, pointing. "The thing that caused all that trouble."

Bobby's other two diaries were hundreds of pages long. This one, I will shortly discover, had only seventeen pages of entries. All that fuss over what was barely a pamphlet.

Then again, they're a dense seventeen pages.

Jen has no memory of getting the diary from Bob Sr. But she does remember reading it immediately, voraciously, and returning to it night after night. She remembers, too, Helen asking for it back, though the tensions didn't start immediately. At first, everything was fine. Helen even gave her the engagement ring Bobby had bought for her. It was awkward and unceremonious—"He'd have wanted you to have this"—but Jen was grateful, and she wore it everywhere for months.

At some point, though, Helen started getting more vocal about that diary. "In hindsight, I don't know what my problem was," Jen says. "I was probably in pain and also grasping for control and wanted something of his that no one else had. It seems kind of ridiculous now. It's just how I felt at the time—that it was mine and I wanted it to be mine and I didn't want anyone else to have it. It probably felt like it was all I had left."

What I had to understand about those awful, leaden days, Jen says, is that she wasn't just depressed. She was wretched—"double grieving," as she puts it, for her mother and then her future husband. When her mother and Bobby died in rapid succession, she fell into a deep depression, though she did her valiant best to conceal it. She still has anxiety attacks to this day. "When something upsets me," she says, "it goes downhill fast."

Which all makes perfect sense, I say. The only thing I can't understand is why she refused to transcribe the nonpersonal parts of Bobby's diary for Helen. That's not the act of a depressed person or a grieving person. That's the act of someone who's angry. She must have been upset with Helen for some reason, no?

Here Jen pauses. Then she starts measuring her words. "This isn't a knock on Helen at all," she says. "I'm so beyond it. But at the time I remember resenting that she said, 'You're going to be okay, because you're young.'" Jen recognized that there was a difference between their two losses. "But it felt like she was saying my grief was less important than hers. I know it was coming from a place of extreme pain, but I remember thinking, *How does she know I'm going to be okay? What if I'm not okay? What if I have a different kind of not-okay?*"

One thing you don't say to a person who's mourning, Jen tells me, is that they're going to be okay. She might have added: nor do you say that to a depressed person. Depression does that—convinces you that you are never going to be okay.

"Now I get it," she says. Because of course Helen was right. Jen did find love again. But at the time, she was convinced that she wouldn't. She considered freezing her eggs. Once, in a moment of near-hallucinatory panic, she wondered if she could get impregnated with Bobby's DNA from strands of hair he'd left in a comb.

"It just would've come out better if she'd said: 'This is really sucky for you. And I'm sorry. Chances are, you'll meet somebody.' I guess there was just a nicer way to say it," she says. "However she said it set me off. Just because of my own personal shit."

I ask if it's possible that Helen *did* say those things, though she may have said a few artless things too. Maybe Jen missed them—or heard insults that weren't necessarily intended as such—because she'd grown up in a house that required an extra set of threat detectors, given her father's volatility.

"A hundred percent," she says. "It was probably me regressing into a little, you know, tantruming child. I was mad at the world. Of course she didn't intend to hurt me. She's the nicest person."

She and Helen are more similar than either of them realizes. Like Helen, Jen believed, at the time, in hiding her grief. Like Helen, she today takes refuge in the idea that Bobby's soul is rattling about somewhere. "I'm really showing my woo-woo side here," she says, "but I think that he'll be back, and I'll be back, and we'll finish our unfinished business."

And like Helen, she has learned to let a lot of things go. That's one of the most ruthless lessons trauma teaches you: You are not in charge. All you can control is your reaction to whatever grenades the demented universe rolls in your path. Beginning with whether you get out of bed. "And that's where I started my day, literally," she says. For years.

Today, Jen is choosing to hand me Bobby's diary as I'm walking out the door and heading back to New York. She has zero reservations about it. She says she'd like to have the original copy back, but there's no rush; the McIlvaines are free to read all of it, free to make as many photocopies as they'd like.

"I would have done it years ago," she tells me. "I think about them all the time."

Before I leave, I ask if she remembers where the phrase *Life loves on* comes from. She looks at me blankly. "I don't even remember him *saying* that. Is it in a book that he liked or something?" Tried that, I say. Searched Google Books. Nope. "Or was it a hymn?" Hymns aren't my strong suit, but I don't think so. I tell her that the McIlvaines are certain Bobby wrote it somewhere, but never mind, this is not her problem. I'll keep looking.

• • •

Memories of traumatic experiences are a curious thing. Some are vivid; some are pale; pretty much all of them have been emended in some way, great or small. There seems to be no rhyme or reason to our curated reels. We remember the trivial and forget the exceptional. Our minds truly have minds of their own.

Jeff, for instance, remembers that Jen stayed at his parents' house for half a year after Bobby died while Helen says it was one week, and Jen thinks it was probably two months.

Or here's another: Jen remembers that Jeff gallantly slept in Bobby's childhood bedroom while she stayed with them, so that she wouldn't have to be traumatized by waking up to all of Bobby's things, while Jeff remembers *her* sleeping in Bobby's bedroom and bravely waking up each day to all of Bobby's things.

And strangest of all: though no one can remember where *Life loves on* came from, everyone—and I do mean everyone (Jen, Jeff, Bob Sr., and Helen)—once knew.

It's from Jen's eulogy. Which she based on Bobby's diary. The one she kept for twenty years.

"This past week I have been searching for some sort of comfort to get me through the shock of losing the love of my life," she told the mourners at Queen of Peace Church. "I came across one of Bob's journals and as I opened it, I said to myself, 'Please let there be something in here that will comfort me.'" Then she described finding this passage, which Bobby had written as her mother was dying. She read it aloud.

It is OK for people to die. It hurts, and it is a deep loss, but it is OK. Life loves on. Do not fear for those who are dying. Be kind to them. And care for them.

"Life loves on," she repeated to the crowd. "After I read this, I vowed that very instant to love on in my life, just as I had made a promise to my mom to never let her be forgotten. It was a way that I could extend a life cut short."

The only reason I know this is because my brother found a copy of Jen's eulogy. Jen had tossed hers out. She is not, as she says, a saver.

Somehow she'd completely forgotten those words, as well as their provenance. And the McIlvaines had forgotten where they came from, too, even though Helen wears them in an engraved bracelet and Bob Sr. enshrined them on his skin.

Then I remembered what Helen told me about Jen: *She became a nonperson to me.* She kept the words. But not Jen. She buried her future daughter-in-law too that year, just as she did her son.

• • •

Helen recently told me a story about a long weekend she'd spent with Jen, maybe ten days before Bobby died. The whole family was vacationing in Cape May. She, Bobby, and Jen were sitting on the beach, staring at the waves, with Bobby in the middle. It was a moment of gentle bliss. Helen turned ever so slightly toward Bobby to run her hand through his hair. But at that exact same moment, that very second, Bobby turned to do the same to Jen.

It was then that Helen realized Bobby wasn't hers anymore. "I said to myself, *You gotta go take a walk and look at the real estate on the beach*," she told me.

In Bobby's early diaries, the McIlvaine family may show up everywhere. But not in this diary. This diary is primarily about two things. And one of them is Jen.

> February 18, 2001: I love her, deeply. We communicate so well. We resolve splits between us so well. And all of this means a lot.

> April 11, 2001: I miss Jen. "Big" part of my life, or descriptions of how much she means to me do not suffice.

> April 22, 2001 [two days after Jen's mother died]: I am so sorry, Jen. So sorry for your hurt. I know it is hard. I'll be here by your side—here to love you, to listen to you, to hold you when you need to cry.

It's no wonder Jen didn't want to part with this diary. Or that she read it every night.

Helen recognized this immediately. I sent her a couple of xeroxed copies after I returned to New York.

"The Jen piece was huge to me," she says, when we have a chance to talk. "I thought of this in the middle of the night: She loses this guy that she loves—and most importantly, who loves her. Now, where is the *proof* that he loves her? I mean, okay, the mother gives her the ring. That's good. But there are these wonderful words: *I love her deeply.*" She marvels. "I never thought about that. Never. That she needed that, that validation."

She also recognizes what the diary is missing. "He didn't say, *I love my parents too.* He said, *I love her deeply.*" Bobby was all grown up.

Helen now wonders about her own behavior in those awful months. She tried to show Jen affection. But she'd only had sons. She didn't *speak* daughter. And that reserve she was describing to me earlier, the reserve I didn't believe she had—it was very real. "What happens is, I have intentions sometimes and forget to say the words," she says. "She had to guess what was in my head."

At any rate, Helen is now clear on one very important point. "It would have been beyond Jen's ability, even if she was in a good mood, to say, 'Okay, here, I'm giving it back.' I really would have had to give her at least pieces of that, somehow. That wasn't for me to own. I really mean that."

For years, Jen had been painted as a villain for holding on to this diary. Yet there never would have been a dispute if she had already been Bobby's wife or perhaps even his official fiancée. But Jen was suspended between worlds, without influence or status. "It must have felt horrible," Helen says.

The final entry in Bobby's diary is dated September 6, 2001. It fills the whole page. When I first read it, I was disoriented. Then I realized what it was. "I feel completely unprepared. Should I rehearse?" it begins.

> It should go something like this: Do you have a few minutes to talk? First, I'd like to say that it has been a pleasure—or maybe a great experience—or do I mention Jen first? Or, I have developed a very strong relationship with Jen, and along the way it has been great to spend time in Michigan . . . OR . . . yes—I've had the chance to grow close to Jen, and after a lot of very serious thought, and after talking to her too, I felt that it is time to make a commitment to her. OR—after a good deal of serious thought . . . AND . . . out of respect for you as head of the family . . .

What I was reading was a script. Filled with fits and starts, but eventually he got there. Bobby was struggling to find the words to say to Jen's father, whom he'd see on September 9, to ask for her hand.

· · ·

At some point, not long after Jen gave me Bobby's diary, I sent a note to my editor, telling him that I had found, at long last, the elusive *Life loves on*. I took a photo of the passage and sent it to him.

Amazing, he texted.

But then, three pulsing dots in a bubble. He was still typing.

Except . . . I think it is (sort of) a misapprehension. Look how he writes his I's in other words. I think it says "Life **lives** on." But hard to say for sure . . .

It wasn't hard to say. He was right. I went through the whole diary again. On just the page before, Bobby had written, *I lived too long without thinking of "the markets" to suddenly care.* But it looks like "I *loved* too long . . ." His *I*'s look like backwards *J*'s, which can be mistaken for *O*'s, while his real *O*'s stand alone, like baby moons.

I texted Jen the same photograph I sent my editor. At first, she didn't see it. Then she did. Her initial reaction was the same as mine: anxiety, despair in the form of an expletive. Then:

Still makes me smile

Me: What does?

Jen: That the people close to him saw and felt what they needed to. And that's ok. You know?

I did. The phrase certainly sounded like something Bobby *could* have said. It was very Yoda, and Bobby was definitely very Yoda, spouting his little aphorisms about the drives of the human heart. To me, it was the difference between the spirit of the law and the letter of the law, or maybe what we do when we intensify the color of an image on our iPhone. We're not trying to create a fake; we're trying to align the image with the one that already lives in our memory.

We are always inventing and reinventing the dead.

You could make a case, weirdly, that Jen's withholding of the diary for all these years turned out to be a blessing. If she'd given it to Helen, it's possible Helen would have tucked it away in her safe for ten years and barely read it, just as she did the other two diaries. Or maybe she'd have read it, but she wouldn't have *misread* it.

Instead, Jen misread it, formed a eulogy around it, and handed the McIlvaine family an organizing motto for their grief for twenty years.

I still debated not telling the McIlvaines. I mean, the bracelet, the tattoo. But in a phone conversation with Helen soon after, I sensed an opening. I mentioned that I wasn't sure I was going to write about *Life loves on*. She quickly intuited that something was amiss. "Because it was from somebody else?" she asked.

Kind of, I said. And I explained.

Helen was fine with it. She sees the unlikely beauty of this misunderstanding, even how it was a gift. But she holds out the possibility that the phrase still lurks somewhere. She remembers it as *Life* truly *loves on*, for one thing. And it's possible that I could have missed it in the hundreds of pages of Bobby's first two diaries. There are probably some missing diaries, too—why did he stop keeping them in 1995, only to resume in 2001?

So really, who's to say?

·   ·   ·

Life lives on, Life loves on—to me, it's irrelevant. There are far more beautiful observations in the recovered diary than that one, and they're prescient, eerie—much more germane to the McIlvaines' story once Bobby was gone.

Because the other thing his diary is about, the second thing, is grief.

In this way, the diary isn't just a time capsule. It's a crystal ball. Through an extraordinary twist of fate, Bobby spent his final few months thinking about what it meant to live with loss. He saw, through Jen, that it could render you angry, irritable, skinless. He saw that grief could utterly consume. He wondered what the utility of all this sadness was, all this suffering. *Why do we have to hurt so badly?* he wrote. *Is that the way the person we lost would have wanted it to be?*

At one point, he guiltily wished that Jen would just make a choice to seize control of the things she could.

Yet somewhere amid all the passages of exasperation and dread—and many of them are quite detailed—Bobby comes to a much larger realization. It's an epiphany, I'm guessing, that made it possible for him to stick with his plan to ask Jen's father for permission to marry her, though he seriously questioned during those months whether she was ready. The date was August 20, 2001.

There are people that need me. And that, in itself, is life. There are people I do not know yet that need me. That is life.

To me, *that* is the most profound quote from the recovered diary. *That* is Bobby as Yoda. *That* is Bobby at his very finest, his most humane, his most mature. He understood that our commitments to one another are what we're here for—*and that, in itself, is life.* Even when those commitments are hard. Even when they cause us pain.

·　　·　　·

One hesitates to say this. But if there was any path forward for the McIlvaine family, it was probably going to be through Jeff. Helen was careful never to burden him with expectations about marriage or kids—"You cannot put *anything* on the other child," she tells me—and he appreciated that. But it was thanks to Jeff, I think, that

Bob Sr. and Helen started to muddle their way out of the dark. There were people they did not know yet who needed them. Among those people were their four grandbabies. The oldest one is named Bobby.

At twenty-two, Jeff had a profound insight. "I remember thinking on that first day: *I can't let this ruin me.* 'Cause then what would Bobby think? Imagine if he knew that my parents and his brother were never able to recover. Imagine how bad that would make him feel."

He was reflexively answering the very question Bobby had asked as he watched Jen struggle with her grief: *Why do we have to hurt so badly? Is that the way the person we lost would have wanted it to be?* Jeff had a very clear answer: No. He had too much of his own life left to go. "I knew that if this ruined *my* life, *his* whole life was worthless," he says. "I wanted to work very hard to make sure that I had a good life."

It was so hard at first. "I remember I felt a responsibility to not die, which is a weird thing," he tells me. At the same time, he felt guilty for being the child who didn't die, thinking often of the dream sequence in *Stand by Me* when the father snarls "It should have been you" to his surviving son. He told no one at his first real job that his brother had died on September 11 because too many people were eager to share their own stupid stories about that day, always with happy endings. This delayed his ability to grieve for years.

But eventually, he built a rich, fulfilling life. He married a woman who could not only subdue his pain but enter an entire grieving ecosystem. He had four kids—four! two boys, two girls— and oh, the relief of not having to focus on himself!

I ask if he would have had that many kids if Bobby hadn't—

"No. I don't think I would have." Jeff lost his only sibling. He never wants any child of his to be in that position, should lightning ever restrike. "When you go through something like this," he says, "you realize that family—it's the *only* thing."

Those kids are now at the center of the McIlvaines' lives— even Bob Sr., who has chosen a path of daily suffering. As our conversation was winding down, he said something that stunned me: this twentieth-anniversary year—a big one for the people in his world, filled with TV interviews and conferences—may be his last of 9/11 activism.

I wasn't sure I believed it. I remain unsure. This has been his life for twenty years. Still: maybe it's time for a change. "I'm sick of being angry," he told me. "That's the beauty of my life now. I can really separate. I truly can. To be out to lunch with Penelope . . ."

Penelope is his youngest granddaughter. He and Helen had lunch with her every Wednesday after preschool before the pandemic. Jeff and his wife and children rely so heavily on Bob and Helen that they recently rented an apartment five minutes from Jeff's house, though they live less than an hour away.

Helen can't get over having little girls in her life. They have so many opinions! She still gets depressed sometimes. She'll have a beautiful moment, then realize that Bobby isn't here to share it. "But then it'll go away," she says. "I mean, being needed—not everybody gets four grandkids."

Yes. Being needed. That is everything.

. . .

Bobby would have been forty-six this September. Jeff used to have vivid dreams about him, and man, how he loved them. They were brothers again, just talking, resuming their old rhythms and habits. But he seldom has those dreams anymore. "I haven't seen him in twenty years, you know?"

He says he almost wishes sometimes that he could trade his current well-being for the suffering he felt twenty years ago, because Bobby was so much easier to conjure back then, the sense-memories of him still within reach. "No matter how painful September 11 was," he explains, "I had just seen him on September 6."

It's the damnedest thing: The dead abandon you; then, with the passage of time, you abandon the dead.

It's really not surprising that Jeff should have this fantasy from time to time, to trade his happiness for just one chance to see

Bobby again in a warmer hue. As Bobby wrote in that last diary, suffering, or the prospect of it, is the price we're willing to pay for the bonds we make.

Helen has found herself in the grip of a similar reverie. Recently, she was out with her limping group, and as she was looking around the table, staring in gratitude at these women who have held her up these past twenty years, a thought occurred to her. "I wondered, *What if God said, 'Okay, look, we gotta rewind here.' Would we go through all of this again?"*

Would they be willing to relive their same lives, give birth to those same children, fall in love with them and then lose them a second time? "And I know that every single one of them would have said, emphatically, yes."

For Helen, nothing in this world has rivaled the experience of raising her two boys. One of them, Robert George McIlvaine, died before his life truly began. But what would she have done without him, or he without her? For twenty-six years, she got to know this boy, to care for him, to love him. It was a privilege. It was a gift. It was a bittersweet sacrifice. *And that, in itself, is life.*

Georgia Review

WINNER—ASME AWARD FOR FICTION

Set in Karimnagar, India, "Come with Me" is the story of a troubled summer friendship between two teenage boys and the memories it does and, perhaps more importantly, does not leave behind. "Come with Me" was one of three short stories—"After God, Fear Women," by Eloghosa Osunde, and "Copper Queen," by Aryn Kyle, were the others—that won the Georgia Review the fifth annual ASME Award for Fiction. "Transnational in scope, these stories are precise and lush, never clichéd," reads the judges' citation for the award-winning entry. "More broadly, they display a level of vision and sophistication that set the Georgia Review apart in 2022." Nishanth Injam received the PEN/Robert J. Dau Short Story Prize for Emerging Writers in 2021. His first book, The Best Possible Experience, will be published next year.

Nishanth Injam

Come with Me

The first time I saw Salim, the weather report called it one of Karimnagar's hottest summers. Streets bore silence like a curfew. Cows belched and jutted out their tongues for moisture. The ice cream vendor rolled his cart into the shade of the big peepal tree and fanned himself with a wet cloth. The vegetable market vanished at noon and reappeared in the evening. None of this bothered us; we were boys with cricket on our minds.

I was no star, but I had a good arm and could take a running catch. Most of us were thirteen, but there were a few who were older. We were forming teams, tossing who'd get to bat first, and we didn't see him approach.

We heard him before seeing him—"I got the bat."

I turned and stood transfixed. Salim wore a graphic tee shirt that said rockstar. Although it was hot and humid, he had worn a biker jacket that he took off and folded, and as he did, his taut biceps glistened. It was a revelation; I never knew sweat could look so good. He was older, eighteen or so. He had thin lips. Strong thighs. And a sharp nose. I felt my stomach flip and flip, like dice that wouldn't stop rolling.

Salim shook hands with some of the older boys he seemed to know, greeting them with a generic *Aur Bhai*. We drew close to introduce ourselves, and it was apparent he was the sun and the rest of us mere planets destined to orbit around him.

When it was my turn, I told him my name. Salim ran his fingers through his hair and said, "Khan, Salim Khan."

"Like James Bond?" I had seen a James Bond movie on the neighbor's television and was aware of this particular mannerism.

"Whatever," he said in a low-pitched voice. But the quick upward dash of his eyebrows all but told me that I was going to be on his radar, and I couldn't stop smiling.

"Chal, start," the boys screamed, and we were off to field. Salim was on my team, and I watched him field in the short cover position. Hips thrust, back angled forward, he drew my eyes right where they were ashamed to go.

Soon it was our turn to bat. Six wickets down and chasing fifty-seven, the team sent me. Salim stood at the non-striker's end. "Take a single, rotate the strike." Even his shout sounded regal.

The tall, fast bowler sensed my fear and urged the fielders to draw closer. He took a long run up and hurled the ball. I swung and missed.

Salim came over. "What's your name again?" he asked.

"Arun," I said.

Look Arun, swing the bat low and run, I expected him to say.

"Do you have ten rupees? I forgot my wallet; I'll give it back next week."

I nodded and gazed around, letting people think we were having a tactical discussion.

Salim looked eager, and so I put my hands in my pocket. I made a show of looking, even though I knew I didn't have any money. I then curled out my lower lip—I had nothing. He shrugged and strolled back to the non-striker's end.

The ball came, and I swung the bat. We ran, and Salim took the strike. The bowler spat on the ball and rubbed it against his crotch. He took an even longer run up and bowled. *Thwack!* The ball flew beyond the compound wall for a six. Salim held his hand against his eyebrows, and in the shadow cast on his face, I saw the hint of a smile. We won the match with two overs to spare.

I saw him at the vegetable market the next day. I waved at him, but he was busy flirting with the fruit-seller lady. I stared at him for a good minute, and he turned around as if he felt the stare. He lifted his eyebrows, a flicker of recognition. He held guavas in his arms, and his eyes traveled to the person next to me, my mother, and stayed there—perhaps trying to ascertain if the woman next to me was my mother. I interrupted Mother in her haggling to point out Salim. By the time she turned to me, he had walked away, juggling guavas in the air. I wouldn't see him again until a few days later. And I wouldn't be friends with him until a month later, but I was already in love with his swagger. Which I knew I'd never have.

•   •   •

The air was hot and sober like it knew about the Alcoholics Anonymous meeting. Families sat in rows of plastic chairs facing the speakers. Father stared at Mother. This was what he had to endure, his face said. Mother watched him with fear in her eyes. I'd had enough of their drama. I scanned the crowd and saw Salim in the last row. He sat next to his father; they had the same chin. I sidled up to him.

"Why didn't you come to the game?" Salim asked.

"Busy," I said. I hadn't been invited; the boys cared to invite me only when they needed an extra fielder, and I was upset.

"Let's get ice cream," Salim said. We strolled to the ice cream vendor sitting under the shade of the banyan tree, cooling himself with a paper fan. He opened the cart-brief and inserted his hand into it. Out came two ice cream sticks, one yellow and one pink. I paid.

"Your father drinks?" Salim bit off a chunk of ice.

"That's putting it mildly."

Salim laughed, and my chest expanded.

"What does he do?"

Father spent most of his time away from home in a cargo ship that went back and forth between Maldives and India.

"Sailor? How?"

I was tired of the question. But people were always amazed that somebody in Karimnagar, thousands of kilometers away from the sea, became a sailor. I told him the story. One drama-filled night, our extended family chastised Father for not securing a job, and he boarded the train to Bombay in anger to find a job and throw the employment papers at all those questioning him. By the time the train rolled into Bombay, a full twenty hours later, his tongue was so dry he had to seek a watering hole. That accomplished, he woke up in a cargo ship several miles away from land. Upon discovering an unlabeled, unpackaged, and disoriented entity in the ship, the captain put him to work. As long as he worked, no one cared if he drank, and that was it for him. So—people usually exclaim on hearing the story—he did find a job that suited him. But it was only a job, and when he came back home, he drank and called Mother a *randi*.

Sometimes he'd ask me to dance, but the smell would make me nauseous, and I'd refuse to entertain him, and he'd slap me till my gums bled. I didn't tell Salim the stories of those nights; I didn't think it was cool to do so. But Salim sensed something. "You okay?" he asked.

I nodded and looked at my feet. My sandals had a blue in them I became deeply aware of.

He patted my wrist, and a tingly sensation spread across my body.

For the first time, I was sad when the AA meeting was over. I waved goodbye to Salim and went home, the lingering starchiness of the ice stick on my tongue.

·   ·   ·

Days drifted past, not unlike the way clouds made their way across the sky, this movement in time, some mysterious design underway. August rains downed summer heat. The ice cream vendor disappeared. AA meetings got suspended due to a lack of roofed seating space. The playground turned into a pond, complete with ducks, frogs, and paper boats. The vegetable market morphed into vendors with moving carts, blue tarpaulins, and flexible schedules. Father left, and school resumed. A boy in my class quit. Salim stayed.

The cricket group disbanded into separate units, and our unit was persistent enough to play in the minutes untouched by the evening rain. Salim and I, regulars in this group, met by the adda and waited for the rest. By now, the boys had changed their opinion. I was no longer the nerdy kid who couldn't play well; I had important friends. We sat cross-legged, leaning against each other, and talked shit about girls. Someone brought up careers. One boy wanted to serve. *The army will send you back in a box*, we said. Another said he'd start a store. *Good luck with that, we'll be your customers*—we made the sign for no money.

Salim said he wanted to be an actor.

"You want to be a Bollywood star?" I asked.

"I am a Khan," he said, and the boys laughed.

"You need English for that." I stretched my legs. I had seen interviews of Bollywood stars on tv, and they all spoke excellent English.

"English to act in Hindi movies?" Salim chuckled, and the boys laughed at me. None of us spoke English well enough for movies. I let them laugh.

The rain stopped, and we threw the ball around, but mud stuck to the ball and smattered a boy in the face. We laughed and gave up. Earthworms wriggled in and out of the earth, and we gaped at the tiny holes they made.

"Teach me English, I'll teach you how to bat," Salim said, on our way back.

"Who said I don't know batting?"

Salim laughed, a hearty laugh that jumped out of his throat.

"I don't know English." I was thrilled with the idea that I knew something he didn't.

"You know more than any of the other boys; I heard them say you won a prize in school."

"Only because everybody else was worse."

"Teach me." Salim held my wrist.

Warmth gripped my body. "Right now?" I said.

Salim nodded, and somewhere in my arteries, I knew this was dangerous. But something larger than either of us had been set in motion, and I felt determined to see it through to its logical conclusion. As we turned the corner and walked up the street, my eyes fell on the house next to ours. These neighbors enjoyed spying on us. Chachi's red sari, hung up to dry, fluttered in the wind. I hated the sari for being her deputy, surveilling on her behalf.

The gate creaked open. It was just another two-bedroom house, identical in construction to others in the street, with cement floors and circular stairs that were built like a garland, leading to the terrace. The house looked normal, but the walls seemed to betray the drama. Melancholy seeped through them. I wondered if Salim could tell.

"I've heard so much about you," Mother said, handing Salim a glass of lemonade.

Salim gave a coy smile. I looked at Mother, her hair tied into a bun, waiting for our empty glasses, a wide smile on her face. She liked him. Why wouldn't she? She'd think I'd learn from an older boy. I showed Salim my prized possession—a globe I won in school—and my favorite spot, the terrace. From the terrace, I saw Chachi peering from behind the sari. What would she make of Salim?

She'd be scandalized that I brought home a Muslim. Chacha, her husband and a friend of my father, had often expressed the opinion that all Muslims were Pakistanis. He believed they spawned dozens of kids with the intention of taking over India; he acted as though the country's future depended on him, a bank cashier. I avoided them both as much as I could.

Some parts of the terrace had already dried, and Salim sat down at the edge and whistled "My Name Is Joker." I washed my feet at the pump and sat next to him. I hung my legs in the air and water drops fell from my feet, one at a time, onto the potted plant below. Kaali, a stray black cat that hung around our house, strode on the parapet wall. Chacha once said that a single black cat brought a hundred years of misfortune. He urged Mother to consult a priest and determine the best possible way to appease gods.

"What can a black cat do to a house that already has your father in it?" Mother said to me after she nodded the neighbors off.

Everything around me conjured memories and experiences I wanted to share with Salim. There was so much to tell, and the enormity of this task overwhelmed me. I stayed quiet, vacillating between sharing everything and sharing nothing.

Salim raised his eyebrows as if to say, *What's the plan?*

I brought my English textbook and placed it on his lap. He flipped pages—an exasperation apparent in the curve of his lips. He put the book aside and said he wanted to fast forward to the part where he spoke English. I told him everything worthwhile took time.

He squeezed my hand.

I looked at the textbook for a minute, not really seeing anything on the page. There was a tension in the air, a newness, this unfamiliarity. Neither of us seemed to be able to concentrate. I put the text aside and watched men burning wood in the distance. Smoke drifted over thatched houses in the eventide sky. Crows didn't caw, dogs didn't bark, people didn't quarrel, and for the longest time, there was silence and it felt like we were in a picture titled *Two Boys on a Terrace*.

Somewhere, a train sounded its horn and broke the silence. Salim smiled and said he liked the view from the terrace. The train blew its horn again and it was just your regular train horn, but it sounded a lot like the arrival of happiness. Salim placed his arm around me. I pretended to yawn and leaned my neck against his arm. Like a friend. From his armpits wafted a thin scent of dried rice, and I smelled him, and I smelled him again, and I swore it would be the last time I did—I didn't want to be caught, I sensed it was forbidden, but each time I took a breath of it, time stopped, and nothing mattered. My father, my mother, the neighbors, the narrow street, everything was dull and pale in comparison, and I kept breathing until my nostrils with their eagerness had become used to his scent, and my chest grew heavy. I had lost it, and I held my breath to ease the weight of that finality, and when I breathed again, there it was, that whiff of intoxication. I held my breath again and again. It came to me that I had been waiting to answer something about myself, and now I knew what it was, and this filled me with anxiety—there'd be days, months to think about what it meant, I told myself, but I could no longer deny it. This new anxiety settled into my being like the smoke that melded into the sky, darkening it bit by bit. But in that moment, leaning on his shoulder, I pushed everything out of my mind and looked at the eventide sky, wide and unblemished, and smiled as if I were being photographed.

• • •

"Do you want to go to that English movie?" Salim asked the next day. We had seen posters for *Pirates of the Caribbean* at the adda.

"Ooh, that's a good way to pick up English," I said, looking at his light stubble.

Salim's smile took on a teasing quality. "Do you have to ask your mother?"

"I don't have to," I said, punching his arm.

I snuck money out of Mother's purse and we took the long route via the train tracks to avoid being seen by people we knew. The secrecy of this mission increased the thrill I felt in the cinema when we rubbed shoulders. We hid our faces in our hands and when the cinema went dark, we rose in delight. The movie had more action than dialogue, half of which I barely understood. *Pirate* was a new word; we said to each other *hello, pirate* and *howdy, pirate*.

We watched a number of movies, and there were other new things for us to discover. We learned people called 911 in case of emergencies. Sex before marriage was okay. An alien invasion was always on the horizon. We mastered the art of styling our hair like Brad Pitt with a mix of coconut oil and tooth powder. Watching a movie put Salim in an expansive mood. He'd put his arm around my shoulder and tell me what he would have done differently had he been the hero. I'd nod, and we'd go our separate ways. But often,

I'd be the first to bid goodbye. I sensed that Salim didn't really want to go home. All I had to do was invite him home, and he'd come. But then there was the anxiety that never left. And the question of appropriateness. I couldn't really invite him without an excuse, and Salim wouldn't be comfortable coming without the excuse. But the excuse arrived one night, and I felt something stir in my pants. Salim's father was out of town, and Salim said he'd be going back from the movie to an empty home.

We had just watched *The Lord of the Rings* and were fascinated by the idea of a sequel, of a movie not finishing at the end.

"I wish the movie kept going," Salim said, his arm around me.

"Until the morning, right?" I said.

Salim turned toward me. "What?"

"Because you are so scared of staying by yourself in the dark." I laughed.

He held me by the neck and tickled me in the ribs. "My *precious.*"

I wrenched free and ran a few feet ahead. "Do you want to sleep at my place tonight?"

"Will your mother be okay with that?"

"Come with me," I said, wishing for the night to never end.

At home Mother okayed my proposition as I knew she would and brought out extra sheets. And I made his bed, next to mine on the floor. Salim wanted to shower. I opened the bathroom for him and pressed a towel in his hands. I felt my sex grow. I tucked my hardness between my legs and hoped it wouldn't show through my underwear. Salim came back from the bathroom in a towel, naked from the waist up. His body emanated heat, but it was my face that felt warm as I hovered around him, asking if he needed another towel. He had hair all over his chest, a mole on his biceps. I had one in the exact same place and I showed him.

I touched his mole, pushing it with my index finger. "Oh, it is a mole," I said, keeping my face straight.

"What did you think it was?" he laughed.

I gave him one of Father's tee shirts and ran to the bathroom. I couldn't stand it anymore. I went to the bathroom and pulled out my fly. The scent of him lingered and I stood there inhaling it, watching myself grow. The tap was wet, Salim had been naked right in front of it. I moved to touch the tap. The long handle of the tap could have been his shaft and I stroked it again and again, bathing in the scent he left. I perched down and took it in my mouth and cocked my head back and forth, imagining him scrunching his face, and I knew this was wrong, something was very wrong with me, but I could not stop, and with each hold of my mouth, I felt my penis grow harder and harder, and I held my hand to the hardness while I continued to move my tongue over the tip of the handle, licking it in each untouched spot, teasing it, and I closed my mouth around it, working against the handle faster and faster till I came.

By the time I cleaned up and came back, he was fast asleep. I fell on my mattress and lay awake for a long time, torn between wanting to wrap myself around Salim and running away that very night before I got outed. When I finally fell asleep and woke up the next morning, Salim had already left, and Mother was searching the house, turning up plastic chairs.

Mother asked me if I had taken the twenty rupees she had placed in the folds of a magazine that had been on the teapoy. I hadn't, but I felt my stomach tighten, and I saw the same thought cross her eyes. Had Salim stolen the money? I asked if she had kept the money elsewhere and forgotten. And she accepted that as a possibility. But I left for school wishing I could make the money appear. I would somehow detect that the wind had swept the note to a corner. Or Mother would remember where she misplaced the money. Anything really. I knew Salim had money problems—I paid for everything. But I thought he'd ask if he needed the money. I sat through the class with difficulty and returned home.

Mother said she hadn't found the money. I dropped my bag and went looking for him. I figured I'd ask him casually if he happened to see any money lying on the ground that night. I went to his house. The gate was locked. I didn't see him the whole week. Mother forgot about the money. Every day after school, I did the circuit. I went to the playground, the theater, the market, the adda. I spun my globe, wondering where he was. I lost interest in school. No one asked me to teach English anymore; no one squeezed my wrist as he did. Each day I looked for him, the money became less and less important. And I slapped my thighs in anger. What I had done with the tap, my sin, had pushed him away. In the bathroom, I remembered what I had done, and my penis began to expand. I was ashamed; I took a blade, steadied my hand, and put a tiny cut. A drop of blood emerged, and the sight of it stopped my shame. I apologized to him at all the places, for desiring him, for doubting him.

The next week, I came home from school and saw him sitting on the sofa laughing with Mother, as if they were now best friends, as if she were just as important in his coming to our house. I went straight to my room and collapsed by the window. Salim came into the room and put his hand on my shoulder. He whispered *sorry*, and I felt his mouth brush against my ear. A tingly warmth spread through my body.

"I had to go to my father's village on an urgent matter," Salim said.

"What happened?" I asked, continuing to act upset.

"My father began drinking again; we had to take him. He can drink all the buffalo milk he gets there." He grinned.

In spite of myself, I let out a chuckle. "I looked for you everywhere," I said.

"Sorry," he repeated and enveloped me with his long arms. I turned and hugged him. Locked in his embrace, I looked outside the window. A pigeon lay on the neighbor's wall looking for grains. He held me tighter. The pigeon found a grain a couple of feet away on the wall. His hands caressed my back. The pigeon hopped to the grain. He kissed me on the cheek. The pigeon grabbed the grain and flew—not knowing that it lifted into the sky my soul.

Most days, I found Salim at home eating Mother's pakoras, regaling her with all sorts of tales. He'd say that he'd marry a woman like her, making her blush and laugh in a way I'd never seen before, and then he'd turn to me and wink. This only meant I didn't have to explain who we were. I could linger in the painting that was *Two Boys on a Terrace*. January brought my fourteenth birthday. We bought a bubble stick, for laughs, something we both had done when we were much younger, and rinsed it with soap and blew soap bubbles at each other, often grazing each other's feet. We hadn't proceeded beyond what we already did. I hadn't asked if his kiss on the cheek meant more than the affection men sometimes displayed in Bollywood movies. There was time, we'd get there. But I found myself growing in confidence, and I threw away the blade in the bathroom.

Mother baked a cake and gave us money to officially watch a movie. We went to the theater, this time unafraid. Salim copied the gestures of film stars and I copied him. I cupped my palms when I spoke in a low voice, like him. I drank chai in the evening, like him. How was I to know things would change so soon?

Chacha beckoned me the day after my birthday and asked me what Salim's name was. He had seen him around the house often and wanted to know who he was. He knew Salim was Muslim, and this was his way of confirming. Fucking pig.

"Samir," I said and ran.

February followed. Father would return any day—it was time. Dark clouds of rain lurched forward in the sky. Shadows the size of mountains cast gloom everywhere. Vendors in the vegetable market packed up their carts in a hurry. The ice cream vendor was nowhere. The playground was desolate. The cinema had a padlock—temporarily closed for projector repair. I found Salim sitting on the train tracks, throwing pebbles at the track.

"It's only temporary," I said. But I couldn't hide the fear in my voice; it felt like we were train tracks, parallel lines that cannot meet. Chacha would tell Father, and he wouldn't let us meet.

Salim stared at the tracks. "I'm leaving for Bombay," he said. Every pebble thrown at the track made a dull cracking noise I heard again and again.

"When?" I asked. The rumble of clouds silenced everything.

"Soon, I'll come say bye. In a couple of days," he said.

I wanted to leave with him; I had fantasized about running away with Salim. He'd tell me to come to the train station one day. I'd hurry there, forgetting to pack my prized globe. And he'd offer to get it for me. And I'd tell him that I wouldn't need it anymore. And that he was my world. But he hadn't asked me to come with him, and I had too much pride to ask.

Salim stood up and brushed the dirt from his pants. "There's nothing here. I have to go," he said.

I let out a sob. "I'll come with you," I said.

Salim squeezed me on the shoulder and left.

I broke away to the terrace and stared at the Karimnagar-sized nothingness in front of me. I blew soap bubbles alone on the terrace. And I could not think of anything other than the one time Salim and I blew soap bubbles at each other. There were things we wanted to do together. Swimming lessons that never happened. Cricket coaching sessions that got postponed. The trip to his village that never materialized. There were conversations that needed to be had. I wanted to know what his mother was like. What did he do when his father drank, and he was too young? Why did he prefer full-sleeve shirts instead of half-sleeve shirts? What were his childhood stories? What had he done when he was fourteen? Why did he have to use his fingers to push up his hair after he had used a comb? Had he liked me the way I liked him?

The soap bubbles lifted higher and floated away. Through them, some things were enlarged, and some were minimized. I saw Salim's absence looming large, and Salim himself in the distance, shrinking away. The bubbles, it struck me, were like memories; they were not original events themselves, they were illusions. And what could I do—I wept on the terrace—but touch these bubbles and hear them go *pop pop pop*!

• • •

The night Salim was supposed to leave, the cries of a woman woke me up. Cuss words, a chorus of harsh voices. It was past midnight.

A thief had been caught, I thought. But I heard Salim's voice, pleading. I sprang to my feet; he had come to say goodbye.

I opened the door, and in the hall, near the other bedroom, Father had returned. And something had happened. Chacha and Chachi stood watching. Father kicked Salim in the stomach and a shirtless Salim twisted on the floor. It didn't make any sense. Father slapped a crying, semi-dressed Mother in the face and went back to kicking Salim. Had Salim been caught stealing money? Chachi dragged Mother inside the bedroom.

Father bent down and slapped Salim in the face.

"You circumcised bastard," Chacha's voice boomed.

I didn't understand any of it. "Please don't hit him," I said.

Chacha shoved me, and I fell back into the room. "Stay inside," he shouted and bolted the door. No matter how much I tried, I couldn't move. My feet wouldn't cooperate. I couldn't open my mouth either. It was as if someone had bound my legs and gagged my mouth. On the floor, I watched the gap between the door and the floor. Light sneaking in from under the gap fell on my globe, which had somehow fallen on the floor. I couldn't comprehend what I had seen. Why couldn't I move? Something to do with what I had seen in the seconds before Chacha pushed me inside, something to do with Mother appearing not quite herself. I couldn't do anything other than look at the gap. Salim had taken away something of what I had, this much I felt. My body shook and shook on the cold floor of my room as I replayed those final images again and again. Soon, I was no longer sure of what I saw—all those individual images became a hazy film.

An hour passed, and the voices dissolved into silence. When the house fell silent, my body returned to me. I got up and ran away from home.

•   •   •

I never saw Salim again or went to Karimnagar after that. For a while, I worked at a dhaba in Odisha, several hundred kilometers away. The dhaba sat next to the highway and attracted a fair amount of dust and flies. A stray dog slept under the tables and I'd feed it leftovers. The work itself wasn't bad. I'd serve food to customers and scrub their plates. Nights were the busiest and afternoons the quietest. Some afternoons when I was dusting the dhaba signboard or picking at a solitary grain of rice lodged inside the stove, Salim would pop into my head. And I'd briefly wonder what happened that night. Before I could arrive at an answer, I'd feel a sharp pain deep within my chest and I'd distract myself with one task or another. Occasionally, a customer would complain about flies and I'd take a grayed tablecloth and swish at them. But the flies were also like memories. They had a mind of their own, they flew out of reach and returned uninvited; they'd entice, gently whirring in the air, nasty little fuckers.

I tried to forget him. My last night at home, I raised myself from the floor an hour after the house fell quiet. I opened the door and stepped into the hallway. There was no one. I walked past the other bedroom that remained closed and felt sick. I limped outside, there was complete darkness. Kaali emerged from the black of the night and meowed at me. *Come with me*, I spoke to it. And my knees wobbled. A song played in my head—the song Salim used to whistle. "My name is Joker." I danced past the veranda. One step at a time, I shook my legs. Past the house, past the playground, past the adda, past the vegetable market, past the train tracks, past the cinema, past the places he became a part of, past me.

Permissions

Contributors

KAREEM ABDUL-JABBAR is known as one of the greatest basketball players of all time as well as a committed social activist and award-winning writer. As a player, he was the NBA's all-time leading scorer with 38,387 points, a six-time NBA champion, and the league's only six-time MVP. A regular contributor to newspapers and magazines around the world, he now writes a newsletter at https://kareem.substack.com/, where he shares his thoughts on some of the most socially relevant and politically controversial topics facing our nation today. The author of seventeen books, most of which explore African American history, Abdul-Jabbar is currently working on a series of graphic novels focusing on social justice. He is also an award-winning documentary producer and is currently producing a series of specials for the History Channel. His latest, *Black Patriots: Heroes of the Civil War*, premiered February 21, 2022. Awarded the Presidential Medal of Freedom by President Obama, Abdul-Jabbar is also the recipient of the Ford Medal of Freedom, the Rosa Parks Award, the Double Helix Medal and the W. E. B. Dubois Medal of Courage. He holds eight honorary doctorate degrees.

MATTHIEU AIKINS has worked in Afghanistan since 2008 and is a contributing writer for the *New York Times Magazine*. His first book, *The Naked Don't Fear the Water: An Underground Journey with Afghan Refugees*, was published by Harper/HarperCollins in February 2021.

DOTUN AKINTOYE is a writer at ESPN.

RACHEL AVIV joined *the New Yorker* as a staff writer in 2013. She is the author of *Strangers to Ourselves: Unsettled Minds and the Stories That Make Us.*

KATIE BAKER is an investigative reporter for *BuzzFeed News* and is based in London.

HEIDI BLAKE is a senior investigative reporter for *BuzzFeed News* based in London. She is the author of *From Russia with Blood: The Kremlin's Ruthless Assassination Program and Vladimir Putin's Secret War on the West* and the coauthor of *The Ugly Game: The Qatari Plot to Buy the World Cup.*

KRISTIN CANNING is the features director at *Women's Health*, where she writes and reports, as well as assigns and edits, long-form features on health research and technology, women's health conditions, psychology, sexuality, mental health, reproductive justice, women athletes, and the intersection of health, fitness, and culture for both the magazine and the website. She has worked in health media for seven years, holding previous positions at *Health, Self*, and *Men's Health*. When she's not writing and editing, you can find her running, hiking, biking, dancing, reading, road-tripping, camping, listening to podcasts, or planning her next outdoor adventure.

CARINA DEL VALLE SCHORSKE is a writer and literary translator based in Brooklyn. She is a regular contributor to the *New York Times Magazine*. Her first book, *The Other Island*, was a recipient of a Whiting Nonfiction Grant and is forthcoming from Riverhead Books.

MEGAN I. GANNON is a journalist from Long Island who now lives in Nome, Alaska. She often writes about space, archaeology, and the environment.

VIVIAN GORNICK is the author most recently of the essay collection *Taking a Long Look*, which was published in March by Verso Books.

KATIE GUTIERREZ is the author of the debut novel *More Than You'll Ever Know*. Her essays have appeared in *Texas Highways, Harper's Bazaar*, the *Washington Post*, and other publications. Of her work on "The Original Cowboys," she says: "Tracing the history of the vaquero and hearing vaqueros' stories firsthand gave me profound appreciation not just for their ingenuity and resilience but for my own South Texas and Mexican heritage." She lives in San Antonio, Texas, with her husband and two children.

NISHANTH INJAM is a writer from Telangana, India. He is a graduate of the MFA program at the University of Michigan and a recipient of the PEN/Dau Prize. His first book, *The Best Possible Experience*, will be published by Pantheon Books in 2023.

E. ALEX JUNG is a features writer at *Vulture, New York*'s entertainment and culture news site, where he writes about TV, film, theater, internet culture, race, and sexuality. At *Vulture*, Jung has profiled Michaela Coel, Thandie Newton, Bong Joon-ho, RuPaul, John Cho, Padma Lakshmi, and many more, focusing especially on stars on the rise.

J. DREW LANHAM is a conservation ornithologist and endowed faculty at Clemson University, where his work focuses on the intersections among race, place, and nature. He is the author of *The Home Place: Memoirs of a Colored Man's Love Affair With Nature* and *Sparrow Envy: Field Guide to Birds and Lesser Beasts*.

JEREMY ATHERTON LIN is the author of *Gay Bar*, which received the National Book Critics Circle Award in Autobiography. His writing has appeared in the *Yale Review*, the *Times Literary Supplement*, *The Guardian*, and *GQ*.

ZACHARY MIDER is a reporter on the investigations team at *Bloomberg News*, where he has written about climate change, predatory lending, and money in politics. His coverage of corporate tax avoidance was awarded a Pulitzer Prize in 2015. Before joining Bloomberg in 2006, he worked at newspapers in Rhode Island and Connecticut. He is a graduate of Deep Springs College and Harvard College.

ANN PATCHETT is the author of eight novels, four works of nonfiction, and two children's books. She has been the recipient of numerous awards, including the PEN/Faulkner Award, the Women's Prize in the United Kingdom, and the Book Sense Book of the Year. Her most recent novel, *The Dutch House*, was a finalist for the Pulitzer Prize. Her most recent work of nonfiction is *These Precious Days*, a collection of essays reflecting on home, family, friendships, and writing. She lives in Nashville, Tennessee, where she is the co-owner of Parnassus Books.

JENNIFER SENIOR is a staff writer at *The Atlantic*. Before joining the team in 2021, she spent five years at the *New York Times*, first as a daily book critic and then as an op-ed columnist. Before that, she spent eighteen years at *New York*, writing profiles and cover stories about politics, social science, and mental health. Her long-form journalism has earned her two Front Page awards, a GLAAD Media Award and appearances in both *The Best American Political Writing* and *The Best American Nature and Science Writing*. She is also the author of *All Joy and No Fun: The Paradox of Modern Parenthood*, which spent eight weeks on the *New York Times* bestseller list, has been translated into twelve languages, and was named one of *Slate*'s top ten books of 2014.

NATALIE WOLCHOVER is a senior editor at *Quanta*, covering the physical sciences. She has a bachelor's in physics from Tufts University, studied graduate-level physics at the University of California, Berkeley, and coauthored several academic papers in nonlinear optics. Her writing awards include the 2016 Evert Clark/Seth Payne Award, the 2016 Excellence in Statistical Reporting Award, and the American Institute of Physics' 2017 Science Communication Award for Articles.

ED YONG is a staff writer at *The Atlantic*. He won the Pulitzer Prize for Explanatory Reporting for his coverage of the COVID-19 pandemic. Yong is also the recipient of the George Polk Award for Science Reporting as well as several other awards. He is the author of *I Contain Multitudes: The Microbes Within Us and a Grander View of Life*, a *New York Times* best-seller, and *An Immense World: How Animal Senses Reveal the Hidden Realms Around Us.*